LIVING WITH
PETS

LIVING WITH
PETS

A COMPLETE GUIDE

to Choosing and Caring for

All Kinds of Pets

BY

ERNEST H. HART

with Illustrations by the Author

THE VANGUARD PRESS
NEW YORK

". . . and let me therefore seek
all the creatures of the air and
water and earth, and with them
find tranquility."

to my grandchildren in
the order of their appearance,
April, Stephanie, Allan Matthew, and Rhett

A WORD TO THE READER

Though I have included a wide and divergent spectrum of pet creatures in this book, I have been haunted by the thought that somewhere, sometime, someone has made a pet of a species of animal that I have completely overlooked. If this has happened, all I can say is, "Wherever and whoever you are and whatever pet creature you have found that I have omitted, please accept my apologies for not having dealt with it in this text."

I have eliminated some species data which I considered unimportant, for a complete and comprehensive coverage of all the creatures included would have made this book too heavy to lift and too boring to read.

To me the most important part of living with pets is the philosophy behind the act of pet ownership. If approached correctly, pet ownership can expand our emotional horizons to new and delightful vistas, can lead us to challenge old fallacies and bigotries and bring us within the boundaries of kinship and understanding of all life-forms. If only a meager handful of the readers of this book reach this pinnacle, I will consider my labors very much worthwhile.

You must realize that every pet is an individual and may not be entirely true to its species' attitude, just as each person differs in his approach to pet possession. You must also understand the jeopardy inherent in owning a pet that is not of a long-domesticated species. Wild animals instinctively consider man an enemy and can, under certain trying circumstances, even when thought to be completely tame, attack and possibly injure their owners. The challenge lies in overcoming those ancient inherited fears and establishing trust and faith in their stead.

Animals have been a delightful part of my life, lending it a richness that I would have never known without their close and intimate presence. In a world of doubts, when many wonder who and what they are and are burdened with strange fears from their primordial past when man first walked erect, questioned his universe, and learned how to kill his brother, the animals around us have remained steadfast and consistent. They "are" and in their "being" we can take comfort and find a measure of peace if we can but reach rapport with them. Our pets are honest and unwavering in their affection, simplicity, and honesty, so unlike our fellowmen who nourish false premises and exist in confused and elaborate unreality.

I find it a constant wonder that man—the animal supreme who controls the atom, conquers the elements and rides to the stars—should inhabit a contemporary time-sphere with the myriad archiac creatures of the forests, seas, and sky. Perhaps these lesser animals are here to remind us of our humble beginnings and by their very existence counsel caution.

—Ernest H. Hart

Bogotá,
Colombia, S.A.

CONTENTS

PART TWO

THE MANY BREEDS OF PETS

Illustrations

PART
ONE

THE CHOICE
AND CARE
OF PETS

1

How to Choose a Pet

If you picked up this book, we can assume that you are either a pet owner or are on your way to becoming one. In either case you probably need help, assurance, and someone to whom you can turn for guidance and with whom you can discuss, openly and objectively, the problems involved in pet ownership.

That is the purpose of this book.

First let us define what a pet is. The dictionary interprets the word as, "Any domestic or tamed animal that is kept as a favorite and cared for affectionately," and, "A domesticated animal kept for pleasure rather than utility." We can accept these definitions but with some reservations; our interpretation will be applicable to a broader concept.

The selection of a pet is not a step to be lightly taken. Without due thought, research, a sincere weighing of values and a knowledge of all the elements involved, one can blunder seriously and arrive at a point of no return with a badly battered ego, a mutilated checkbook, a damaged and odorous home, a dislike of all living creatures including one's self, a generous number of psychic hangups, and complete disillusionment about pets in general.

On the other hand, if well prepared for pet ownership, and if the pet selected is the right one for you, you can look forward to years of an interesting and fruitful association that will make your life richer and more satisfying and bring you to a closer understanding and more amiable kinship with all living things.

As you can calculate from a quick glance through the pages that follow, there is an almost limitless category of pets from which to choose. The problem is to find the one that fits *you*—a tailor-made creature, so to speak, modeled specifically to your needs.

What shall it be—mammal, fish, reptile, insect? The choice is large. But before we select the pet we must examine you, the prospective pet owner. We must dissect and view you minutely—heart, soul, mentality;

physically, financially, psychologically. Here lies the secret of a perfect fit in pet ownership—temperamental compatibility combined with physical and financial capability.

What Kind of Person Are You?

Are you a quiet, introspective person who prefers his own company and lives a calm, orderly life? Then you will want a tranquil pet that will give you pleasure without intruding upon your solitude. If, on the other hand, you are an ebullient type, excitable and always on the move, your pet should mirror your own effervescence.

Let us assume that individuals mimicking these two divergent types select canaries as pets. The quiet person should purchase a small roller canary, with a song rich in low, sweet-water notes that are a serene background for, not an intrusion upon, thought and study. The outgoing, animated person would be happier with a large, red-factor, English chopper, an active bird with a loud voice, high and insistent.

If these same two people should want a dog as a pet, the introvert had best select a specimen of a quiet breed that would not impose upon its owner's solitude unless requested, while the extrovert would find great satisfaction in the company of a lively, constantly active terrier.

Are you married or single? If single, you have only yourself to please and probably have activities that pleasantly absorb much of the time you would need to lavish on a pet. But remember that pets are marvelous conversation pieces and can lead to very rewarding dialogues with an individual of the opposite sex. The married person must consider the tastes, temperament, and personality of his or her mate and select a pet that both can live with and enjoy. Under these circumstances the choice of a pet can be rather difficult, necessitating a good deal of serious thought and discussion between the matrimonial partners.

The wrong pet can become a source of irritation, angry argument, or can even be the last straw in a serious situation born of some other petty source. In the case of the married workingman whose job keeps him away from home for long periods of time, his wife will, of necessity, have to feed and care for their pet. To perform this chore she must, to some extent, share her husband's enthusiasm for it. Picture, if you will, a woman who abhors mice, rats, and snakes, and whose husband, a dedicated herpetologist, has left on an extended business trip and has instructed her to feed the reptiles a specific number of live mice and rats while he is away. In this case absence does not make the heart grow fonder and the result could be hysteria, and/or divorce, and/or bodily attack, or even a visit by the white-coated gentlemen from the state funny-farm to take the distraught woman away. This, of course, is a drastic instance, but it gives sharpness to the point made.

Do you have children? If so, you must consider the youngsters' association with the pet. A child must not be exposed to the danger of being hurt physically or psychologically by the pet. With some family pets such a consideration can be immediately ruled out, but with others the possibility remains. Both the child and the pet must learn to respect each other's feelings and live in harmony. Children of certain tender ages are impulsive little savages and must be taught by their parents not to hurt household pets. Pain can cause the most mild-mannered animal to strike out blindly in an effort to escape and so cause injury to the child who is inflicting the pain. Children must not be allowed to tease their own pets (or other animals). Some pets are so tiny and delicate that an uneducated or unthinking child can injure or kill them through improper handling.

Can you give your pet the environment it needs to prosper and be happy? Is the place in which you live right for the pet you want? A very small apartment is no place for a very large pet, or one you acquire when young and small that will reach considerable size when mature. Some pets need lots of room for exercise and you must provide the necessary space close by and be willing to take the time needed to allow your pet this activity.

Should you be so unfortunate as to have some disability that curtails your physical activity, it will be necessary for you to select a pet that will not demand or need supervised exercise to keep fit.

The kind of weather you have where you live is another factor to be considered. Climate is important to some pets. If they or their ancestors come from tropical or semitropical climes, they may not prosper in a chilly or cold atmosphere. Some pets need a dry climate; others do best in a humid place; a few can survive only in frigid, arctic climes.

How old are you? Your age is another consideration when selecting a pet. People slow down and their life-style changes with the burden of years. A pet for senior citizens should be one that can be cared for simply and easily and from which they can derive a maximum of pleasure with a minimum of work and worry.

In selecting a pet for a child, be sure it is a creature that the child can pet and handle. Unlike older people who can derive esthetic pleasure through mental gratification, a child finds delight and rapture through his senses. Think objectively when deciding on a pet for a youngster. So often I have heard people say, "We'll have to get a small dog for Junior; he's so little." Wrong thinking! Little Junior can very easily hurt or even fatally maim a small dog. Get him a large dog that cannot be as easily hurt as a small one. But remember—any animal can be injured by a careless child.

What hours do you work? The hours you spend at your job can be pertinent to the variety of pet best suited for you. If you do not arrive home until rather late at night, perhaps one of the many interesting nocturnal creatures may be best for you. They sleep during the day and awaken to activity at hours you can share. Tropical fish and most birds are a pleasure no matter what the hour. And there are many other pets whose feeding and sleeping schedules can be shaped to your own needs.

How much can you spend for a pet? Finally we come to the question of cost and maintenance as we do in all things. Actually the initial purchase price for your pet is not terribly important unless it is so exorbitant as to be ridiculous. Due to scarcity of a species, shipping costs, quarantines and customs fees, some pets are priced beyond the reach of the ordinary man's pocketbook. But in almost every such instance another less expensive pet in the same general species category will make a very satisfactory substitute.

The maintenance of your contemplated pet must also be carefully assessed. Some creatures need special and costly housing; some, special bedding material. Others have exotic tastes in food that must be constantly supplied, that may be difficult to find and, when located, may be expensive and therefore a constant financial strain. There are also pets that prove to be delicate in captivity and will run your veterinary bills up into a frightening aggregation of figures.

These monetary considerations must be explored because some pets may simply be beyond your financial means to own and support and, when this happens, your pet will become a burden and the basic pleasure of pet ownership will be lost in a deluge of mounting costs.

These are some of the most pertinent fundamentals that we must be aware of and understand before taking the initial step toward pet ownership and the mystic rapport between human and pet that usually results. The pact thus formed brings much pleasure over the years and broadens our perception of intensely interesting life-patterns other than our own.

What Is a Pet Owner?

A pet owner is a compassionate human being who feels the need to add another dimension to his or her life-style. A pet owner is generally a person of questing mentality with a desire to reach out into another sphere of experience that will enlarge his ability to care for, and share, the emotional being of another creature. Sometimes a pet owner is an individual who simply wants to revel in a living thing or things of beauty or interest that will enable him to find peace and tranquility in a new and fascinating world.

Why Do You Want a Pet?

Examine your true motives before you purchase a pet. Is it for financial gain? Have you heard of someone who has made a lot of money breeding and selling specimens of the pet you wish to buy and you reason that you can do the same? Take the advice of one who knows and forget it. Very, very few people ever make a lot of money dealing in animals or creatures in the category of pets. Livestock is extremely perishable and losses are frequent. Only someone who has had vast experience in the field and has built up an enviable reputation and following over the years can make any financial gain with pets, and then only as a full-time business where the monetary gains are hard-earned and never too impressive.

Do you wish to own a certain kind of pet because it will bring you the attention of other people and perhaps make you more interesting in their eyes? Are you searching for a pet to help build up your ego? Or do you feel that you have to hold dominance over some living creature and figure that a pet will be ideal for this purpose? Are you simply lonely and in need of another living creature to care for, to share your life? Perhaps you want a fine pedigreed dog for the prestige it will bring, or because you enjoy the thrill of competition in the show ring. Do you feel you need protection and want the kind of pet that will give it to you? Maybe you have lost someone you love and need a pet to care for to give you something to do and perhaps help to fill the empty place in your heart. Or do you simply like animals, have a rapport with them, and find it impossible to conceive of life without them?

Though some may not seem to be, all these and many more are legitimate reasons for owning a pet, because in each instance the pet will fill a basic human need and, in so doing, will create a strong, lasting bond with its owner that will eventually result in a closeness uniquely shared only by a human being and a living creature of another species.

What Is the Best Pet for You?

In the sections to follow the "rightness" of various available pets for certain kinds of people will be explored. But there are other fundamentals that we must evaluate.

Pets can be divided into specific categories from the standpoint of approachability; those you can touch and handle; those you handle infrequently; and those you do not handle at all. In the first category we can include dogs, cats, some birds, rodents, raccoon-family animals, primates, marsupials, some reptiles and amphibians, and farm pets. In the second group we can list some birds, some reptiles and amphibians, and some primates. The third category includes some reptiles, some birds, tropical fishes, and insect pets.

Within the scope of these categories, consideration must be given to the mental and emotional qualities of the individual species among the many varieties of available pets. Dogs, cats (to a certain extent), most of the primates and raccoon-family pets, and the parrot-family birds (*Psittaciformes*), are intelligent creatures that learn to love their owners. They demonstrate this through physical contact—touching, licking, cuddling—and, as an added bonus, the parrot-type birds can be taught to talk. Snakes, amphibians, rodents, some birds, and farm animals can be handled, and while they may engender a feeling of warmth in their owners they do not show any emotional feeling themselves.

There are, of course, pets that are not handled at all, but that can bring the owner much pleasure and aesthetic satisfaction, such as a lovely songbird or a tank filled with beautiful tropical fish. The song of a canary can brighten a home and make human attitudes more cheerful. The exotic shapes and jewel-like colors of the most popular tropical fishes, combined with the colorful and ingeniously arranged environment of the tank (generally a product of the owner's sense of design), constitute an extravagantly beautiful and alien world that brings quiet, contemplative peace to the observer. As any tropical fish enthusiast will attest, when we get taut and nervous due to the aggravations of our modern society, a half hour spent in quiet observation of the fish tank's aquatic world will untangle knotted nerves and relax the mind.

Before we proceed to a more precise knowledge of pet ownership I would like you to be aware of another very important area in which the value of pets is keenly felt. Psychotherapists have used pets in helping maladjusted, physically handicapped, and mentally disturbed children and adults. Psychologists have found that these people, alienated from the so-called normal world, have a terrible need to reach out to some living creature. The animal pet fulfills that need. It gives them love and attention and helps them, gradually and haltingly, to release themselves from the protective shells that are a necessary hiding place for their bruised beings. Through pets many such people can finally be reached and their conditions improved. It has also been reported that incarcerated criminals are much more manageable if allowed to have pets to help relieve the deadly boredom of imprisonment that often turns inward, generating hate and finally an explosion of violence.

To a pet, the physically and mentally handicapped or the old person rejected by society seem normal; the color or ethnic background of its owner mean nothing. The individual who provides love and food, care and protection is, to an animal, never a nonperson because of age or any other classical reason that has cut him or her off from the main area of social grace. A pet never shames or belittles, is never bored by or impatient with its owner. A pet allows the underprivileged in all areas to retain their dignity, their individuality, and identity as human beings. Often, particularly to the aged, a pet is the last remaining link with life, or, for the mentally ill, with reality.

Today our materialistic world with its complexities baffles and frightens many normal people and often alienates and rejects them. To find love, belief, and a reason for being, they turn in despair to basic simple things. They turn to the animals, to their pets, and through them attempt to find their lost faith in themselves and their world.

Your Obligation to Your Pet

Before we discuss basic obligations I must remind you that your pet is not human, so please do not think of it as having human attributes. If you do, you will never find a common ground upon which the two of you can meet. A fish is a fish, a dog a dog, a parrot a parrot, a human being a human being, and each is separated from the others by the gulf of specie evolution. The tendency among scientists and trained animal observers is to be completely objective in their approach to animals in order to avoid any inclination toward anthropomorphism. We who own and love our pets are not cold analytical observers, and we do not put our pets under a microscope. We love them as pets, and allocate for them a special segment of our lives, but we *must not* humanize them, for the fact that they are not human is what makes them precious and special.

Your pet is a dependent in the truest sense of the word. It will depend on you, its owner, for all the necessities to sustain life—food, water, a place to sleep comfortably. In short, you are obligated to create a complete specific environment for your pet that, in the case of long-domesticated animals, has been proven best or, for the more exotic or unusual pet, one that mimics its natural life-style. If your pet is in the latter category, study its authentic habitat and attempt, within reason, to supply it with food that contains all the elements the animal utilizes in the wild, and with surroundings and climate most suitable to its needs.

You must also supply affection and understanding and through proper care help it to achieve a full and happy existence. Most pets require grooming and must be kept free of external and internal parasites. You and you alone are responsible for your pet's well-being and you must plan your own activities to conform to its needs. Food must be supplied at regular intervals, and the pet's quarters must be kept clean or you risk the danger of illnesses and infections that breed in filth. It is never a good policy to have someone else do the dirty jobs for your pet. Take care of it yourself, for the person who grooms, feeds, and cleans a pet's quarters is the most important person in the world to that pet and the one to whom it will give its affection.

You also owe your pet protection from outside sources such as children with sticks, grownups who tease, and some pets must even be protected from each other. If your pet's quarters are so built that they are easy to clean, if you keep utensils stacked and handy, and if you adhere to a schedule, the time involved in caring for your pet will not be too great. Certainly it will be spent in a very worthwhile occupation— learning more about, and coming closer to, your pet.

Yes, there is always a certain amount of work to do and time that must be spent with your pet. But remember this, for it is important: *you must never allow yourself to become so enmeshed in obligations to your pet that you become a slave to it.* If this happens, the joy of pet ownership becomes a mockery.

All animals, including man, are creatures of habit and you can guide your pet's activities into habit-designed channels. Sometimes a degree of strictness is necessary to reach a desired end, but first make certain that the animal understands what it is you want it to do. Often failure to obey is not disobedience but simply ignorance of what is wanted. Your pet may not be a bad pupil; maybe you are a bad teacher. Even when firmness is necessary, it should be tempered by patience and kept free of harshness. Permissiveness with pets, as with children, generally leads to the pet getting the upper hand and becoming difficult to live with. Therefore, through conditioning or habit-forming training, the pet owner must control his pet. When he succeeds, his pet will be a pleasure to own and live with.

Your Pet's Obligation to You

There should be reciprocation in the owner-pet relationship. The pet must, in return for your fondness and proper care, give you affection and pleasure by learning to behave in a proper manner. If your pet is chronically nasty and you can make no advancement in establishing rapport with it, or if it is destructive and cannot be trained after a decent interval of trying, then sell or give it away and find another that will be friendly and offer you what you want and deserve.

First, of course, try patience and fortitude and attempt to reach your pet through association and good care. But if the pet does not respond after reasonable time and effort on your part, then it is ridiculous to keep it, for its lack of response will only aggravate you more and more until it becomes a pest rather than a pet. Such an experience could destroy your faith in the joy of pet ownership.

Your Pet's Body and Its Functions

The body of your pet is composed of a multiplicity of specialized cells. Some cells remain static, others constantly renew themselves, and unless they are affected by accident, disease, incorrect nourishment, or obesity, they work as a harmonious whole.

The skeleton is the basic supportive structure of the body. It also acts as a protective shell for important and easily damaged inner organs. Drastic form changes in breeds and species (mutations), are first registered in this bony framework. The bones vary considerably in size, shape, and structure, some being solid, others hollow or filled with marrow, and the long bones artfully combining several skeletal substances. All these bones fit together as though very carefully engineered to form a very ingenious foundation for all the other elements that constitute the body of your pet. Not all pets have the same number of bones. Birds, for instance, have clavicles (collarbones) just as humans do, but dogs and cats lack collarbones.

Muscles and tendons clothe the skeleton, hold it together, and allow certain parts of it to move. To flex, and thus attain mobility, a muscle must be attached to two different bones. There are some muscles (striated or smooth) designed to aid in the continuous involuntary work of the organs, blood vessels, digestive tract, and other sections of the complicated internal system. These muscles are involuntarily controlled by the body.

Between the muscles and the covering skin is a subcutaneous layer of connective tissue, composed of elastic cells through which run blood vessels, lymph vessels, fat substances, and nerves. This layer is hidden by the sheath of the outer skin from which grow hairs, feathers, or scales, according to the beastie it covers.

Various glands affect the skin and help to protect it. Sweat, sebaceous, and oil glands perform this service to the highly sensitive skin that reacts to touch, pain, and variations in climate.

Within this highly organized body of your pet is the central machine, the heart, that must keep beating or death follows. This most important organ is a fantastically efficient four-chambered pump that receives blood and jets it out into two huge arteries which act as pipelines, distributing this life-giving fluid, along with oxygen, to all parts of the body. The blood flows through smaller veins, arterioles, and capillaries, nourishing, bringing life, and picking up wastes from the cells in its journey.

The blood itself is actually an organ composed of specialized cells and fluids. Like a benevolent river it flows through the body, purveying nourishment, carrying off dangerous carbon dioxide, and distributing necessary oxygen. Within the plasma (liquid) of the blood float balanced red and white cells, coagulants to stop the loss of blood through disease or injury, and chemicals necessary for health.

As the blood courses through the veins, it is purified by body filters, the most important being the spleen. Lymph is moved along by the natural bodily movements of the pet.

The lungs are the most important part of the respiratory system. They work closely with the blood in the transference of carbon dioxide and oxygen. To a limited extent they also aid in the control of body temperature. Two bronchial tubes, with their subdivisions (bronchioles and air sacs), are also important segments of the respiratory system.

The digestive system, as you might expect, varies greatly in the many class divisions of the creatures we call pets. Some pets have teeth; others don't. Some confine themselves to a diet of vegetation, while others must have meat. Certain pets can digest substances that others cannot. The tongue, the throat, the stomach, the crop, the intestines, the liver (also concerned with other life functions), the pancreas—all play important roles in turning food into energy, promoting growth, and sustaining the life processes that govern the pet's being. Peristalsis, a wavelike, contractive motion pushes the intaken food along the digestive system to its inevitable distribution.

The glandular system is tremendously important as the regulator of bodily functions. Glands, being essential to the breeding cycles of your pet, and the cause of sexual development, are necessary to the perpetuation of the species. Glands also stimulate growth, cause skin and coat changes, affect labor in pregnant animals, and regulate the metabolism of carbohydrates. The glands, when they are not working properly, can cause abnormalities. The pituitary, adrenal, thyroid, and parathyroid are important ductless glands. The prominent mixed ductless and ordinary glands are the pancreas, ovaries, and testicles.

The nerves carry messages between the brain and all parts of the body, triggering most conscious activity. They can be likened to the telephone wires that touch every corner of a city, radiating outward like living antennae, pulsing with messages of all kinds from the common center which, in living creatures, is the very complicated brain. The largest bundles of nerves are in the spinal column.

The huge and fearsome prehistoric dinosaurs that ruled a forming earth millions of years ago possessed brains so tiny that they were practically useless, and the theory has been advanced that these great reptiles reacted to stimuli directly through the ganglia (clusters of spinal nerve cells) rather than with their undeveloped brains. From the way some people I know feed and care for their pets, and the old wive's tales they believe about them, I am of the opinion that tiny brains did not vanish completely with the dinosaurs.

The eye, ear, and nose (and in some creatures prehensile tail, hands, antennae, tongue, and whiskers), are the sensory organs that aid the pet to see, hear, smell, and touch. This is not a book on anatomy, so I will not go into detail about the various elements of sensory control, except to say that the nose is only the visible part of the scenting (olfactory) apparatus. The hidden and most important parts are highly complicated. In some creatures recognition through scent is mandatory for survival. Some animals (wolves, the big cats, et cetera) hunt by scent; others hunt by sight (hawks, eagles, et cetera), and acute hearing helps many wild creatures find food or warns them of approaching danger. Many pets are color-blind and live in a world of graduated gray, black, and white. Fishes, most students agree, are able to discern colors much as humans do.

Pets, like humans, are of one sex or another—male or female. Sometimes the sex of a pet is not important except to other pets of the same species, but often it can also be important to you. For instance, if you want to train a pet budgerigar or cockateil to talk, better purchase a male since the male talks much more readily than the female. In falconry the female eagle, falcon, or hawk, is the fiercer of the sexes and is, therefore, selected for this most interesting of sports.

Of course, if you intend to breed your pets, their sex is eminently important. Sexual differences are sometimes very obvious, in other cases not outwardly recognizable at all, and in certain pets not readily perceptible until maturity has been reached or the oncoming breeding cycle brings color changes that make the sex distinction obvious.

Suffice it to say that there are two sexes in all species and they beget young that mirror themselves. The female produces eggs, either inside or outside of her body, and the male produces sperm to fertilize the eggs. Some pet species breed easily in confinement; some are difficult to breed; others will not breed at all in an artificial environment.

Though this very rapid run-through of the parts of a pet's body and their functions may have seemed redundant to you, it is really a necessary reference section. It can help to pinpoint ailments and also make us realize that we are not so terribly different from our pets after all!

Classification of Animals

While you are still in a soporific state of boredom from your brief lesson in anatomy, I will sneak in another necessary item: the scientific method of classifying all creatures. Many specialty books use Latin names to identify animals, birds, or what have you, and, if you understand the scientific classifications, the exasperating bewilderment usually associated with such listings will be changed to a superior smile of learned satisfaction.

Every known creature has a scientific Latin name that provides absolute identification. This eliminates much confusion because many different common names are given to the same animal in different areas. The Latin names also express the relationship of the tremendous variety of creatures to one another.

We begin with an all-encompassing division term *Phylum* (*Phyla* in the plural). For instance, if we use *Phylum* in conjunction with *Chordata* (the Latin word meaning "notochord," which refers to what we might call the primitive backbone), the master division *Phylum Chordata* includes all backboned animals—mammals, birds, reptiles, amphibians, fishes.

Next we have the *Class,* in which are grouped creatures having a common evolutionary basis that makes them alike in important features. Thus the *Class Mammalia* means that class embracing mammals, and includes animals that have body hair and mammary glands for suckling their young. In this class we would then list primates, rodents, and marsupials. Placed in their own classes would be species of birds, reptiles, and fishes.

Narrowing our description still further, we arrive at the *Order.* To continue with mammals as our subject, we consider the meat-eating mammals (as opposed to vegetarians) and find they are placed in the order *Carnivora,* which includes all doglike animals, all cat creatures, hyenas, and the various weasels.

Family is a grouping of still smaller units. Continuing with carnivorous mammals, the cats would be grouped under the family *Felidae* because each is a cat (*felis*). Some cats, however, have certain common characteristics not shared with others, and so they are separated into different *Genera* (plural of genus is genera). For instance, the lion, tiger, jaguar, and leopard are placed in the genus *Panthera*. The cheetah is in a different genus, *Acinonyx* (*jubatus*); and the domestic cat, the bobcat, ocelot, and puma or mountain lion are given the generic name *Felis*. The genera *Felis, Acinonyx,* and *Panthera,* being all cats, are grouped together and classified under the family name *Felidae.*

Last, we have the species, which is a group of animals with one or more similar characteristics distinguishing them from similar groups.

To further clarify this litany, let us trace the ocelot backwards through this Latin maze. The ocelot is of the species *Paradalis,* genus *Felis,* family *Felidae,* order *Carnivora,* class *Mammalia, Phylum Cordata.* So, through the Latin scientific name clues, we find out where any particular creature fits into nature's scheme of living things.

2

How and Where to Buy a Pet

Before You Buy

Pets can be purchased from breeders, pet shops, or commercial zoos. Many of the wild creatures, native to the area you inhabit, need not be purchased at all but can be caught in their natural environment when young and tamed and trained to become good pets.

Before buying learn as must as you possibly can about the pet you have chosen through books and conversation with individuals who have expertise in handling the specific animal. Beware though of false authorities who profess to know all there is to know about the creature you have selected but who, in truth, are all wind, and full of old wive's tales. If at all possible, when going to select your pet, inveigle into accompanying you someone who is really somewhat of an authority on the breed or species you have selected.

The seller should supply you with a guarantee as to the age and quality of the animal and with a health certificate. He should also specify that you have forty-eight hours in which to have the pet examined by your own veterinarian. If not given a clean bill of health by your veterinarian, the seller should guarantee that your money will be refunded upon the return of the pet.

Check the surroundings of the pet shop, kennel, cattery, aviary or commercial zoo for cleanliness, and, before you buy, make certain (through earlier inquiry) that the dealer has a reputation for honesty. Whatever pet you choose, buy the best specimen you can afford, even if a superior one costs a bit more than you had planned on paying. Purchasing the pet is a basic, one-time cost, but for the rest of the pet's life you will have to pay for its food, veterinarian bills, and other miscellaneous costs. It is wiser to spend your money over the years on a fine specimen that will give you esthetic enjoyment than on a poor or mediocre one.

Buying a Dog

Take the advice of a man of vast experience in the dog game and do not buy a puppy from a pet shop. Such puppies are often breeder's discards. You can buy a much better, and certainly a more valuable, youngster from the kennel of a private breeder at approximately the same price. You will also have the decided advantage of being able to see the dam (mother) and possibly the sire (father) and related stock to give you some measure of the worth of the animal you purchase.

Check with your local all-breed kennel club to locate a breeder in your vicinity who produces the breed in which you are interested. Ask the club when the next close-to-home dog show will take place. Arrive at the show early and haunt the areas where owners and handlers of the breed of your choice congregate. When these people are not busy preparing their charges for classes, ask any questions you can think of that will help you garner a better knowledge of the breed you have selected. In short, make a pest of yourself and be certain that before you leave the show grounds you have acquired a good-sized list of successful breeders within easy driving distance of your home, as well as a copy of the American Kennel Club's standards and description of the breed you want to buy.

Armed with this description and standard, pay particular attention to the list of faults and disqualifying deficiencies. Then begin to make the rounds of the kennels on your list. Take note of the environment and condition of the animals in each kennel. Is it sanitary and are the dogs clean and healthy? Are the grown dogs true representatives of the breed? Are they happy and filled with the joy of living? Once you've checked locally do you yourself feel that the breeder is honest and trustworthy? What guarantees will he give you if you buy a puppy or dog from him and what price is he asking?

The price of puppies and grown stock varies according to the breed, its popularity at the moment, availability, age, and size (the larger the dog the greater the upkeep for the breeder and eventually for you). Top show stock is expensive. Pups from show-winning parents will cost much more than those bred from pet stock. But the fact that the breeding of the animal is of high caliber, with many champions appearing in the pedigree, does not insure that all the puppies in the litter will be fantastic animals. Even the greatest of champions produces much more ordinary than superior stock. The chance of acquiring a really good animal is increased though when the parents and the lineage behind them are distinguished.

WHAT AGE? WHAT SEX?

Are you interested in a puppy or a grown dog? Male or female? Most prospective dog owners think only in terms of a puppy that they can mold to their own wants and personality, which is reasonably good thinking. But the puppy must be housebroken, taught to behave properly, and its end potential as a true representative of its breed cannot be completely assessed until it is fairly well grown. An older dog will probably be housebroken and have been taught some home and kennel deportment. If not, the older dog will be much more easily and rapidly trained in these areas. It will also have attained enough maturity to exhibit clearly all its virtues and faults. So, in buying an older animal, you would not be selecting as blindly as you would when purchasing a puppy. The older dog (eight months to approximately a year and still really only a puppy) will soon fit into your mode of living as nicely as would the puppy of from eight to ten weeks of age, and will be easier to care for and train.

The sex of the dog you select is a matter of choice, arrived at by the addition of plus and minus attributes. Male canines are larger, usually more noble of aspect, generally more aggressive, and a bit more stubborn than females. Bitches (the proper term to designate the female dog and one you must learn to use without trepidation) are usually sweeter, softer in temperament than males, willing to please, and yet protective when necessary.

The bitch comes in season (or heat) twice a year and must then be isolated from the amorous advances of eager males in the area; the stains she leaves in her wake on the rugs must be cleaned up. She can also, of course, be bred during this period and produce a new generation of cute youngsters. There is an old axiom that bitches come in season twice a year, but male dogs are always in season. Actually each sex offers more that is plus than minus and the selection must be yours.

HOW TO CHOOSE A DOG

You are a person of some taste, are you not? You like nice things; you have a lovely home, fashionable clothing, and all the accouterments of discernment and discrimination. Into such an atmosphere you cannot bring a canine that introduces a jarring note to the symphony of your life-style. You must psych yourself into purchasing a really fine specimen of the breed of your choice. The reasons are many and valid.

When you buy a dog, you are making an investment in companionship, devotion, and perhaps in the protection of yourself, your family, and your goods that will stretch over a period of years. You are buying love and must give it in return. If this sounds like a marriage ceremony, that idea is not far from the mark, for this canine you are about to adopt must be cared for in sickness and in health, must be loved and cherished until death do you part.

Let us assume you have chosen the breeder who seems to have excellent stock and who is honest and earnest in his breeding ideals and in his dealings, and you have gone to him with intent to buy. If it is a puppy that you desire, select one that is gay and happy, that approaches you without fear, that is alert and inquisitive. Avoid like the plague the pup who sulks in a corner or runs away with tail tucked under its belly when you reach out to pet it.

The puppy should be plump without displaying a huge, swollen belly. The skin should be loose and pliable, the coat healthy looking. It should exhibit no maturation from the eyes or the wet, cold nose. Watch as it plays and romps to make certain it is not limping. If the puppy hops like a bunny with hind legs together, using its front legs to pull its body forward, it is quite possible that it has hip dysplasia, an orthopedic ailment that is prevalent today in almost all breeds but greyhounds.

If you select a more mature but still young dog, compare him with the top dogs in the kennels. Is he sound? Is he typical of the breed? He, too, should show no fear, be friendly and bright-eyed, and move freely, albeit still with puppy clumsiness. Examine his mouth. Is his bite correct and does he have a full complement of teeth? If a male, does he possess both testicles; do they hang evenly in the scrotum?

HOW MUCH SHOULD YOU PAY?

A pet-type puppy in most breeds should not cost more than $75 and quite often can be purchased for less. A puppy of show type will cost comparatively more. Such a youngster, with an impressive pedigree indicating a fine genetic heritage, will be priced from $200 and up, depending upon the breed. In keeping with the rapidly rising costs of dog foods and other essentials, prices could quite possibly be higher by the time you read this.

An older puppy or young dog might cost slightly more than a good young puppy, but not necessarily so. The reason for such a seeming discrepancy may be simply that the breeder has kept from a former litter a good youngster that hasn't quite lived up to his promise as a candidate for top show honors and he will sell this "teenager" at a realistic price to make room for other promising young stock. The lucky buyer can, under these conditions, often purchase a very handsome young animal at a good price.

Scrutinize the young dog or puppy you select very carefully for any disqualifying or grave faults as listed in the American Kennel Club

(AKC) standard for the breed. No dog is perfect. Obviously cosmetic faults of the moment, such as shedding of the coat, are not important, but genetic faults of structure or temperament that cannot be corrected must be avoided.

THE PEDIGREE AND GUARANTEES

When you purchase a purebred dog or puppy, you should be supplied by the seller with a three- or four-generation pedigree, an individual AKC registration certificate, a health certificate, a record of the treatment the dog has received for worms, what kind and when vaccinations have been given (distemper, hepatitis and leptospirosis vaccines are given together in one dose and there is a separate vaccine for rabies), and what diet the breeder has been feeding.

The pedigree is a record of the animal's lineal ancestry and is a valuable document to both breeder and owner. If you explore deeply the genetic background of the dog—a requisite for all breeders of fine stock —you can evaluate faults and virtues that are handed down from generation to generation. Delving into the ancestry must be completely objective or the reason for the study is lost in a haze of wishful thinking and the desire to enhance the individuals listed with virtues that they did not possess.

Wild canines can be acquired through animal importers and commercial zoos. They must be gotten when very young if they are to be turned away from the inner call of their wild heritage and tamed and trained. Their innate fears and savagery will surface if they are not constantly handled and fashioned to the ways of domestication.

Where and How to Acquire a Cat

If you want a common, so-called alley cat, you will find any number of people whose family house cat has been more companionable than cautious and has had a litter of cute kittens. These folks will be more than willing to give you a kitten for absolutely nothing. Or in the daily pet-column advertisements in your local newspaper you will usually find kittens being offered free to a good home. This is a price you certainly cannot better. I must warn you that any dyed-in-the-wool fanatic cat fancier will indignantly inform you that there is no such thing as a "common" cat.

If, on the other hand, you are looking for a purebred, pedigreed puss, you had better find a cattery where a professional (or skilled amateur) breeder produces the kind of cat in which you are interested. This fancier will also be able to tell you where and how you can join a club dedicated to your breed, or an all-breed cat club, and where to procure the most pertinent and informative literature about the breed of your interest. A pet shop can also supply the same information and quite possibly the kitten you want. In both the cattery and pet shop look and smell with an eye and nose for detail. Are the premises and the animals clean and well cared for? Is there a sickly odor permeating the premises that your nose knows emanates from filth and illness? If so, leave immediately through the closest exit and search elsewhere for the pet of your choice. Wherever you buy that precious cat, do not leave until you have managed to get all the free advice you can possibly absorb.

Test the hearing of any white cat or kitten that you wish to purchase. Charles Darwin initially reported the fact that white cats with blue eyes are usually deaf. London scientists found that, when very young, white, blue-eyed kittens tend to have normal hearing, but as they mature seventy-five percent become deaf.

If your fancy leans toward long-haired cats, attempt to learn if the parents were completely docile, for some long-hairs strongly resent grooming. However, if they are not thoroughly and frequently combed out, their coats become a tangled garden for fleas and lice and are soon beyond the stage when grooming utensils can help. If the parents are quiet and permit comb-and-brush attention, chances are good that their progeny will also if first groomings are handled delicately.

HOW TO CHOOSE A CAT OR KITTEN

Should you decide to purchase a purebred cat, make yourself familiar with the official standard for the breed you admire. Attend local cat shows, and steep yourself in the lore and characteristics, mental and physical, of the specific breed. Select a cattery that specializes in that breed and see what they have to offer. It is wise to ask the aid of the breeder when selecting a purebred kitten because individual lines or strains within a breed can vary. The breeder knows how kittens from his strain will mature.

Select a cat or kitten with evident bounce and vitality, one that comes to you readily and is bubbling over with verve and playfulness. Grown cats, of course, do not "wear their hearts on their paws" and will exhibit a certain dignity. Check the coat, eyes, mouth, and nose to make certain there is no sign of illness, which will be evident in maturation from the eyes and nose (the latter should not be hot and dry), debility, sluggishness, and a dull coat. Sniffles can accompany any of these symptoms.

The same advice holds true in the selection of an ordinary house cat. Though such felines are given free and it is not polite to "look a gift cat in the mouth," it is wise to do so before you take it home.

WHAT PRICE SHOULD YOU PAY?
The current price for cats and kittens varies greatly, from zero for mixed breeds to a rather goodly sum for purebreds. In most catteries good pedigreed stock will cost over $200. Show-type kittens carry divergent price tages, according to the popularity and availability of the breed. Good Siamese kittens sell for about $75 and up; Himalayan youngsters have an asking price of $100 and up; Persians, $150 or more; and young Balinese from $200 upward. These prices will no doubt change with the shifting desirability of certain breeds.

PEDIGREE AND GUARANTEES
Purebred cats from reputable catteries should have a pedigree. Every pedigreed cat or kitten should be registered with an organization that exists for the purpose of assuring the buyer of the authenticity of that cat's bloodlines. Such organizations have a record of every purebred litter born in the United States. There are, at the moment, five such feline registration associations in this country; the largest, the Cat Fancier's Association, also keeps a stud book and foundation records. The pedigree is particularly important if you contemplate breeding or exhibiting your stock in the future. Insist upon being provided with this record.

You will also want a health certificate with your new purchase, and I suggest that you make certain the kitten has been vaccinated to protect it from infectious diseases *especially infectious enteritis.* Be sure that, if necessary, the cat or kitten has been wormed by a veterinarian and pronounced clean of these internal, dangerous pests.

AGE AND SEX
Kittens, both male and female, are malleable little creatures that can be molded by you to fit your environment. In a house with children, a kitten can easily adapt to—and even enjoy—the frenzied social activity that accompanies young humans. An older cat, sensitive to noise and disliking confusion, might resent such frenetic surroundings. I sympathize with this attitude, since I myself am one of the "old cats" who find it difficult to accept for any extended period of time the pitter-patter of a multitude of little feet, the shouting, screaming, yowling, and generally boisterous activities of children.

A kitten, of course, has to be trained, while a grown cat generally does not. Given the necessary freedom, an older cat will adapt to a new environment within a few weeks and is, in general, much less trouble than a kitten.

If you contemplate ownership of one of the wild cats, a kitten can be your only choice and the younger the kit the better. *Do not* purchase one of these creatures if your sole object is an ego trip, or if you know in your heart that you are not gifted with the special ability to find rapport with animals (and only a select few people are). Association with a feral pet, if you are not one of those special people, can only end in disaster.

The sex of your cat or kitten can be determined in a simple, easy way. The male, or tom, has under its tail two small dots that resemble a colon (:), while the female exhibits an upside down exclamation point (¡).

You have, I am sure, heard the term "tomcatting" applied to a male human. Strangely enough it has the same connotation when applied to a male cat. If your pet is a mature male and has not been neutered, he will go courting. He will roam the streets and alleys looking for a female cat that is in heat, fight over her, and return home in the wee hours dirty, unkempt, bitten, scratched from fighting for the lady's favor, drunk with love and possibly infected. He will also taint (or "spray") the air with an odor that is cologne to female cats but anathema to humans.

The simple solution to this problem is to have your tom neutered. It is not expensive surgery and your veterinarian can do the job quickly. It is best to have this surgery performed when your cat is between four and six months of age. It will remove his desire to roam and will turn him into a clean, sweet pet and a complete homebody. Even a valuable exhibition-quality male can be neutered if he was purchased as a pet and companion. Of course if you are a breeder, such a male is an asset to your cattery and should remain whole to be used at stud to sire fine litters of show-quality kittens.

Should you buy or fall heir to a male of any of the wild species of felines, he should most definitely be neutered. When I mention wild cats, I am referring to servals, ocelots, and such wild relatives of the feline family, not domesticated cats that have taken to the wild. Of the latter there are two kinds: those that have gone back to a natural way of life in the woods, and those that have become bums in the city— mangy, slinky outcasts from society, living on garbage and prowling dark alleys like feline winos.

The female cat—called a queen by breeders—if a fine, purebred specimen, is a vehicle for the propagation of her kind and so has intrinsic value. Female cats produce and care for their young with much less trouble than most animals. If your female pet and companion is of mixed ancestry—or even a purebred that you don't want to breed—you can eliminate the bother of prowling toms, loud serenades of love, the raucous "calling" the female indulges in when mature, and periodic litters of kittens, by having her spayed—surgery that is not expensive but is definitely final.

Purchasing a Bird

When you contemplate buying a bird, visit a breeder of fine birds, a bird ranch, or a really good pet shop owned by someone who knows quality birds. If the bird you want is a popular breed, you can probably find a successful breeder of that specific species without too much trouble. A contact of this kind can be of immeasurable worth to you, for many hobbyists have a fund of valuable lore that they can impart.

Write a list of pertinent questions to ask the seller. Make certain that you have the right kind of cage or can purchase one where you buy the bird. Cages are fashioned to house different kinds of birds. Perches must be of the right size and set with the correct spacing between them. To give you just a slight idea of the necessary differences to be found in cages for two of the most popular birds: canary cages have a section for bathing and hooded food cups attached to the outside of the cage, while budgerigars feed from open cups inside the cage and will not use a bathing utensil. Do not buy a cage that has a peaked or pointed top with the vertical wires gradually joined at the top of the peak. Many birds climb upward, insert their heads through the wires and, in so doing, strangle themselves.

Buy the food being fed the bird at the breeder's or pet shop and make certain to take home any necessary supplements. Do not buy packaged food at the supermarket for your bird. Viability of the seeds is usually below par. Purchase fresh seeds in bulk at the breeder's, pet shop, or the nearest feed store. The last named may not have the seed in the proper mix so, unless you wish to buy several kinds of seeds separately and mix them yourself, it is best to find a place where you can purchase fresh, ready-mixed seeds designed particularly for your avian breed. Specific gravel or grit—which performs as teeth would if the bird had teeth, grinding the food in the crop—will be needed. Cuttlebone, a mineral block, and perhaps some kind of live food or a special nectar will be needed, according to the breed you have chosen.

The feeding of specific species of birds is a long and varied subject that would take up too much space here and cannot be generalized. Definitive coverage will be given in the section devoted solely to avian pets.

When selecting your bird, regardless of species, make sure its feathers are smooth and glossy, that it is active and giving voice, not sitting fluffed up without moving. Check the droppings on the floor of the cage for normalcy (which varies with the species) and observe if the bird's crop is full, its body rounded and the breastbone not obvious. Buy as fine a specimen as you can afford. Cheap birds are never worth more than you pay for them, but a fine bird is always valuable.

If the bird is of a species that you will handle, try to buy one that has been aviary bred and, if possible, hand fed. Many species are, of course, caught wild rather than being bred in captivity. Pedigrees can be supplied with some birds (such as budgerigars) if they are of top show breeding lineage.

AGE AND SEX

The age of a bird can be very important. Many avian creatures must be bought when quite young if you hope to successfully tame and train them to become satisfying pets. When young, birds will become acclimated quite rapidly to a new environment. With many species it is best to attempt to acquire a chick that has only recently left the nest but is successfully feeding itself.

The sex of a bird is significant in many ways. Usually males, or cock birds, are much more colorful and beautiful than hens, and the mating displays some males indulge in are nothing short of fabulous. In many families the males, not the females, are the songsters. Hen birds are more prone to bite and are not as easily tamed as are males, and last, but certainly not least, in most of the talking species the cock and not the hen becomes the accomplished vocal mimic. I mentioned that these facts are "usually" so. I used that word because in a few species the reverse is true and the hen is the more colorful of the pair. In other species the birds are most difficult to sex and appear to be exactly alike. Of course, if you intend to breed birds, the hen becomes as valuable to you as the cock bird.

HOW MUCH SHOULD YOU PAY?

The amount you will have to pay for your pet bird will vary greatly, depending upon the species and availability of the bird of your choice. Some of the more common finches can be purchased for as little as $5 to $10 a pair, if they are easily bred and commonly available. Macaws and cockatoos, at the time of this writing, cannot be bought for less than

$500 for a single specimen—and prices ascend into thousands of dollars for superb specimens already trained and talking. Remember, though, that these birds will probably outlive you. Many species of birds will not breed freely or at all in captivity and must be imported from their native heaths. As a result their price is quite high. Most macaws, cockatoos, and a host of other birds are imported from countries that, in an attempt to conserve their wildlife, have stringent laws regarding the export of their fauna, hence few of their native birds reach these shores. The result is a rapid climb in the value of such birds. Some of the truly rare exotics probably cost more than the average hobbyist can afford or is prepared to pay.

Buying a Rodent

Rodents are best bought in pet shops or from breeders. Some of the more exotic species may be found for you by an animal dealer who imports such creatures for public or private zoos. Since this mammalian order is so exceedingly large in number and elastic in size, the choice is indeed wide.

Rodents that are destined for pet status should be as young as possible when purchased. But if you contemplate a breeding program, it is best to select older animals of prime breeding age that are guaranteed to be a pair (a male and female of the same species). For either purpose the animals you buy should be in the best of health: active, exhibiting glossy, healthy coats (not patchy, indicating skin disease), and with good appetites and normal stools.

The cost of most of the common, or more available, rodents is not at all high and will not put a strain upon your finances. Exotic rodents that must be imported from far countries will necessarily be higher in price.

Purchasing Tropical Fishes

The best place to buy tropicals is from an aquarium pet shop or a hobby breeder who specializes in ornamental fishes. When selecting your fishes, examine each one thoroughly to make certain they are healthy, of good size, and well fed and plump. Young adults are your best buy, for they exhibit mature size and color. Signs of illness are emaciation, drawn-up stomach, abnormal lumps of any kind, clamping of fins, swimming on one side, obvious veils of fungus on body or fins, distended eyes, abdominal swelling, rubbing against objects in the tank, open sores or whitish pimples, lack of balance, shaking while remaining in one place, and rough scales (see, Diseases of Fishes).

THE COST OF FISHES

Fishes vary greatly in price. Some, such as the lovely discus fishes, are always rather expensive. Common guppies are relatively inexpensive, yet fine guppies from top show strains can sell for $30 or more for a trio. New mutations are inevitably highly priced until a large number have been bred. Because tropicals are fairly delicate and fancy specimens cost quite a bit, it is best for the neophyte to begin with less costly specimens and learn the art of tropical-fish keeping from the cheapies. After gaining valuable experience, the newly crowned aquarist can advance to keeping and breeding some of the more delicate, expensive, and exotic tropicals.

Where and How to Acquire Reptile Pets

Reptiles do not have to be bought; they can be caught by the hobbyist, one of the few pets of which this is true. Of course this method of acquisition limits the enthusiast to those reptile species native to his locale. If the hobbyist or herpetologist desires more exotic serpents, such as the beautiful boas or pythons, then he must purchase them from a commercial animal dealer or pet shop that has such snakes. Reptiles of this classification are quite expensive.

Trading snakes from your area with collectors from another section of the country (or the world) is an excellent means of enhancing your collection. Snakes are not allowed to be shipped through the mails, so, should you arrange trades, your reptile must be strongly boxed and sent by express with a suitable descriptive label on the box. Reptile dealers issue catalogues and bulletins describing new stock; some even send monthly mimeographed lists describing new stock and listing prices for exotic and rare reptiles.

If you live in a seaport city, let it be known at the docks that you will pay a reasonable sum of money for snakes that inevitably arrive on fruit boats from the tropics, stowed away in bunches of bananas. On the piers, when they appear during unloading, they are immediately killed. Exotic young boas and other snakes from far countries can sometimes be purchased inexpensively this way, though they would cost a great deal if bought through regular channels.

When snakes are collected in the wild, specie selection becomes relatively unimportant. You do not select; you catch what you can and later hope to trade with other hobbyists for what you want. State museums usually issue pamphlets naming the species of reptiles prevalent in a specific area. This gives you some idea of the kind of snake you are likely to collect when reptile hunting in these areas. Learn the habits of the species that pique your interest and you will have a much better chance of success. Never hunt for snakes during inclement weather; when it is extremely hot or very cold, they stay hidden. During the cold months reptiles hibernate. A flour bag, with a shoelace sewn near the mouth to draw it tightly together, is the easiest method of transporting your catch. If you are hunting water snakes, you will need a copper-wire noose attached to a long noose-pole for the capture.

WHAT AGE REPTILE?

Young snakes are the easiest to work with once they are caught. They quickly become used to you and permit handling more readily than older reptiles. Whether the snake is caught or bought, look it over carefully, particularly for *external parasites* and *mouth diseases*. If you are buying, reject the animal that exhibits symptoms of such diseases. If you collect one that is infested or infected, treat it as advised in the section on reptile diseases.

Sex does not seem to be of importance in the selection of a reptile as a pet. There is little evidence that the sex of a reptile effects differences in habits or temperament.

Buying a Primate Pet

WHERE AND HOW TO BUY

There are several kinds of pet shops, some catering mostly to tropical-fish enthusiasts; some that sell remedies, cages, and equipment for pets, animal books and perhaps a few birds. Bu there is another category of pet shop that stocks many kinds of animals, sells foods, cages, and all the necessary paraphernalia for animals and birds. This is the shop to look for when you wish to purchase a primate pet. Another place to seek is the animal dealer's, but that type of business is usually available only in large cities. Whichever of these you select, be certain that the owner keeps his place clean and odor-free and has a fund of knowledge and understanding of the pet he has for sale.

Be certain that the monkey you buy is young and of a species that will remain gentle and sweet-tempered in maturity. Handle the primate you fancy and examine it carefully. Be sure it is one that has not been teased, that trusts humans, exhibits a desire to be cuddled and petted. It should be bright-eyed, lively, and inquisitive, with clean glossy fur, never patchy, dull, or ragged in appearance. The tail should be full and with the pelage characteristic of the species.

Examine the animal for lice, fleas, or body eruptions, and scabs. The primate's skin should be clean and the animal should not emit an objectionable odor.

WHAT SEX TO BUY?

Sex is important in the selection of a primate pet. A female remains much more evenly tempered than does a male and is more loving and docile upon maturity. In the wild state all primates conform to definite, complicated social and group organizations that center around the alpha or dominant male. Males, therefore, develop the arrogant, domineering alpha characteristics and can become dangerous.

How to Acquire a Raccoon-Family Pet

The kinkajou, lesser panda, and cacomistle must be bought from an animal dealer or pet shop that features exotic animals. In the United States a coatimundi will have to be purchased from the same source, but in South America they are more readily available. Raccoons are bred in the United States for their pelts, and fine baby 'coons can often be bought from a breeder. They can also be found in pet shops. Frequently those available in shops are from nests found by night raccoon hunters, a popular fall sport in this country.

AGE AND SEX

All of the raccoon-family creatures can be tamed and trained by an owner who has a special way with animals, but it is best to acquire a very young specimen. If you can possibly find one before it is weaned and bottle feed it yourself, it will never really have to be tamed.

The best sex to select is a moot question. If you can choose between several youngsters, select the most docile and affectionate, regardless of sex. I have been told that the male coati when old cannot be trusted, but in my own limited experience I have found the male more reliable than the female which, I have observed, has a tendency to behave erratically in maturity. All living creatures vary in individual temperament. The kinky kinkajou of either sex, if gotten when young and properly handled, remains a quiet and affectionate pet. Raccoons can be mischievous rascals and, unless kept chained in a specific area while in the house, or kept under surveillance, can cause damage to curtains and other household items.

How and Where to Buy Hoofed Animals

The many and varied species of what we call farm animals are most likely to be found for purchase on (of all places) farms. The domestic varieties of sheep, swine, goats and cattle generally belong on farms as pets of farm people. Deer and antelopes can occasionally be bought through animal dealers but, with a few exceptions, do not make good pets. They, like farm animals, need space to roam. (Remember "Where the deer and the antelope play"?) Exotic hoofed mammals are difficult to keep unless you own a farm or a lot of land. But if your fancy leans toward an odd-toed hoofed pet, buy it young and select a female. Bulls, boars, stags, rams, and billy goats are often belligerent—and smell gamey. I grant you that little lambs, small calves, and tiny piglets are exceedingly cute, but they grow up to be big, stupid sheep, cows, or swine that love to wallow in mud.

The odd-toed hoofed animals present different problems of purchase. Horses, ponies, and their relatives can usually be bought from private owners, stables, or breeders.

Should your emotions exceed your sense and you want an even-toed hoofed mammal, it can probably be purchased from a farmer on a pound price basis. If your fancy embraces deer or tapirs and such, you will have to pay a dealer a set price according to their availability and the price he has paid to import the animal. Examine it for any evidence of poor health and do not buy if such evidence is present.

SELECTING A BREED

Your riding ability, age, and intent have a great deal to do with the breed of equine you should purchase. We will pass over the zebras and other wild equines and think in terms of those generally available as pets and/or riding or driving animals. From this view the thoroughbred, Arab, Standardbred, and some American Saddlebred horses are generally considered "hot" animals and could be difficult for a novice to handle. On the other hand, Arabian horses have for generations been the pride and pets of the desert sheiks. Arabian pedigrees are carved on ivory tablets and the animals share the tents of their indulgent and swarthy masters.

Experienced horsemen will tell you that, after wintering out, the only two breeds of horses that will come to them when they call, and enter the pasture with a pan of oats, are quarter horses and Tennessee Walkers. In my own experience I have found Morgans to be generally docile also. Remember that stallions can be tough and dangerous animals, so mares and geldings (neutered stallions) should be your choice for riding or driving.

If you are selecting a pony for a child, be very certain that it is well-mannered and gentle. Sometimes the smaller ponies are too tiny to have been trained by a grown and knowledgeable horseman. As a result, the ponies are not as reliable as they should be.

I suggest that you take with you someone who has had experience with horses and can aid you in selecting a sound, manageable animal, free from vices. The connotation of shrewdness accruing to the title "horse trader" should be taken seriously. The Latin words, *Caveat emptor* (Let the buyer beware) are the horse trader's motto. Spend some time with the animal before you buy. Check its teeth, and hooves and, if possible, find out the name of the veterinarian that has taken care of the animal. Ask the vet for his professional opinion of the horse's health. Only then should you begin to estimate the animal's monetary worth.

AGE AND SEX

Hoofed animals other than horses, ponies, mules, asses, and burros should be acquired when young. Specimens not of domesticated species should be bought when just old enough to eat by themselves—before they can instinctively turn to the ways of the wild.

DOMESTICATED HOOFED ANIMALS

Horses, ponies, mules, asses, and burros, on the other hand, should not be purchased when colts or youngsters. It is best to buy an animal that is three years of age or older and that has been trained in good manners and deportment. An equine up to eight years of age is considered young and possesses the strength and agility of youth. Geldings generally have the best temperaments and are more manageable than either mares (female horses) or stallions. Mares are next in docility. Stallions are quite difficult to handle and some are as savage as tigers. Occasionally you will find a horseman who has a strange rapport with equine males—old-timers in the horse business refer to such an individual as a "stallion man." I would advise that you select a well-mannered gelding as a pet and riding hack.

A jackass is a male donkey. A mule is the hybrid offspring of a jackass and a mare and is inevitably sterile.

COSTS AND OTHER CONSIDERATIONS

The cost of an exotic hoofed pet will vary with its scarcity and the distance it is shipped. Farm-type pets (calves, lambs, kids, pigs, sheep, cattle) can probably be purchased on a pound average basis. The cost of mules, asses, or burros depends upon their utilitarian abilities, temperament, and availability.

The price of horses and ponies differs greatly with the breed, training, and purpose for which the animal is to be used. A stakes-winning Thoroughbred, Standardbred, or Quarter Horse can command a fantastic sum. Top show horses of any breed, fine jumpers, hunters, working Quarter Horses (cutting and rodeo mounts) and top Arabians are all very expensive. But a decent riding horse or pony (not too old but trained and in good condition) can often be bought for from $300 to $500.

Beware, however, of low prices. You will quickly find that the initial purchase price is a veritable bargain compared to the cost of maintaining the animal from month to month (see Chapter 3).

Buying Mustelines and Viverrines

The animals embraced by these two mammalian families are not often thought of as pets, yet there are some species, particularly among the mustelines, that make admirable pet material. Most of these animals must be purchased from animal dealers. The scent glands that make many of them obnoxious as pets can be surgically removed.

The general care of both mustelines and viverrines is much the same except that all the viverrines are inhabitants of tropical lands and therefore must be supplied with warmth throughout the year. All of the mustelines are hardy creatures that adapt readily to changing or cold climates.

HOW AND WHERE TO BUY

Today ferrets have entered the pet realm. They are in demand and being sold by pet shops and animal dealers. Since ferrets are basically domesticated creatures, they will, if acquired when young, tame without undue trouble. Ferrets are also used in some areas (mostly on the European Continent) to hunt rabbits and hares.

Both badgers and otters make excellent pets if tamed when young, though few ever become pets. Otters are exceedingly playful creatures, their antics graceful and humorous. I have known of several otters that have given a good deal of pleasure to their owners. But they are rather frenetic, always moving, and so not a good companion for someone who wants a quiet and peaceful pet. They don't become bored if kept in pairs so that they have constant company.

WHERE TO GET A SKUNK

Baby, or kit, skunks can be purchased from animal dealers, pet shops, breeders, or, perhaps, from a hunter who has caught a wild kit. I do not recommend the last-named means of acquiring a baby skunk, for wild-caught kits could have been exposed to rabies. The commercial breeder is your best contact. He might have an unevenly marked kit that you can buy for a good price. If you buy from a pet shop or animal dealer, attempt to determine if the kit was originally purchased from a breeder or if it was wild-caught. Also find out if it's been descented!

AGE AND SEX

The best age at which to buy a skunk is when it is about five or six weeks old and able to feed itself. Give it a concoction of evaporated milk, a little water and a fine puppy feed. The mixture should be the consistency of medium cream. Dip small pieces of bread in it and offer them to your new pet.

Sex is not important in buying a kit. Both sexes seem to have a fairly even temperament.

BUYING VIVERRINES

These animals (mongooses, civets, genets, et cetera) all come from other countries and are therefore expensive. They are also very rare because their importation into the United States has generally been barred. I would, therefore, recommend that you set your heart on the acquisition of some other species of pet.

Where and How to Buy a Marsupial

It would be easy to suggest that you go to a marsupial market for your purchase, but the truth is that marsupials are hard to come by. Only one species is easily available and that is the Virginia, or common, opossum that ranges throughout the greater part of the United States. Occasionally other species, imported from Australia, the home of the marsupials, can be found in pet shops or at animal dealers, but not very often.

If you are fortunate enough to find a specimen of the marsupial you want, look it over carefully for the usual signs of good health and temperament. Buy only a young marsupial or one that has had a lot of human handling and is perfectly tame. Opossums can often be found in the woods and sometimes you will find a female, killed by a car, at the side of the road with her myriad family of babies still clinging to her. Rescue these youngsters, pick the individual you want for your own pet, and sell the remainder to a pet shop to be sold to other marsupial lovers.

If you can find a young marsupial (the younger the better), it will be fairly easy to mold it to your own desires. Mature animals, even of domesticated varieties, are often not malleable and may have developed tricks of deportment or quirks of character that you may eventually find too difficult to live with.

Insect and Miscellaneous Pets

WHERE AND HOW TO GET THEM

Insect pets can be found all around us. They are so numerous and adaptable that they will undoubtedly inherit the world. Find them where you can. Your own backyard or the woods nearby are both teeming with insects just waiting for you to adopt and make your own.

Among the miscellaneous category of pets, I have seen tarantulas and bird-eating spiders in pet shops. Some native species of bats you can catch yourself if you can find where they live and capture them during the daylight hours when they are asleep. Armadillos can also be had for the taking in Mexico, Texas, and Florida. The rest of the animals in this category will have to be bought from an animal import house, will cost a good deal of money, and would generally be happier in a zoo than in your hands.

CHAPTER
3
Housing and Environment

A good deal of trouble can be avoided by giving serious thought to the proper environment for your pet. If you have selected the ordinary domestic pet, such as a dog or a cat, you have no real problem. But if you yearn to own—or do own—a more unusual pet, you must study its habits, find out how the species survives in the wild, or exists happily in zoos, so that you can supply it with the best environment for good health, contentment, and easy care.

Any housing or cages you build or purchase should be large enough for the creature's complete comfort. If your pet is one that habitually chews wood, use the very hardest kind of wood for its house and enclosure or, if necessary, use metal. Build its quarters well, with no wire points or edges that can cut either you or your pet. Seal these edges, if necessary, with wooden or metal strips.

Floors of cages, wherever possible, should have slide-out metal trays for easy cleaning. Cement or builder's sand over a cement base is ideal, in most cases, for outside exercise runs. Cement can be flushed down with water and sand quickly shakes off the feet of your pet. Utilize every means that you or anyone else can think of to provide an easily cleaned and sanitary habitat.

If cleaning your pet's quarters becomes a nasty, dirty job due to a lack of forethought and sanitary construction, you will tend to procrastinate more and more when it comes time to clean the house or pen until—for the sake of your pet, your neighbors, visitors, and your own esthetic senses—the job becomes an immediate and horrid necessity.

Your Dog's Environment

When you bring that precious puppy or dog home, have everything ready for his reception. A commercially manufactured bed can be bought or you can just place a spare piece of carpet in the spot where you want the animal to sleep. Have two pans ready, one for food and the other for water. They must always be in the same place. I suggest you put a rubber mat under the pans to keep the area under and around them clean, and to keep them from sliding.

Small puppies need lots of sleep so, if you have small children, allow them to play with the puppy only until it is tired and then retire him to his bed for a nap.

If you decide to keep your dog outdoors, build a run for him, using substantial wire for the fencing and strong posts set in cement to hold the wire. Make the run long enough to allow him a modicum of exercise and high enough to keep him from jumping out. Soil cement or regular cement makes a good run base. A couple of inches of builder's sand on top of this is ideal as it is easily removed with the dog's stools and new sand substituted. Periodically, to clean the run of worms and their eggs and offal of any kind, the sand can be completely removed, the cement underneath surface-scorched with a blow torch or scrubbed with a liquid cleaner (a strong disinfectant, kerosene, lime, or borax solution), dried, and a new layer of sand applied.

Another efficacious run surface can be made by raking in small to medium white stones, the kind used decoratively around plants. One need not use cement as a base for this run. The dirt surface must first be treated with a grass killer, then about 3 to 4 inches of the stones raked over the ground evenly. The dog's stools on this surface are simply hosed into the ground below the stones every day, and once every two weeks the stones should be given a lime or chlorine treatment. Simply buy a bag of lime, scatter it over the surface, and hose it down. When grass begins to grow up through the stones, flow kerosene over the run and any grass will be killed. A run is really a necessity as it provides a safe place for your animal, keeps him controlled in a specific area, and, without supervision, allows him exercise in the fresh air (if there is any of this scarce commodity still left any place in the U.S.). Be sure there is an area of shade in the run, where your dog can find shelter from the sun in hot weather.

If you use cement or sand-cement runs and scoop up the stools, deposit them in a pit dug for this purpose. Cover with a layer of soil and disinfectant, or use one of the commercial substances designed to dissolve such material quickly. Also don't forget to disinfect your shovel or "pooper-scooper." Dogs tend to defecate in a fairly limited area in the the run, so keeping it clean will not be too drastic a chore.

YOUR DOG'S HOUSE

Build a doghouse that will fit conveniently in the run and locate it at the end farthest away from the section where he defecates. A dog's house is his castle and lends a sense of security to his days. It is also a very handy hideaway if he is in his run when you are away from home and there is a sudden, unseasonable change in the weather. The house then becomes a cosy shelter where your pet can doze away the time until your return.

If you live in the Northern states where winters are severe and snow and heavy frost are hazards during certain months, build the house as small as your pet's size will permit. Keep the ceiling low to allow just enough space for him to circle around and curl up tightly. Line the inside with insulation board. Give your dog plenty of hay, straw, or pine shavings to burrow into and nail a piece of burlap across the top of the door or opening so that it will swing back in place when the dog enters or leaves. If you follow these instructions, the animal's own body heat will keep his quarters snug and warm.

It is a good idea to build a porch onto the doghouse with part of the roof overhanging to create shade. The porch will provide a sheltered platform on which the dog can lie when rain has soaked the run or when the sun is too hot. The back section of the roof of the house should be hinged (a piece of tire tubing nailed over the place where the sections meet will keep out the rain), so that it will swing up and over to give you easy access to the inside for quick cleaning. A piece of rubber matting or heavy oilcloth nailed to the floor is easily cleaned and flea powder sprinkled under the bedding will keep the house free from other, unwanted occupants.

Paint the house with a good outdoor blue or gray paint (colors not favored by flies). If you build the house yourself, perform your modest carpentry as close as possible to the area where the house will eventually be placed. This is particularly important if the breed of dog you have selected is a medium or large one. You will find that the house, when completed, will be quite heavy and any attempt on your part to drag or carry it any distance is an invitation to a double hernia.

A water pan or pail should be attached to the wire on the side of the run so that it cannot be dragged or carried by the dog, thus spilling the water and soiling the receptacle. Weighted aluminum or steel pans are best and do not chip as does porcelain. Keep the pan clean and filled with fresh water. Situate it, if possible, where it can be reached by a hose.

Housing and Environment for Felines

Arrange a special place in the house for your new feline pet and have it ready when you bring him home. An enclosed box with a front opening and a high lip to keep the bedding from falling out makes a fine bed and gives the animal privacy. Hinge the top of the box for easy access to the interior to make changing the bedding an easy chore. (Adequate bedding can be found in pet shops.) Instead of a box you might prefer a cage in which to keep your pet, at least until it becomes familiar with its new surroundings. This temporary cage can be a carrying case, always a handy article when you own a cat.

Next to the cage or box arange a litter pan of plastic or enamel, containing one of the excellent sanitary products manufactured specifically for this purpose. Receptacles for food and water can be plastic, but aluminum is better because it cannot be scratched or bitten apart.

After you bring your pet home, offer it some warm—not hot and not cold—milk. All food fed to cats should be warm or at least room temperature. They dislike very cold food. Cats often pull bits of food out of the dish, so a sheet of rubber or even plain newspaper should be placed under the food and water pans.

A scratching post should be provided for your cat immediately. Make it (or buy it) tall so that puss will have to stretch when using it. Kittens love to play and they will climb all over their toys. Nylon carpeting makes a particularly good surface for a post. Catnip, derived from the leaves of a plant related to the mint family, is harmless to your pet. Applied to the post, it will attract your cat and keep him from ruining your furniture. (If he persists in scratching the furniture, you may have to have him declawed.)

If you own one of the wild felines, a securely built area in the garage —or an arrangement which allows the animal access to an enclosed porch area or outside run—is an excellent idea. One advantage of such a plan is that the litter box can be kept outdoors so that odors are not much of a problem. Cats, large and small, are excellent climbers, so any outside accommodations you provide for your wild feline pet should have a secure roof of heavy wire.

Cages and Environment for Birds

Generally speaking the cages built for specific kinds of birds are too small and are designed to please the human eye rather than provide comfort for their occupants. Birds need flying room to keep fit; the ornamental, particularly the decorative round cages, do not supply the space a pet bird needs. So make certain that the cage for your bird is large enough and supplied with perches of varying thickness so that the pet's feet are not cramped from using one size perch. Do not use so many perches in the cage that you block the flying room. Natural branches are preferred by some aviculturists. Very active birds need proportionally larger cages than birds of a more phlegmatic temperament. A stand can be provided for some of the larger parrots (macaws, cockatoos, et cetera) rather than a cage, and there are many toys manufactured that can keep your pet amused during daylight hours.

If you build your own cage, use welded wire fabric of a rectangular mesh that is strong enough to house even fairly large, hook-beaked birds that are veritable fiends at wrecking wire. Many species of birds, particularly the psittacines, will utterly destroy wood, so use metal main braces, or seal with aluminum the edges that are available to the bird. Do not make the cage doors so large that a bird can escape over your arm when you have your hand inside the cage. Feathered pets that are handled, once tamed and trained, should have one or more perching stations around the house to which they can fly. To allow for flight space, cages should be long rather than tall.

Supply wood for chewing. Pieces of soft white pine for the bird to chew can be placed inside the cage, clamped or chained to the wire, or attached to the stand. This will give the bird exercise for his beak and keep him from gnawing on other exposed wood. The bottom of all cages should be a metal tray that slides out for easy cleaning. Supply paper or clean sand for the floor.

Feeders and waterers can be of many kinds. Plastic feeders are ornamental, attach handily to the cage, and are inexpensive, but most aviculturists prefer open, shallow seed pans. The low, red-clay dishes into which flowerpots are set come in many sizes and make excellent food dishes for birds.

Tube waterers that attach to the outside of the cage are perfect for their purpose. Birds tend to foul the shallow trench of a waterer that projects into the cage, so fresh water must be supplied about every other day and the waterer cleaned wth an ordinary bottle brush.

To supply the proper environment for your bird, study the care, food, climate, and habitat supplied by successful breeders of the species. If the environment is not correct, most species will not breed, so you can be sure that the successful breeder is doing many things right. Research the original habitat from which the species came. The progenitors of a large majority of birds inhabited tropical or semitropical lands. If your pet is in this classification, it will probably need warm quarters all year round and might be susceptible to respiratory ailments if it becomes chilled. Many birds, of course, become tolerant of new climatic conditions; others are very hardy and adjust readily to a new environment. Budgerigars are a prime example. Though they originated in Australia, they can become quickly accustomed to a cold climate. Budgies can be kept in outdoor flights the year round in New England

and seem not to mind the cold even when it becomes so frigid that the water in their pans freezes solid.

Never place a caged bird in front of a window during cold weather or at night; the glass itself holds the cold. There is always air leakage around a window and drafts of any kind are not good for our feathered friends. Cover your pet's cage at night if you wish, but if you do, be consistent and cover it *every* night. It will keep him warm during the wee hours and the noisy little rascal will also be quiet so that your sleep will not be disturbed. If you desire to hang the cage out-of-doors so your pet can bask in the sun, be sure to place it in an area where there is also some shade to which the bird can move if it becomes too warm.

You can make your bird's abode extremely interesting and decorative by adding plants of the correct kind and some pleasing rock formations. Plants and other decorative elements should be similar to those that are native to the natural habitat of the bird or his wild ancestors. In jolly old England the exhibiting of exotic birds of all species is an intense and popular competitive hobby. The cages in which these birds are shown are beautifully ornamented with plants, rocks, and branches cleverly arranged. Be certain that the materials you utilize will not be harmful to the bird should he nibble a bit. There are some birds that will eat or wreak havoc upon any flora you attempt to use for decorative purposes in their cages. Such species are exhibited in plain cages with just gravel or seeds covering the floor.

To control mites or lice spray under the bottom tray of the cage and the ends of the perches wth a liquid manufactured for this purpose. For cleaning the normal small- to medium-sized cage a 2-inch paintbrush becomes a broom for sweeping out seeds, and a square-end cement trowel or spatula is handy for scraping the bottom of the tray to clean it of debris.

Your Pet Rodent's Environment

You can build or buy housing for most rodent pets. For rabbits the hutch should have wire on the front and a wire door, or wire on three sides and a hinged frame with a wire top. Most successful hutches have in the past had a wire floor through which the animal's droppings fall to the ground (if it is kept out of doors). If you use the wire floor, supply a small square of plywood upon which your rabbit can rest. Because of the newest studies made of the ingestion of rabbits, however, the wire floor would seem to be less efficacious. Wooden legs should be attached to the hutch to lift it high enough off the ground to make it easy to clean the hutch and to feed and supply drinking water to the inhabitant. Many rabbit owners favor the commercially made all-wire cages. They have proven to be the most sanitary. If you breed your rabbits (plural since breeding takes two, and very plural after breeding), the nest box for the doe should be large and well ventilated.

Each rabbit you acquire should have a hutch of its own, the size depending upon the size of the occupant. A rule-of-thumb requires the hutch to measure about 3 feet long, 18 inches deep, and 18 inches high. If your hutch is outdoors, provide some shade and protection from feral animals. If you live in a climate of seasonal change, provide a cover and heavy straw to keep out the cold. Rabbits are wood chewers, so if the cage or hutch is of wood, cover with thin aluminum all edges that the rodent can gnaw.

Gerbils, hamsters, rats, and mice can be housed in metal cages that are easily cleaned and that can be bought in most pet shops, or in an old aquarium that leaks when water-filled. To keep your pet in and all other animals out, be certain to attach a wire or hardcloth cover that can be easily removed. Use wood shavings, hay, cedar shavings, or "kitty litter" for bedding, but do not use newspaper—the ink can prove harmful to your pet.

Supply your gerbil with a piece of burlap to tear up. If you have only one or two gerbils, clean the cage thoroughly about once every two weeks. Do *not* use cleaning sprays or liquids that have been manufactured for canines. A cage with a wire-mesh floor about 2 inches above the slide-out tray bottom allows defecation to drop through to the tray and makes for better sanitation. When cleaning, use hot water and a good detergent; disinfect and finish the chore by spraying with a rodent or feline flea and louse eradicator.

Rats cannot be kept with other rodents, for they will attempt to kill them—and usually succeed. *Cavies,* bless their little hearts, do not climb, jump, or gnaw wood. They get their kicks from just running around, so they must be given a larger floor space than other rodents in proportion to their size. In your cavy's quarters build a ramp or two connected to an upper shelf where he can perch. Your *cavy habitation* can be of solid wood with the top of open (wide-mesh) screening. One 24 x 12 inches x 12 inches high is suitable for one pet cavy. A good size for one male (boar) and five or six female cavies (cows) is 36 x 30 inches x 15 inches high. *The British Hamster Club* designed a hardwood box 24 inches long x 12 inches wide x 12 inches high that is called the *Oldfield Pen.* It is considered ideal for housing hamsters.

If you plan to keep several rodents, the separate cages you keep them in should be built so that they will stack, one on another. A feeding chute attached to the exterior of the cage can eliminate the constant opening of the cage doors to supply fresh food.

For your pet *Chinchilla* a simple cage made of 1-inch wire mesh, 15 to 18 inches high with 2 to 4 square feet of floor space, and with a floor of ½-inch hardware cloth will do fine. Here too a feeder that can furnish food from outside the cage should be used.

Hamsters, rats, mice and gerbils appreciate an exercise wheel in their cages. They also enjoy cardboard tubes and cans from which the tops and bottoms have been removed.

Some of the larger rodents need more space if they are active animals. The *Agouti* needs a rather large cage in which a box with an open end is set for sleeping quarters. The placid *Capybara* and other rodents that spend much of their time in water, need lots of room and a small body of water. Capybaras need a small pond, while a sunken bathtub will supply the needs of a *Nutria*.

Squirrel cages should be about 5 feet high and supplied with upright pieces of 2 x 4's or heavy branches for them to climb on. Flying squirrels need the same kind of cage, with vertical branches to which they can glide or "fly," and enough cage width (at least 4 feet) in which to do it. If you study the natural environment of rodents, you will be able to duplicate closely their wild habitat and provide them with a healthy and happy life.

All rodents should be given a block of hard wood on which to gnaw. The branch of a fruit tree that hasn't been sprayed is good for this purpose. The activity keeps them occupied and aids in grinding down their constantly growing front teeth. Wood or bark from the branch of a fruit tree can also add roughage to their diet.

Aquariums for Tropical Fishes

The aquarium in which tropical fishes are kept is much more than just their house and environment. It is closely linked to their beginning, intimately interwoven into the fabric of their life and death, in the same sense that the air we breathe is essential to our lives. For this reason the aquarium cannot be divorced from the species and given separate status here. I have therefore incorporated this alien, watery world, in which fishes move suspended, with the section devoted to the varied species of tropical fishes.

Reptile Housing and Environment

There are two kinds of cages or habitats for reptiles: the terrarium, which is decorated and arranged to mimic the inhabitant's natural environment, and the simple, unadorned exhibition cage. To a great extent the selection of habitat for a captured snake is not completely in the hands of the hobbyist because there are very specific requirements for the surroundings of many serpents if they are to survive and prosper. Therefore the hobbyist must be able to identify the particular reptile, know the conditions under which it exists in the wild, and reproduce those conditions in the terrarium.

Snakes of medium to large size and the larger lizards are generally not very active and will do well in an exhibition-type cage. But the smaller snakes, turtles, small lizards, and crocodilians need environment, temperature, humidity, and light that parallels their natural habitats. Of course the larger snakes and lizards also need these last three essentials but supplied in a plain enclosure with a tree trunk and branch or shelf upon which they can torpidly nap. For the smaller reptiles you can purchase plastic- or metal-framed terrariums with a heat reflector or screen on top. Within the terrarium you can create a miniature world that closely resembles their natural habitat. If you have several snakes in your collection, remember that all reptiles kept together must be of a similar size, for large snakes will eat smaller snakes and big lizards will dine on small lizards. This is not cannibalism. In the world of reptiles it is simply a way of life. Snakes and lizards of the same size can usually be kept together and, if they are water snakes, turtles of equal size can be their companions.

SNAKES

Terrariums (or vivariums) for snakes can be divided roughly into three habitat classifications: forest, bog, and shoreline. Snakes that normally make their homes in any of these three environments will do well in terrariums fashioned to their needs. Desert snakes need only a well-ventilated terrarium with a few inches of sand on the floor and perhaps a rock or two. To lend the scene a touch of reality you might furnish a piece of dry wood and a small cactus plant for interest. This terrarium can be of glass with a framed screen top.

The *forest* or *woodland terrarium* can be the same basic type of tank as the desert one, but should have only a 2-inch layer of sand and over it one inch of leaf mold topped with 2 inches of garden soil. A shallow pan for water, with the top edge even with the loam, should be sunk in the floor. A few plants taken from the woods, a piece of wood, dried bark, and a couple of rocks will add to the scene's reality. Remember to leave living room for the inhabitants and don't become so carried away with your own amazing decorating talent that you forget your reptiles must make this their home. Use a hand spray to keep the plant foliage freshened and keep the ersatz pool filled with fresh water.

To create the atmosphere of a bog simply use any kind of moss for flooring, supply a water pan and, if you wish, add a fern or two and a rotting piece of wood. For the *shoreline terrarium* divide the floor area equally between land and water, with the land sloping into the water. Use your fertile imagination in decorating your terrarium or, if it pleases you, leave it as plain as possible so that the accent is on the inhabitants. Purchase or build a terrarium large enough to supply plenty of room for your pets even after it is decorated. Of course some snakes are phlegmatic and do not need as large an area as do more active species.

Outdoor cages can be constructed by the fancier fortunate enough to live in a tropical or semitropical clime. They are particularly suited to boas and other large reptiles. Enclosures for tree-climbing snakes should be high with a post having stout horizontal sections projecting from it, or the trunk of a large tree with a few heavy limbs can be used. A shelf, as mentioned before, should also be supplied and there should be a large pan of water on the ground. The post or tree and the shelf provide the reptile with a place on which to rest above the ground. *Anacondas* need a rather large area of water in their enclosures for they are water boas. All snakes, incidentally, are good swimmers.

Handsome terrariums can be bought for the smaller reptiles or old aquariums can be converted to their needs. If you are handy, you can construct your own terrarium by building a well-screened box with a glass front. The tops or lids of all small terrariums should be of the sliding or hinged type and should have some mechanism for locking or bolting the cover securely in place.

CROCODILIANS

If you have acquired a baby *crocodilian,* place it in a shoreline terrarium with half water and half land and enough of both to allow the animal room to move about freely. The air temperature should be from 70 to 90 degrees Fahrenheit and the water should be kept at room temperature. Feed small chunks of meat, small frogs, shrimp and earthworms and put some small minnows in the water. Never feed the crocodile with your fingers. Use instead a photographer's wooden forceps to hold any food with which you want to coax the reptile. The young 'gator will grab the food and eat it in the water. About a teaspoonful of food a day is enough until the creature reaches approximately 2 feet. Some of these small *Crocodilia* absolutely refuse to eat and finally die. But if yours lives and prospers, please heed my advice and find a zoo, aquarium, or animal dealer to whom you can give the critter before it becomes too large (about 3 feet) and injures you. There is a legend that the sewers in New York City harbor many *Crocodilia* that were dispatched to that lovely environment by disillusioned former owners. Some years ago I owned a baby caiman which reminded me so constantly of the wife of a friend of mine that I finally gave it away in disgust. My friend has since been divorced and is living happily ever after. The order *Crocodilia* embraces crocodiles, caimans, and alligators.

TURTLES, LIZARDS, AND FROGS

Most reptiles are easy to care for if given the proper environment. Many *land turtles* can be tethered outside or, if your garden is completely enclosed and escape-proof, can be allowed to roam freely.

The shoreline terrarium that shelters the crocodilia, should also be used for *red bar* and *painted turtles, ribbon* and *water snakes.* All can live together in harmony if they are of like size. *Desert terrariums* can shelter *chameleons, horned toads,* and *gopher tortoises* together in a communiy. *Iguanas* also do well in the desert terrarium and will enjoy the company of other *lizards, turtles* and *snakes* of equal size. But to keep iguanas really happy, supply them with a walled area of treelike plants on which they can climb. Leaves of low trees with thick vegetation are relished by the larger iguanas, particularly if you spray or sprinkle them with sugared water.

Skinks and fence lizards fare best in a woodland or forest habitat. *Wood* and *box turtles* need the forest terrarium environment. You can put in with them some lizards and small snakes that also fit this type of habitat. Some turtles need a bog terrarium with peat moss and a glass cover to insure higher humidity, mimicking a summertime swamp. A mixed bag of reptiles can be exhibited in such a terrarium with lizards and snakes of equal size. *Milk snakes* and *water snakes* of the correct size are also at home in such an environment.

If you have bought a commercial "turtle tank," change the water every other day and be sure to replace it with water of the same temperature (from 75 to 80 degrees Fahrenheit) as the drained water. The water depth should be enough to allow your pet to swim freely. A rock that juts up from the water or a piece of drifting stick on the surface will allow Mr. Turtle dry spots on which to rest or nap.

Wood frogs and most spring peepers require a forest terrarium, though some spring peepers prefer a bog terrarium. Do not overcrowd them. *Green* and *bull frogs* need a shoreline atmosphere. All amphibians can be kept in a large terrarium that has areas imitating the various necessary environments. Turtles and lizards of equal size can be added to make a varied and, hopefully, happy family. The *bog terrarium* is the proper environment for your pet *salamander*.

Primate Housing and Environment

Your pet primate should be given a special place of its own, a one-room house-like box in a quiet spot to which it can retreat and rest. Monkeys are, as I am sure you know, essentially arboreal, so your pet will need an enclosed area in the center of which you have constructed a tree of cement. If you were smart, you would have built the enclosure around a live tree with strong branches. There, in their tree, they can swing, climb, and cavort as they do in the wild, indulging in needed exercise and releasing some of the abundant energy they possess.

If you live in the tropics, the enclosure can be of wire, outdoors. If your resident climate is chilly or has varied seasons, a room in a house can be stripped and arranged for your pet's comfort and fun. A few species can even be allowed to play outdoors in wintertime, but most primates are tropical or semitropcal creatures and prone to respiratory diseases if they become chilled. If your primate pet is one of a very small species, a large boxlike, wired enclosure that can be moved either inside or outside the house, with climbing and swinging space, can be built. Make certain the size is adequate whatever the enclosure, for monkeys are the original "swingers" and need room to indulge in their activities. It is important that all doors, all parts of the cage contrivance, and all locks you may use be well made and strong, for primates are also the greatest escape artists ever known and can find a way out of their habitat if there is any weak link.

At the beginning of your association with a primate it is best not to have other pets visibly sharing your affection. Once the two-way affection between you is established, many pet primates also form a real bond of friendship with the family dog or cat. In the wild, primates travel in large family groups or bands for protection against their many enemies on the ground, in the trees, and in the air, and become wild with fear if left alone. When adopted as a pet, the family, its dogs and cats and other pets become the primate's surrogate band or family. Treat your pet primate much as you would treat a child and remember that the animal is highly intelligent and extremely dexterous.

Supply your pet primate with toys that are of fast color and that cannot possibly hurt him. Like children, primates are fascinated by toys and will spend hours playing with them, enjoying the feel and sight of the varied shapes and sizes of the playthings and, in so doing, relieve their boredom.

Housing for Raccoon-Family Pets

For raccoons, coatis, cacomistles and lesser pandas, a strong wire pen about 6 x 10 feet x 10 feet high is about the correct size for one individual or at most a pair. All the *Procyonidae* are arboreal so need a good deal of height for their ramblings. A tree, real or ersatz, with strong limbs for climbing, should be a part of the built-in accommodations. A large container, kept filled with fresh water and securely fastened so it cannot be spilled, is a necessity. For raccoons and coatis a tub should be supplied for bathing. This can be sunk into the ground, but it must have a drainage outlet so that dirty water can be flushed away and fresh, clean water supplied. An enclosed house set on stilts 3 to 4 feet off the ground should be built inside the enclosure. This house, 4 by 4 or 5 feet and 4 feet high should be supplied with fresh hay for bedding.

The outdoor area should have a cement or hard-packed dirt floor. The attached house should be built with a slanted, hinged roof for drainage and easy cleaning. Be very sure that all doors and outlet areas are tightly locked and make both the house and the cage as secure as possible, for both the raccoon and the coati, with their clever front paws, are, like the primates, veritable Houdinis in the art of escaping from enclosures.

If you live anywhere but in a tropical or semitropical climate, an indoor cage is necessary for kinkajous, cacomistles, and some coatis (those that come from the lowlands, not the mountains of South America).

The kinkajou needs only a wooden box on top of a high shelf in the house or outside a small boxlike pen hung on a wall; there it will sleep the day away. At dusk it awakens, yawns, and begins prowling. The kinkajou, in the house, is not at all destructive as are raccoons and coatis, so it need not be constantly watched. If you need a cage in which to confine your kinkajou during the night, make it about 4 x 4 x 3 feet deep and about 3 feet off the ground at its base. Keep your kinkajou's quarters dry and away from drafts, and be sure the temperature of its living area is not less than 70 degrees Fahrenheit.

When building (or having built) any enclosures or cages for animals, use your good common sense in their design and make them easy to clean and decontaminate. It is essential to the good health and happiness of your pet to keep the area in which it lives scrupulously clean, so wash its quarters thoroughly with soap and hot water, disinfect the premises twice a week, and change all bedding at least three times a month.

Housing for Hoofed Animals

All hoofed mammals need an outdoor shelter and an area for exercise and grazing. Their stable must give them protection from the elements and easy access to hay, grain, and water. Straw should be provided for munching and bedding material, and the whole area must be kept clean and fresh with no buildup of sodden material. Otherwise you invite hoof trouble and other diseases. A program of fly and rodent control is important, and exposed wooden surfaces in the shelter should be painted with a wood-chewing inhibitor. *Tapirs* need an area of water and, generally speaking, a pond is a necessity on any land where hoofed creatures are kept.

Housing for Mustelines

Ferrets are rather restless animals and should be given a cage large enough to permit them the activity they need—one that is about 3 feet wide, 5 feet long, and 2 feet high—and a smaller, attached enclosed house that holds sweet hay for bedding. Keep your ferret's quarters clean and you will avoid unpleasant animal odors and an unhealthy beast.

Should you acquire a pet badger, it must be kept outdoors on a cement floor sunk well beneath ground level so that the animal can have enough top dirt to build a "sett" or burrow. Cement sides built up a foot above the surface of the run and down rather deeply are also a must to keep him from digging his way out. The enclosure or cage should be quite large (at least 8 feet by 6 feet) and of heavy wire. Supply your badger with fresh nesting grasses and sweet hay daily.

Otters need a wooden house just big enough to hold them comfortably and a body of water close by of a size that will allow them full opportunity to indulge their playfulness and constant activity.

A large box or cage, open at the top, should be your pet skunk's private dwelling. Never allow him to bite or nibble at your hand. He must learn immediately that the human hand is the bringer of good things—of food and caresses—and must never be bitten. You can reach in from the top of the box to pet him. Give him fresh hay as bedding and if there is an unpleasant smell, it will be your fault—not your pet skunk's—for not keeping his quarters clean and disinfected.

Viverrine Environment

Housing for your viverrine pet should be large enough for comfort, built well for protection and to keep him from escaping, and created for easy cleaning. Runs should be of strong wire, set deeply enough below the surface to prohibit an escape through digging. The pen floor can be hard-packed sand, sand-cement, or cement. Logs on which viverrines can climb, large rocks, and low bushes, lend an air of naturalness to their habitat and have a decorative quality. A ceiling of wire will help prevent the inmate from climbing out.

Marsupial Environment

The habitat you create for your marsupial pet depends upon the species you select. If it is basically an arboreal creature, its quarters must have height and contain a tree or facsimile into which it can climb to find contentment. If you select a marsupial that spends its life on the ground, the surface of the enclosure you build can be broader and not of great height. The surface structure also depends upon the creature's habits in its own environment. Remember that you are dealing with a tropical animal that needs warmth for survival.

Insects

The housing and environment necessary for some of the insect and miscellaneous pets you will find incorporated in the text on these creatures.

Actually the application of a little common sense to the housing and environment you supply your pet, whatever species it may be, is all that is necessary. Make its quarters comfortable, escape-proof, easy to clean, and provide it with the correct temperature, natural or artificial. The wild-type pet should be supplied with an environment that reproduces as closely as possible the terrain and habitat it—and its ancestors—have enjoyed in their native state. The end accomplishment is to make the pet happy and comfortable in the environment you supply.

4

The General Care of Pets

General care consists of the day-to-day chores that you must undertake to keep your pet looking and feeling its best. The creature you have selected to share with you your way of life and your leisure moments is dependent upon you for its care almost as much as a tiny, helpless human baby depends upon the loving care of its mother to keep it clean, happy, and content.

Supply your pet with good and constant care and you will reap the incalculable harvest of your pet's good health. It will look and smell good, the latter attribute a highly desirable by-product of good care from an esthetic point of view.

Use your voice constantly when with your pet or when working around his quarters. It forms between you a connecting link of sound which can strengthen the bonds of affection. Used correctly, your voice can soothe and pacify and create a quiet atmosphere of trust between you. Move slowly and deliberately so pets do not become alarmed. I always speak softly and continually to the flock of birds in my aviary while I go about my chores of feeding, cleaning, watering, and examining nests and youngsters. I well remember looking up one day to find a friend peering in at me through the screening that forms the top of my bird room, a man whose interest in birds is nil. He was watching me with a rather strange expression on his face and when I called a greeting, he mumbled something, shook his head, and walked away. Ever since that day he has looked at me sideways and queerly whenever we chance to meet, which is not as often now as formerly.

Most animal pets have coats that need grooming. Purchase the correct tools and get your pet accustomed to the coat-care ritual by approaching it as a game or a time of happy rapport between you. During the grooming process examine your pet thoroughly, particularly for any signs of skin disease.

If your pet needs bathing, use the same psychological approach as you do with grooming. Be quietly cheerful and use your voice to convey an easy camaraderie. There are all sorts of soaps for pet bathing, with new ones appearing on pet-shop shelves almost weekly. There are cake soaps and liquid shampoos, some medicated, some vermicidal; soaps that need rinsing and some that don't; canned lathers and detergents. Bathing can be indulged in almost anytime regardless of the weather if your pet is well dried (down to the skin) before being exposed to an inclement climate. If the weather is particularly chilly, you may want to take advantage of one of the dry shampoos that are worked into the coat and then brushed out for a cursory cleaning. *Birds* can be feather-cleaned with a commercial spray or plain water. *Fish* we will allow to fend for themselves in this department. When shedding time arrives, your pet's coat will need extra care and grooming. Birds molt. Snakes and lizards shed their skins, and their needs during these periods will be more fully explained in the sections devoted to these creatures specifically.

Some pets will need their nails clipped. A strong scissors with blunt ends, a nail clipper, or a specially designed animal nail clipper (usually for dogs) should be used for this chore. Sometimes *birds* need both their nails and beaks trimmed. The trick in trimming both beak and nails is not to cut so far back that you nick the vein. This hurts your pet, causes the vein to bleed, and makes your pet wary of the whole clipping routine. So do not cut off too much of the nail at the beginning. Incidentally, should you nick a vein, the blood coagulates rather quickly, particularly if aided by the manipulation of a styptic stick, so don't be unduly alarmed if, at first, you prove to be less than a virtuoso with the clippers.

Teeth should be examined periodically. Tartar should be removed, and broken and loose teeth taken care of (a job for your veterinarian). Hard-baked dog biscuits can be fed to many pets in addition to their regular diet to aid in scraping tartar loose and to keep the teeth and gums healthy. Sometimes the two front teeth of *rodent* pets grow so long that they must be broken off with a cutting pliers to the proper length and filed smooth. A rodent's front teeth never quit growing, so unless you supply them with something to gnaw on to limit that growth you will have to cut them.

Examine your pet's eyes. Sometimes they become injured by bedding material or caked by secretion or dust. Wash them gently with warm water and a soft cloth. The application of a mild antiseptic agent or ophthalmic ointment can have a soothing and healing effect. If inflammation, purulent discharge, excessive blinking or pawing at the eye, or any other outward sign of eye distress persists, it could indicate any one or more of many ocular ailments and should be treated by your veterinarian.

Keep your pet's ears clean, assuming it is not a bird, a reptile, amphibian or fish. A little warm olive oil on the end of a cotton swab will loosen caked dirt. Follow with another swab dipped in alcohol to remove the oil and freed soilage. Mites and canker can affect the ear passages. If your pet scratches at its ears and persistently shakes its head when its ears appear to be clean, it could have a deep-seated infection or infestation that should be treated by your veterinarian.

Canine Care

There are some elements in the general-care category that must become more specific for certain pet creatures; the dog is one such animal. Yet, in a broader sense, much of the specialized canine information given here can readily be utilized in the care of other mammals. You will find this overlapping to be true throughout the areas dedicated to specific elements of care, feeding, housing and breeding of the various and widely divergent species given recognition in this book.

It behooves the reader, therefore, to focus attention upon all creatures in these areas, not on just the one beastie that has caught his interest. The reason for the more intimate and helpful knowledge we have of some species of animals lies in their commercial or scientific value. Dogs and cats, for instance, are commercially "big business" and much time and money goes into research for products to sell their respective fanciers in a highly competitive market. Fur-bearing mammals such as the chinchilla, and farm animals that are economically important, providing milk, meat, and eggs, are also spotlighted by scientific research at the highest government level. Other mammals, such as the primates, cavies, rats, rabbits, et cetera, are used directly in scientific research and have been accorded a great deal of intimate study to find an environment in which they will flourish. From these sources we obtain data and adapt it to the environment we supply other creature pets that have not achieved the commercial or scientific limelight.

Grooming is very important in the care you give your dog, and is predicated upon the structure of his coat. A short, close coat merely needs brushing with an ordinary brush and a "hound's" mitten (which has wire, in the palm of the glove). Long-haired and wire-coated breeds need their own special grooming tools to keep them trim and typical. There are charts available that illustrate how to pluck and barber such breeds, and those who exhibit them can give you further tips on trimming and grooming. Poodles, cockers (American), and wirehaired terriers are most difficult to clip, trim, or pluck correctly and may have to be taken to canine beauty salons for correct coat styling.

Bathing your dog can be indulged in whenever his coat becomes odorous or dirty. During the shedding periods more than the usual grooming should be done, using a stiff brush and, in some instances, a saw-edged currycomb to remove loose hair. White areas can be enhanced and whitened by the application of a white chalk sold for this purpose. Dust or rub it into the white parts of the coat, then brush out the surplus to remove any yellowish cast and make white whiter. Sprays can be bought that will condition the coat and give it a high gloss. Daily grooming removes dirt, dust, dead hair and skin scales and, through the massaging effect it has on the skin, eliminates the need for frequent bathing and helps keep your canine pet looking his best.

In the General Care section I listed many of the materials used for bathing animals. For your dog, a good flea and tick dip after the bath is smart insurance. Follow the manufacturer's instructions on the label, rinse well, and dry thoroughly.

Do *not* use soaps or shampoos manufactured for humans. As a matter of fact it is wise to check the ingredients in dog soaps and shampoos for the skins of humans and dogs differ. So select cleansers from your pet shop shelves that are alkaline skin cleansers and manufactured specifically for dogs.

Paints can be washed out of a dog's coat with whatever vehicle is recommended as a thinner or solvent. Alcohol will generally remove enamels and some varnishes. Some glues can be removed with nail-polish remover. Kerosene will remove tar, but must be quickly washed out with warm water and a bland soap to prevent skin irritation. Last but by no means least, skunk odor can be obliterated by washing the animal (the dog not the skunk) in tomato juice and walking in the hot sun.

A squirt of Vetalog salve in each ear after cleaning will aid considerably in keeping your pet's ears free from canker. If ear trouble does make its appearance and persists, consult your veterinarian, for canker can become deep-seated and chronic.

Overgrown nails can ruin the compactness of your dog's feet and cause lameness. Use a "guillotine" nail clipper. They are manufactured in two sizes, one for small and medium-sized canines and the other for larger breeds. Buy a dog nail file and file from above downward to smooth any roughness after cutting.

Some owners brush their dog's teeth even as you and I brush our own teeth. Dog biscuits and soft rib bones are a good substitute for brushing, for in masticating them the teeth of the canine pierce the material, the tartar is scraped from the teeth and the gums are massaged. As a bonus, biscuits and soft rib bones help keep the dog's stool firm.

Your dog needs exercise and it is up to you to see that he gets it. Walking the pet on a leash is good for both of you, but not enough exercise for your dog. Train him to chase and retrieve a ball or a stick. This will allow you to stand in one place until your throwing arm begins to ache, while your pet will receive an adequate amount of exercise. Some dogs, confined to an enclosed area, will "run the fence" continuously and in this manner get plenty of exercise.

The Care of Cats

Make your home safe for your cat or kitten. This is the first rule of care for your feline pet. Cats are curious creatures and love to investigate all things that attract their attention, and generally all things do. They like to nibble on plant leaves, so be sure that you have no plants in their reach that can poison them such as mountain laurel, poinsettias, African violets, rhododendron, philodendron, and oleander. Cats also relish a bit of grass (lawn grass that is), so do not allow your pet access to your yard after it has been sprayed with any kind of insecticide. Teach your puss not to chew on electric cords or explore electric outlets. This could lead to a shocking experience.

Groom your cat once a day, removing all the dead hair possible, thus helping to eliminate the danger of "hair balls" forming in the cat's stomach, the result of swallowing loose hair as puss grooms himself. You can purchase the proper grooming utensils in most pet shops. I advise a rubber brush for Siamese and other short-haired breeds. A piece of soft chamois rubbed over the coat as a final touch to the grooming procedure brings out the gloss.

Most short-haired cats like to be groomed and enjoy the attention, but long-haired felines are another matter. They often thoroughly dislike being groomed because it pulls at the base of the hair follicles and hurts. Using the proper tools for this chore and being ever so gentle during the grooming process helps a good deal. A long-toothed steel comb and a stiff bristle brush are basic equipment for long-hair grooming.

There are special cat shampoos available, wet and dry. If you bathe puss, keep him warm and out of drafts for several hours after the bath. An electric hair dryer works wonders on long-haired cats if the coat is fluffed as it dries. Groom thoroughly when the coat has completely dried.

When handling your cat, do not pick it up by the scruff of the neck or by its legs or paws. Slip one hand under its chest, holding the front legs with the fingers of that hand. Cup the hindquarters with your other hand and lift the cat up, holding it close to your body. If you have children, they should be taught that this is the only way a cat or kitten should be handled.

Most cats exercise themselves by climbing or playing with their toys. If you live in the country and allow your cat outdoor freedom, he will get as much exercise as he needs. If you keep tabby in an apartment or house in the city, supply him with a post to climb, toys to play with, and train him to a collar and leash so that you can take him out for walks.

Cats, unlike dogs, are very independent creatures, and their care involves providing them with all the elements of cleanliness, a place of their own for sleep and rest, and a sanitation pan which, for your own sake as well as your cat's, must be frequently cleaned and changed.

Bird Care

Birds are not really difficult to care for. Some of them, particularly the lovely, but tiny, finches, apear to be very delicate, but with the proper care and diet they prove to be robust little creatures.

Learning how to handle a bird properly is quite important. The slightest excess of pressure on the bodies of smaller species when they are held in the hand can damage them and result in their death. All small birds should be held gently with the fingers curled around their bodies so that they lie snugly in the hand without undue pressure. The head of the bird should project between the index and middle fingers which should be held in a slightly curled position. Handling is necessary for examination, transferring a bird from one cage to another, and sometimes to administer medication, dust on parasitic powder, or to trim nails. To handle the larger species, whose claws or beaks can inflict nasty wounds, wear heavy leather gloves and immobilize the bird by wrapping him in a thick bath towel. It generally takes two people to handle any of the large birds, particularly if they object strenuously.

Use a bird-louse and mite spray under the bottom tray of the cage to help control these minute blood-suckers. If you use the mite and louse spray on the bird, direct it under the wings. A 2-inch paintbrush makes a good broom for sweeping the bottom of the normal small cage free of seed husks and other debris, and a square-end cement trowel or spatula is handy for scraping the bottom tray of droppings.

Keep your bird clean by spraying it with water or any of the good commercial sprays that add gloss to the feathers and often contain mite and louse inhibitors. If you begin with plain water, keep it warm and use a very fine spray, soaking the bird well. If you wish, you can work up from a warm- to a cold-water spray over a period of days, spraying every other day. The cold-water spray tightens the feathers and the bird takes on that "finished" look so necessary for the exhibition bird. Some of the smaller Psittacine birds will roll up in a wet piece of lettuce, cleaning their feathers in this unique manner. Canaries and many other species of birds will keep themselves clean if supplied daily with a special bathtub that can be attached to the cage. When wet, most birds will begin to preen, thus aiding in the cleansing process.

When your pet begins to molt, give it a bit of extra care. Add to the vitamin and protein content of the food to aid it in growing its new, colorful cloak. A bird's feathers are almost pure protein, so to grow new ones they need this important food element in their diet.

There are blocks that can be hung in your bird's cage that will help your pet to keep its beak honed to normal size.

Bird species are so fantastically numerous and the particular care necessary for many species so varied and so much a part of their very existence that further elements of care peculiar to certain species have been incorporated in the text describing the many breeds of birds available to the seeker of an aviary pet.

General Care of Rodents

The coats of most rodent pets can be kept looking well by periodic brushing with a soft brush. *Abyssinian cavies* can be combed with a metal comb such as that used for long-haired cats. Smooth the hair of your pet with the palms of your hands from nose to tail—the oil on your hands will lend the coat a glow.

To bathe your pet rodent, dissolve a good white, mild soap in boiling water; cool until it is lukewarm, then wash the animal thoroughly, being careful that none of the soap mixture gets in its eyes. Rinse thoroughly, using clean, warm water, until all the soap has been dissipated. Towel dry the beastie and keep it in a warm place until it is completely dry.

Chinchillas should be supplied with a dust pan of sand and talcum powder. Mix ¼ commercial talcum powder with ¾ washed fine white sand. The dust pan should be about 11 inches in diameter and 3½ inches deep. The little chinchilla will bathe in this mixture and keep his precious coat clean and conditioned.

Slobbering or an excessive wet discharge from the mouth is indicative of "Slobbers," not a very effete word, but one that certainly tells the story without beating around the bush. It can be caused by malocclusion of the incisor teeth, mouth abscesses, or softness of the teeth. The basic cause must be treated. But if the problem is caused by malocclusion, or if for any reason the incisors grow too long they must be cut off with sharp, side-cutting pliers. By supplying wood and pumice stone in the animal's house so that it is constantly available to the pet a lot of tooth trouble can be avoided.

If your rodent appears listless and unwell, put him on one of the medicated foods used for rabbits or chinchillas. Always have fresh water for your pet, made available in a gravity feed bottle not an open container which he will quickly soil.

A healthy rodent feels round and soft and heavy for its size. An emaciated rodent is a sick one.

General Care of Tropical Fish

The general care of tropical fish is an integral segment of the entire aquaria concept from which it cannot be divorced. Interwoven and linked so closely with other elements that are a part of the essence of survival of the varied multitude of these jewels of the watery worlds, their care must become a part of the special section devoted in this book to tropical fish, both fresh-water and salt.

Caring for Reptiles

The obvious reaction to the above heading by a good many people will be "I don't care for reptiles—at all." But to those of you who have fashioned a hobby based on reptiles I caution: Handle snakes gently and with care. All wild-type creatures will react in the same self-defensive fashion: Even though they are pets and frequently handled, they will strike if they are startled or roughly grasped. With thumb and forefinger of one hand grasp the reptile gently but firmly directly behind the head. As you lift it from the prone position, support its body with your other hand about midway of its length.

SNAKES

Snakes periodically cast off their skins. The intervals at which this natural phenomenon occurs depends upon the reptile's growth rate. As an indication that shedding is about to take place the color and pattern of the snake's skin becomes dull, the reptile becomes torpid and the eyes have an opaque appearance. No food or water is taken during this period, which can persist for up to two weeks. The preliminary stage over, the reptile's eyes clear, it becomes active, rubbing its head and snout against anything in the terrarium that is rough, and presently the skin along the lips becomes broken and the serpent literally crawls out of its old epidermis and emerges in a brand-new, shiny coat.

Pet or captive snakes frequently find it difficult to rid themselves of their old skins and must be assisted. A large rough and grainy rock in the terrarium, against which the reptile can scrape, is often all that is necessary to complete the shedding process. If this does not help, place the pet in an aquarium containing about two inches of water and a piece of floating wood upon which it can rest its head. Leave the snake there overnight so that the skin can become softened by the water. Large, phlegmatic types such as boas should be covered by a wet cloth that must be re-moistened periodically if the boa crawls out from under it. After a day of this treatment your pet should be capable of casting off its water-softened skin.

If all else fails, a piece of fine sandpaper rubbed gently across the reptile's snout will cause the shedding process to begin. If the snake is totally unable to shed its old skin, it will die—a very rare occurrence I might add. This whole process is looked upon with extreme envy by many women beyond the years of youth.

LIZARDS

Many of the lizards will not drink from a pan or other receptacle of water, so it is necessary to sprinkle or spray water on the plants within the terrarium. Do not pick up any lizard by its tail, for this appendage is extremely fragile and can easily break off. Remarkably the body cells will form a new tail, though sometimes the regenerated member might become bifurcated and the lizard sport two tails. In rare instances three tails will form to replace the one that was lost, a unique exhibition of both cell specialization and ridiculous redundancy.

Natural sunlight for most of the day is an essential segment of lizard care. Be certain that the terrarium is placed in an area that will provide this necessary element. But also be sure that the terrarium is constructed so that there is a section of shade as a refuge for the reptile when the sun becomes too hot.

Primate Care

Most primates prefer being picked up by their hands. This is particularly true of spider monkeys, gibbons, and many of the long-armed lemurs. Contrary to popular belief, primates are essentially clean creatures and spend a good deal of their time grooming themselves. A daily grooming by the pet owner will keep the primate's coat glossy and clean and will also form a bond of intimacy between owner and pet.

In the wild the grooming process is a form of ritual social intercourse between the members of a primate band. When you indulge in the act of grooming your pet, you are subscribing to this ancient, instinctive rite and reaching toward a closer, mutual understanding. The daily grooming and examination insures that any skin rash or eczema will be recognized early and quickly discouraged.

Teeth that need care should be the burden of your veterinarian.

Caring for Your Raccoon-Family Pet

General care for the *Procyonidae* pet follows the same formula I have prescribed for pets in general. The daily handling of your raccoon-family pet during the routine of grooming and examining is an essential part of the animal-human relationship and will keep your pet tame and affectionate.

Because of their high order of intelligence the *Procyonidae* are curious, active creatures and should be provided with playthings such as hard-rubber balls, clam shells, and hard dog biscuits. Remember that *procyonidae* are nocturnal and therefore rather sluggish by day, sleeping away many of these hours. But they become lively at night and can get into as much trouble as a monkey can. Being nocturnal, they have excellent night sight, but they are color-blind. All night creatures lack the faculty to see color, for in the darkness all colors become only values of dark and light, or black and gray, so the ability to discern color would be an unnecessary visual burden.

Hoofed-Animal Care

All hoofed animals need pasture on which to browse and a natural source of water. Tapirs particularly need an area of water to keep their skins moist. Hoofed animals of the equine family must be cared for through the use of special equipment.

Family Equidae animals will need their hooves pared down and most will have to have new shoes supplied periodically. Use a currycomb to remove caked mud and dirt; a body brush for dandruff, dust and surface dirt; and a water brush for the feet and legs. A hoof pick will keep the hooves clean. A sweat scraper, a mane-and-tail comb, and a grooming cloth and towel are all necessary equipment. The feet of all hoofed animal pets should be examined every day and cleaned if necessary.

The control of flies, mites, ticks, lice, and grubs is an essential of hoofed-animal care. There are several kinds of flies; two basic kinds of lice, sucking and biting; several kinds of ticks and mites and also the mosquito. To control all these pests takes a sound program that involves four basic ways of using pesticides: fogging, using a mist blower; application directly to the animal through direct hand sprays or dust bags; premise sprays; and fly baits.

Exercise is essential to the health of your hoofed pet. A harness and leash can be employed for some of the even-toed animals and some of the larger creatures in this category can be trained to the touch of a long wand or stick. A lunge line is of great value in exercising colts and horses or even-toed mammals that have been trained to wear a halter. Actual riding and/or driving of herbivorous animals that have been trained to saddle or harness is the best of exercise. All the equines fall into the category of animals that can be ridden or driven, but one can also similarly train other hoofed creatures as well: Llamas, cattle, goats, deer, and even sheep can be used in this fashion.

General Care of Mustelines and Viverrines

These animals need no special care other than that given to all furred creatures. Some of them sport scent glands that emit unpleasant odors that make them less than a likely candidate for a pet. But such glands can be removed just as successfully as those of the skunk and the offensive odor thus eliminated.

Marsupials, Insects, and Miscellaneous Pets

Care of these follows the pattern of generalized pet care. A rule of thumb could be: if it has fur groom it; if it has eyes, ears, and teeth, clean them; provide it with a comfortable home that imitates the temperature and environment of its natural habitat, and feed it properly and well.

5

Feeding Your Pet

Since we are here concerned with such a wide range of species, no simple, all-encompassing feeding rules can be formulated. Some pets eat fruit and vegetables, others meat; others consume insects, seeds, fish, worms; still others a host of other foodstuffs. There are many kinds of prepared commercial foods that can be bought for many pet creatures. These are the best and most nourishing to feed and should be used as the whole or a good part of your pet's diet.

Prepared foods are the end result of years of testing and scientific blending by dietary specialists employed by large commercial food manufacturers. These foods have been stringently tested under controlled conditions. Wholesome food elements designed to take care of all your pet's nutritional needs are combined and packaged by research personnel, working with many species of laboratory animals. Such food elements can be bought by the pet owner. There are also frozen, canned, dried, and freeze-dried foods for pets. Actually just about every method for preserving and packaging foods for human consumption has also been utilized by pet-food manufacturers.

Whatever you feed, make certain that it is fresh and not contaminated. I am referring now to fruits and vegetables specifically. It is always best to wash such foods to remove contaminants in the form of poisonous pesticides and bug killers that may have been used as sprays to control the many insects which feast on growing foods.

Many pets, not of a strictly domesticated, bred-by-man species (and referred to here as "wild-type" pets) eat in their native habitat foods that can be supplied by their owners; for instance, the various greens, fruits, nectars, barks, insects, and meats that are a part of the diet of many wild creatures. But often a study of the ingredients found in manufactured diets fed to other pets, perhaps of the same genus, reveals that they are very similar in food values to the diet you are feeding your pet in a basic form. If this is the case, wouldn't it be wise to attempt to coax your pet to eat the prepared, manufactured food, perhaps at first for taste appeal, mixed with some of the edible elements with which it is familiar?

Your pet will be healthier and live longer if you do not allow it to become obese. It is a known fact that most pets will consume 10 to 25 percent more food than is necessary to keep themselves in good physical condition. Test to find out how much food is needed to sustain your pet at its best weight and feed only that amount and no more. Young, growing pets and pregnant or nursing females need comparatively more food than the stable diet fed adult animals. Those that are ill or recovering from illnesses will also need more food than the healthy adult. Studies have shown that many pet owners who are themselves overweight tend to allow their pets to follow the same pattern of overeating in which they themselves indulge. If you are in this category, why not slim down with your pet?

Nutritionally any substance that is utilized by your pet as a source of energy, a regulator of body activity, or a body-building material, can be considered food. All creatures need certain food elements for a well-rounded diet. To be complete your pet's meal should include the following essentials:

Protein for lactation, growth, recuperation. Animal protein is found in fish, meat, eggs, and dairy products; 20 to 25 percent needed in diet.

Carbohydrates for energy. Found in cereals, vegetables, sugar, and honey; 70 percent maximum needed in diet.

Fat stores vitamins E, K, A, and D. Causes longer retention of food in stomach. Fat is found in butter, suet, cream; 10 to 15 percent needed in diet.

The exact vitamin and mineral requirements are not always known and can vary due to a number of factors. But if you are supplying a well-balanced diet, you can be assured that your pet is absorbing all the vitamins and minerals necessary to keep it healthy.

One of the most important food essentials, and the least expensive, is water. Consider the fact that about 70 percent of your pet's body is composed of this liquid, that the blood that carries nutrition to the body cells is mostly water, that water bathes the cells, brings valuable substances to them, carries away waste products, and helps to regulate body temperature by evaporation, and you will have some idea of how important water is to your pet in addition to being a thirst quencher. Water is truly liquid life to all creatures on this planet, including you, me, and our pets.

Water content in foods varies to a great extent, so fresh water must be constantly supplied to your pet, unless it is a fish or an amphibian.

Many brands of animal food of the "pudding" variety contain as much as 75 percent water. Dry or dehydrated meal, pellets, and biscuits average about 7 percent water. It does not take a Solomon therefore to understand why pets fed on meal, pellet or biscuit foods require more drinking water than those fed on canned foods. With a little thought you will also, I am confident, come to the conclusion that, since water is free it is much less expensive to feed your pet on the dry-type foods and add the necessary water than on canned food that contains a very high percentage of water.

But the great number and variety of pets included in this book make it obvious that dietary essentials will vary greatly with the species, and a diet that is completely adequate for one species of pet will be sadly lacking in essentials for another. Therefore diet balance is completely and irrevocably bound to specific specie needs and no one balanced diet will fit the requirements of all pet creatures.

Feeding Canines

The dog is a carnivorous animal and his teeth are fashioned for severing and tearing flesh. But he cannot thrive on meat alone despite the evidence of his teeth. Wild individuals of the family *Canidae,* to which our dogs belong, kill and eat herbivorous meat mammals, rodents, and birds, but they do not eat the muscle meat alone. They consume the whole animal, including the prey's bone marrow, inner organs, stomach and intestines filled with digested vegetable matter, connective tissue and fat, bones and blood. The wild canine absorbs the rays of the sun and drinks from the waters of free-flowing streams and so, through his natural life-style, ingests a well-rounded diet that includes all the food factors necessary to keep him healthy. Add to this the fact that he must hunt for, and run down, his prey, providing him with the exercise necessary to keep him entirely fit and you have a prescription for total health and vitality.

FEEDING THE PUPPY

A good commercially prepared puppy food should be the basis of your pup's diet. To this add melted fat or butter (equal to about 15 percent of the total weight of food fed). Cod liver oil and calcium phosphate should be added in the correct dosage for his weight. Be sure not to overdo the oil or calcium. Consult your vet before giving more oil. Warm evaporated milk can be used in an amount that will give the meal a heavy cream-like consistency. Some freshly ground or canned meat can be added for taste appeal, but not so much that it dwarfs the total amount of commercial puppy meal, which is the basic essential food. Feed this mixture four or five times a day until the puppy reaches the age of three months. If you prefer, one of the meals can be of plain warm milk. From three months on, gradually cut back the number of meals fed, feeding less liquids and more grain meal. When your pet is about six months old, you can switch from puppy meal to a well-balanced, high-protein standard dog meal or kibbled food and use water as a mixing ingredient rather than milk.

FEEDING GROWN DOGS

By the time your canine pet is a year old he should be fed only one main meal a day (at your convenience) plus a breakfast of a few dog biscuits and some milk. The size of your dog must be a consideration in his feeding program. Small breeds mature earlier than large ones so the small breeds can be fed like mature animals much before specimens of the medium or large breeds of canines. Taking this fact into consideration the regimen of feeding I have recommended will supply your pet with a diet containing all the essentials in the correct ratio.

Supplements, vitamins, minerals, et cetera, should be added to the diets of dogs that are ill or recuperating from surgery or sickness, of pregnant or whelping bitches, of frequently used stud dogs, and of puppies of the giant breeds. Your veterinarian will advise you about which supplements to use and when to use them.

Deficiency diseases, such as rickets and anemia, are caused by a lack of dietary essentials. Hookworms, lice, and some illnesses can result in deficiency diseases. By removing the cause and supplying the missing food factors or supplements in the diet you can effect a cure.

Feeding Felines

Feeding your cat has been made an easy chore by the wealth of commercial—complete dry and canned (or "pudding") foods—available on supermarket shelves. Cats can be trained to eat just about everything that people do, so you can occasionally vary their diet by supplying some leftovers from your own table. If you feed your cat a dry ration and find that he does not maintain a desired weight level, mix up to 25 percent fresh meat, fish, canned tuna, salmon or sardines, or a "pudding" food high in fish or meat by-products. Grown cats do not need milk as a permanent additive to their diet.

Feed twice a day, morning and evening. Many cat owners like to vary the diet at each feeding, but this is not at all necessary. Your feline pet will probably enjoy a tidbit of melon occasionally and loves to eat grass. Instead of the latter, which may have been chemically sprayed, a little fresh spinach or other green vegetable shredded fine and mixed in the food about twice a week will be relished.

FEEDING KITTENS

Kittens begin to eat solid food at three to four weeks of age and can be fed regular cat food from then on. Kittens and pregnant queens should be offered all the food they can eat at each meal, for they must have a high rate of food consumption during these critical stages in their lives. Make certain that cats, when young or pregnant, have added vitamins and minerals, particularly calcium and vitamin D. Kittens should be fed several small meals a day instead of the two recommended for grown felines. As they grow older, gradually increase the amount fed and decrease the number of feedings until at about five months they are being fed two meals a day. Always feed your cat at the same time and in the same place, for felines are haughtily insistent upon regularity in all things. Cats do not care for cold food, so if your pet, particularly if it is a kitten, should refuse its meal or not eat with gusto, warm its food and you will probably see a distinct change in its attitude at mealtime.

Food for Birds

The families of birds are so many and so varied in their dietary needs, and their food intake is to such an extent correlated with their mode of life and environment, that I considered it best to give this phase of avian culture more definitive coverage in the section devoted wholly to the vast aggregation of our feathered friends. (See Chapter 11.)

Diets for Rodents

Have specific feeding times for your pet rodent and feed only at those times. Twice-a-day feeding is adequate except for young stock and females that are bred or are nursing young. There are a great many kinds of food that your rodent pet will accept and relish, but to supply him with the balanced diet that is necessary to keep him fit and healthy it is best to give him a commercially prepared food. The evening feeding is the most important one, for rodents are basically nocturnal creatures and feed at night.

A rodent's food should have a high level of quality proteins arrived

at through a judicious amino-acid balance to help reduce the incidence
of fur-chewing (very important to breeders of chinchillas and other rodents that bear valuable or semi-valuable pelts).

Supply at each feeding only the amount of food your pet will consume
readily and completely and your rodent pet will never be called a "fat
rat." Most rodents will relish some extra hay to eat. Rabbit breeders
generally fashion a very simple hay manger that can be copied for all
rodents. The commercial mix you feed can be supplemented by a pigeon-
feed mixture that contains grains, seeds, corn, and other edibles that
your pet will relish. There are manufactured foods of the pellet type
made specifically for rabbits, hamsters, and chinchillas that can serve
for all rodents. If your pet is not one of the rodents for which a special
diet is manufactured, try the foods made for other rodents and watch
which of the various ones he especially likes, then stay with that particular mix. Also supply your rodent pet with a spool of rock salt on
which to nibble.

You will find it rather difficult to feed your hamster just a given
amount at each feeding because the little rascal will take food out of
the feeding dish and store it in the corners of his cage to consume at
leisure. Make sure *you* recall precisely what has been fed.

RABBITS, CHINCHILLAS, AND CAVIES

Rabbits, according to size, will consume about three to eight ounces
of commercial food per day. *Chinchillas* eat about three-quarters of an
ounce of commercial food daily, plus hay, a handful of 50 percent
alfalfa and 50 percent oats, and a heaping teaspoon of alfalfa pellets.
Greens and carrots can be offered every other day. *Cavies* should be
given commercial pellets plus fresh greens such as dandelion, alfalfa,
spinach, clover, celery tops, and small pieces of apple. Do *not* feed,
onion, potatoes, or peppers. Timothy hay is good for them, and a mixture of oats, dry corn, and bran is relished. If you have more than one
cavy and decide to breed them (or they themselves succumb to romance), feed the pregnant females bread soaked in milk in addition
to the regular diet.

HAMSTERS

Hamsters are excellent trenchermen and will eat almost anything you
offer them. If you follow the same diet-pattern that is used for rabbits,
you won't go far wrong. Hamsters, however, do not need extra hay.
Again a good pellet food should be the mainstay of the diet. Hamsters
also enjoy grains, greens, bread and milk. These little tykes need to

be fed only once a day. Do *not* feed citrus fruits, onions, cabbage, or garlic. If you breed hamsters, add a few drops of vitamin E to their food.

GERBILS
Gerbils will consume about 1 to 2 teaspoonfuls of food per day. Feed a commercial rabbit, chinchilla, or hamster food; some fresh, sweet hay, seeds (sunflower seeds are the gerbil's favorite), and grains. No fresh vegetables are necessary to keep your gerbil healthy.

RATS
Rats are omnivorous creatures, one of the reasons for their survival over the ages despite persistent attacks on them by man. Feed your pet rat a commercial pellet food, sour milk with bread, a bit of fresh greens, and a piece of apple three or four times a week. Hard-shelled nuts are excellent for them to gnaw on. *Mice* can be fed on the same diet recommended for rats. They are also fond of budgerigar seed mix. *Wild rodents* can be fed foods similar to those ingested by their domesticated cousins with a few added dietary supplements. For example, *squirrels* should be supplied with nuts in addition to their regular diet, and the *capybara* is fond of a variety of vegetables, stale bread, hay, and succulent underwater plants.

Food for Tropical Fishes

Today there are foods of all descriptions available for fishes. Modern food manufacturers lay before the aquarist a bountiful supply of gourmet treats utilizing the latest methods of freeze-drying foods. Protein and organic foods are also available. Hatchable eggs, infusoria powders, starter cultures of many kinds of worms, and balanced-diet dried flakes are all offered. One can purchase freeze-dried tubifex worms, daphnia, brine shrimp, liver, red worms, algae, combinations of all these fish goodies, and many more. There are special formula foods for specific species of fishes, homogenized and pelleted food, all scientifically blended to give your fishes a balanced diet with all the proteins, carbohydrates, fats, minerals, and vitamins in correct proportions to meet your finny friends' requirements.

NATURAL FISH FOODS
Infusoria are the foods on which all fry (baby fishes) feed. These microscopic single-celled organisms provide fodder for fishes of all kinds in the first stages of growth. With full growth, the larger tropicals and

some of the characins prefer larger animal food such as *crustacea, worms, small snails, insects,* and *smaller fishes.* Live food should be fed at least once a week to all tropicals to keep them healthy. Fed to young fishes, live foods produce greater and faster growth. Except for the hardy live-bearers and a few species of egg-layers, live foods are necessary for breeding success. Yet some tropicals prefer a vegetable diet.

WORMS

Earthworms make fine food for fishes. They can be fed whole or cut into halves or thirds for smaller fishes, and (honestly) you can buy a shredder that will cut the worms into small pieces for very small fishes.

Tubifex worms are always relished. Bought in a pet shop, they will have been cleaned and will be ready for use. *White worms* can be bred in a window box filled with good soil. They will multiply rapidly. The box can be kept in the cellar, garage, or garden. Add humus and oatmeal to the soil and feed the worms cottage cheese, mashed potatoes (without gravy), and milk-soaked bread. You can also purchase a worm separator that will cleverly force the worms to leave a lump of soil and fall into clean water in a jar out of which they are taken to feed the fishes.

Microworms are minute nematodes that are easy to produce. Buy a starting culture, divide it into two portions, and place each in a glass jar into which you have mixed minute oatmeal, wheat-germ powder, water and baker's yeast. Keep the jar where it is quite warm (80 degrees Fahrenheit). One culture will last about two weeks, so keep subdividing and you will always have at your disposal microworms from the original culture. *Gammarus pulex* and *Asellus aquaticus* are large shrimplike crustaceans that survive well in salt water and so are fine food for salt-water tropicals.

CRUSTACEANS

Daphnia, also called water fleas, are small crustaceans that appear in warm weather, crowding stagnant pools where they can be scooped up in a shallow net. They can also be bought, in season, in aquarium and pet shops. Daphnia make excellent food for fish and are especially relished by goldfish. But do not consider them a complete diet for tropicals. No one type of food can be so considered. There are other crustaceans that tropicals will relish, but none are as important to the diet as daphnia.

Another important crustacean, *brine shrimp,* are exceedingly important to aquaculturists. The minute eggs of this tiny creature can be bought dried and then hatched in a shallow pan of weak salt water (6 teaspoons of salt to a gallon of tap water). Quick hatching occurs if the eggs are kept in a 70- to 75-degree Fahrenheit temperature. You can keep the shrimp themselves in a mix of salt, epsom salts, baking soda, and water. Feed them yeast and they wil grow well, reaching maturity in approximately six weeks. Brine shrimp will reproduce readily, giving you many more live shrimp to feed to your fish.

PREPARED FOODS

Many fish cultists prepare their own foods for fish. Some years ago I bred show guppies from the famous strain of the late authority, Paul Hahnel, and I prepared my own feeding formula. I mixed ground beef or lamb liver (20%), Pablum, an enriched baby cereal (50%), hard-boiled eggs (10%), shredded shrimp or crab meat (10%), freshly ground spinach (10%), calcium phosphate and fish-liver oil (one-half teaspoonful of each). These ingredients were ground into a paste, flattened and fashioned into pancakes between sheets of waxed paper, and frozen until needed. When finished they looked good enough to eat! But it is only the fanatic hobbyist breeding top specimens for exhibition who mixes his own food.

When feeding prepared foods, do not feed more than the fish will clean up in about five minutes. Siphon off any that is not eaten and that has sunk to the bottom of the tank. Fish should be fed small amounts of food frequently, and they will eat with greater gusto if the temperature of the tank water is about 80 degrees Fahrenheit than if it is lower. If fed live food, they will do fairly well on only one feeding a day, but multiple meals and less food per feeding are more desirable.

Even though tropicals can oblige you by going without food for about two weeks when you are on vacation, it is far more preferable to have a friend feed them when you are absent for any length of time. It is a smart idea to make up small packages of food that your surrogate hobbyist can feed them at each meal. If you do leave your fish during your vacation, plant some live tubifex worms in the gravel and behind and under rocks where the fish can seek them out while you are absent.

There are *floating rings* into which you can deposit flakes and dry food and so keep it reasonably centered in the tank, and there are *worm feeders* through which worms can be fed easily. There is also a newly developed fish food that sticks to the glass wall of the tank and remains there while the denizens nibble at it to their little fishy heart's content. This handy device obviates the need for siphoning off excess food from the bottom of your tank.

There is, in short, everything manufacturers of things for aquarists can think of to make you, your fish—and the manufacturers themselves —happy.

FEEDING MARINE FISHES

Salt-water fishes should be fed only food that they will accept eagerly. They are, of course, carnivorous and all the live foods offered to freshwater tropicals can be supplied to these denizens of the deep, but they must *never* be overfed. Except for live foods, feed only an amount that they will eat in about three minutes and no more. Then immediately remove all uneaten food with a siphon or dip tube. Some marine fish eat a great deal of algae, a food that should be produced in the tank by the artificial light and sunlight you provide through proper positioning of the tank.

Sea anemones can be fed clam juice, shrimp, beef heart, mussels, or fish flesh cut into thin strips, or two 3-inch earthworms per week. Place the food on the anemone's mouth opening or tentacles.

Feeding Your Reptile

SNAKES

Undoubtedly the most difficult area of care for the reptile hobbyist is feeding. More than half of all snake species require live food. This means that mice, rats, and other rodents, small birds, and frogs must be found. Most snakes can be pursuaded to accept freshly killed birds and small mammals, but even so there is still the problem of procuring them. And the proper food must be fed to allow your pet to continue a normal rate of growth and to remain healthy. To give you an idea of what is required in the food area, some of the larger serpents, *anacondas* and *reticulated pythons* (when fully matured to a length of over thirty feet) will consume a forty-pound animal, deer, pig, sheep, or what have you, a week.

For the smaller reptiles that are usually kept as pets, you can, if you live in the country, set traps to catch rodents. Mice can be caught just about anywhere. Since some snakes will not eat unless supplied with live food that they can personally kill before ingesting, the hobbyist is left with the choice of maintaining several breeding pens of rodents or contracting someone in the area who breeds such stock and will sell him the necessary food animals. The difficulty is that many breeders of rodents are repulsed by the idea of their pets being used as snake food. Another alternative is to contact an animal supply house and once a week pick up, or have delivered, the number of live creatures you need. Often research laboratories have surplus stock that they will be glad to let you have.

If you intend to breed your own food animals, you will find sections of this book devoted to the entire spectrum of breeding and husbandry of the many creatures you can utilize as live food for reptiles. In the process of such an enterprise you might also become interested in some other pet creatures and derive a twofold pleasure from your undertaking. If you need food for *water snakes,* tropical fish are easy to find, for the world seems filled with aquarium hobbyists.

Frogs are also simple to obtain and are the staple diet of several species of aquatic and semiaquatic snakes. *Never* buy the brightly colored pickeral frogs that many dealers stock in quantity. They secrete an acid substance deadly to reptiles. Bait dealers can supply you with earthworms that are relished by many snakes and other reptiles, or you can dig or breed worms yourself. Some snakes will consume mealworms and white worms, both of which are readily available at aquarium pet shops. These worms can also be bred in quantity by the snake fancier.

Be careful when feeding rats to snakes. The common rat is an exceedingly vicious creature and has been known to attack and kill fairly large snakes to whom it has been served as food. I know of an incident where a herpetologist friend of mine turned two large rats into an enclosure to serve as food for a medium-sized but expensive boa. The boa ate one and then became torpid and somnolent and, while in this state, was attacked and killed by the other rat.

TURTLES

Feeding turtles is an easy chore. One can purchase several different kinds of commercially prepared foods for them as well as ant eggs and other turtle goodies. An occasional feeding of small bits of raw beef is beneficial, and mealworms are always a welcome addition to the diet.

FROGS

While they are in the tadpole state, frogs do well on fish foods, algae, daphnia, brine shrimp, and a host of other types of tiny water life, many of which can be bought at your pet shop in various forms—fresh, frozen, or dehydrated.

When frogs reach maturity, bugs and worms of almost any kind will be relished. A species as large as the bullfrog will consume spiders, crayfish, snails, grasshoppers, beetles, wasps, bees, dragonflies, and a host of other flying, hopping, crawling, and swimming creatures. Big frogs and toads will eat little frogs and toads and, being true gourmets, will enjoy an occasional meal of small live Snakes, Terrapins and Alligators. All frogs are voracious, but the bullfrog is ridiculous in this respect, for he will even eat small mice, birds, and little ducklings.

Mark Twain made a bullfrog the hero of his famous story of the frog jumping contest in Angel's Camp, Calvera County, California, and every year a Bullfrog Jumping Contest is held in that area to commemorate

the story. Mark Twain's tale elevated the bullfrog in the United States
to a kind of homespun hero status. Actually the bullfrog should be
known for its appetite rather than its jumping ability.

SALAMANDERS AND NEWTS

These reptiles can be fed the same foods recommended for frogs.
In the salamander and newt terrarium you can also keep frogs of
approximately the same size. Of course snakes should not be introduced.

Food for the Primate Pet

Your pet primate needs vitamins, particularly vitamin D, and other
food elements equivalent to those he ingests in a natural environment.
There are commercial monkey foods fashioned into large pellets that
were developed by scientists who, in their research, work with large
numbers of primates. These pellets provide a completely balanced
diet and should be used as the basic food for your primate.

The foods that the various species of primates eat in their wild habitat
are mentioned below to allow you a choice of additives to the basic diet.
These can be fed about twice a week to add zest to your pet's mealtime.
Often primate pets that are ill or just not consuming enough food can
be tempted by an offering of natural food. Milk is always relished by
primates, and large, hard dog biscuits can be given them to gnaw on.

SHREWS AND LEMURS

These little creatures will eat most anything, including insects, fruits,
leaves, snails, frogs, lizards, eggs, rice, plant bulbs, bark, and milk.
Tree shrews have even been known to consume hot spaghetti. It is
only a rumor that they demand Chianti with this meal; they are not that
shrewd. *Lemurs* are partial to guavas and bananas. The way-out *aye-aye*
taps on branches with its elongated third finger and listens for the sound
of disturbed grubs moving about inside the branch. He then inserts the
long, thin finger and hooks the grubs out with his claw. He will devour
the larvae of many insects and has a sweet tooth that can be satisfied
only by a meal of sugarcane.

LORISOIDS

These primates relish insects (especially meaty ones), plant shoots,
leaves, and some flowers. They also dine on bird's eggs, small animals,
and green nuts. *Tarsiers* ingest live grasshoppers, lizards, newborn mice,
and small bird's eggs.

NEW WORLD PRO-PRIMATES

These animals also feed on a great variety of food. The tiny *marmosets* are too small to nibble much off the large commercial monkey pellets, so they can be given strained baby foods and mealworms augmented by bananas. In the wild they consume insects and tender fruits. *Douroucouli* and *sakawinkis, sakis,* and *nakaris* eat fruit, snails, frogs, nuts, insects, bird's eggs, and honey. The same foods can be fed to *squirrel monkeys* with the addition of crabs and anything else you can think of in the food category.

TRUE NEW WORLD MONKEYS

New World monkeys such as the *spider monkeys* and *capuchins,* are partial to milk, apple, banana, carrots, bread, and a variety of fruits. *Woolly monkeys* will consume all the foods that delight the spider monkeys and capuchins with an added bonus of insects and grubs as appetizers. *Howlers* prefer a diet of wisteria leaves, green palm nuts, and some green vegetables. They are not much interested in fruit.

From a perusal of their dietary habits it is evident that the six genera and approximately twenty-four species of primates and pro-primates found in South and Central America have very catholic tastes in food selection.

OLD WORLD MONKEYS

Macaques, the guenons and patas monkeys will eat just about anything that can be labeled food, including leaves, pine cones, all kinds of fruits and fresh farm products, insects, nuts, and bird's eggs. Macaques are also fond of figs, pomegranates, scorpions, sweet potatoes, and crabs, while *DeBrazza guenons* go ape over tree gum and small lizards, particularly geckos. Patas will ingest everything in the line of food that the monkeys just mentioned will, and for variety like a few beans and berries, a small bird now and then and, like the true gourmets they are, mushrooms.

Langurs and colobus monkeys are primarily leaf eaters. As pets both these primate species can be fed fresh, raw vegetables, particularly the leafy varieties. *Vervets,* of the guenon family, eat milk corn, flowers, vegetables, fruits, seeds, berries, and—I can vouch for the fact—are also fond of toast. These monkeys frequently wash their food before eating it.

Mangabeys in their wild habitat select a diet of seeds, palm nuts, leaves, all varieties of fruits, and vegetables. They also like milk, fed to them only in captivity of course. As pets, these monkeys, are quite easy to feed.

Baboons, drills, and mandrills all eat the same kinds of varied foods in their native environment. Moving in groups, they consume large quantites of vegetables, roots, tubers, insects, eggs and chicks, small burrowing mammals, leaves, tree bark, scorpions (they nip off the sting with their fingers before eating), grasshoppers, lizards, and hares. Sometimes they will catch and dine on small monkeys, killing and skinning them before indulging in their monkey-meat feast. If the opportunity presents itself, they will eat newborn Thompson's gazelles and will occasionally hunt, run down, and kill older Thompson's gazelles for a change of diet.

Gossip has it that the Romans had a unique method of capturing baboons. They would stake out vessels filled with wine which, during the night, the baboons would drink with gusto. They would become completely smashed and pass out, whereupon the wily Romans would simply pick them up and put them in cages where the baboons would eventually awaken to a huge hangover and the realization that they had made monkeys of themselves.

THE LARGER PRIMATES

Gibbons are the only species of large primates in which we are interested as pets. They love figs and all other kinds of fruit. In the wild they will also dine on bird's eggs, young birds, and ants. A gibbon that has reached pet status will enjoy an occasional meal of boiled potatoes, lettuce, and various fruits with the accent on bananas. They are very choosy about their food, examine every bit closely, and delicately remove any bad spots they may find.

Raccoon-Family Pet Diets

All *Procyonidae* pets should be fed twice daily, once in the early morning and again in the evening, the latter meal as soon as they awaken to their nocturnal awareness. If you are home during the day and want to keep your pet from sleeping away the daylight hours, a light luncheon of fruit will cause it to awaken.

In the wild state *raccoons* eat a great variety of foods including rodents, frogs, lizards, small birds, fish, shellfish, crabs, small snakes, nuts, berries, corn, fruit, vegetables, and grains. The favorite food of the *crab-eating raccoon* is (you guessed it) crabs—land crabs, that is. Incidentally, if you have any small pet caged birds in the house, always keep them in an area unavailable to your raccoon-family pet. With their very clever front paws they can easily open any cage, catch the bird and dine with pleasure on this fine feathered morsel.

The lesser panda, or cat bear, though classified as a carnivore, seems to eat very little, if any, meat. It prefers leaves, vegetables, fruits, eggs, milk, and butter; the latter two staples it steals in the mountain villages of its habitat. Both the *Coatimundi* and the *kinkajou* consume a great variety of foods in their native environment, similar in scope to that eaten by the raccoon.

When tamed, domesticated, and treated as a pet—assuming the animal is acquired when quite young so that its tastes and feeding habits can be shaped by you—your pet raccoon, coatimundi, and kinkajou should be fed a mixture of a good, high-protein dog food, rabbit pellets or monkey pellets, nuts, fruit, raw vegetables, corn (particularly for 'coons) and occasionally some table scraps, fish and meat. If you are fortunate enough to have a *lesser panda* as a pet, feed the same diet, but eliminate fish, meat, and table scraps and substitute for these foods a greater percentage of rabbit pellets, greens, fruits, and an occasional egg. Some pure fat (beef suet, melted butter, or lard) can be added to the diet of all raccoon-family pets, and milk can be given whenever it is available. Vitamins can be added upon the advice of your veterinarian.

Feed at each meal only the amount of food your pet can readily consume within a half hour. *Raccoons* and *coatis* are rather greedy animals, waste a good deal of food, and have a taste for candy, peanuts, and dried fruit, particularly prunes, of all things. Such food items can be utilized as treats or rewards during training.

Food for Hoofed Animals

Oats, fresh hay, and specially prepared feeds should be given to your domesticated ruminants. A cattle ration that can be hand-mixed and that will keep cattle in top shape is composed of 70 percent cracked corn or ground milo, 15 percent crimped barley, 10 percent crimped oats, and 5 percent molasses. In addition, feed a daily ration of clean, fresh hay. There are brood-cow and creep-feeding calf programs, and starting and finishing programs.

Feed your hoofed pet three times daily; provide a salt block and always plenty of fresh water. Hay occupies an animal's time, keeping him from becoming nervous or bored. There are a large range of commercial foods used in regular "programs" that are excellent and particularly needed by pregnant females, young growing stock, and animals that need building up due to illness. Ruminants in these categories generally need more than just a maintenance diet, but be careful that you do not over-supplement.

GOATS, BURROS, AND SHEEP

All hoofed animals need an outdoor shelter and an area for exercise and grazing. The grazing area should be rich in good grasses and alfalfa. *Goats, burros,* and *sheep* seem to be able to find sustenance on poor grazing land but will, of course, do better in richer pastures. Ewes at lambing time should be supplied with supplementary feedings of oats and wheat.

HORSES

There are many good horse-feeding programs presented by the manufacturers of commercial feeds, but they are often expensive. If you use a bit of old-fashioned horse sense in your feeding program, you will do fine. If you have more than one horse, try to feed them individually so you know the level of food each intakes. In this way you can maintain the body condition and weight individually. Make certain that feed-room doors are locked or you might find your pet foundered. Feed should be at shoulder level or lower, the natural position for horses to feed, and don't overfeed. If you change your feeding program, do it gradually so that you do not upset your animal's digestive tract with a sudden change. Large rocks, about baseball size, in the feedbox will slow down the horse that has a habit of eating too fast. Feed only hay that is properly cured. Coarse hay can keep a nervous horse occupied. So can a companion animal such as a goat, dog, or cat. Restless equines are the chewers or cribbers. Feed horses at regular intervals and remember that general care and feeding go hand in hand.

Feeding Mustelines

FERRETS

All ferrets are carnivorous, but the domesticated pet can be fed on dog food mixed with meat and with some vitamins (particularly B 12) added. Albino mustelines and the mink mutations bred on ranches are prone to anemia, which can be rectified by dietary additives.

BADGERS

Your badger's diet consists of much the same menu as the other mustelines except that he also favors bulbs (plant not electric), acorns, earthworms, apples, grass, berries, and cereals. Ears of wheat and corn are also relished.

OTTERS

In the wild otters feed mostly on fish, frogs, snails, and crayfish. If you have a pet otter, feed it dry dog food mixed with about 50 percent raw fish. Fish heads and live frogs can also be supplied.

SKUNKS

Skunks in the wild enjoy a varied diet, which includes fruits, grains, buds, berries, worms, insects, turtle eggs, and small mammals. The diet of your pet skunk should consist of three-quarters high-protein dog food and one-quarter meat. Table scraps and a vitamin supplement can be added.

Viverrine Diets

The Viverridae are all carnivorous, their menu encompassing many kinds of rodents. There are a number of viverrines that enjoy killing and eating snakes, a habit that would seem to be as dangerous as dining at your local hash-house. A good dog food mixed with meat is the best diet for your pet viverrine.

Feeding Marsupials

Like the creatures that feed upon it, much of the flora of Australia is specific to that island continent and not found in other countries. As a result, herbivorous animals brought from Down Under have been difficult to feed properly with the foods to which they have been accustomed. The *koala's* diet consists of the leaves of a few particular eucalyptus trees (which smell like cough drops) not grown anywhere else in the world but Australia, so the little Australian Teddy Bears did not do well when removed from their native heath.

In captivity it has been found that, when acquired young, koalas and other marsupials can fortunately be induced to consume food other than that to which they have been accustomed in Australia. They seem to prosper on foods manufactured for rabbits and cats. If the marsupial pet is carnivorous, meat should be added to its meals. If it is herbivorous, fresh vegetables and fruits will prove beneficial as additives. Supplements of milk and vitamins are an aid in keeping a marsupial healthy.

A dietary rule of thumb for all marsupials is to feed them a diet similar to that which is eaten by the mammals they mimic. The opossum hunts during the dark hours for small mammals and birds and relishes fruit and eggs. The *bandicoot* is a nocturnal prowler that hunts small, live prey which it pounces upon and pummels with its front feet, until the unfortunate victim is reduced to a broken pulp. The catlike marsupials are also carnivorous, while the *brushtail opossum* is largely vegetarian. *Kangaroos* are browsers not unlike our hoofed mammals. Those marsupials that are insect and ant eaters can be fed milk, bread soaked in milk, and finely ground meat.

Miscellaneous Pets

The diets indulged in by the miscellaneous pets vary as greatly as the species incorporated in that section, so I have joined their feeding habits to the specific information about each individual species.

6

Medical Care for Your Pet

To insure your pet's continued good health and longevity, it is wise to take it to your veterinarian at regular intervals for a health check. When you do, try to take along a small sample of its stool. Your veterinarian can spy trouble and nip it in the bud before it becomes serious or chronic, saving you both money and the anguish associated with illness. Your veterinarian will, upon request, give you a list of, or supply you with medicines and other special items that can be important to the health and continued well-being of your pet.

You should keep on hand the usual first-aid kit which, for the more common pets, should be supplied with assorted bandages (one of 6 inches can also be used to fashion a muzzle), salves, thermometer, antiseptic powder, alcohol, a roll of 1-inch adhesive tape, cotton swabs, tongue depressor (which can also be used as a splint for small animals), surgical scissors, a jar of Vaseline, enema equipment, tweezers, ophthalmic ointment, Kaopectate, peroxide of hydrogen, methiolate or betadine, aspirin, mineral oil, rubber-tube tourniquet, tranquilizers or sedatives with instruction on dosage and, last but not least, the telephone number of your veterinarian.

Remember that when your pet is ill or injured it may not recognize you and, in its blind and abysmal agony, may revert to primitive instincts, biting or scratching anyone who touches it. It would be wise, therefore, when it is under the stress of pain and fear to muzzle or bind its jaws and handle it with extreme care. Use your voice as a soothing instrument and to make the animal aware that you are sympathetic. Also make certain to leash your pet quickly under these circumstances so that it can't escape, run blindly abroad, and hide, an atavistic habit even dogs display when hurt badly.

Below are two lists for easy reference: one for general first aid; the other of poisons and antidotes. These are only emergency measures that might help to save your pet. But you should still consult your veterinarian.

Emergency First Aid

Automobile accident	If gums are white, internal injuries are indicated. Wrap blanket tightly around body. Treat for shock and take to veterinarian immediately.
Bites (tooth wounds)	Shave area. Flow betadine or methiolate into wounds with eye dropper. Consult veterinarian.
Bone fracture or break	Splint if limb involved. If break is in any other part of body, keep pet immobile, get to veterinarian. If back injury is suspected, lift pet with body in straight line and carry on flat board.
Burns	If minor, apply cold water and dress with cold, strong tea liquid. If severe, take to veterinarian.
Choking	Bone or wood can form suction on roof of mouth or lodge in throat. So can chunk of meat. Pull out with fingers. If you can't, take to veterinarian immediately.
Cuts	If minor, clean with peroxide. If severe, apply pressure bandage and take to veterinarian.
Dislocation	Keep immobile and rush to veterinarian.
Drowning	Treat for shock. Apply artificial respiration. Lay pet on side and push down with hands on ribs, releasing quickly, every three or four seconds.
Electric Shock	Treat for shock. Give artificial respiration while someone else drives you and pet to veterinarian.
Heat prostration	Lay pet flat on side and keep pouring cold water over him. Use fan aimed directly at pet during treatment. Drop ice water on tongue. Give cold water enema. Cold towels on stomach and skull, and get to veterinarian.
Insect bites	Apply cold-water cloth to swelling area. Give pet an antihistamine tablet (same as used by humans). Call veterinarian for advice.
Poison snake bite	Rush to veterinarian immediately for treatment. If he is not available, cut ⅛"-deep X over bite with knife and drop potassium permanganate into

fang holes. If on limb, use tourniquet above bite releasing periodically. Keep immobile; movement increases circulation of venom.

Shock   Keep pet quiet and in darkened area. Cover with blanket and soothe while taking to veterinarian for stimulant.

Poison and Household Antidotes

Acids   Acid must be neutralized. Give orally 2 teaspoons baking soda in 10-ounce glass of water.

Alkalies   Neutralize by giving teaspoon lemon juice or vine-
(cleaning vehicles,   gar in 10-ounce glass of water, orally.
etc.)

Arsenic   Antidote Epsom salts (25 percent solution)

Bug poisons   4 teaspoonfuls salt in 10-ounce glass of water
(Thallium)   given orally. Several glasses if possible.

DDT   Antidote-peroxide with equal parts of water orally. Follow with enema.

Food Poisoning   Antidote-peroxide of hydrogen mixed with equal
(botulism, garbage,   parts of water, given orally to make pet vomit.
etc.)   Follow with enema.

Hydrocyanic Acid   Dextrose or corn syrup, followed by lemon juice
(laurel leaves, etc.)   in water—(a 50-percent solution) given orally.

Lead   Epsom salts, given orally.
(from lead-base
paints)

Mercury   Three raw egg whites mixed with a 10-ounce glass of milk. Given orally.

Rat Poisons   Give peroxide of hydrogen orally to induce regur-
(Phosphorus)   gitation.

Strychnine   Give sedatives—phenobarbital, Nembutal.

IMPORTANT: Check poison container for antidote on label before administering the antidotes in this listing. If container not available, use antidote listed above and rush to veterinarian immediately.

Incidentally, I do not advocate the practice of veterinary medicine by neophyte pet owners any more than I would encourage the layman to diagnose and treat himself or any member of his family for any illness more drastic than a slight cut, bruise, stomachache after Thanksgiving, headache, or hangover. The practice of amateur medicine is an invitation to disaster. These listings, and those in the section on pet diseases are for the sole purpose of educating you to recognize the symptoms of sickness and the gravity of various diseases so that you will get your pet to your veterinarian before it is too late.

Administering Medicine

When your pet is ill, your veterinarian will give you specific medication to administer. This is not a difficult task if properly handled, so do not face it with trepidation. Believe me, it is generally a much easier task than giving medication to an ailing child.

This generalized information pertaining to the administration of medication is applicable to most mammals.

PILLS AND CAPSULES

Pills and capsules can be wrapped in a piece of food that your pet is particularly fond of. Have another piece of bait clearly visible so that your pet, in his eagerness to get at the second piece, will bolt down the piece containing the hidden pill. If the pill or capsule is too large to hide in the food, or if the pet will not accept it in this manner, then you must resort to a less sneaky technique.

A little practice can make you quite efficient in forcibly administering pills and capsules to your pet. Take a second or two to review the moves you will have to make, allow your nervousness to flow away and take a deep breath to promote calmness and tranquility. Sit your pet in front of you; generally a table or box can be utilized to put your pet in an easier position for you to handle. If possible, envelope the pet's head by curving your left hand over it. Tip his head upward and, with your fingers between the animal's teeth near the back of his jaws, exert pressure to make them open. Hold the capsule or pill in your right hand and with the forefinger of the same hand, pry the pet's jaws wide open and drop the pill or capsule far back on its tongue, deep in the throat. A pencil can be utilized to push the pill back; be sure, however, to use the *eraser end*. Close the animal's mouth quickly and massage the throat. Generally when the tip of the tongue appears between the front teeth of the animal's closed mouth, it signals the fact that he has swallowed the medication.

LIQUID MEDICINE

If you are not experienced in administering liquid medicines, you may need the help of another person to hold the animal. With the pet sitting in front of you in the same position as in the paragraph above, lift the pet's head up and gently pull out the skin at one corner of the mouth. This forms a pocket or funnel into the mouth. From a small bottle into which you have previously poured the medication, allow a thin but steady trickle to flow into the lip pocket, while you still hold your pet's head up. A little practice will have you shooting the stuff into the side pocket like an old pro. A stomach tube can also be used to administer liquid medication, but the mere idea of attempting to give medication in this manner makes most novices nervous, so it is best to stick to the lip-pocket method.

POWDERS

Powdered medication is seldom used today, but should it be prescribed by your veterinarian, the easiest way to administer it is by mixing it in the animal's food or in a liquid suspension.

EYE MEDICATION

Gently pull the lower lid of the eye outward and squeeze the necessary amount of ointment into the pocket formed. Release the lid and the ointment will spread over the entire eye as the animal blinks. Liquid eye drops can be administered in the same way.

Enemas

A common bulb syringe can be used for an enema unless your pet is fairly large, in which case a douche bag or hot-water bottle, converted to douche use with a rubber hose to fit the bag, will do the job. Grease the rubber tip of the hose with Vaseline and hold the bag high to command a constant flow of liquid. The tip of the hose must be inserted well into the animal's rectum. An efficient enema can be made with two tablespoonfuls of salt and a quart of plain warm water, or a quart of warm, soapy water can be used.

Using a Thermometer

The ordinary rectal thermometer is as efficacious for your pet as it is for you. Calm your pet before taking its temperature. Shake the thermometer down, dip the tip in Vaseline, hold the tail of your pet up and insert the thermometer three-quarters of its length into the rectum. Hold your pet's tail up or keep your hand under its stomach so it can't sit down. Leave the thermometer in for about two minutes, remove, wipe clean with cotton, and read. Most normal pet temperatures are about 101 degrees Fahrenheit. Your thermometer will indicate normal to be 98.6, which represents normal human temperature, so ignore it. A canine's body temperature will be between 101 and 102 when normal. A feline's temperature will register 101.7 degrees.

Tourniquet and Pressure Bandage

If your pet sustains a deep wound that is bleeding profusely, apply a tourniquet at the nearest joint between the wound and the heart as you rush it to the veterinarian. Do not put a tourniquet around the neck to top the flow of blood from a head wound. A pencil can be used to tighten a tourniquet to cut blood loss. You *must* remember to loosen it every five or ten minutes. This is imperative as a tourniquet can cause damage to nerves and blood vessels.

A pressure bandage rather than a tourniquet is my preference. Take a wad of sterile bandage and, if the wound is spurting blood profusely (arterial bleeding), put pressure directly on the wound. If the bleeding is slower but continuous (vein bleeding), pressure can be applied on that part of the vein closest to the heart, about one or two inches or less above the wound. The pressure must be constant until the animal is in the hands of the doctor.

Immunization

Immunization is one of your veterinarian's best weapons against disease and you should be aware of the various types of immunizing agents.

There are many kinds of immunizing agents or biologicals. They are actually antibodies (substances that react against foreign bacteria) and antigens (substances introduced into the body to stimulate the production of antibodies) of disease organisms which have been scientifically catalogued. Antitoxins and antiserums are actually antibodies that have been recovered from the blood serum of animals that have contracted harmful bacteria or viruses. The protection such antibodies produce is fairly brief.

Vaccines are antigens of bacterial or virus-caused illnesses. They are grouped into three classifications: alive, modified live, and killed, and they provide long-term protection.

Bacterins stimulate antibody production and are killed antigens (bacterial), as are toxoids. The difference between them is that the bacterins are produced from the bacteria themselves while the toxoids are fashioned from the toxins of the bacteria.

Most virus vaccines are altered live viruses, changed to make them safe to use, and are called modified live-virus vaccines. Killed virus vaccines are slower acting and are safer to use under certain stress circumstances, such as when it is necessary to provide specific protection to a pregnant animal.

Vaccines that are a combination of two or more antigens are called polyvalent vaccines and are effective when wide-range virus and bacterial protection is necessary.

What you have learned so far is generalized information that is applicable to most pets. But illness and disease is as wide in its implications in the pet area as it is in humans. The difference lies in specie variety. Different ailments affect different kinds of creatures, and so we must segregate the various pets and their ailments and give them separate attention, always remembering the generalized information so that it can be applied to our own specific species of pet if it becomes necessary.

Dog Diseases and Ailments

Today, because of the position the dog has been given in society and the family circle, and in consideration of the costs of purchasing and caring for fine specimens, treatment for canine illness equals and sometimes surpasses that given to sick humans and must meet the highest medical standards.

As soon as you purchase your puppy or dog he should be given a thorough examination by your veterinarian, who will, at this time, set up a program of protective (and combined) vaccinations against distemper, hepatitis, leptospirosis, and also rabies. This will effectively eliminate the possibility of your pet ever being struck down by those frequently fatal virus and bacterial canine diseases.

Always watch for signs of unthriftiness (illness) in your pet. Loss of appetite, poor coat, diarrhea, constipation, vomiting, anemia (distinguished by palish-white gums), lack of normal activity, obvious lameness, listlessness, hanging tail, maturation from eyes and/or nose, dry nose, lack of healthy pink color of gums, a hangdog expression and general weakness, are all signs of ill health and evidence that your pet needs the practiced administrations of a veterinarian.

Your dog should have a pulse rate of 90 to 100, and a respiratory frequency of 15 to 20 per minute, the same as you and I.

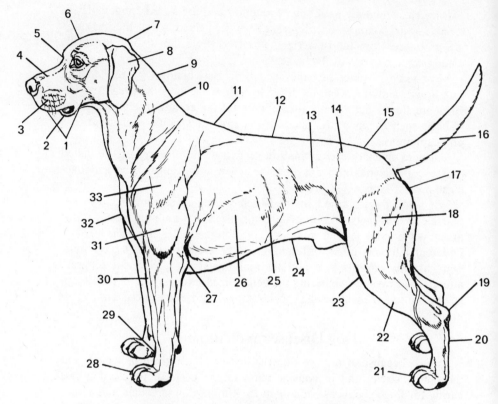

EXTERNAL ANATOMY OF THE DOG

1. Lower jaw. 2. Corner of lip (flews). 3. Muzzle. 4. Foreface. 5. Stop. 6. Skull. 7. Occiput. 8. Ear. 9. Crest of neck. 10. Neck. 11. Withers. 12. Back. 13. Loin. 14. Hip. 15. Croup. 16. Tail or stern. 17. Point of haunch or buttocks. 18. Thigh. 19. Point of hock. 20. Hock. 21. Hind foot or paw. 22. Lower or second thigh. 23. Point of stifle (knee). 24. Abdomen. 25. Ribs. 26. Chest. 27. Elbow. 28. Front feet. 29. Pastern. 30. Forearm. 31. Upper arm. 32. Prosternum (breastbone). 33. Shoulder blade.

EXTERNAL PARASITES

There are internal and external parasites that prey on your pet and must be eliminated or the health of your dog will suffer. Of the external pests, the most common is the *flea*. They bite; cause irritation, dermatitis, and anemia; act as an intermediate host for heartworm; carry tapeworm eggs and other diseases to the dog, and can also infest your home.

Lice are also a hazard to your dog. They, too, can cause anemia, dermatitis, tapeworm, et cetera. Control of fleas and lice is an important owner function. The premises, as well as the dog, must be divested of these parasites and control must be carried out diligently on a year-round basis.

For the house pet the easiest way to prevent fleas and lice is to apply a flea- and louse-killing dip after the pet has been bathed with a flea- and louse-eliminating soap. Within a week apply one of the many liquid or powder sprays specifically manufactured to kill these pests. Use the same spray and powder in and around the animal's bed. Dips are actively effective for up to ten days, sprays from five to seven days, so spray every five days until all fleas and lice are eliminated.

Ticks are ugly blood suckers that are a menace to your dog, can infest your home, and are very difficult to eliminate. If you feel them on your dog, remove them manually by grasping the tick and pulling steadily. Or you can use tweezers. Once removed, flush them down the john as they are not easily killed. The large ticks are female; the small active ones, males. Special dips and sprays can be purchased to rid the dog of these pests, and a tick spray bomb can be set up in the house. You must depart the premises until all fumes have dissipated. Pay particular attention to the dog's ears and between its toes where ticks generally hide. You may have to spray the area outside around the house where your dog customarily walks and plays. For this chore a strong concentration of Sevin is efficacious.

INTERNAL PARASITES

There are several species of *worms* that can infest your dog and the ways in which infestation occurs are many. Worm parasites can enter the animal by penetrating the skin, via prenatal infestation, by ingestion, and through transport hosts. Dogs that have parasitic disease exhibit unthriftiness, dull coat, diarrhea, eye maturation, underdevelopment (in puppies), and often anemia.

The most common kinds of worms that can infest your dog are *roundworms,* dangerous to puppies but generally not to older dogs; *hookworms,* whose massive infections can cause circulatory collapse and death; *whipworms,* which can be eliminated only by repeated treatment; and *tapeworms,* helminths that need rather harsh treatment to be eliminated.

These worms, as well as *coccidiosis*—a parasitic protozoa that infests the intestinal tract and is quite deadly to puppies—can be recognized through microscopic fecal examination by a trained technician. If worms are confirmed, your veterinarian will treat your dog with specific medications and, if necessary, advise supportive treatment.

The pet owner must act as the intermediary whose job is parasitic prevention and control. He must, through sanitation in the environment and keeping his dog from exposure to new sites of infestation, break the links of the chain of infestation caused by the life cycle of these vicious parasites. Nursing and supportive treatment by proper diet, with added vitamin, protein, and mineral supplements, is also an important owner function. Pet owners should *never* attempt to diagnose or treat an animal with worms. The result of amateur treatment can be disastrous. Your veterinarian is the only one qualified to treat helminth infestations in your dog.

Heartworms are deadly creatures, long worms that crowd the dog's heart and large arteries, that develop from microfilaria (larval) introduced into the bloodstream by the sting of a mosquito. At one time confined to the Southern states, the incidence of heartworm has now spread throughout the country. Arsenicals and antimony are the drugs most generally used to combat them. But the best treatment is prevention. Your vet will take a blood sample and if it indicates that your dog is free of heartworms, you can begin preventative treatment with a pill or liquid served in the animal's food. In the Northern states, where winter eliminates mosquitos for several months of the year, this treatment need be given only during the months when mosquitos become prevalent.

SKIN DISEASES

Diseases of the skin are often difficult to diagnose, treat, and cure. Some infections are so complicated that many weeks of treatment may be required before control is established.

Mange is one of the most easily diagnosed skin disorders. There are three species of mange mite that infest dogs: *Demodex folliculorum,* or red mange, is certainly the most difficult of the three to treat. If too much of the body is involved, the prognosis will probably not be good. Years ago a dog exhibiting red mange would have been destroyed as incurable, but today, with modern medical treatment, the majority of cases can be controlled and cured if recognized and treated early.

Sarcoptic mange can be diagnosed through skin scrapings and cured through the use of an effective insecticide contained in a skin-lotion base. Adjunctive therapy involves medicated baths and, usually, an oral insecticide.

Ear mange (Otodectic cynotis) is related to the mites that cause skin mange. Within the ears a discharge occurs that is black and oily with blood and results in secondary ear canker unless cleared up before it becomes chronic. Your veterinarian will clean out the ears and treat them with an insecticide that generally contains antibiotics.

Ringworm is a fungal infection of the skin and is, therefore, not really a worm at all. There are three kinds of ringworm (*dermatophytosis*) that affect dogs. All are communicable to humans, as manifestations of "athlete's foot."

Treatment consists of first disinfecting the area where your dog sleeps and burning its bedding to remove the possibility of transmission of the fungus to you and your family and to prevent reinfection of the dog. Long-haired dogs may have to be clipped so that medicinal baths and local applications of specific ointments can reach the affected skin areas. Sometimes the use of griseofluvin, an oral fungicide, is necessary as a supplemental treatment.

Dogs often exhibit "hot spots," a form of *moist eczema* most often occurring during the hot summer months. Cleanliness is important and systematic anti-inflammatory drugs and antibiotic treatment are successfully used. Summer dermatitis seems to be a syndrome, rather than a specific skin disease, aggravated by bacterial growth in raw areas. A series of treatments involving corticosteroids, lotions, powders, baths, and flea antigen injections are all generally employed to achieve relief for your pet.

Pyoderma is a type of bacterial infection that often attacks puppies. It is labeled "acne" and is usually a staph-type infection. Cleanliness is important and medicated baths and a topical lotion or powder are used in treatment.

Dogs also have *allergic dermatitis* caused by allergies to pollen, inhalants, grasses, insect bites, certain foods, and flea saliva. Tests can be made to isolate the allergic agents. Then one of the new desensitizing vaccines can be employed as treatment. If this condition is severe, a common antihistamine cold tablet can help to relieve it until you reach your veterinarian.

Hormonal skin conditions, *seborrhea,* and other infrequent types of dermatitis can affect your dog and must be treated by your veterinarian.

BACTERIAL DISEASES

Bacterial diseases can be identified by examining cultures taken from the source of infection or from the blood when the infection becomes generalized. The basic attacking medications are the antibiotics, specific or wide-range, or in combinations.

In humans *leptospirosis* is known as Weil's Disease. Rats are the carriers and those animals that recover from the disease are generally carriers for the rest of their lives. They spread the disease through their urine. An affected dog must be isolated and a thorough program of rat control in the area should be launched. The spirochetes of the disease affect the liver and kidneys. Treatment involves the use of wide-range antibiotics and immunity serum.

A protective vaccine given early in life and incorporating protection against distemper, hepatitis and leptospirosis is a must for every dog.

Tetanus bacteria, commonly called lockjaw, produce poisons that are extremely deadly. The bacteria multiply rapidly where there is a lack of oxygen. Because of this fact punctures, where oxygen fails to reach the inner depths of the wound, are most dangerous. Treatment consists of thoroughly cleaning and disinfecting all deep wounds, followed by the administration of tetanus antitoxin. Penicillin given orally or hypodermically aids in killing the bacteria.

Tonsillitis is, in itself, not a dangerous disease, but is often a symptom of some other disease (such as hepatitis). The symptom of tonsillitis is an inflammation of the tonsils that is of either bacterial (*streptococcus*) or virus origin. Treatment is carried out through the use of penicillin or any of several of the antibiotics.

Brucellosis is becoming one of the "popular" ailments, since some owners of stud dogs of a few popular breeds became aware of its existence. It is a venereal disease that effects cows, pigs, sheep and, we now know, dogs. Testes infection in males and abortion in females follow this bacterial infection. Diagnosis is made through the blood of the affected animal and a wide spectrum of antibiotics is standard treatment.

Pneumonia, though listed here under bacterial diseases, takes many forms. It can be viral in nature (interstitial pneumonia, a manifestation of distemper), caused by fungus (mycotic), a parasitic invasion (verminous pneumonia), or a typical bacterial pneumonia. The use of antibiotics, the newer fungicides (for mycotic) and treatment and elimination of the cause (distemper, internal parasites, et cetera) are basic.

VIRAL DISEASES

In this category we find the most dreaded canine diseases caused by the smallest of organisms that, over the years, have taken their vicious toll of canine lives. Dedicated veterinarians and medical scientists, after intense research, gave definitive recognition to these insidious microorganisms and finally found the medical means to combat them and, more important, to protect mammals susceptible to such viral diseases through the medium of vaccines.

True *distemper* is known as *Carre's disease.* It has probably killed and crippled more dogs, particularly puppies, than any other illness. Because of the terrible mortality rate of distemper, and the sweeping contagion it brings in its wake, protection against it is a vital necessity for all canines. Symptoms are nasal discharge, eye discharge, general unthriftiness, failure to eat, diarrhea, dry hacking cough, and hard pads. All or some of these symptoms may be present. Protective distemper vaccine, combined with hepatitis and leptospirosis vaccines (*D-H-L*), can be given to a puppy as young as six weeks of age. Most puppies have maternal immunity to distemper while very young and, while temporarily immune, are resistant to distemper vaccine; yet if one waits too long there can be a susceptibility gap during which time the pup, if not protected, can contract the disease. Safe immunity can be achieved through new treatment that utilizes human measles vaccine (found efficacious in warding off distemper) followed at the correct time with D-H-L vaccination. Remember that vaccination does not bestow lifetime immunity as previously thought. An annual vaccination must be given to make immunity positive.

I have often wondered if the injection of special vaccines into the dam's amniotic fluid while the puppies are in the fetal stage would confer a degree of after-birth immunity against these deadly diseases. So far this seems unfeasible.

If the dog does not succumb to the vicious distemper virus, he will probably die of shock, other effects of the disease, or an uncontrollable secondary infection. A survivor of distemper (and there are very few) generally exhibits some form of nervous defect or convulsions. Treatment must be left to the trained administrations of your veterinarian.

Hepatitis (*infectious canine*) attacks the liver, causes a rise in temperature, and congestion of the mucous membrane. In acute cases it results in sudden death. The virus can be found throughout the body of the victim in the early phase, but after the animal has recovered it remains in the kidneys. The urine of the affected dog is a source of primary infection to other canines for many months.

Treatment of hepatitis consists of using serums to battle the virus, antibiotics to halt secondary infections, vitamin B complex, and drug therapy.

If the combination distemper, hepatitis, and leptospirosis vaccine is administered, your pet will be fully protected against all three diseases. This is much less expensive, and certainly a great deal easier and less agonizing both for you and your pet, than treating any of the dread diseases innoculation prevents.

Rabies, also called *hydrophobia* ("phobia" meaning fear which, combined with "hydro," expresses a fear of water or liquids) is the scientific, and more descriptive term for this horrible and deadly disease, which can affect the brain cells and nervous systems of all mammals, including man. The rabies virus is present in the stricken animal's saliva and is transmitted to another body through a bite, scratch, or any slight wound, then migrates by way of the nerves to the brain. The span of incubation for the virus is from fifteen days to a month. Rabies is easily spread and it has been speculated that the virus can even be airborne in areas where infection is exceedingly heavy. Bats, especially, are known carriers (making vampire bats particularly dangerous). So are squirrels, raccoons, chipmunks, skunks, and many other common mammals.

The only real control over this dread disease is protection for your pet through a specific preventative vaccination. Two kinds of vaccines are used, giving immunity for from one to three years, depending upon the vaccine. In many states rabies vaccination is mandatory. If caught early, a new series of vaccinations can be given to victims of the disease with hope of success. Hyperab, an anti-rabies serum, provides immediate short-term protection for a human bitten by an animal suspected of being rabid. Hyperab takes the pain out of treatment and eliminates the drastic and serious adverse serum reaction that previously affected approximately 90 percent of those treated by the old method that employed a series of injections.

There are many other diseases that affect our canine pets, but they are illnesses or anomalies that only your veterinarian can cope with. Heart disease, cancer, bone anomalies, and many more ailments are in this category. Some diseases are fairly specific to certain breeds. But there are a few other miscellaneous ills that you should be aware of because they affect many breeds and rapid recognition by the owner can make a great deal of difference in the eventual prognosis.

BLOAT OR GASTRIC TORSION

Large breeds of dogs, much more than smaller breeds, have a definite predisposition to gastric dilation and torsion (turning) of the stomach. This condition in which the abdomen distends grossly and the victim's respiration is affected occurs quite suddenly. Rapid relief must be given or the animal will die. It is necessary, therefore, to rush your pet to the veterinarian the moment you become aware that it is the victim of bloat.

In simple dilation, specific drugs and stomach tubing can alleviate the condition. But if true torsion is present (a 90 to 180 percent twist in the stomach) and the ends of the stomach are pinched off, immediate surgery is necessary. To prevent shock, intravenous drips are useful. Calcium IV and adjunctive treatment are necessary to aid recovery.

CONSTIPATION

Generally constipation (a hard, dry stool that must be forced out or cannot be passed at all) is caused by dietary ignorance. The most common cause is the feeding of bones. Contrary to widespread belief, dogs do not need bones to prosper. In fact they are not at all good for your dog and should not be fed.

Feeding dry foods or dog biscuits without sufficient water available is another cause of constipation. Sometimes long-haired breeds will lick the anal region in an attempt at cleanliness and in the process ingest enough hair to cause a blockage in the bowel. Anal gland infection and tumors that block the anal passage are other causes of constipation. Both must be treated by your veterinarian.

For simple constipation the introduction into the diet of laxatives, buttermilk, whey or bran, and an immediate dosage with mineral oil is indicated. An enema can bring quick relief. Prevention of repeated attacks of constipation lies in proper feeding, more frequent grooming of long-haired breeds, and periodic cleansing of the anal glands.

DIARRHEA

A loose, watery bowel movement is often a symptom of other disease. Take your dog's temperature. If it registers normal, the condition may be only a temporary one caused by diet, excitement, or eating disagreeable food. In such case use a tightening agent such as Keopectate. Withhold water, but be careful that your pet does not become dehydrated. In place of water substitute cooled, boiled milk (to which corn syrup can be added), and add hard-boiled eggs, boiled rice, dog biscuits, and large kibbles to his regular diet. If the condition is not corrected within a few days, seek the advice of your veterinarian.

CONGENITAL AND INHERITED DISEASES

A congenital disease is one that is present at birth. It may be inherited or due to physical factors, such as a disease contracted by the dam while pregnant, dietary deficiencies of the pregnant bitch, toxicity, et cetera. Such diseases can also be latent and not obvious until the young animal has grown.

An inherited disease is transmitted through the genes, which are the biological units that dictate and transmit all hereditary features. Some inherited diseases are not visible at birth but develop later. Obvious inherited anomalies are harelip, umbilical hernia, deafness, orchidism, et cetera.

Deafness is usually genetically associated with white hair color, albinism, and dilution of hair color. White dogs and white cats with blue eyes frequently exhibit deafness. Dalmatians are troubled with occasional deafness and an inherited kidney abnormality. Umbilical hernia and eye troubles are common in Pekingese. Rhodesian Ridgebacks, due to the abnormal hair pattern on their backs, are susceptible to the formation of a type of inherited cyst. Congenital heart disease is also common in dogs. Dysplasia, certain kidney malfunctions, epilepsy, eye diseases, and many other ailments are inherited completely or in part.

CAR SICKNESS AND VOMITING

Some dogs become ill when riding in a car for any great distance. By beginning with short rides and working up to longer distances with intermittent rest periods, this distasteful problem can often be overcome. If this simple procedure fails, drugs must be resorted to. There are some antihistamines that will help to control side reactions. They do not depress the animal and, therefore, should be tried first. Depressants, such as tranquilizers and phenobarbital, will generally bring relief to your pet and a happier journey to you. Before giving them to your pet you should get your vet's approval; at the same time ask him to specify a proper dosage.

Vomiting is, of course, associated with car or motion sickness. But there are many other causes, some quite dangerous. A dog will vomit or attempt to vomit, for instance, if he has ingested poison. In the latter case, he should be rushed to your veterinarian for immediate treatment.

Quite frequently your pet will eat grass and then vomit a whitish liquid containing the ingested grass. Do not be alarmed, for this is merely your pet's method of relieving a sour stomach.

Diseases of Felines

Though most cat illnesses may parallel those summarized in the section on dog diseases, they must nevertheless be given full recognition here as treatment and medication often differ between the two species. Because of their huge popularity as pets, I feel that both dogs and cats deserve complete coverage in this important area.

EXTERNAL PARASITES

Fleas are a serious health hazard to animals. They cause loss of weight; patchy, dull coats; and contribute to the spread of skin disease. More seriously they are carriers of tapeworm larvæ, heartworm larvæ and bubonic plague. There are four types of fleas: human, cat, dog, and sticktight. All are dark brown in color and can be easily seen on the

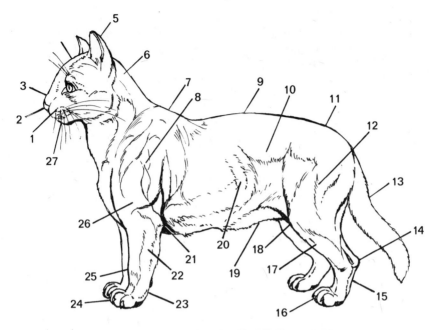

EXTERNAL ANATOMY OF THE CAT
1. Muzzle. 2. Nose. 3. Foreface. 4. Skull or forehead. 5. Ear.
6. Neck. 7. Wither. 8. Shoulder. 9. Back. 10. Loin. 11. Croup.
12. Thigh. 13. Tail. 14. Point of hock or heel. 15. Hock.
16. Hind foot. 17. Second thigh. 18. Stifle or knee. 29. Abdo-
men. 20. Ribs. 21. Elbow. 22. Foreleg. 23. Pastern. 24. Fore-
feet. 25. Wrist. 26. Upper arm. 27. Lower jaw.

cat's skin by parting the coat. They need warm, moist weather in which
to hatch.

To rid your pet of these tiny monsters, use any of the good manufactured flea powders. These can be found on the shelves of your pet
shop. You need not cover the cat with the flea eradicator; simply dust it
on the animal's stomach (where there's less hair) and the fleas, which
travel all over the host in any twenty-four-hour period, will eventually
walk through the lethal powder and die. Be careful of the well-advertised
flea collars, particularly if your pet is a kitten. I recommend that you use
the flea powder followed by a bath and a rinse in cat flea dip, another
product you will find in your pet shop.

Lice must be controlled. These small, gray vampires can bring death to a whole litter of kittens if the infestation is large enough, so it behooves you to make sure that the queen is free of all external parasites. Generally the cat flea powders and dips will also eradicate lice. For further control shake some of the flea and louse powder under the cat's bedding.

Ticks are a problem to all animal owners. Not only do they infest the cat, but, like fleas, they can also infest the house, hiding under rugs, laying eggs, and multiplying to such an extent that an exterminator sometimes has to be employed to get rid of them. Ticks are usually picked up outdoors by your cat, so if his area of outside activity is limited to the yard or garden, you can spray the grass and bushes with Sevin (double its normal strength) to clear out the ticks. Do not let your pet near the section sprayed for at least a week; it might eat grass. The spray could be disastrous should the cat ingest it. Tick bombs can be used in the house.

Flea and louse remedies will not harm ticks. You must use a cat tick dip and make sure you get the liquid between his toes where ticks often attach themselves. Also check your cat's ears for ticks. They are very obvious: the small brown active ones are the males and the large gray ones the females. They can be picked off by hand, but are difficult to kill manually.

While there are several kinds of *mange mites, red mange (Demodex canis)* and *sarcoptic (Sarcoptes scabeii)* are most prevalent. Red mange was, not so very long ago, a serious and usually lethal disease. Today your veterinarian can cure it. The mange begins on the forehead and under the eyes, also on the cheeks and front legs, causing bald spots that become red and raw, causing a thickening of the skin. The mite reproduces at a fantastic rate and treatment, therefore, must begin at the first onslaught. Sarcoptic mange mites also reproduce prodigiously, but the cure, in your veterinarian's capable hands, is relatively easy. There is a cat mite *(Notoedres cati)* that infests both cats and rabbits and is quite similar to sarcoptic mange.

Ear mange mites (Otodectic mange) cause a crumbly wax to form inside the ear where there is also great irritation. Though there are products commercially sold to use on ear mites, if you see your pet shaking its head and scratching at its ears, I suggest you allow your veterinarian to cope with this problem. Deep-seated ear infection can result from amateur treatment. Clean ears generally discourage ear-mite infection.

INTERNAL PARASITES

Inside its body your pet can be attacked by many kinds of parasites. *Roundworms, hookworms, whipworms,* several kinds of *tapeworms,* and *coccidiosis,* are a few of the internal parasites to be coped with. The worst thing about these helminths is that your pet can reinfest himself time and time again through the worm larvae that he passes or walks in, spreading and finally ingesting it again or having it penetrate through the skin or feet. If your tabby is unthrifty in appearance, take a small portion of a fresh stool to your veterinarian so that he can determine what kind of worms your pet is harboring and give specific medicine to eradicate them. A second worming will be necessary to eliminate worms that have hatched from eggs not passed during the first worming. Your job will be to clean your cat's quarters thoroughly and supply fresh bedding and new material in its sanitary tray.

Coccidiosis is a protozoa, not a worm, but it can cause considerable damage to its host. Your cat is susceptible to three forms and all are self-limiting in character. Diarrhea occurs intermittently and there may be fever and severe systemic reaction. Your veterinarian will make his diagnosis by fecal examination and prescribe specific medication and supportive treatment.

DEFICIENCY DISEASES

Anemia and *rickets* are the most common deficiency diseases. Anemia results from a diminished supply of red cells in the blood due to various causes. Hookworm or a heavy infestation of lice and/or ticks can cause anemia: toxins produced by these same parasites can seriously aggravate your pet's condition. Other causes of anemia are a lack of iron and/or copper, protein deficiency, and inadequate vitamin-B-complex factors.

Rickets is caused by insufficient calcium, phosphorus, and vitamin D. For anemia, remove the parasites and give supportive vitamins rich in iron, copper and the B-complex factors. For rickets, which causes malformation of the skeletal structure in all living creatures, supply the missing but necessary agents by adding calcium phosphate and irradiated fish-liver oil to the diet. If your cat or kitten is being fed a good balanced diet, it will not become a victim of deficiency disease.

VIRAL DISEASES

Feline distemper is almost always fatal to cats. According to one prominent veterinarian this is the disease often referred to as feline enteritis or infectious feline panleukopenia. In my humble opinion feline panleukopenia is a disease separate from distemper. The symptoms are much like those accompanying severe cases of other diseases, but stricken kittens may succumb in less than twenty-four hours. There are no medical means to combat this murderous virus. The only safety for your pet lies in prevention by early vaccinations of feline distemper shots. While a dreaded killer of kittens, feline distemper is not common in older cats.

Rabies is another vicious killer of animals and also a disease that can be communicated to humans. Cats can get rabies by being bitten by a rabid dog (the canine's saliva carries the dread virus), or from rabid rats that the cat kills. Again we have a virus disease for which there is no known cure other than a series of shots—if the disease is recognized immediately. The old Pasteur treatment, which was said to be worse than the disease, has been replaced by new and less drastic means to combat the disease before the severe encephalitis symptoms appear. Prevention in the form of rabies serum vaccinations is the key to life here. The disease occurs only one fifth as frequently in cats as it does in dogs.

Viral pneumonia (*Pneumonitis*) is a highly contagious disease. There are valid reasons to believe that it can be transmitted from human to cat and vice versa. The use of the newer wonder drugs, supported by good nursing, can effect a cure. There are several kinds of pneumonia that can affect your cat and treatment can vary with the different viral strains. The virus seems to be inhibited by tetracycline antibiotics. Pneumonitis, or feline infectious rhinotracheitis, can be controlled by vaccination.

BACTERIAL DISEASES

Leptospirosis, a disease spread by rat urine, has been identified in two forms, both of which are highly dangerous. Prevention through vaccination is desirable. For treatment, good results have been obtained with penicillin when the disease was diagnosed in an initial stage. Unfortunately, the disease is not usually diagnosed before severe damage is inflicted. At that point it results in death or permanent invalidism due to extensive damage to the animal's liver and kidneys. The symptoms of leptospirosis are bloody stools, vomiting, and very definite jaundice (evidenced by pale gums).

Tetanus bacteria thrive in an oxygen-free environment and can grow in any deep wound. If your cat sustains such a wound (usually from a bite), take him to your veterinarian for treatment and a tetanus shot to avoid the possibility of lockjaw (tetanus).

Inflammation of the lungs, high temperature, difficulty in breathing, rasping breath, loss of appetite, prostration, are all signs of bacterial pneumonia, which takes its toll of feline lives. Penicillin and some of the newer drugs must be administered by injection. Even cured animals sometimes exhibit the symptoms of pleurisy and emphysema after recovery. Force-feeding is at times necessary and a full range of vitamins and strengthening foods must be administered to combat the debilitating effects of the disease.

OTHER AILMENTS

If you suspect your cat has a *hairball,* you can purchase a product at your pet store that will take care of it. Petromalt is used by many cat breeders for this purpose, but is not the only effective product.

Diarrhea is usually either a sympton of disease or the result of inbibing some food element that upsets the digestive system. The reason for it must be found and eliminated. Boiled rice and hard-boiled eggs in the food will help control the bowels. *Constipation* can be relieved by milk of magnesia or mineral oil. This is a condition not at all uncommon in cats.

Abcesses should be surgically debrided (dead tissue removed) and drained, then flushed daily with antiseptics and antibiotics until the wound heals.

The *Feline urological syndrome* (which appears as general unthriftiness) is a common clinical problem in cats. If it is not controlled, it results in death. Your veterinarian will prescribe a special diet, treatment for control, and sulfa drugs to combat secondary infection.

SKIN DISEASES

There is both a dry and a wet eczema to which your cat can fall prey. *Dry eczema* is characterized by a very arid condition of the skin accompanied by intolerable itching. *Moist eczema* causes wet discharges, which become encrusted and spread rapidly. Both eczemas cause hair loss and constant itching. Scratching and biting at the affected areas compounds the problem by resulting in fungus and other forms of infection. Let your veterinarian treat your pet before too much of the skin area is involved.

The affected areas of *ringworm infection* can be seen as fairly even ovals. The disease is extremely contagious, and is caused by a fungus. The condition, therefore, must be treated with a good fungicide. Skin scrapings and microscopic study can aid your veterinarian in forming a diagnosis and initiating the proper treatment. On the Continent successful treatment has been reported using sodium acid sulphate and sodium thiosulfate. Griseolfulvin orally administered for thirty days and tinactin cream used topically constitute recommended treatment.

There are also skin diseases caused by allergies. Tests will indicate what factors are causing your pet's allergic reaction.

Remember: your cat grooms itself by licking, so when using external

The Elizabethan collar, which fits around the animal's neck, prohibits it from tearing off bandages or licking off ointments and salves.

medications be careful that the medication will not harm it if ingested. Or make an "Elizabethan" collar to foil its efforts to reach its body with its tongue. Before giving any patent medicine to your cat, consult your veterinarian and *never* give a cat aspirin. It reacts upon felines as poison.

A cat may have nine lives, but they can all be forfeited to any of the deadly diseases that take their yearly toll. Only you and your good sense (and your veterinarian of course), stand between a healthy cat and one that is sick or injured. Incidentally the pulse rate of a cat is 100 to 120; respiratory frequency is 24 per minute.

RESTRAINT

Sick and frightened cats will often claw and bite while being treated. To eliminate injury to the owner and helper, a heavy towel can be thrown around the cat to hold its legs and feet immobile. Or a cat bag can be made of heavy material with a drawstring at one end. Cut holes in the bag to accommodate the tail and to allow for administering enemas et cetera and four other holes through which the cat's legs can be freed. One leg or foot at a time can be handled in this manner for nail clipping or tending an injured limb. If all four legs and feet must be confined, simply twist the bag around so that the leg holes are on top.

Cats are generally vigorous, healthy creatures and remain so if properly fed and cared for. But like all living things they can fall ill. When or if this occurs, rely upon the expertise of your veterinarian rather than the advice of well-meaning, but inexpert, friends or your own undirected medical fumbling.

Diseases of Birds

It is imperative that the owner be able to recognize an ailing bird almost the moment the pet becomes ill. In many cases a few days of the proper home treatment can cure a bird that might become fatally ill if the owner is not keen enough to recognize the initial signs of sickness. It is much easier to prevent sickness through cleanliness, good husbandry, and proper diet than to attempt to cure an ailing bird, which is heir to numerous diseases, many of them of the kind that affect mammals and others that are specific only to birds.

The signs of sickness are generally quite obvious. The color and condition of the bird's stool changes. In many species that have fairly compact stools of neutral color the bowel movement of the ailing bird becomes liquid and green. Any bird that is ill will indicate its condition

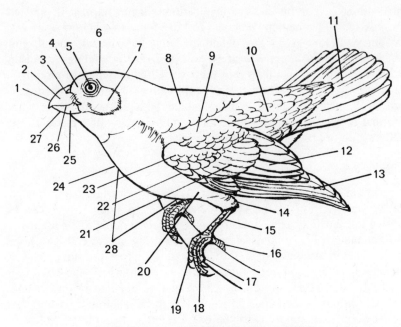

EXTERNAL ANATOMY OF A BIRD
1. Culmen. 2. Upper mandible. 3. Nostril. 4. Lores. 5. Iris.
6. Crown. 7. Ear coverts. 8. Mantle. 9. Scapular feathers.
10. Upper tail coverts. 11. Retrices. 12. Secondary remiges
("secondaries"). 13. Primary remiges ("primaries"). 14. Tibia.
15. Tarsus. 16. Hind toe. 17. Outer or fourth toe. 18. Middle
or third toe. 19. Inner or second toe. 20. Flank. 21. Greater
wing coverts. 22. Ala spuria (bastard wing). 23. Lesser wing
coverts. 24. Crop. 25. Lower mandible. 26. Cutting edge of
mandible. 27. Gonys. 28. Breast.

plainly by its lack of activity, dullness of its eyes, and a puffing up of the body feathers. The sheen of the sick bird's plumage is gone and he sits huddled and apathetic on the perch. If you find him puffed up and unmoving on the bottom of the cage, he is a very sick bird indeed—and needs immediate treatment.

WHAT TO DO

Your first action, if the sick bird is in an enclosure or cage with other birds, is to isolate him. Watch the other birds for any sign of illness. If a small bird, he should be put in a hospital cage that has been heated to 85 to 90 degrees Fahrenheit. Mix one-half Brewer's yeast and one-half Aureomycin (chlortetracycline, tablet form) crushed to a powder-like consistency and sprinkle it on whatever food the bird likes best and will still eat. Or the antibiotic can be purchased in soluble form and stirred into his water. For pigeons and larger birds both can be administered daily by hand. Generally this antibiotic-dietary treatment will put your bird on the road to recovery, but if he does not respond satisfactorily within three to five days, he should be taken to a veterinarian who has had some experience with bird diseases (a rather rare species of veterinarian) and who will diagnose the disease and begin specific treatment. If you are breeding birds, I must tell you frankly that in most of the smaller species any bird that has become quite ill, even if it eventually recovers, is practically worthless as a breeder thereafter. They never seem to recover their breeding ability. The pet bird that is cured can live happily ever after, but when a breeder is ill for several days and "goes light," I waste no time putting him down unless, of course, he is an import or a particularly valuable bird. Under the latter circumstances, I do all I can to bring him back to health.

THE HOSPITAL CAGE

Hospital cages can be bought or you can build one yourself, using an old cage or a small box as a base. Build a false bottom in which you can install a light bulb. No perches are necessary. The top and three sides should be solid or covered with insulating cloth or board. Drill a few holes in the solid sections for ventilation. The front section should be of glass so that the patient can be watched. Fashion in one end of the solid sides a door big enough to accommodate your hand and the food dishes that are to be put on the floor of the cage. Don't forget to attach a clip inside the cage to hold a tube waterer. Hang a thermometer on one inside wall and use whatever watt bulb is necessary to obtain and sustain the 80–90 degrees Fahrenheit you need.

If you don't have a hospital cage or if you are the type of person who waits to build one until you suddenly have a sick bird on your hands, put the ill bird in any small cage, drape three sides with a heavy towel and use a small lamp, preferably a gooseneck desk lamp, which has a pliable neck that can be bent to allow the heat from the bulb to be directed into the interior of the cage through the exposed side.

Heat, quiet, good food, and the treatment outlined are the prerequisites to bringing an ailing bird back to health unless the ailment is drastic and that rare veterinarian mentioned earlier is needed.

BACTERIAL DISEASES

When your pet bird is ill, it is almost impossible to diagnose his ailment by any outward manifestation. Bacterial and virus diseases in birds can be found only through laboratory analysis. Once this has been accomplished, your veterinarian will know how to cope with the disease.

Paratyphoid (or salmonellosis) is a typical avian bacterial disease. The pet bird isolated in the home seldom contracts the disease. Birds are more often infected in stores, pet shops, and breeding aviaries where many birds are in close proximity. The disease can cause death within a week and will spread rapidly through a large aviary; it can destroy more than 60 percent of the feathered inhabitants. Survivors are generally carriers. Injections of streptomycin seem to be rather successful for pigeons who have contracted paratyphoid.

Other avian bacterial diseases are: *typhoid, staphylococcosis, erysipelas, pullorum, tuberculosis, streptococcosis, fowl cholera, roup,* and *pseudotuberculosis*. The mortality rate from these diseases is very high and in many cases survivors are carriers. *Erysipelas* attacks pigeons.

VIRAL DISEASES

Newcastle disease, bird vox, bronchitis, leukosis, ornithosis (often called *psittacosis*), and *fowl pox* are all virus diseases. Newcastle disease is a highly communicable and deadly ailment that can wreak havoc in aviaries and commercial flocks of fowls. Ornithosis (also called parrot fever, though it can attack any species of aves), is communicable to humans and produces one of the most deadly of known toxins. Many of the new antibiotics seem to be helpful, but treatment of any bacterial or virus disease is questionable as to effectiveness, and recovery of affected birds is, in my opinion, very doubtful.

OTHER DISEASES OF BIRDS

A note to you who indulge in the exciting sport of falconry; remember that large and medium-sized predacious birds eat pigeons and rabbits and can become infected with diseases carried by their prey.

Infectious enteritis is a deadly disease particularly lethal to finches. Specifically it is an infection of the intestinal lining. The bird looks ill and "goes light." Complete isolation in fresh quarters and treatment with sulphamethazine is sometimes helpful.

A fungus disease, *aspergillosis*, does not spread through flocks as do so many other diseases. It will attack only an occasional bird, affecting its lungs. Since there is no known cure, the disease is almost always fatal.

RESPIRATORY DISEASES

There are three basic respiratory diseases that affect birds: *infectious coryza, bronchitis,* and *pneumonia.* The aftereffects of these ailments are sinus disorders and asthma.

There are specific symptoms associated with these diseases: sinusitis, depression, sneezing, discharge from the eyes and nostrils, labored breathing (indicative of pneumonia) and wheezing (a symptom of bronchitis). Treatment consists of warmth, quiet, and the injection of penicillin into the bird's breast.

MORE BIRD DISORDERS

Diarrhea is generally not an ailment in itself but an indication of illness. If the bird seems healthy and is eating well, it could, however, be a dietary aberration. Add boiled rice to your pet's menu and quit feeding greens for a few days. If the diarrhea continues, medication can be found on the shelves of your pet shop.

"Going light," a term used to indicate that a bird is rapidly losing flesh, is indicated by the sharp delineation of the breastbone. This condition is, like diarrhea, a symptom of disease rather than a malady itself. I have not as yet seen a bird fully recover from this indication of disease.

Sour crop (evidenced by regurgitation) indicates some kind of digestive upset. Clean all the eating and drinking utensils and treat by stirring a teaspoonful of baking soda into a quart of water and using this mixture to replace drinking water. *Soft molt* (a partial molt) is caused by abrupt changes in temperature. Attempt to keep your pet always in the same place in the same room to eliminate the chance of a temperature change.

Oil-duct obstruction results from a clogging of the oil gland opening, which is situated where the bird's back and its tail merge. The oil secreted from the gland is used by the bird for grooming and preening. When obstructed, inflammation results. Use a matchstick or toothpick to create gentle pressure that will squeeze out the plug that is sealing the opening.

Bumblefoot is an ailment that causes swollen, painful feet and lumpy disfigurations. It is generally due to dietary imbalance coupled with a lack of exercise and has some relationship to gout in humans. Better allow your veterinarian to cope with this malady.

Egg binding can happen to a pet hen bird as well as to a breeding hen.

There are a number of causative agents. It is most important to relieve the female as quickly as possible of the egg that she cannot expel or she will exhaust herself trying to lay it and will die. First, using an eye-dropper, oil the bird's vent with olive oil, then put her in a hospital cage. If the latter is not available, place her on a hot water bottle that is filled with hot water. A second treatment, which I hesitate to suggest to the novice, is finger manipulation to bring the egg down and out. The obtruding membrane must then be gently pushed back into the vent. A drop of belladonna applied to a swollen vent after the egg has been passed will cause it to shrink back to normal size.

French molt is, in my opinion, a deficiency disease that affects budgerigars particularly and sometimes other psittacines such as love birds and cockatiels. Young chicks coming out of nest boxes should be fully clothed in their junior feathering. If they are the victims of French molt, however, the flight and tail feathers drop out. Sometimes these feathers grow in again, but repeatedly they are lost. Some birds are so badly affected by the disease that all the body feathering is twisted and distorted and the bird has a sorry, moth-eaten appearance. Such specimens should be humanely killed, for they will lack in growth, never be normal, and generally succumb before they reach maturity.

I spent several years in experimental research on French molt, keeping controls and testing every one of the many theories that had been advanced by authorities in the field. My final results indicated that some parent budgerigars possess an inherited inability to produce all the necessary dietary factors in their "crop milk" when feeding their young. This results in French molt. For the first thirty days of a chick's life there is tremendous competition between the explosive body growth and the production of feathering to clothe the growing body. Feathers are almost pure protein and there is very little protein in the general diet given to psittacine birds, so the crop milk fed the chicks lacks the necessary keratin proteins and affiliated amino acids and unsaturated fatty acids or vitamin F. The diet I have outlined for budgerigars can help alleviate the pressure on the parent birds to synthesize the necessary food factors from their own bodies into the crop milk. However, the genetic factors that produce the disease—triggered by dietary insufficiency—still remain and will be inherited by a percentage of the progeny.

Shock and *heart attack* must be accepted as parallel manifestations of the rapid metabolism of birds. They often result from inexpert handling or plain fright. While a bird is being treated for injuries, it will sometimes go into shock and never recover. At other times, if put back in a cage and allowed to rest in a dark, quiet place, the bird will gradually get over the shock.

Canker develops in your bird's throat due to the presence of a harmful protozoa. It is a disease that affects pigeons particularly and sometimes raptors that prey upon pigeons. Palmetto Canker Treatment Tablets, a medication developed by Wendell M. Levi, kills the protozoa in the bird's digestive tract.

Fits affect caged mynahs and soft-bills. Generally the causes are incorrect diet, lack of exercise, or overexposure to direct sun rays. Many of our pet birds have progenitors that inhabited tropical jungles where they were protected from the sun's rays by the sheltering shade of the lush jungle growth. Our pets have inherited a need for the same protection, so make sure your pet is able to reach a shady spot.

INTERNAL PARASITES

Roundworms are very common bird parasites. I treat my flock of budgerigars twice a year with piperazine, a liquid worm eradicator that is nontoxic and can be used in the food or on seeds. *Tapeworms* and *flukes* can infest birds, but there is no known safe medication to expel them. Eventually, the bird will succumb.

Coccidiosis is caused by a single-celled protozoa and is most prevalent in birds that are in outdoor aviaries or cages where wild birds can visit, defecate, and pass these internal parasites on to their domestic kin. Weakness, loss of appetite, and loose, bloody stools are all indicative of coccidiosis. Sulphamethazine in the drinking water for not more than a week may help.

The eggs of internal parasites, and often the parasite itself, can be seen and identified in a stool smear under a microscope.

EXTERNAL PARASITES

Tiny *red mites* are ardent bloodsuckers no larger than a pinpoint. They generally attack the smaller birds such as finches, canaries, and budgerigars, though they are really no respecters of size. Red mites are prevalent also in nest boxes where chicks have hatched. *Feather* and *quill mites* chew on the feathers directly and can do a lot of damage to plumage. *Lice* are tiny, gray marauders that bite and can drive a bird into a frenzy if the infestation is acute.

All these vicious little arachnids can be easily controlled by specific sprays and powders applied on the breast and under the wings of your pet and also in its cage, particularly in corners. Apply the remedy, which can be bought in pet shops and feed stores, weekly until all signs of the vampiric invaders are gone.

Scaly leg is also caused by a mite. This one infests the scales of birds' legs and feet. Treat the problem with aureomycin salve or any good commercial product designed for eradication of the scaly leg mites. *Scaly face* can be an extension of the scaly leg infestation, but it can also be caused by a fungus. If the latter, treat with the application of a mild fungicide on the affected area. Your vet can determine if fungus is the cause.

In modern pet shops you will generally find specific medication for a host of bird ailments. If purchased and used without very definite results within a short time, take your bird to the veterinarian for treatment. Liquid appetizers (tonics that can be bought at pet shops) are worthwhile trying when your bird is ill. Hydrogen peroxide and Monsel's Salts are coagulants useful in the control of bleeding and should be added to the aviary first-aid kit.

DISEASES OF GAME BIRDS AND FOWL

Whether you are producing game birds for commercial purposes or have one or two as decorative pets, you must try to prevent disease through sanitation particularly the control of flies, rats, and mice. To kill harmful bacteria, viruses and fungi, *first* clean the housing area thoroughly with soap and hot water. Then use a disinfectant made for this purpose. Control disease germs that utilize water as a spreading agent through a drinking-water sanitizer. Control flies, mice, and rats through bait you can buy at the feed and grain store.

The most prevalent diseases affecting game birds and fowl are *blackhead,* treated through the use of hepzide or dimetridazole (emtryl) in the water. *Coccidiosis* is treated with sulfaquinoxaline in the drinking water, the preventative level of SQ used here will also help to prevent *fowl cholera. Chronic respiratory diseases* should be treated with antibiotics such as Terramycin and Aureomycin in the drinking water. Breast injection of penicillin is sometimes used when the disease is not chronic. Check with your veterinarian for proper proportions and doses. *Ulcerative enteritis* (quail disease) responds to Terramycin, tylosin or bacitracin, 1 gram per gallon of water for prevention, 2 grams for treatment. Streptomycin at 5 grams per gallon is also efficacious.

WOUNDS AND FRACTURES

All birds at one time or another suffer wounds, which, if severe enough, will require attention. Dirt and damaged tissue can cause gangrene, so the wound must be thoroughly cleansed and sulfathiazole powder sprinkled directly into it. Should a muscle be torn, allow your veterinarian to perform whatever surgery is necessary.

A broken wing or leg bone is not too difficult to attempt to mend unless you become all thumbs at the mere thought. Pull the leg or wing out very gently until the broken ends meet and align as they did before the break. Then apply splints to hold the bones in place and tape, but not so tightly that you cut off circulation. For small birds splints can be fashioned from toothpicks, matchsticks, or small strips of cardboard. For larger birds tongue depressors are good, and for very large birds wooden splints can be whittled to size. *Compound fractures* need the practiced touch of your veterinarian. So do *abscesses* and *tumors*.

ADMINISTERING MEDICINE
Medication for birds can be given in their drinking water or their food. Complete control of dosage can be achieved by holding the bird and dropping medicated liquids, pills, or capsules directly into its mouth. Dr. Allan H. Hart (referred to as "my son, the veterinarian"), after a bit of experimentation, found the ideal method of administering liquid medicine. A piece of plastic tubing—for most birds use a size utilized in hospitals to administer a blood transfusion to a child—is adjusted to the end of a hypodermic syringe barrel from which the needle is removed after the proper dosage of the medication has been drawn up into the syringe. Bend the tubing slightly. Then, holding the bird in one hand (or with an assistant holding the bird if it is a rather large species), put the tubing into the bird's mouth (over the tongue) and gently push it down into the crop. Then slowly push down the plunger of the hypodermic syringe until all the medication has flowed into the patient's crop.

Though the disease picture is necessarily grim, let me lift your spirits with the knowledge that birds bred in captivity, and well cared for, seldom contract the ailments listed here, particularly not those that are truly dangerous.

Diseases of Rodents

Rabbits and chinchillas have been bred for exhibition, meat, and pelts, and, in the selection for these attributes, resistance to some ailments has been neglected or has been inadvertently selected for along with certain desired physical traits. I will list the most prevalent rabbit and chinchilla diseases, since these ailments can affect any or all the *Rodentia* though, as I mentioned earlier, they generally do not.

RABBIT DISEASES
Contagious rhinitis, the real so-called snuffles, was a very troublesome disease before the discovery of antibiotics. Many rodents acquire "colds" that are actually manifestations of rhinitis. The first signs of the disease

are a running nose and sneezing, followed by a thickened nasal discharge. In severe cases the lymph glands of the neck and throat enlarge and become very tender. The disease is bacterial in origin and frequently coccidia will be mixed with the bacteria (which is usually Pasteurella type). The patient will generally recover, but injections of penicillin, sulphamethazine, streptomycin or Aureomycin will aid in shortening recovery time.

Coccidiosis (hepatic) is a common destructive parasitic disease. Rats and flies, contaminated food and water, or the eating of dirty bedding contaminated with cocysts are the usual means of spreading the disease. Licking of the feet and contaminated fur as well as indulging in coprophagy (an integral part of the animal's feeding process) also spread the ailment. Five species of protozoan parasites of the genus *Eimeria* cause coccidiosis. Four of these species affect the intestine; the fifth affects the liver. The functions of the liver become impaired, producing the symptoms of the disease. Sulfaquinoxaline in water or feed (0.03 percent) and sulfamerazine or sulfamethazine (0.5 percent) in the feed are used in treatment. Reinfection is always possible.

Rabbit syphilis is *not* contagious to humans, but is a true venereal disease contracted through copulation. Nodules with scaly, moist crusts that scrape off appear about the prepuce and there is a swelling of the surrounding tissue. Does exhibit lesions around the vagina. The disease will yield to a single quarter c.c. dose of procaine penicillin, usually in sesame oil.

Acute heat can affect all rodents, yet when they show indications of snuffles (displayed as a mucous discharge), sniffles (which appear as general cold symptoms), or any cold-like ailment, they should be isolated immediately and kept in a warm place at a temperature of 85 to 90 degrees Fahrenheit. The hospital cage described in the section on bird diseases will serve wonderfully well for sick rodents (page 103).

Septicemia has a duration of from one to ten days and is accompanied by diarrhea, loss of appetite, nasal rhinitis, and a temperature rise of from three or four degrees. For identification of the disease a bacterial culture must be made. There is a process of serum immunization that should be looked into. Streptomycin is effective, to some degree, if the disease is caught before it has advanced too far. When septicemia breaks out in a colony of animals, fowl-cholera serum is often recommended.

These are the most prevalent diseases of rabbits. There are others that are not so often seen, such as *infectious pneumonia, myxomatosis* (a rare disease), *Bang's disease,* and *nasal catarrh.* All should be treated by your veterinarian.

AILMENTS OF CHINCHILLAS

Chins are sensitive to heat and can become stricken with *heat prostration*. To counteract the effects, reduce the body temperature by applying cold cloths to the stomach and head and feeding very cold salt water (2 teaspoonfuls of salt in a 10-ounce glass) with a medicine dropper. This treatment can be used for any rodent that is affected by heat. There are vaccines available that have been developed to combat various chinchilla ailments. Ask your veterinarian about them.

Colds, which can be contagious rhinitis are accompanied by wheezing, a discharge from the eyes and nostrils, and nose irritation. They should be treated with antibiotics by your veterinarian. Change the rodent's diet to roughage, fresh greens, and milk and add a large dose of vitamin C. *Kidney and liver ailments* are sometimes caused by faulty diet or hepatitis, inflammation of the liver or kidneys, cirrhosis, or nephritis. Allow your veterinarian to pinpoint the disease and treat it specifically. *Pneumonia* should also be treated by your vet. He should lance any *abscesses,* which are caused by mixed pathogenic organisms deep beneath the skin in the body tissue, for it must be done under antiseptic conditions. Chinchillas are often affected by *cysts.* These sacs are sometimes filled with bacteria or parasitic eggs, which your veterinarian will aspirate or surgically remove. *Bloat or torsion* can be fatal. If it occurs, rush your pet to the veterinarian for treatment. It is usually caused by a twisting of the stomach, by bacteria, or by food that is too solid for young chins.

OTHER RODENT DISEASES

Ear infections can also be fatal to any rodent pet—especially so to chinchillas—so rush it to the veterinarian if this occurs. *Constipation* can be caused by too much concentrated dry food, by intestinal infection, or by lack of fluids. Give your pet a few drops of mineral oil, correct his diet, and see that he gets more exercise. *Diarrhea* is often a symptom of some other intestinal ailment. If binding foods and ½ dropperful of Kaopectate do not bring relief within thirty minutes, take him to the veterinarian with a stool sample. *Fever* and *fits* are both indicative of something drastically wrong with your pet that only your veterinarian can cope with. *Broken bones* also require a professional's touch.

Skin diseases can result from various types of *eczema* caused by fungus, or *scabies,* which causes itching and scratching and results in bald and raw areas. Take the tyke to your veterinarian so he can make a scraping of the skin to determine exactly what is causing the irritation and treat it accordingly. If it is a fungus, it must be treated with a fungicide. If it is due to other basic causes, the treatment will be entirely different. *External parasites* such as *fleas, lice,* or *ticks* can cause a good deal of damage to your pet. They can also be the culprits in cases of skin disease. Try to purchase, at your pet shop, a good parasitic powder to apply to your rodent pet, one that is made especially for rodents. If you can't find such a powder, purchase a mild, nontoxic parasitic powder manufactured for cats. Do *not* use *any* medication that has been manufactured especially for dogs.

Gerbils are prone to the development of *sore noses.* The treatment is the application of an antibiotic ointment to the sensitive area and the addition of a vitamin powder to the food.

If you have more than one rodent pet and one of them becomes ill, you must isolate the ailing one immediately and begin treatment. When treating your pet for any illness, including an infestation of external parasites, destroy all the bedding it has been using and thoroughly scrub and sanitize its cage and all the utensils with which it has come in contact.

Your pet rodent may become infested with *internal parasites.* If it becomes listless and its appetite is irregular, this could be the beginning symptom of any number of ailments, including these parasites. When you visit your veterinarian, take along a small sample of the beastie's stool to be checked for internal parasitic invasion.

Tuberculosis can break out in a colony of *cavies.* So can *dysentery* and *generalized blood-poisoning diseases.* Isolate all sick animals and disinfect everything while treating the ill animals with specific medication recommended by your veterinarian. All rodents are subject to infestation by *coccidiosis.* They lick their feet and reinfest themselves. Besides specific treatment, sanitate completely and put the pet or colony on a wire floor so that defecated matter can fall through the wire. Also screen them from contact with flies. Remember that rodents are singularly free from disease, but to keep them that way a program of cleanliness, frequent examination and correct diet is necessary. Be careful in feeding to wash thoroughly any fresh greens or fruit. Most vegetables and fruits are sprayed with disinfectants containing phenol, which can poison your pet. Moldy hay is also a cause of rodent poisoning.

Tropical Fish Diseases

Protozoa cause most of the diseases of *tropical fishes,* so the wide-spectrum antibiotics such as Chloromycetin and tetracycline are the most successful in treating fish diseases. Prevention is, of course, the best medicine and fishes that are knowledgeably cared for are seldom victims of illness. The difference between fishes and other kinds of pets

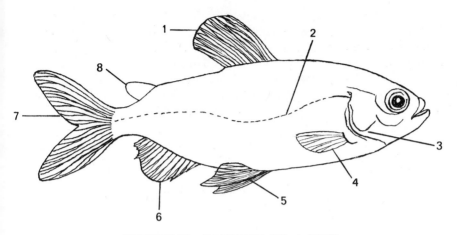

EXTERNAL ANATOMY OF A FISH
1. *Dorsal fin.* 2. *Lateral line.* 3. *Gill cover or operculum.*
4. *Pectoral fin.* 5. *Ventral fin.* 6. *Anal fin.* 7. *Tail or caudal fin.*
8. *Adipose fin.*

when illness strikes is a very grave one; you do not seek the advice and skill of a veterinarian. You, the hobbyist, must be the doctor; you must recognize the disease and select the method of cure. There is one definite plus to the treatment of ailing fishes—for practically all of the most prevalent diseases there is a ready-made remedy that can be bought at a pet or aquarium shop.

White spot or ich is quite common and is caused by a protozoan which develops as white specks all over the fish (actually they are blisters) making the fish itch intolerably and finally to become listless. Ich is quite contagious and some species of fishes are more susceptible to the disease than others. To cure, bring the temperature of the tank to 80 degrees Fahrenheit, purchase a specific medication for ich and use as directed. Or you can use 5 drops of a 5 percent solution of medical *methylene blue* to the gallon (of water in the tank). An even more certain cure is 100 mg of *Chloromycetin* per gallon of tank water.

Shimmy is usually the result of chilling or foul water. The fish remains in one spot, swimming or "shimmying" without forward movement. Clean the habitat and bring the temperature up to about 85 degrees Fahrenheit. Then dose with a specific manufactured medicine.

Fungus of various kinds attack fishes that are hurt or in ill health. A cottony, whitish veil appears all over the affected fish. This too is a very contagious disease, so isolate the affected fish in your hospital jar. The hospital jar or tank should be devoid of any decoration and well aerated. It should be made of clear plastic and sterilized after each use. But before putting the fish in the jar, immerse him for 30 seconds in a solution of 4 grains of *malachite green* or *brilliant green* (zinc free) to one gallon of water. An easier way of treating fungus is to purchase a specific medication from your pet shop or friendly aquarium man and closely follow the directions on the label.

Fin and tail rot and *mouth fungus* are diseases that look like fungus attacks but are actually caused by bacteria. In *mouth fungus* a white line begins to form around the affected fish's lips. When this becomes visible, begin treatment immediately. Fin and tail rot can be recognized by a ragged, moth-eaten look of these parts. These bacterial diseases must be treated with dispatch, for they spread rapidly. Since they are of bacterial origin, they should be treated with penicillin, about 50,000 to 200,000 units per gallon of water. Remove the affected fishes and treat them in the hospital tank. Again a commercial product can be bought for treatment.

Flukes attack both tropicals and cold-water fishes. These are not digenetic flukes that require an intermediate host. They fasten onto the fish's skin and gills and cause the poor creature to thrash about maniacally until exhausted. Flukes spread rapidly and are difficult to eradicate. A commercial remedy can be purchased and used for treatment. Or put the infected fish in a container with ⅛th grain per gallon of potassium permanganate and leave it there for several hours. Meanwhile treat the aquarium by siphoning off a good deal of the water; don't forget to siphon the bottom of the tank particularly to remove flukes that have fallen.

There are several types of *dropsy* that affect fishes. The outward manifestation of dropsy is a bloated appearance throughout the body of the fish. There is no known truly effective treatment, so it is best to quickly destroy a victim of this illness. Closely watch the other denizens of the aquarium since there is evidence that some forms of dropsy are caused by a contagious virus.

Velvet (also known as rust disease) is caused by a protozoa and is much like ich in appearance except that the spots are smaller, are yellow and move. This disease is fatal to young fish. Remove those affected to a separate small tank and treat the same as with ich but, if you use methylene blue, double the amount. Treatment should last for from one to two weeks.

Swim bladder disease is accompanied by a complete loss of physical balance. There is no known cure. *Tuberculosis* is characterized by a gradual wasting away and extreme emaciation. At the moment there is no cure for this disease either. *Neon disease* affects several of the *tetras* and *glowlights* and manifests itself by a fading of body hue until the glow line of the affected fish has lost all color. This too is an incurable disease. All of these diseases are contagious and affected fish should be removed from the tank or eliminated.

Itch (*ichthyophonus*) is caused by a fungus-like organism that infects the fish internally through infected food and water it has ingested. The blood acts as a carrier for the disease, distributing it throughout the body. The infected fish rubs against objects in the tank as though itchy. Treatment consists of the use of a commercially prepared medication that can be purchased in an aquarium or pet shop. Para-Chlorophenoxethol is a specific for itch, but rather difficult to prepare, so it is best to use an already prepared medication.

Skin slime is a self-descriptive disease. It is often accompanied by faded color and clamped fins. The causative agents are a variety of protozoa; treatment consists of mixing 2 grains of hydrochloride into a gallon of water. Add this medicated water to the aquarium in three equal doses at twelve-hour intervals. This is actually a quinine bath for the fish.

Anemia and loss of color are generally due to poor husbandry. Make certain the aquarium is clean and that the filter and aerator are performing properly. Then begin feeding live food and heavily vitaminized dry food until the fish are back to normal.

Fish lice are external parasites that gnaw and infest the fish's flesh. The *anchor worm* is another such parasitic invader. Treat infested fish with the same medication as recommended for flukes.

In every instance of disease remember to bring the temperature of your tank water to approximately 80 degrees Fahrenheit to help hasten the cure.

Diseases of Marine Tropicals

Make absolutely certain that any salt-water tropical you purchase is healthy when you buy it. See that it is sleek and sassy and in full color, never thin and faded in hue, and be sure it harbors no parasites or fungus. Marine tropicals become ill with the same diseases that affect fresh-water fish. Most of the troubles that marine aquarists have to contend with are parasitic infestations. It is best to isolate any sick fish in a prepared hospital tank.

Ichthyophonus, which looks like tiny white spots, is a dangerous disease caused by algae spores. Try raising the water temperature to 86 degrees Fahrenheit and add a prepared copper-sulfate solution. Shut off the filter. Actually there is little chance of saving the stricken fish, but if it is a very beautiful or expensive one, it pays to try. Another treatment you might attempt is 5 drops of 5 percent methylene blue per gallon of water with a prepared mixture of streptomycin and penicillin.

Branchiophillus is also caused by an algae spore. Tiny white spots around the gills identify this disease. Cut off the filter, drop the temperature to 68 degrees Fahrenheit and treat with a prepared copper-sulfate solution.

Ichthyophthirius in marine tropicals can be treated exactly as described for fresh-water fishes.

Popeyes (*exophthalmia*) can be caused by a lack of complete nutrition. Shift fishes to a clean aquarium and feed a different range of food that includes vegetable matter, cereal, and live foods. You might try the Holly Commercial Mixes. Drop the temperature in the tank about 5 degrees, adding three tablespoons of salt per gallon of water. Use aeration and leave the fish in the solution for 72 hours. A *flagellate* that attaches itself to the fish's skin (*oodinium ocellatum*) can cause a deadly epidemic in your aquarium. A prepared copper-sulfate solution should be used to combat this scourge.

Diseases of Reptiles

All living things are susceptible to disease and infection of some kind —and reptiles are not excepted. External parasites particularly are always a cross to be borne by all forms of life. It would be a comfort to know that all the blood-sucking, disease-carrying, tiny, tormenting arachnids had external parasites of their own to plague them. But justice being what it is, this is not so.

SNAKES

Snakes are among the healthiest of vertebrate creatures in captivity, so disease is generally no big problem. The real trouble lies in the fact that very few veterinarians are truly qualified to treat sick snakes. The rare veterinarian who is a herpetologist or a reptile hobbyist is truly a godsend to his fellow serpent fanciers.

To begin, we can eliminate all ailments that affect mammalian legs and feet. The eyes of a snake are generally well protected by the upper brow, and, because of its simplified skeletal structure, the incidence of bone fractures or breaks is almost nonexistent.

Snakes definitely do have *external parasites* and tropical reptiles in particular harbor these tiny, crablike arachnids. Peer closely at the scales of an infested snake and if it looks as though it has been sprinkled with pepper, you will know it is infested with mites. Observe your pet's skin for a few minutes and you will see the parasites move. What you see is by no means the total parasitic population, for just as many, or more, have burrowed deep into and under the scales. Parasites can cause a great deal of trouble, including deep-seated infection. They are highly mobile so the reptile must be immediately isolated and any others you may have should be carefully watched for the first sign of infestation. If you are a collector, whenever you procure a new snake, be certain it is in excellent health before you allow it to come in contact with any of your other serpent pets.

To cure external parasitic infection, segregate the affected pet and thoroughly swab him with a mild antiseptic such as Betadine, Listerine or Mercurochrome. Then clean the quarters he has been inhabiting with parasitic powder—and get all edges and deep into corners. Next wash the powder out and sanitate completely, washing with hot water and non-detergent soap and rinsing again in clean water. Meanwhile gather a few of the mites and take them in an envelope to your veterinarian for identification. Have him prescribe a dip or powder for eradication that will not harm your pet and that can be used whenever this trouble reoccurs.

Pulmonary tuberculosis is rare but can follow in the wake of repeated chilling, dampness, and an untended habitat. Early manifestations of the disease are asymptomatic. It can be quickly fatal unless treatment is immediately instituted. If your pet is infected with tuberculosis bacillus (*mycobacterium tuberculosis*) and is a valuable snake, take him to your veterinarian. He will be able to decide if the trouble is tubercular or if the ailment is another pulmonary disease. He will then prescribe specific medication. If your pet *does* have pulmonary tuberculosis, Isoniazid is the drug of choice, used in combination with other drugs such as streptomycin, para-aminosalicylic acid, ethambutol, cycloserine, viomycin, and several other antibiotics. Supportive nursing consists of lots of sunshine, heat, a very dry environment and, if available, ultra-violet light.

Another very lethal disease, called *mouth rot* or cankermouth, is prevalent in reptiles, particularly boas, pythons and all poisonous snakes that are captive and "milked" for their venom. Mouth rot is caused by a bacterial infection and manifests itself by a small red spot on the mouth of the snake. This spot, unless treated immediately, becomes larger and angrier, developing into an ulcerated lesion. Eventually the condition works deeper, affecting the bones of the jaw and killing the gum tissue (necrosis). If the disease is allowed to advance this far, it is almost impossible to cure. If treatment begins early, a cure can be effected.

With cotton held by a forceps apply an antibiotic cream or aqueous solution three times daily at three-day intervals until the infection is cured. Your veterinarian might want to give supportive treatment, using an antibiotic through intermuscular injection. Older drugs that were previously used for this condition were Sul-met and sodium sulfamethazine. Segregate the infected reptile, since this condition is contagious.

Rapping on the front of a snake's cage or terrarium seems to be a custom of most visitors. Do not allow it. This constitutes teasing and can ruin your pet's disposition. If the snake becomes irritated enough to strike out and hits the glass or wire front of its cage with its snout, it can cause a nasal or oral injury that will have to be treated.

Examine the mouth, inside and out, and the eyes of your pet at least once a week, and remember that proper food and care, cleanliness, warmth, sunshine, and dryness will keep your pet healthy and free of disease. One fact I must mention in reference to food: snakes can go on incredible fasts seemingly without suffering any harm. Some of the large reptiles (pythons and giant boas) have fasted for nineteen months. Authorities claim that snakes can, without doubt, survive a fast of two and a half years.

TURTLES

Turtles and other reptilia are not difficult to treat. The first thought when disease attacks your turtle should be to provide additional warmth for the patient. Either place the terrarium where the warming rays of the sun can reach it, or situate a lamp so that its heat is directed into the turtle's habitat.

Diseases of the eyes can be treated with a commercially prepared ophthalmic solution that can be bought at a pet shop. One such medication has been specifically manufactured for the eye troubles of turtles, lizards, salamanders, and terrapins. Follow the directions on the label faithfully.

Fungus diseases are treated by dipping the patient in a mild medical bath and then painting the affected area with a fungal medication. Again a commercially prepared product can be found on the shelves of your local pet shop.

Turtles are hardy creatures if given the correct environmental conditions and properly fed. They are perhaps the longest living of all reptiles, outliving even the crocodilians that are noted for their length of life. Aquatic turtles, particularly young terrapins, can develop soft shells. They need lots of sunshine. All aquatic turtles need *copper* ions in their water if the soft-shell condition is to be alleviated. A few copper pennies in the water are all that is necessary. Turtle shells, particularly those of young turtles, need calcium for growth and to sustain them upon maturity. Calcium blocks can provide this needed mineral, or powdered calcium or bonemeal can be purchased and added to the turtle's food. Turtles are not nocturnal creatures and all are oviparous, or egg-laying, reptiles.

FROGS AND TOADS

Frogs and toads seem to be singularly free of disease. Young tadpoles are sensitive to abrupt changes in temperature. Toads enjoy having some water that they can absorb through their skins even though it is known that they can go for long periods of time without water.

Diseases of Primates

Primates are cursed with all the diseases—and generally a few more that they garner in the wild state—that are the heritage of man. Most primates are rather delicate in captivity and are particularly prone to respiratory diseases, their major cause of death. In captivity and as pets, they do much better in tropical or semitropical climates, with the exception of one or two species whose native environment includes seasons of cold and inclement weather.

When your pet primate becomes ill take it to your veterinarian. New medication and methods of nursing are constantly replaced by those being used at the moment and only your veterinarian is informed of their worth and usage. The best way to treat diseases in primates, as in other animals, is to prevent them. This much to-be-desired condition can be arrived at through correct husbandry and by supplying the pet primate with the proper environmental factors under which previous generations of the species have thrived.

Some of the most pertinent facts about your primate's health, of which one must be made aware, are: the good-natured sakis show a high percentage of parasitic infection; monkeys can go into penicillin shock just as humans can if they are allergic to this drug; they can have rheumatoid arthritis and develop diabetes, ulcers, and eye cataracts. Monkeys are also susceptible to heart disease, athereosclerosis, aortic ills, plaque, fat, or chloresterol deposits, kidney failure and influenza, which is deadly to primates. If this sounds to you like a review of human diseases, you are correct—it is—but it is also a list of the ailments and diseases we share in common with our cousins, the primates.

INTERNAL PARASITES

Some of the most prevalent forms of parasitic infestation in primates are *pinworm* (*oxyuriasis*), which is treated with pyrvinium pamoate (the drug of choice) or piperazine citrate, a mild drug used to eradicate roundworms in canines. *A nematode, strongyloidiasis,* can be successfully treated with gentian violet. The taste of the specific is disagreeable, but if mixed well with any berry syrup, it will be more palatable to your pet. *Schistosomiasis* is a parasitic fluke that is also common to man in certain parts of the world. It would have to be diagnosed and treated by your veterinarian.

Thorny-headed worms cause occlusion of the intestines, perforation of the intestinal wall with resultant peritonitis. This infestation has been reported in both *squirrel monkeys* and *marmosets.* Cockroaches have been found to be the intermediate host of these worms, so roach control is imperative.

Thiapendozole is considered an efficient drug against *cesophagostomum.* The anthelmintic is also highly useful against strongyloides.

RESPIRATORY DISEASES

Pneumonia can be bacterial, viral, or mixed viral and the only way your veterinarian can diagnose the disease correctly and prescribe specifically is by taking a blood sample from your pet and making a culture. Supportive treatment consists of humidification of the air, fluid intake, and codeine administered to control coughing. Drug allergy should be ascertained and oxygen may be necessary.

Bacterial pneumonia can be treated with penicillin G or tetracycline, cephalothin, chloramphonicol, or oxycillin. The choice of drug is dictated by the bacterial agent involved. In *Klebsiella pneumonia,* kanamycin, cephalothin, and gentamycin are drug specifics. Tetracycline is generally used in *primary atypical pneumonia.*

Influenza is exceedingly lethal to primates. It is an acute viral infection characterized by respiratory and constitutional symptoms that result in a sluggish, generally sick-looking animal. There are several viral strains that produce the disease and the viruses of all are airborne. Give aspirin for accompanying fever, headache, and myalgia. Antibiotic therapy is indicated, usually penicillin G or erythromycin. Prevention can be achieved through vaccination.

OTHER DISEASES

Herpevirus, in humans commonly exhibited as shingles, cold sores on the lips, or chicken pox, is seemingly prevalent in *marmosets* and particularly virulent in *white-lipped marmosets* and *squirrel monkeys.* The last-named primate, often shipped with marmosets from South America, shows a high mortality rate from this viral disease, which also seems to have great virulence for the *owl* or *night monkey.* Oral ulcers are suspected of being an associated Herpe-T infection in New World monkeys.

Should your primate pet break out in a *measle-like rash,* take him immediately to your veterinarian and do not assume offhand that it is a form of eczema. Several kinds of respiratory diseases dangerous to primates are caused by viruses that produce skin rashes.

FIRST AID AND OTHER MEDICAL ADVICE

When your pet needs an anesthetic, the most commonly employed are generally the most successful. However some research laboratories have reported that they have had the best results with fluothane administered by a Fluotex combined with Boyles anesthesia machine. Oral administration of capsules, or the use of stomach tubes for liquids is not always highly successful with primates. The alternate suggestion is the use of a tube inserted through the nose. For an average-sized rhesus monkey use a Bardic, size 8 French feeding tube. Baby primates will readily accept flavored oral pediatric therapeutic agents.

The rectal temperature of a primate is normally 100 to 100.1 degrees. If your pet has a fever, it can be brought down, as it is in humans, by administering aspirin, one tablet every four hours for a primate the size of a baboon. Grade dosage down in proportion to the size of your pet. When you use a rectal thermometer, it will take only about a minute to get a true reading. Don't worry too much about slight variation. It doesn't matter much if the temperature is 100.20 or 100.40.

Medicinal tablets should be crushed and fed mixed with a strong-tasting wet-type food that your pet particularly enjoys. When administering liquid medication, stir it into a drink that your pet is very fond of but is treated to only occasionally. Above all, when administering medicine of any kind, be nonchalant because your pet will sense tension in you and immediately become nervous and wary.

If you have to give your primate an *enema,* use about 3 to 6 ounces (according to your pet's size) of warm water in which you have dissolved a piece of mild soap until the water has taken on a milky look. If your pet is under a veterinarian's care, he may advise you to use some other liquid in the enema.

Suppositories should be slipped completely into the rectum. A word of caution: never give your pet an enema, and never use a suppository or any cathartic unless you have first consulted your veterinarian.

For *cuts, burns,* and *bites,* the best treatment is to wash the affected area thoroughly with warm water and clear soap, then rinse with clean water. Cover the cut or wound with a clean bandage to keep dirt away. The bandage should be snug but not tight. Unless the wound is superficial, it is advisable to have it examined and treated by your veterinarian.

For *burns* immerse the affected area in very cold water. Do *not* use any ointments, salves, oils, or other greasy substances. Cover with a wet, clean bandage and rush the patient to the veterinarian for treatment.

Believe it or not, monkeys, the finest of brachiators, sometimes fall from trees and sustain a *broken limb*. Your vet will set the limb and splint it so that it will mend properly.

Sick and hurt primates can self-inflict serious wounds in sheer panic, pain and anguish, so handling them when they are in such a condition is not easy. Heavy leather gloves will help and a thick blanket can be wrapped around them to keep them immobile. For complete restraint, your veterinarian will tape the monkey to a plywood, cross-shaped board. The arms of the patient are outstretched and taped to the horizontal section and the legs are taped to the vertical piece. A strap around the middle can also help. This holds the primate in a position where he cannot injure you or himself and can be easily treated.

Illnesses of Raccoon-Family Pets

The raccoon family has its share of diseases that, as a pet owner of animals falling within the scope of this species, you will have to cope with. Specifically it is your job to be able to recognize the initial signs of sickness and be quick to treat your pet, or have it treated, before ailments can become chronic or lethal.

EXTERNAL PARASITES

Fleas, lice, ticks and other external parasites are the bane of all animals and their owners. Specific powders, lotions, and dips are available for eradication and control. Those used for felines are also excellent for raccoon-type mammals. I suggest you hark back to the cat-disease section for most of the information you will need to treat your *Procyonidae* family pet against these pests. Remember parasites are also present in your pet's bedding and surroundings and must be eliminated in these areas for complete control. Mange mites should be treated by your veterinarian.

INTERNAL PARASITES

Your pet can harbor numerous kinds of *worms*. It is no easy chore to rid it of these internal parasites since reinfestation usually occurs repeatedly, particularly in raccoons and coatis that pace back and forth through their stools. The drugs used as specifics are, except for round-worms, necessarily harsh. Take a small sample of your pet's stool to your vet and allow him to determine the kind of worms your pet has and to prescribe the treatment necessary to control and eradicate them. Absolute and continuous cleanliness is a necessary adjunct to control.

VIRAL DISEASES

These are deadly diseases that need prevention rather than cure. *Rabies* is the worst offender and is a terrible disease that is communicable to humans and all other mammals. Please see *Diseases of Cats*, p. 94. Treatment for virus diseases contracted by raccoon-type animals should follow in dosage, medication, and care the pattern suggested in the parallel section for felines.

BACTERIAL DISEASES

These illnesses include *tetanus* and *bacterial pneumonia*. The latter disease, along with *viral* and *mixed viral pneumonia* and other respiratory diseases such as *influenza* and *pulmonary* tuberculosis, are always a danger when you own a pet whose natural habitat is tropical and you are in an area of drastic climatic change. The raccoon is hardy and not as susceptible to these diseases as the coati-mundi, the kinkajou, and the crab-eating raccoon. The last named is a southern cousin of the *Procyon lotor* and cacomistles that come from a northern range and are also not likely to become affected by respiratory diseases. Your veterinarian will prescribe combinations of antibiotics that have proven efficatious for these illnesses. Raccoon-type mammals that are from tropical environments have to be watched. Lesser pandas and some coatis live at high altitudes and are therefore more accustomed to chillier weather.

DIARRHEA AND CONSTIPATION

Digestive upsets can cause *diarrhea,* but sometimes it is a symptom of some other disease. To find the cause, examine the diet you are feeding. If the condition can be corrected through a change of diet, then your troubles are over. If not, watch the animal carefully for the development of some other illness and consult with your veterinarian.

Constipation can be relieved by giving a teaspoonful or tablespoonful, depending upon your pet's size, of mineral oil or milk of magnesia given orally. Diet can also cause this malady, particularly if you are feeding too much hard, dry, or densely fibrous food. Lessen the percentage of dry foods (pellets) and feed more fruits.

SKIN DISEASES

Eczemas, dry or wet, can spread rapidly. During the daily grooming you will be able to catch any beginning skin disease before it can become widely spread. Your veterinarian can take skin scrapings and prescribe specific treatment to eliminate the condition before it takes too strong a hold.

Ringworm, evidenced by oral areas of fungus infection, can be cured by a good fungicide. Your pet will lick any affected areas it can reach, so the medication used must not be harmful should he ingest it.

Diseases of Hoofed Mammals

It is much easier to prevent illness than to cope with it once it has taken hold. There are available an assortment of effective vaccines for use in the area of preventive medicine. These vaccines can thwart tetanus, strangles in horses, equine encephalomyelitis, leptospirosis, virus abortion, enterotoxemia, and distemper. Antibiotics incorporated in the food promote growth and aid in disease prevention.

Bruises, abrasions, and *lacerations* should be promptly attended to. Shave the hair around wounds, flush with a warm 50 percent saline solution, and use a moist dressing for healing. For deep wounds that need suturing, call your veterinarian. Punctures should be cleansed with hydrogen peroxide and tetanus antitoxin must be immediately given. Strains and sprains should be treated with cold applications to reduce inflammation, followed by hot applications and hand massage with a mild liniment, plenty of rest, and a localized analgesic. Rest and the use of a local pain-killer also apply to torn muscles.

Thrush is an infection of the frog of a horse's foot, and is caused by standing in unsanitary conditions in the barn or stable. Clean the area in which the animal lives and treat the hoof with a medication prescribed by your veterinarian.

Colic originates in the digestive tract, causes pain, restlessness, and loss of appetite. It can kill. Sometimes there is inflammation of the stomach, diarrhea, gas and bloat (or torsion). Call your veterinarian immediately and always keep on hand a good colic remedy to bridge the gap between the onslaught of the disease and the vet's arrival.

Colitis is a very serious—often fatal—disease. *Equine encephalomyelitis* (sleeping sickness) is a viral disease carried by blood-sucking insects, particularly mosquitos. It is *not* communicable to man. Prognosis is not good.

Influenza will yield to antibiotics if promptly treated, or it can be vaccine-controlled. Hoofed animals that show the symptoms of a cold

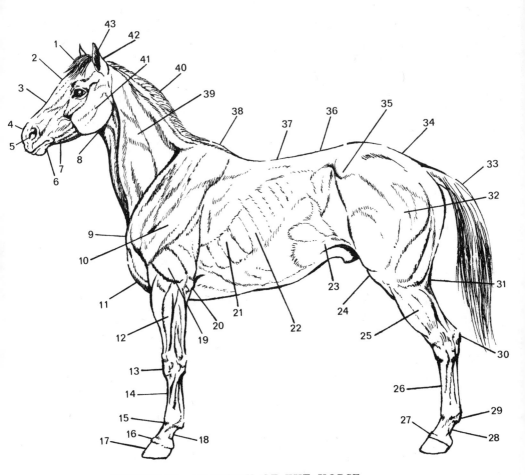

EXTERNAL ANATOMY OF THE HORSE

1. Foretop. 2. Forehead. 3. Nose. 4. Muzzle. 5. Nostril.
6. Chin groove. 7. Lower jaw. 8. Throttle. 9. Sternum. 10.
Shoulder. 11. Breast. 12. Forearm. 13. Knee. 14. Front cannon. 15. Fetlock or ankle. 16. Coronet. 17. Hoof. 18. Pastern.
19. Arm. 20. Elbow. 21. Chest or Barrel. 22. Ribs. 23. Flank.
24. Stifle. 25. Gaskin or second thigh. 26. Hind cannon. 27.
Coronet. 28. Pastern. 29. Fetlock (feather). 30. Hock. 31.
Quarter. 32. Thigh. 33. Tail. 34. Croup. 35. Point of hip. 36.
Loin. 37. Back. 38. Withers. 39. Neck. 40. Crest. 41. Cheek.
42. Poll. 43. Ear.

should be watched closely, for they could indicate influenza or other viral respiratory disease.

Swamp fever is another dangerous virus disease that reduces the red-blood-cell count. The virus can be carried by animals that indicate no evidence of the disease.

Infectious bovine rhinotracheitis is also caused by a virus. Treatment consists of controlling secondary bacterial infections through the use of antibiotics usually put into the drinking water. Prevention can be attained through vaccination and an annual booster shot.

Blackleg-malignant-edema can also be prevented through specific vaccination. Penicillin in massive doses with supportive antibiotics and sulfonamides is the treatment. Veterinary assistance is necessary to provide surgical drainage if pertinent and to supervise treatment.

Vaccinate all lambs and young calves to prevent enterotoxemia, the over-eating disease. There is a drug that is an effective corrective medication for lambs.

Diphtheria should be treated with antibiotics and the patient given complete rest. *Infectious keratoconjunctivitis* (pink eye) is treated with medicated powder while the victim is isolated to keep the disease from spreading. Fly control is an important element in preventing this disease.

INTERNAL PARASITES

Hoofed animals can harbor many kinds of internal and external parasites. Unthriftiness, weakness, coughing, anemia, colic, and roughness of coat are indications of parasitic infection.

Your veterinarian will treat your pet with specific drugs (anthelmintics) that will rid the animal of whatever kind of worms it is harboring. *Bloodworms* (*strongyles*) are dangerous parasites that infest the large arteries and can cause blood blockage. The artery wall can be weakened by these helminths to such an extent that it may rupture and cause death.

Roundworms can be gotten rid of with proper medication. With maturity, the animal generally becomes immune to the parasites. *Pinworms* cause irritation in the anal area, and *bots* are the larvae of the botfly. The latter enter the animal's stomach when it licks the area where the fly's eggs have been laid. The eggs hatch and the larvae attack the stomach lining. A program of parasitic prevention can be launched that will keep the problem manageable. Routine worming in the spring and the fall will also aid in the constant battle against helminths.

EXTERNAL PARASITES

Lice can be controlled with sprays and powders. *Ticks* are a nuisance and can carry *Rocky Mountain spotted fever* and the blood parasite responsible for piroplasmosis. An infected animal becomes a carrier. Spray pesticides, dips and tick powder are the answer to this problem. *Ringworm* can be communicated to you, so wear gloves when handling the affected animal and when using medication. Iodine or a specific veterinary medication should be used.

Sanitation and good management are the most important disease preventatives for all hoofed animals. When disease does rear its ugly head, be on the safe side and call for the expertise and experience of your veterinarian.

Ailments of Mustelines

Skunks and other mustelines can become infected with most of the ailments dogs and cats (particularly cats) are heir to. These include all the deadly viral and bacterial diseases. Inoculations against these dread destroyers are the major means of protection. Discuss this with your veterinarian, especially in reference to rabies and the distemper-hepatitis-leptospirosis triumvirate. Meanwhile, if you possess a pet musteline, please peruse the pages on cat diseases (p. 94), studying the symptoms and advice.

Ailments of Viverrines

Viverrine diseases are quite similar to those infecting mustelines. Therefore the area embracing feline diseases is also applicable here.

Marsupial Medical Advice

Unfortunately we know very little about the diseases of marsupials. If kept under ideal conditions, in sanitary surroundings and a tropical environment, they seem to be hardy and not prone to disease.

If kept in an inclement climate, these creatures from the past will be susceptible to respiratory diseases. If this occurs, your veterinarian, through a blood sample and culture, will be able to determine the exact kind of respiratory illness and treat it accordingly. Supportive treatment will consist of warmth, fluids, and lots of loving care.

External parasites are always a nuisance and affect all creatures, even marsupials. Should your Down Under pet become infested, turn to diseases of cats (p. 94) and follow the suggestions given there for external or internal parasites, and other diseases your pet may become subject to.

Your veterinarian, unless a graduate of the Sydney School of Veterinary Medicine, may not be entirely conversant with marsupial medicine. But he does know how to treat sick animals and if he follows a course of treatment similar to that prescribed for cats, he should, in most instances, do well for your pet. Certain marsupials that mimic rodents should be treated medically as rodents. Browsing kangaroos can be given the same sort of treatment that would be dispensed to a mammalian hoofed herbivore, with account taken of the size and weight of the marsupial.

Medical Advice for Insects and Miscellaneous Pets

"Medical treatment for insects?" you ask. I am afraid that very little can be done in the way of medication for ill insects. The very thought of doctoring an insect is rather ridiculous and leads to ludicrous surmises and questions such as: Can a flea become the victim of external parasites or smaller fleas, and can those fleas have . . . and so on, ultimately leading to the couch of the closest psychiatrist.

For those varied creatures in the miscellaneous section that may become indisposed or ill, depend upon your veterinarian for help. I don't think that those of you who have pet tarantulas, vampire bats, and creatures of like ilk will ever be listed among your veterinarian's favorite people, but I am sure he will supply what you need—all the elements of exacting medical aid for which the profession is justly known.

CHAPTER
7
Training Your Pet

Basic training is actually educating your pet to be a good citizen. In the process you teach your precious pet to live in harmony with you and to assume a comfortable place within the framework of *your* life-style.

The secret of quick and easy animal training lies in a definitive knowledge of how it is accomplished. Four words form the foundation upon which all training is built: control, consistency, conditioning, and patience.

When you train your pet, you condition him to perform a certain action in response to a key or signal given by you. This can be either a spoken command, a hand signal or both. All animals, including man, are creatures of habit and by conditioning your pet to react to your command you are shaping his response into a habit.

Control is a necessary adjunct to molding the conditioned reflexes. But before you apply it to training you must learn how to control yourself completely. When you lose your temper during training, when you shout, become exasperated, and angrily reprimand your pupil, you confuse and frighten the pupil. If the animal does not obey, it generally means that he has not been conditioned to react properly to the given command. He needs to be taught, not punished. The fault is yours, not his.

Control is accomplished through a meeting of the minds, a rapport between you and your pet. You must completely capture his attention so that he will react to your every word and gesture during the act of training. Once the pupil has learned to respond to a command correctly, insist on his obeying the same command with alacrity—*always*. If you don't, you will begin to lose the control that is so important.

Consistency in training is closely linked to control and conditioning. You must use the same command—*always*—if you wish to get the identical response from your pet. Do not, for example, call the pupil to you by commanding, "Here" one time, and "Come" the next.

You must also be consistent in everyday living with your pet. Never allow him to perform an act in the house that is contrary to your wishes.

If, for instance, you have trained your pet to keep off the furniture and he ignores or forgets your teaching and jumps up on the living room sofa, never be too tired or listless to scold him and make him get down, letting him know by the tone of your voice that he has committed an offense.

Patience must be coupled with consistency and repetition. One must be extremely patient during the training process, repeating the lesson over and over again, quietly and firmly, until the pupil has been conditioned to respond correctly. If the instructor loses patience, he loses control and nullifies all that has been accomplished before.

Training periods must be short, for animals, like children, possess a rather brief attention span and after half-an-hour your pet will grow weary of the whole process.

Fish, reptiles, and insects are not trainable to any great degree. But training our canine friends has, rightly, become an important and exceedingly valuable part of the utilitarian concept of dog ownership. Living so closely with man, a dog's deportment must be exemplary. And, at this time when, in the flow of centuries, the clock has turned back and medieval crime and violence are accepted as indigenous to our society, the dog has a very real role to play as a protector of his master's home and possessions and even of his life and the precious lives of his family.

Training and Showing Your Dog

Every dog should be trained. Your pet should have, at the very least, rudimentary or basic training to make it a good citizen and a well-behaved family dog. If you have a child, you must train it in good manners and behavior; you must do the same with a puppy. The difference between training a child and training a puppy is one of time: the human youngster is tutored over a period of many years, but the canine adolescent must be taught proper deportment within a year or two.

Many puppies bought as show prospects never achieve the physical potential for which they gave promise as youngsters. Frequently the owners of such animals decide to work their pets in the training ring. Often such dogs become fine performers at obedience trials and their owners reap a much richer reward in satisfaction, competition, and closer rapport with their pet than had the dog become a show specimen.

Words of command in training must be simple. Each must have a sound clearly different from the other. "Sit," "Down," "Heel," "Stay," "Come," "Stand," "Jump" or "Hop," "Bring," et cetera are all excellent examples of one-word commands. When giving a command, preface it with the dog's name. The sound of it instantly brings his active attention to you and he is alert to the command. The exception is the "Stay" command when the dog's name is *not* used, since inaction is desired.

The tone of your voice when giving training commands should be divorced from your normal speech. It must be stronger and more decisive, a "training voice" that your dog will recognize immediately and know that serious business is at hand. Be sharp when you scold him and soften your voice for praise. Use your voice as an instrument to play on your pupil's auditory sensitivity in order to elicit the proper response.

Intelligence and sensitivity varies in dogs as it does in all living creatures. Sensitive pets must be handled with greater care during training than more aggressive animals. The ability to learn and perform depends upon the character of the pupil and is limited by the breed's inherited functional abilities and size. It would, for instance, be ridiculous to try to teach a hundred Chihuahuas to pull a sled when a Malamute will do it instinctively and alone. And it would be next to impossible to train a collie to point game or a pointer to herd sheep, simply because each of these breeds has, over many generations, been selected to do a specific job. The ability to do that job has been locked into their genetically inherited behavior patterns and no amount of training can change it.

Keep training periods short. Ten-minute sessions are enough at first. Lengthen the time as you proceed and quit when your pupil indicates that he is tired of the whole thing. But take just a few minutes more to command your dog to perform an act of training that he knows and does well. In this way you both end the session on a high note of triumph.

Reward your pupil with a show of affection, a happy petting and rubbing of the ears and neck, a smile and words of praise, such as "Good boy," when he has completed an exercise well. Never omit this indication of your pleasure at his cleverness and he will always attempt to please you to gain this reward. Both praise and correction should be administered immediately following the act that prompts them.

I do not advocate actual punishment in the process of training. It introduces a negative element to the conditioning concept. A quick, forceful jerk on the leash is enough to bring your pupil into line and to correct him. In the process of training you *praise* and *correct* your dog; you never *punish* him. I have two German shepherds, a male and a bitch, both German imports, that I have used on television and in exhibitions. Both are fully Schutzhund trained (in obedience, tracking, locating lost objects; in finding a criminal, attacking upon command in the face of gunfire; holding, releasing, or escorting the criminal to a given place), and never have I found it necessary to punish these dogs. I praise and sometimes correct them, but never do I punish them. They are under complete control at all times, can be taken anywhere, are wonderful house and guard dogs, and love children, but, if it becomes necessary, they can be more dangerous and effective than a loaded gun.

THE MECHANICS OF TRAINING

The equipment you need for basic training is simple: a 4½-foot-long leather or webbed leash and a chain-link collar. The pupil must always be on your left side, the hand loop of the leash over your right thumb, the slack gathered in your right hand, which should be held comfortably near the right side of your middle section so that the leash can be jerked sideways or upward without awkwardness. Your left hand is down at your side and can hold the leash lightly as it flows down to the dog's collar leaving about a foot of slack. All the actions with the leash will be done by your right hand. The left hand is used essentially for pet-praising, pressing for sits, and a signal or two. You will need a light dumbbell and jumps later, but for the basic training discussed here you need only the collar and leash.

Do not try to train a just-fed dog. He will be sluggish and will not respond as he should. When his stomach is empty, he will be eager to work and quick to respond to commands. Do not feed a puppy immediately after a training session. Give him time to settle down before offering him his meal. Older dogs can be fed a light meal after training and will consider it a reward.

EARLY TRAINING

The first important words of communication between you and your puppy are his name and the words "No," and "Shame," "Come" and "Good." Your pet's training has already been started by the breeder who, after the pup and his nestmates had been weaned, brought them their food. Generally the breeder makes some kind of special sound or call to which the pups respond, knowing it indicates that food is about to be served. Thus a conditioned reflex has been triggered and your pup's training begun.

Housebreaking is the first order of business after bringing home a little bundle of furry joy. Alas, the little one, once brought into the home, seems to become less of a puppy and more of a bladder and bowel wrapped up in fur. But never despair. With a little knowledge housebreaking becomes an easy chore.

Try to purchase your pup so that you bring him home on a weekend and have two whole, glorious days to make him feel at home and to housebreak him. The pup will play and sleep, eat and sleep, and in between these activities will piddle and defecate. You will observe that he has to relieve himself after drinking, eating, and sleeping, so take him at these precise times to the area you want him to use for this purpose.

Paper-breaking is easy to accomplish, particularly if the pup was raised in a nest of paper. Habit will urge him to go on the same surface he was accustomed to using before you brought him home. Put the paper in the bathroom on a tiled, easy-to-clean floor. Watch the puppy constantly and the moment you see him begin to assume the telltale position, scoop him up, take him to the paper and hold him there until he does what he is supposed to do. Then praise him lavishly, making a huge fuss over this sterling accomplishment. If he goes on the rug before you can do anything constructive about it, show him what he has done and tell him "No," and "Shame," in a scolding voice. Then take him to the paper, put him on it, point to it, and tell him kindly that this is "Good."

Now is the time to psych the little rascal out. Take a bit of his stool and put it on the paper in the bathroom and, the next time he indicates that nature is calling, take him to the paper. If he thinks he has used it before, he will use it again. Do not be too quick to remove soiled paper from the bathroom. Leaving some will be a reminder to the little scamp that "This must be the place."

When the time comes that you want to train him to relieve himself outdoors, simply transfer some of the soiled paper from the bathroom to the outside and anchor it with a rock or stone. Take the puppy to it and praise him extravagantly when he uses it. Gradually, over a period of time, reduce the size of the paper until it vanishes completely and your smart puppy is evacuating on old mother earth.

Breaking the puppy to the outdoors immediately is easier if his first early weeks were spent in an outdoor pen. Use the same technique as in paper breaking and rush him outside the moment he shows any sign of wanting to relieve himself. Do not clean up the yard too quickly because the puppy must be taken to an area he has already used if you want him to repeat his performance.

Until the pup is thoroughly housebroken you can save yourself trouble by confining him at night and when you are not at home to a single small room, preferably the bathroom, which is easily cleaned and contains little that can be gnawed and chewed.

Feed your puppy only at regular intervals so you can, to some extent, control the intake and evacuation of food, and, until housebreaking has become an accomplished fact, offer him water only after meals. The use of baby suppositories can also facilitate housebreaking by giving you control over the time the animal will defecate.

The eating of their own feces (coprophagy) by some puppies and occasionally an older dog is a habit that should be changed as quickly as possible for both health and esthetic reasons. The cause is sometimes boredom and the availability of dried feces to play with. Sometimes it signals a lack of some essential in the diet. I have thought that this objectionable habit could be due to a residual archaic memory of a mode of eating practiced by ancient mammals and thought to be lost in the process of evolutionary selection. This procedure, known as *refection,* may have left a vestigial instinct that has echoed faintly down through the ages. Refection was reported to be practiced by rabbits and hares in 1882, but the research was overlooked, then rediscovered in 1939. To give you briefly the gist of that research, it was reported that rabbits graze and the food thus consumed is partially digested and enriched in the process with B-complex vitamins. This incompletely digested substance is subsequently forced out of the body as soft stools and then reingested by the animal. During its return passage through the digestive system the valuable B vitamins are absorbed, the digestive pattern becomes complete, and waste matter is voided.

To cure coprophagy absolute and immediate cleanliness is necessary. Clean up as soon as the animal voids, leaving nothing to attract his attention. Break the conditioned chain in this manner and you shatter the habit the dog has formed. Applying a highly objectionable substance such as hot red pepper to stools left in the yard can also aid in effecting a cure. When necessary, I use the initial suggestion, for I have found that seasoning stools is definitely not my thing.

COLLAR AND LEASH TRAINING

Put a narrow, soft collar on your pup and have him wear it constantly. Purchase one that is inexpensive, for he will soon outgrow it. After a day and night of just wearing the collar, tie a long piece of heavy cord to the collar. When he has dragged and stumbled over the cord for a few days, he will be partially leash trained without any effort on your part. Now remove the cord, snap a leash to his collar, and take him for a walk. Be gentle and do not drag him by the leash to make him follow you. Allow him to move wherever he wishes and *you* follow *him.*

The next step is to urge him to go your way with short jerks on the leash and cheerful calling. Once he becomes used to this and moves with you, wait until he sits, then step away from him, face him with the leash at arm's length and through short jerks on it urge him toward you. The command is "Booboo, come!" issued in a lilting, cheerful voice. Praise Booboo extravagantly when he responds. Next use a rope or leash three times the length of the first leash so that you are farther away from your pupil and train him to come to you in the same manner.

If the pup is running loose and he ignores your call to "Come," don't chase him or you will destroy all the success you may previously have had in making him come when called. Squat down, extend your hand toward him, and give him the command quietly. If he still will not obey and moves farther away, then turn from him and run in the *opposite direction,* calling to him by name to "come" as you do. Chances are he will immediately rush after you to join in the fun. *Praise him* for coming. Do *not* chastise him for not having come before. If you do, he will think that you are scolding him for *coming* to you. This may sound rather confusing to you, but take my word for it, it makes sense to the puppy.

To train your dog to "Sit" (on your left side remember), when he is standing next to you in the "Heel" position, press your left hand down on his croup, forcing his hindquarters down as, with your right hand, you lift up on the leash, holding it directly over the animal's head. After he has learned to sit without pressure on his croup, correct the position if necessary so that he sits squarely. Repeat until he is prompt and perfect in this exercise. This is a very important lesson as it is the basic position from which many future command movements begin.

"Heel" is also a basic command. With your dog at your side in the sit position, step out and away from him with your *left* foot first. Jerk on the leash and command "Adolph, heel" (assuming his name is Adolph, a name which in humans we associate with a heel). By stepping away from the pupil with your left leg you withdraw a measure of the intimate support that was his while in the sit position at your side. Step out briskly and keep him moving close to your side through sharp, directive jerks on the leash. Your left hand can be used to pat your side encouragingly. Repeat the command "Heel" as many times as necessary to hold his attention. Each time you come to a very decisive stop command him to "Sit," prefacing the word with his name, until he automatically sits the moment you come to a halt. Soon the "sit" command will no longer be necessary when moving at heel.

Once the pupil has learned to heel well, vary your pace while working him and make right and left turns without allowing him to lag behind or surge in front of you. Walk your pet in the heel position on the street and in crowds until he has been conditioned to heel perfectly under any conditions.

To teach your dog to "stay" you give the command while the pupil is at "Sit." Command "Sit-stay" and bring your left hand down with the palm close to the dog's nose. Keep your hand in this position as you step away from your pet on your *right* foot. Then move slowly in front until you face him. Return to him and repeat the lesson. When he performs well, don't forget to give him the praise he expects.

The command "Down" is also executed by the dog from the "Sit" position. If the animal is small, push down on his shoulders until he is in the down position, then praise him. If he is too large to push down in this manner without a struggle, give him the command, "Sit-stay" and move away on your right foot to face him. Grasp his front legs at the pasterns and pull them toward you, out from under him, making him fall into the "Down" position. Another way to accomplish the same result when you are facing him and he is in the "Sit-stay" position, is to step on the leash with your left foot close to his collar while holding the leash rigid with your right hand, thus forcing his forequarters down to the ground into the required position.

"Down-stay" is simply a combination of the "Down" and "Stay" commands. When you return to your pupil in the "Down-stay," circle around him to the correct side (left) and with a slight jerk upward on the leash command him to "Sit." Thus you combine a series of commands that are easily executed by your dog.

"Come" can be executed from the "Sit-stay" and "Down-stay" exercises. From your position in front of the animal give the "Come" command (always remembering to preface a command with your dog's name) and with a few smart jerks of the leash urge him to you. When he has obeyed the command and is directly in front of you, tell him to "Sit." Then, moving him through leash manipulation and a slight shifting of your feet and body, bring him to "Heel" in the proper position on your left side and then "Sit."

Combine all these newly learned lessons every time you work your dog and always end each session with the exercise that he does best. Don't forget to praise him at the finish of each exercise, for this is his reward for doing them well. If he can accomplish the above exercises within a reasonable period of time (which varies with each breed) and do them well and gaily, he has the makings of a well-trained dog.

With the knowledge you have gained here of the basic principles of training there is no reason why you and your pet cannot go on to more advanced training and finally, if you so desire, into obedience competition. The American Kennel Club publishes a pamphlet with all the rules and regulations of obedience competition and the rewards you can reap from such an endeavor are more than worthwhile.

Through your local kennel club you can find very inexpensive obedience classes close to home that you can attend with your dog. You will be in the company of other novice dogs and handlers with the same goals as yours.

One more thing: you *can* teach an old dog new tricks. Any dog of any age can be trained to be a good citizen. Training removes many of the barriers that exist in the human-animal relationship, so treat yourself to the wonderful communication that is shaped between a dog and its master-trainer through the medium of obedience training.

SHOWING DOGS

If you are fortunate enough to own a dog of the necessary nobility, gait, and verve, one that is so close to his breed standard of perfection that he can compete successfully in dog shows, you will enter a whole new exciting world. Here your pet will meet with the elite of dogdom and compete with dogs of known excellence and breed lines that boast the names of great champions and producers of an earlier day.

To compete in such exalted company you must bring your dog to perfect condition (show bloom). It must be properly clipped, stripped, or barbered if it is necessary for his breed to be so finished for competitive exhibition; he must be trained to move and stack (stand) correctly in the ring for examination by the presiding dignitary, the dog-show judge, a personage all-seeing and all-knowing, whose decisions in the ring are completely and unalterably final.

As a novice you may wish to have the pleasure of handling your dog in the show ring yourself. This you can do in match shows and reap enjoyment and exercise from the experience. But, sad to say, the truth is that today very few dogs—even top animals superbly ready for competition—ever win consistently and almost never attain champion distinction when owner-handled. To reach the status of a champion and be consistently Best of Breed or Variety and so be eligible to compete in the groups, an animal should be shown by a professional handler who, of course, charges a rather stiff fee for his services.

A dog wins points toward its championship when, after winning in its class, it defeats all other class winners in its sex and goes Winners Dog or Winners Bitch. The number of points it wins depends upon the number of animals entered in its sex on the given day. If your dog defeats the winner in the opposite sex, it becomes Best of Winners and is entitled to the number of points toward its championship acquired by the defeated dog of the other sex if that number is greater than your dog has won in its own sex. No points are given for Best of Breed. But should it attain this honor, go into the group and win the group, it will be awarded the greatest number of points won by any other breed representative it defeats in the group. (Five points is the limit given for any show win.)

Of course your Cinderella dog could go on to Best in Show . . . but not very likely. It is your privilege to dream a bit and bravely demand "Where is it written that my dog *can't* go Best in Show?" My answer must truthfully be, "In the book of odds, Baby."

Should your dog become a Champion, if a male he could be well patronized as a stud, a happy event that will bring in a nice revenue in stud fees. A bitch honored with the Champion prefix will be considered a valuable brood animal and her whelps should command a good price. There is also, of course, the prestige that accrues to the title and that can be invaluable to a kennel or breeder.

This then is the show ring, where you will enter into an alien and exclusive society, flaunting its own language of shows and judging, points, winnings, circuits, breeding, genetics, handlers, trophies and imports. Be warned though: once you have been bitten by the show-ring bug you will never recover and might even infect your entire family with the same disease, because competition—for old, middle-aged, or young—lends spice to life and the thrill of winning cannot be surpassed. It was once said by a particularly stupid detective (not Charlie Chan) that, "No one commits suicide who has a future champion puppy in his kennels. This is moider." I think the last three words referred to the decision of a popular dog-show judge.

Training and Showing Your Cat

When training your kitten, be gentle but firm, always utilizing the same commands in the same tone of voice. Remember that cats are exceedingly independent creatures and cannot be roughly pushed into obeying. If you are reasonably certain that your kitten understands a command and can accomplish the act you request, make sure—through patience, firmness, and (if necessary) a bit of coercion—that he performs it.

The first word your kitten will learn is its name, when you call it to be fed. Add the word "Come" to the name and, since eating is a pleasurable experience, he will soon learn to "come" when called.

The second word he should learn is "No." A loud hand-clap and a vehement, "No" denotes your displeasure should he do something of which you disapprove. Some experienced cat breeders combine a squirt from a water pistol with the angry, "No," to accent their displeasure.

"Good boy" (or "girl" as the case may be) is next on the list. With these very few words you can control a host of your cat's actions. You can call him to you, keep him from running out the door, show your displeasure when he does something wrong and your profound appreciation when he obeys a command or does something right. You can—in short—

relate them to many other dos and don'ts he must learn if he is to become a good citizen and a delightful pet.

HOUSEBREAKING

Cats are naturally meticulously clean creatures and are, therefore, easy to housebreak. Take your kitten to the sanitary litter pan after eating, after he awakens from a nap, after playtime, the first thing in the morning and the last thing at night. In the beginning do not be too quick to clean the sanitary facility, for he must be able to identify its use by scent. Use the words "No," and "Good boy" to indicate your feelings in reference to the way he performs in this area and he will soon be using the tray regularly.

A cat that is allowed to go outdoors should still be litter trained in case he is kept indoors during inclement weather or when you are away from home. Incidentally, it is my opinion that a cat can lead a perfectly happy contented life when confined to the house and not permitted to run free. He is much safer when not exposed to the myriad hazards of the great outdoors.

TRAINING TO LEASH

First allow the cat to become accustomed to the collar or harness he will use. Do not use a harness if the animal is a show specimen as it tends to cause irritation, pushes the elbows out, and gives the owner less control over his charge. When the cat has become used to the collar, clip the leash on and take him out for the first time at night. Cats are much more at ease in darkness than in light. After a few nights, begin to take tabby out in daylight. Correct his mode of locomotion when on lead by short jerks on the leash, not by pulling or dragging him. He will soon learn to walk calmly and sedately at your side and to enjoy his outings.

ADDITIONAL TRAINING

You can make your cat "sit" upon command simply by repeating the word over and over as you press downward on his croup, forcing him to the sit position. Once he sits letter perfect to your command, keep him in this position and hold a bit of food or his favorite toy above his head until he sits up reaching for it with both front paws. As he does this tell him to "Sit up!" So a new trick is soon learned by conditioning your pet's response to your command.

A cat can be taught to retrieve by playing with him and his favorite toy, throwing it a short distance until he fetches it and brings it to you. Toys are essential to a kitten's enjoyment of home life. They help to give him exercise and intrigue and occupy his time for hour after hour.

EXHIBITING CATS

If you like cats and competition here is an area of the cat fancy that you should explore. There are, as in all competitions, some disappointments, but there can also be great satisfaction and rewards in the quest for ribbons and awards at a show. To breed or own a finer specimen of your chosen breed than anyone else has yet been able to produce or own is an accomplishment in which you can take pride.

Cat shows are held throughout the country under the patronage of local cat societies or one of the larger registration organizations. They are held in public halls and armories and are one- or two-day affairs—generally two. At these exhibitions you will see the cream of catdom, beautiful felines that are the result of sincere efforts by knowledgeable breeders to produce superior specimens in the various breed categories and so improve the line, bringing glory to their catteries.

Entries in these shows generally close about a month before opening date. If you have previously been an exhibitor, you will probably receive an entry blank in the mail. If not, and you wish to show your pride and joy, contact the show secretary for an entry form. Shows are listed in the major cat magazines and include the show secretary's name and address. Each show consists of an All Breed Show (the various breeds judged separately), as well as Short-Haired and Long-Haired Specialties.

When traveling to the show with your cat, carry him in a cat carrier made specifically for this purpose. Line the carrier's floor with disposable diapers for sanitary reasons and supply the cat with water during the trip. Take him to the show well groomed, and in good coat and correct weight. Clip his nails before you start off. It will be appreciated by the judge. Do not use oils on his coat; some cats are highly allergic to oil.

Cover the front of his cage with clear plastic to protect your pet from handling by strangers. Tom cats will often bite probing fingers at a show. Decorations for your cat's cage at the show should be adjustable and made of washable material. And don't forget to take along food for your pet and receptacles for food and water. Listen for the announcement of the beginning of your breed judging and for your cat's number to be called. The shows have stewards who will take your cat to the judging cages.

Kitten classes are judged first at the show, followed by novice classes, open classes, champion and grand champion classes, then neuters. The number of entrants dictates the number of champion points a cat can garner at any given show. Classes are divided by sex and color and the winners' points and ribbons go to the cats that have achieved class wins (competing against each other) and then have defeated their competition in the winners' classes. To achieve the title of champion, a cat must win its points under three different judges in all-breed competition, and must have won at least one specialty show. Grand championships are awarded to cats that have won best champion under three different judges. One point is awarded for each three champions competing.

A veterinarian examines all cats before they enter the show room and no entry may be benched until he issues a card signifying that the cat is in good health and therefore cannot endanger the health of the other entries.

All competing cats are taken, as their class is called, to large wire cages in the area where the judge presides. The judge takes each cat out of its cage, examines it on a central table, compares it with others in its class, and then awards the ribbons. Spray cleaning of the table and the judge's hands takes place after each cat is handled and the cages are cleaned before the next class is placed in them. Go to the next show advertised in your neighborhood. I am sure you will be intrigued and interested in the cat-show mystique.

Training Birds

The training of birds is also a complicated, many-faceted affair because of the diverse areas into which it leads us—from teaching one species to talk to training another to fly in a certain fashion or for a distinctive purpose. As with canines, the particulars are too varied and too closely correlated to the breeds of birds to be less than completely individualistic. Therefore specific bird training must be presented in the chapter that embraces the multitude of feathered creatures.

Training Rodents

If you attempt to train your rodent, it will not require a great deal of time or concentration, since the learning ability of your pet is limited. One cannot teach a mouse to attack upon command, a rabbit to talk, or a cavy to walk at heel. A few small feats may be achieved by watching your pet and, through rewards of food, trying to have it indulge on signal in some specific maneuver that it does by itself, such as sitting up to receive a bit of food.

Training Fish and Reptiles

Training fish and reptiles is a lost cause. Any attempt to teach these creatures to react to training can only be the overture to colossal frustration.

Training the Primates

Primates should be trained in much the same manner in which you would train children. Remember that you must teach your primate to acquire correct habits, and habits are formed through repetitive actions triggered by conditioned responses. Once a habit is formed, it becomes part of the life-style of the creature and can be broken only by eliminating the chain or pattern of events that caused the formation of the habit.

Be firm when necessary and, through moderate strictness, without harshness or overbearing severity, and by virtue of temperate permissiveness without weakness, you will be able to shape the deportment of your pet. End each training period with an act that your pet has learned well and enjoys doing so that the session ends on a note of fun, friendliness, and triumph. The use of small tidbits of food as a reward for good behavior can be indulged in and often works well.

If your primate pet seems to have difficulty learning, do not immediately accuse the little beastie of being stupid. Actually primates are exceedingly intelligent and any seeming lack of intelligence is probably your fault. Assess yourself. Check all the basic principles of training enumerated in the generalized section at the beginning of this chapter and evaluate your ability in the use of these tenets. Never attempt training too soon after you have acquired your primate. At the beginning of your association simply feed your pet well, give him a great deal of affection and understanding and, when you reach a plateau of rapport (and you will be aware of it when it happens), gently begin to mold his habit patterns to your own design.

Primates, like many children, sometimes attempt to bite when frustrated or angry. A professional trainer of primates and several scientists who constantly handle monkeys in their work have informed us that the best cure for this behavior is to bite the monkey back immediately. This seems to be an eminently wise and satisfactory way to terminate such monkey business. (I have also been told that this method works with dogs that bite.)

Training a Raccoon-Family Pet

A baby raccoon-family pet is easily trained. Put a soft collar on him and use treat foods as a reward for good behavior. Young, but not infant, animals are a bit more difficult to get started. Offer the treat with your fingers as a preliminary to stroking and scratching the youngster's head. All your movements must be slow and gentle and you should speak quietly during the whole process. Your voice, your hands, your whole being, and the love you project are vehicles you must use correctly to gain the little creature's confidence. Above all try never to frighten him inadvertently through a quick movement, gesture, or loud vocal sound.

Never allow the youngster to bite, even gently and in play. It can bite its toys in play but never your fingers. Generally speaking you can use the same training methods on your raccoon-family pet as you do on your dog or cat but with greater caution and calmness. These creatures are intelligent and highly sensitive to word sounds and what they convey, so if you wish to discipline your pet, scold him and return him to his cage or place of confinement to indicate your displeasure with his deportment; *never* strike him with your hand. These are all gregarious creatures who enjoy companionship. When divorced from their own kind, they will seek the comfort and companionship offered by their human friend. In so doing they make themselves available to training by that friend.

Hoofed-Mammal Training

The various hoofed animals differ greatly in their ability to absorb training. Those that have been domesticated by man over the centuries are most easily trained because selection has been made for animals that will accept training and profit from it.

To respond to hand, voice, rein, and foot signals, or to come when called, are the basic facets of hoofed-animal training. The most exasperating exercise I can think of is chasing an animal who does not come when called and does not wish to be caught. For the sake of the owner's blood pressure the hoofed pet must be taught to come when called. The easiest way to accomplish this is through the use of a primary animal need—food. Call your pet by name every time you bring its food and it will soon associate food with the sound of your voice and its name and come to you. If it seems a bit reluctant at first, withhold its food for a day and it will soon respond to your call with alacrity. Carry a tidbit of some food that it particularly relishes, such as sugar cubes, a bit of carrot or apple, and it will not be long before your pet comes galloping to you the moment you appear.

The training of hoofed beasties for shows or fairs necessarily varies with the species. The most complicated training exercises are confined to the equines and the areas of training differ widely. Some horses and ponies are shown in halter classes; some on the flat in Eastern or Western classes; others are trained as hunters or jumpers and some, such as Quarter Horses, in cattle-working classes. There are three- and five-gaited and walking-horse classes; barrel-racing, hackney, and roadster classes; haute école and many other specialized activities that equines can be trained to perform. Training in any of these areas takes time, patience, and the advice and aid of someone experienced in a particular type of schooling. The various methods, approaches, equipment, and authoritative knowledge in the specialized fields would fill a book as large or perhaps larger than this one.

Training Mustelines and Viverrines

Handle your pet musteline or viverrine daily if you want it to remain tame and amiable. Stroke it, feed it tidbits from your fingers and, through the medium of food, teach it to come when called.

Perhaps the most easily trained of the animals in these two categories is the skunk. The training advocated for this musteline of doubtful renown can with some variation be utilized for all the creatures of the families *Mustilidae* and *Viverridae*.

To train your pet skunk to collar and leash, purchase a soft collar and allow the youngster to wear it constantly. In a few days attach a leash to the collar and take him out into the back yard. Do not pull on the leash to guide him as you would a dog. Instead carry him outside, put him down close to your feet and shuffle them to get his attention; then slowly, with short steps, move away from him. He should follow.

During training you must remember that skunks are very nearsighted and, if you get more than a few feet away, they will not be able to see you clearly. Also remember that the skunk is not a domesticated species and can be easily frightened, so never punish the kit. Carry with you a piece of food, some tidbit that the kit especially favors. Reward him with it and caress and praise him when he performs well. Don't forget . . . no punishment, only reward!

Housebreaking your pet skunk will not be very difficult. Use a pad of newspapers and take the kit to it to evacuate immediately after eating, drinking a lot of liquid, and after waking from a nap or his night's sleep. If you keep your pet in an outside (or inside) enclosure, put the papers in one corner of it. A skunk in an enclosure will always use a corner of its abode as a latrine. See the section on housebreaking a cat (p. 139) and follow the same pattern. Once a skunk is completely housebroken, you may be able to teach it to use a cat litter box, though usually a skunk will dig in it and scatter the litter about.

One plus to be added to the skunk's score as a pet is the fact that he adapts readily to a small apartment. Normally nocturnal, this basic behavior pattern can be changed if you make it a habit to play with your pet during the daylight hours. It might be wise, though, to buy an easily cleanable cage in which to confine your pet skunk at night, just in case instinct urges him to roam in the wee hours.

Insects and Miscellaneous Pets

In the area of training insects I must leave the particulars to your fecund imagination. But just a word of caution: never chastise a recalcitrant insect by slapping it with your hand.

To train those creatures in the miscellaneous-pet category that are capable of reacting to training, I suggest that you follow the generalized training advice imparted in the section of specialized training for cats and raccoon-family mammals (pp. 138 and 142).

All animals are learning machines to a greater or lesser degree, and so are fairly good training material. But those we term the lower animals have limits to the amount they can learn. That is where man, the highest animal, differs from all the others, for he keeps on learning long past the stage at which other animals quit. I grant you, however, that some of the knowledge he absorbs is dangerous to himself and other creatures and would be better left unlearned.

8

The Art of Breeding Animals

Breeding animals must not be merely the multiplication of a species. It must have as its goal the betterment of a breed toward a higher plateau of excellence (in terms of adaptation to its environment) through the utilization of knowledge of the genetic material with which you will work. That is where the fascination of breeding animals lies—in the manipulation of the microscopic elements of life itself—the genes. For with some knowledge of their behavior and how they can be molded to change in pattern and aggregate results, you, the breeder, can become a sculptor in living material. Sounds dramatic, doesn't it? Well it is!

Effecting changes or rearrangements in the germ plasm of a living creature is of paramount importance in the breeding of better food animals and valuable exhibition and sporting stock. But even in the breeding of creatures that have not reached these high estates, it is thrilling to breed for wanted virtues or work with new mutations for specific features.

Something about Genetics

To be a successful breeder you must have at least a rudimentary grasp of the elements of genetics. Space limits all but a brief discussion here, but hopefully there is enough to lead you in the right direction and throw some light on an area of knowledge that is a necessary tool to success.

Every living cell in your pet's body contains a package of chromosomes, within which nestle the genes, the units of heredity that Gregor Johann Mendel, the father of genetics, brilliantly (and correctly) theorized shaped the essence of all living things. Chromosomes are paired and each living creature receives one set (50 percent of its chromatic design) from the male and the other 50 percent from the female. The genes within the chromosomes are also paired and in combination these microscopic bits of chemical material completely control the physical and psychological development of the creature in which they reside, and dictate the inheritable material it will pass on to the next generation within the limits of random selection during the process of fertilization.

The genes are inviolate and can be affected only by some cosmic rays, mutation, and a hostile chemical environment. Sex-linked characteristics are carried by the sex cells* so certain recessive factors, mostly benign and relating to color and some other characteristics, or occasionally congenital afflictions (in humans hemophilia and a type of color-blindness, et cetera), can be hosted by the dam but affect only her male offspring.

The genes are the abject servants of a nucleic-acid spiral molecule called DNA (deoxyribonucleic acid), which, through its code-like arrangement of chemical subunits, dictates the hereditary pattern of all life forms. This "code" is passed on by DNA to a similar molecule, RNA (ribonucleic acid), which carries out the dictates of DNA and directs the body chemistry, growth, and specialization of each cell.

The genes, guided by their nucleic-acid dictators, create dominant and/or recessive formats that actually mold the creature they affect and give it individual status. Penetration of the gene effect can vary, resulting in modified intensity; and a pairing of similar recessive genes for any one trait can give the recessive genes the same visibility that dominant gene factors enjoy (dominant traits are always visible, never hidden as are recessive traits).

A few traits are determined by simple Mendelian dominant and recessive alleles, but generally the factors that govern any section, small or large, of the living creature are a complex of interlocking genetic agents. Even when recessive genes pair and become visible, they do not become dominant but remain recessive, subject to the rules that apply to recessive factors, just as dominants work according to the rules that govern their effects on living tissue.

The pet breeder must think of his animals not in terms of lovable individuals but as the living custodians of specific inheritable material. He must understand that every breeding animal is in effect two animals, the visible one that he sees and can easily assess in terms of faults and virtues (the phenotype), and the invisible pet that is the product of the total gene complex (the genotype) that can come into focus only through objective study of the animal's genetic background in relation to its known ancestry, and the results it produces when bred.

When breeding animals, the pet breeder must divorce himself from all

---

* The sex cells are not chromatically paired as are other cells. In mammals the male sex chromosomes are designated as XY, the female XX, but in fish, birds, and insects the male chromosomes are XX and the female XY.

human reference and concentrate on improvement of the species, a far more intelligent approach to race continuity than is favored by man with his hit-and-miss gamble (or gambol) called marriage. Don't misunderstand me. I am not knocking marriage and would not personally have it any other way. I simply wish to point out that chance mating is not the way to improve the animals over which we have some genetic control. If we are going to attempt to play God, we should do it correctly.

Breeding Techniques

The various techniques available to breeders follow tested patterns. Any of these practices, followed intelligently, can result in breed betterment. Generally the canny breeder finds that he can use his knowledge of all or any of these techniques at various times, or balance one against another for the best results.

Inbreeding is utilized when complete stability of the inheritable genetic material is desired. It is achieved through the breeding of brother to sister (the closest inbreeding), father to daughter, mother to son, and half brother to half sister. This practice gives the breeder the closest possible control over the progeny. It does not produce faults or degeneration, it merely accentuates to the greatest degree the faults and virtues inherent in the stock used. To the breeder, the strongly inbred animal represents a very simplified breeding formula. Selection is very important, for only animals with the least number of known faults should be selected for inbreeding. This method is at the root of all known breeds, for it is the quickest way to establish wanted types, but it is capricious and, since it can reproduce both the best and the worst in your stock in the same offspring, it should be indulged in only by a master breeder.

Backcrossing is another kind of inbreeding, in which the breeder crosses back constantly to one very fine male specimen to intensify the type. Generally the best daughters of a stud are backcrossed to him, then the best daughter from that breeding, and the best daughter from all subsequent breedings. All male geneological lines will be stopped by the name of this exceptional stud.

Linebreeding is distant inbreeding that gives the breeder some control over type, but not the intense control reaped from the close inbreeding described above. Linebreeding consists of concentrating on families or strains to create a similarity in type through the selection of breeding partners that have one or more common ancestors in their genetic background. The breeder must select partners carefully, for they should be prototypes of the animals upon which he is linebreeding or the reason for the exercise is lost. Intense linebreeding can result in strong prepotency (the ability to pass on similar characteristics) and almost as much control over type as inbreeding. Through linebreeding a breeder can form a "strain" of animals that all have some features in common, providing personalized recognition.

Outcross breeding is the mating together of two animals that have no common ancestry (heterozygosity). Usually this type of breeding is indulged in to bring into a line wanted characteristics that are necessary to correct faults in the line. The breeder has no control over the results of such outcross breeding. He can only hope that the needed virtues appear in some of the offspring so he can then cross the new progeny back into the line to hold these corrections through linebreeding. Some fine individuals are produced through outcross breeding, but they are seldom good breeding animals since favorable genetic combinations have been dispersed and uniformity is gone.

Outcross breeding promotes individual merit, concentrates recessives, promotes greater health, strength, and vigor, but the individual lacks in breeding worth, while bringing new, needed genetic qualities to the line. If one of the pair of animals utilized in this type of breeding is line- or inbred, the breeder can have much more control over the progeny.

Heterosis has been used with much success in commercial fields (agriculture and the breeding of meat animals). Close relatives, usually brother and sister, are mated and this inbreeding is continued over several generations. Then two of the inbred lines are crossed and the result is complete heterozygosity or completely unmatched gene pairs. The heterozygous progeny are generally larger, more robust, better breeders and producers than the original pair. In short, they exhibit all the virtues of hybrid vigor. I indulged in experimental heterosis with some of my budgerigars and the birds produced were beyond my original expectations and won many trophies for me.

Canine Breeding

With the foregoing generalized breeding knowledge completely absorbed (I hope), we can delve immediately into the more pertinent mechanics of dog breeding for the neophyte.

The brood bitch that is a top producer of good and typical stock is a jewel of great worth to the earnest breeder. She is the hope for the future of the line and she must be the best that you can possibly find. The bitch will come in season twice a year and should not be initially bred before her second or third season. To keep her vigorous and healthy it is best to skip every other heat period and not allow her to nurse more than six or seven puppies per litter. Before she comes in heat have her checked for internal parasites and wormed if there are any present. Worm larvae in the bloodstream can cross the placenta of the pregnant bitch and affect the unborn pups. Feed the bitch a well-rounded diet, increasing her intake as the whelps within her grow, but do not feed so much that she becomes obese.

Counting from the day of the first red vulva discharge, the bitch will accept the stud dog from the eleventh to the eighteenth day (this can vary somewhat). Ovulation occurs during the sixteenth to the eighteenth days. The bitch should be bred, therefore, between the fourteenth and eighteenth days, every other day by the stud if possible, until she refuses to accept him. A sure sign that she is ready and will accept the stud is indicated by the vulva which becomes swollen and flaccid. The bitch also becomes flirty, lifts and holds her tail to the side, and swings her hind end toward the stud. From a vaginal smear your veterinarian will be able to tell you when ovulation will occur and thus eliminate some of the imponderables from the mating game.

If your bitch is a maiden, she should first be bred to an experienced stud dog. It is amazing how inept many highly bred dogs can be at so basic an act as breeding. Often the animals must be assisted by their owners in consummating the breeding. Once a tie has been made, hold the bitch and quietly soothe her and, with your hand or leg under her, keep her from sitting down until the tie has been broken.

Keep your bitch under close surveillance after she has been bred to the desired stud, for, if she is not completely over her acceptance period, another dog can breed to her and she will have a mixed litter. Before you can finish uttering a curse she can be bred by some stray mutt and blissfully tied for an hour while you stamp around on the ragged edge of apoplexy. It is just such charming little episodes that lead earnest breeders to ulcers and the brink of insanity.

The stud dog needs no special care other than a nutritional diet and exercise to keep him in excellent physical condition. Though the brood bitch is important to the individual breeder, the stud dog is of vast importance to the breed as a whole. If we assume the average litter consists of five whelps then, if a brood bitch is bred every season (which is much too often), she will produce ten puppies a *year*. A popular stud dog can be used three times a week without strain, and sometimes even more. Using the same figure as we have with the bitch, we see that the stud can sire fifteen puppies in a *week*. The influence of a fine stud dog therefore is numerically tremendously greater than that of a brood bitch.

The first time you breed your young male make certain it is to an older bitch who has been bred several times before and is an easy and complacent breeder. This first breeding can shape his destiny as a stud, so it must be a pleasurable experience. Use him first, if you wish, when he is about fourteen months old, but very sparingly until he reaches the age of two. After that he can be bred often, so long as his vigor and health is not compromised.

THE PUPPIES

The whelps (puppies) develop in the horns of the uterus, not the fallopian tubes. They will be born approximately fifty-nine to sixty-three days after the breeding. The bitch's whelping box should be ready and she should be introduced to it and allowed to sleep in it several days before she is due to whelp. A railing around the inside of the box, high enough for a young puppy to slide under will help to keep the bitch from crushing a youngster against the sides of the box. Bedding in the whelping box can be shredded paper, oat or rye straw, et cetera.

As whelping time approaches, the bitch will become restless and will refuse food. She will whelp each puppy individually in the membranous fetal envelope or caul. The umbilical cord will be attached to the placenta. If the fetal caul is not ripped open by the bitch (or ruptured as the pup is being born) and the umbilical cord is not chewed off by the dam to one to one half inches from the pup's belly, then it will be the breeder's job to do. He must also dry each pup, force its mouth open, put it on a teat, and see that it begins sucking shortly after it's born.

If the bitch takes more than two hours between pups call your veterinarian. He will give her an injection after she has finished whelping to make her expel any last pup that may be hiding far up in the uterine horn, or a bit of placenta that has been retained. Dewclaws can be snipped off on the second day after birth with a small manicuring scissors. Healthy pups are generally quiet, suckle frequently, and have shiny coats. Pups that are not well or are not getting enough milk from the bitch are restless and cry a lot.

When the pups are about three weeks old, begin weaning them by feeding them warm milk with melted butter the first day. Add a good grain puppy food the second day to form a creamlike consistency. After a week on this diet add some raw meat, calcium, vitamin powder, and a good grade of cod liver oil to the diet. If the bitch regurgitates food, do not be alarmed. It is an atavistic impulse, the way in which wild canines begin the process of weaning puppies away from their own body milk.

You should have the whelps completely weaned by the time they reach five weeks of age. At this time feed them all they will eat four to five times a day. You will find that most of the day is filled with mixing food, feeding, and cleaning the area in which the puppies live, and you will wonder "Has it all been worth the effort?" To answer your own question, compare the best male puppy in the litter with his sire and the top bitch puppy with her dam. If each is better than, or equal to its parent, then yes, it has been all worthwhile.

Incidentally, I have found that neophyte breeders indicate shyness during the process of breeding their bitch to a selected stud. Remember, please, that by breeding you are attempting to refine your breed. So look upon the animals merely as receptacles of certain worthy genetic factors you wish to perpetuate and the act of copulation simply as a mechanical necessity to reach your goal.

The breeding of fine dogs is a worthwhile hobby and is truly an enriching part of the whole dog-world concept. You are not truly a dog afficionado unless you have experienced the excitement, drama, exhilaration and sometimes tragedy of whelping a litter of puppies.

I must mention here a new and valuable drug, Ovaban, the Pill with which you can control estrus in your female dog. This means you can control her heat and keep her from attracting males and becoming pregnant.

The Breeding of Felines

The earnest cat breeder, to achieve his goal, must first absorb all that he can about the breed he has selected and must, during this process of study, adopt and foster within himself a completely objective approach to every aspect of the hobby. The purpose of this approach is to keep the breeder from forming erroneous opinions that are based on hearsay and superstition and not on fact and objectivity. By being objective the breeder will be better able to assess the faults and virtues of his stock and so know how to breed for continual improvement of the line.

The second step in the breeding of fine felines is to learn enough about genetics, as it applies specifically to cats, to be able to use the rules of this science intelligently in eliminating faults and increasing virtues in your stock. Basically you will attempt to breed your queen to a stud that can help correct the faults she exhibits and which you know are in her breeding line.

To start a cattery you should purchase the best stock you can find no matter how high the price may be. With top stock, a working knowledge of genetics and breeding principles, and the correct environment (plus a little luck of course), you should prosper as a breeder.

Physically your cattery should be a room that has access to a screened porch, or a building that is insulated against extremes of heat and cold.

The floors and walls should be composed of materials that can be easily washed and sanitized. A colony breeding arrangement works very well: five to six queens can be maintained by one male, or twelve to fifteen females with two or three studs. Do not overcrowd the quarters. You will need hot and cold running water, a tub or other bathing facility, and a drying cage. If at all possible, and you have sufficient room, segregate one section of the cattery solely for the act of breeding.

Several females can be kept together in a large cage and separated and put into smaller whelping cages when they are individually about to become mothers. The room and all the accommodations must be kept scrupulously clean. Proper ventilation must be considered and there should be shelves supplied at different levels for the cats to jump up to in order to nap. Cages should be built so they are easy to clean and there should be space for necessary storage. Have within arm's length a first-aid kit containing every kind of medication and equipment for emergencies. Kittens should be kept caged until they are ten to twelve weeks of age.

Instead of using towels or shredded paper in the nursery pens where your queens have their kittens, use the largest-size disposable diapers. They are very absorbent, easy to dispose of, and also insure greater cleanliness in the kitten cages.

Breeding Birds

This subject could be fashioned into a huge tome by itself. I include it here because many people who buy a pet bird become so involved with it that they eventually turn to breeding birds as a hobby—and no one could possibly find a more absorbing, fascinating, and satisfying pursuit.

To breed birds of any kind the pairs must be in top condition, feathers full and gleaming, eyes bright, the cocks strutting and displaying, and the hens interested in the mating performance of the opposite sex. They should be fed supplements that will enable them to produce and adequately feed strong and healthy chicks.

The various species of birds exhibit different indications of their sex which you must learn to recognize. A rule-of-thumb analysis would be that cock birds are generally more vividly colored than hens, are usually larger, have bigger heads, and are given to strutting. Yet none of these secondary sex characteristics hold true for all species of birds, so seek the advice of an experienced aviculturist if the breed of your choice lacks identifying sex definition.

Not all breeds of birds can be bred in captivity. It is wise for the novice to acquire experience working with birds that are easily bred. Your breeding room, breeding cages, nest boxes, and flights must be fashioned for the breeding use of specific species of birds, since every breed needs specialized equipment and environment or they will refuse to cooperate. Every season, it seems, a fancier someplace in the world succeeds in breeding a species that has never before been bred and has been considered not breedable by aviculturists. Triumphs such as this add particular zest to the bird-breeding concept.

I suggest that your initial breeding attempt be made with budgerigars or cockatiels if your interest is in breeding psittacine birds. Canaries, zebra finches, star, shafttails or any other of the easily bred finches should be your subjects if your interest directs you to this type of bird. Discuss your needs and aspirations with other breeders, who will probably be able to direct you to the proper place to purchase all the equipment you will need. Breeders will, perhaps, show you how to build your own cages, flights, and nest boxes. Buy for your breeding stock the best you can afford, for your basic breeding birds will produce stock that, in general, mirrors their own genetic worth.

Once started in the breeding of birds, you will probably seek social intercourse with other breeders through fanciers' clubs, and you will begin to hear words such as "dominant," "recessive," "genetically pure," "bloodlines," "sex-linked," "mutation," and many others. They are all part of a new vocabulary you will learn that is based upon the processes of breeding and the science of genetics. When you have acquired some knowledge of these most interesting subjects, it will bring new scope to your horizons and will make the breeding of your feathered friends so fascinating that it will become less of a hobby and more of a way of life.

In the sections dedicated to the vast variety of bird species you will find more intimate details of the manner in which many of them breed, their gestation periods, the environment necessary for breeding success, the number of eggs and young they produce, their care of the young, and the individual mechanics of reproduction and propagation.

Breeding Rodents

Usually hobbyists begin with one pet and become so charmed by that individual that they soon begin to breed the species, or perhaps some interesting commercial aspects in such breeding capture their interest. Whatever the reason, before launching a breeding program, it is well to know as much as possible about the subject as it applies to the species you intend to breed.

BREEDING RABBITS

When the doe is ready to breed, she begins to rub her head and throat on anything that is handy. When she displays these signs, she should be brought to the buck every twelve hours until a breeding is consummated. Generally mating takes place within a few minutes after the buck and doe are introduced. Do not leave them unattended because they might indulge in battle.

As soon as the mating has taken place, return the doe to her own hutch. Actually the production of egg cells in the doe overlap, so she can be bred at almost any time, provided she is in good condition. The buck, like Dickens' Barkus, always "is willin'." The gestation period is approximately thirty-one days and a well-conditioned doe will kindle (give birth to) from six to ten young.

New Zealand junior does can be bred at five months and junior bucks started when about six months of age. I would not advise allowing a doe to have more than four litters a year. Does will produce for three or four years, occasionally up to six years. After a doe kindles, wait until she leaves the nest; then examine the young and remove any dead or imperfect babies. If the doe becomes nervous, give her food to quiet her down. The babies are born hairless and look like tiny embryos. Their eyes will remain closed until they are approximately ten days old.

Keep the bucks in the coolest portion of the area where your animals are kept. They can become sterile in high temperatures (85 to 95 degrees Fahrenheit).

Sexing rodents is often difficult for novices. If you turn your rabbit on its back, you will be able to determine its sex, for the testes are quite obvious in the buck. They are two swollen bean-shaped objects that form an inverted U meeting at the top. The female has an inverted pear-shaped swollen area.

BREEDING CHINCHILLAS

Chinchillas can be bred when they are nine to eleven months old, and seem to have no specific mating season, though they apparently breed more readily in November, December, and March. Though pair mating is practiced by many breeders, these little beasties are polygamous and harem breeding is indulged in by many of the big farms. In the latter method one happy male may serve from five to ten females. The gestation period is one hundred and eleven days and a female produces about two litters a year. Usually she has two youngsters, but a litter can vary from one to six babies. The female will come into heat about every thirty-five days and will generally breed again within a few hours after having her litter. Chinchillas naturally live on the bleak slopes of the

Andes Mountains in South America and the long gestation period insures the young against being born in an embryonic state. Instead, after a gestation period almost four times that of the rabbit, they are born furred to keep them warm and with eyes open so they can see their surroundings. Within a few hours they are able to scamper around. In the wild a litter consists of five to six young.

BREEDING CAVIES (GUINEA PIGS)

The breeding of cavies is a simple procedure. I would not breed them under six months of age, even though they are capable of breeding before this. Young boars (males) can be kept together until they are mature. Then separate them and never allow them to be together again or they will join in battle. The sows (females) should be put with the male in the breeding pen for about thirty days and removed as soon as they indicate pregnancy. At this time a female should be given a hutch of her own. The period of gestation is about sixty-eight days and the litter will average about three young, though it can be more or less. A healthy, strong sow can produce about five litters a year. The young are born fully coated, with teeth and open eyes and within an hour after birth they are gamboling in the hutch. The young should be weaned when they are about three and a half weeks old and the males and females separated and kept in their own hutches, for they are capable of breeding at a very young age, before they have reached adult strength with its commensurate ability to produce well. To be sure of the difference in sexes turn the cavy over and you will find an obvious round and swollen area where the sexual organs lurk. These are the testes of the male or boar. The sow is flatter in this area.

BREEDING HAMSTERS

Hamsters seem to produce many mutations, which adds to the excitement and interest of breeding these fine little rodents. For this reason pair breeding is more to be desired than colony breeding. With pair breeding you know exactly which is producing what and you can further the production of mutations and control all your matings. Always bring the female to the male for breeding—preferably at night, for the hamster is a nocturnal creature. If they fight when introduced, watch them closely and separate them if the battling becomes too furious. Then try again the next night. If they are amiable toward each other, they can be left alone.

The female comes into heat about every four to six days and stays in for about twelve hours. If the female won't allow a breeding to be consummated, try her again . . . and again . . . and again. Or try other females until one does allow the male to mate with her. Sometimes a virgin female, when put in with an older male, becomes frightened of the "dirty old man" and falls on her back emitting great sobs. Remove her immediately and wait a few days. Then return her to the same male, so that he won't begin to think that he has lost his manly charm or "machismo," and fall into despair.

The actual breeding will last from fifteen to twenty minutes, after which the female should be returned to her own cage. Female hamsters are quite belligerent and stood for women's rights long before their human counterparts took up the cry. Before introducing the female into the male's pen it is a good idea to clean his quarters of all food including his hidden caches. Unless this is done, the female will begin to eat, filling her pouches. After she has eaten her fill, she will want out and will repel all the male's advances.

Colony breeding needs a 3- to 4-foot long breeding pen. Three males are placed in the pen together and after they appear to be at home the females are introduced. After about twelve days the females (assuming they are pregnant) are removed and each placed in her own pen.

BREEDING GERBILS

Gerbils, unlike rats, mice, and most other rodents, are monogamous and mate for life. Do not introduce the unfamiliar pair you want to breed to each other by putting them in the same cage. Put them in adjacent compartments with a wire partition between them, allowing them to become acquainted and their ardor to mount until they seem to have achieved a good relationship. Then put them together. To be sure that you have a true pair and are not putting two males or two females together—which will get you nowhere as a breeder—check for the telltale signs of different sex. The female has a rounder body and the vulva is closer to the anal opening. The male has a much more pointed posterior, the scrotal area is darker, and the scrotal pouch obvious.

The gestation period is approximately twenty-five days and the average number of young in a litter is about five. The young, as are those of the rabbit, are born hairless and blind like tiny embryos. This is also true of the babies of rats and mice, but the young of the gerbil develop more slowly. They reach maturity in about twelve weeks; at the end of twenty days their eyes begin to open. You can leave the male parent in the cage with the female when she has her litter, as both parents will care for the young, teaching them survival tactics as well as how to relax and play. After the youngsters have been weaned and are on regular food they can be taken from the parents (who by that time will probably be starting a new family) and put together in a large community cage. When these youngsters reach the age of three months, they will begin to select mates and pair together. This must be observed carefully for, as mentioned earlier, they mate for life. The pairs, which have grown up together, can be put in their own cages for breeding.

If the dam has a large litter, she will distribute them in different corners of the pen, thus discouraging competition between siblings during the time of nursing. The parents and babies should be left undisturbed until the young have opened their eyes because the dam is usually quite nervous about her babies and does not like interference.

MICE AND VOLES AT BREEDING TIME

Breeding mice for genetic purposes is like shooting fish in a barrel . . . you can't miss. Put your buck (male) mouse in a cage with a doe (female) mouse when they are between two and three months old and let nature take its course. The doe will indicate her pregnancy in the usual way by her swollen stomach. Put her in a cage by herself and give her a private nest box with a variety of nesting material such as frayed rope, bits of wool cloth, and cotton. Do not handle her or her babies when they arrive. See that she is getting a well-rounded diet and extra milk. The gestation period is approximately twenty days.

Of course if you are just breeding for additional pets several pregnant females can be kept in the same cage. Each will have her own litter and all will cooperate in raising the young. The average number of youngsters in a litter is seven and they are born blind, nude, and embryonic-looking. They develop rather quickly, however, and can be weaned when about a month old. Generally breeding mice is no problem. The big question is how to make them quit breeding. A single pair of these tiny rodents can produce about a hundred and twenty-five youngsters each year.

Voles in the wild have many enemies, therefore the death rate of their progeny is quite high. To insure the survival of the species the gestation period of voles is only eighteen days and they have four to five litters a year with three to six young in every litter. Like most rodents the babies are naked and blind. They are weaned at two and a half to three weeks and become sexually mature at the tender age of four to five weeks.

BREEDING RATS

Rats are fantastic breeding animals. If they weren't, they would never have survived over the centuries mankind's continuous attempts to eliminate them. One pair of rats in the wild could possibly produce in three years millions of descendants. The domestic and tamed rat's reproductive ratio can be controlled by the breeder. Thank heavens! The gestation period is about twenty-one days and you need do no more than put a male and female together to be sure of pregnancy. The females have no definite period of heat and can be bred at any time. Female rats do have an estrus cycle of about five days, but it is a continuing occurrence, so if a female is not impregnated during one cycle, she will be during the next one. One male can be used as a stud for up to ten females. As early as ten weeks after their birth young rats are sexually mature and ready to produce their own families. Their most productive time is between the ages of three to ten months. After they reach the age of eighteen months, their reproductive life is over. The pregnant female should be given her own cage in which to have her litter. Wean the babies, starting when they are about two weeks old, by offering them cooked oatmeal soaked in milk. After weaning, at about five weeks, the young should be separately housed according to sex. Sexing is not too difficult as the male rat shows definitely the heavy scrotal sac between the hind legs and the tail.

SQUIRRELS AT BREEDING TIME

Squirrels engage in a strange mating chase before courtship, which begins early in spring, and sometimes even as early as January. Several of the wild rodents chase each other in and out of trees and around the ground, making low coughing-like sounds. Finally they pair off and the actual mating takes place in March or April. The pair busily prepare a nest for the coming family. Once completed, the male evidently considers that he has done all that can be asked of a male squirrel to perpetuate the race and he has no more to do with the family. After a forty-day gestation period, four or five young are born—blind, naked, tiny pulsing bits of flesh. A covering of fine hair grows within ten days and they are nursed for five weeks, after which their mother tells them never to darken the nest again and kicks them out while she prepares alone for her second litter. Not infrequently one can find albino or the black, melanistic specimens in the squirrel nest.

Chipmunks are the best known of the ground squirrels. If you have a chipmunk and contemplate breeding it, you must provide enough depth of earth in the pen to enable a pair to create an underground burrow, for it is there that the male seeks out the female and the breeding is consummated. In the wild the time of breeding is from February to April and the young are born about thirty-one days after the act. There are two to eight babies in a litter and they remain in the nest about a month before venturing forth with their dam. After six weeks these intrepid tykes go off on their own. The female generally has two litters a year.

The largest of all rodents, the capybara, has a single litter a year after a gestation period of from 119 to 126 days and produces from two to eight progeny. Like the cavy (whom it resembles in giant size), the young are born in an advanced stage of development, fully coated, eyes open, and able to gambol shortly after birth. The babies remain in the custody of the dam until the next breeding season.

Breeding Habits of Fresh-Water Tropical Fish

Because they are so varied in their mode of reproducing, each group of tropicals will have to be examined separately. In their natural habitats many species spawn communally, but when placed in the aquarium's limited confinement, the majority will spawn in single pairs. The fertilized eggs of some species hatch within twenty-four hours, but others will take several months. Some fish bear live young while others lay eggs. With such reproductive variation, it becomes necessary to group the varieties in terms of their diverse breeding habits.

THE LIVE-BEARERS

Live-bearers are free breeders with an incubation period dependent upon the temperature of the aquarium. Gravid (pregnant) females deliver young more rapidly in water at 80 degrees Fahrenheit than in that of 65 degrees. Generally males in this category are smaller than the females, are more vividly colored, and flaunt long, decorative fins. They also possess a gonopodium, which is the male fish's sex organ and is a rodlike modification of the anal fin. When the sexes are mixed, live-bearers will breed at quite an early age.

Live-bearers are easy to breed, but they are also avidly cannibalistic and means must be devised to keep the fry (babies) from being devoured by their loving parents and any other concerned relatives who may be present. Floating plants thick with foliage in which the fry can hide is one answer to the problem. Or the gravid female can be placed in a small separate tank previously made ready for her conception and filled with protective plant life. Once she has had her brood, she can be removed and returned to the home tank. If she has her young in the home aquarium, the fry can be removed by scooping them up with some of the water into a cup or glass and transferring them to an unoccupied tank where they will be safe. Breeding traps are also designed to protect the newly born from the end result of child abuse. The female is placed inside the so-called trap, which is a smaller tank with a narrow slit in the bottom, and as she gives birth the fry fall through the slit into the safe water of the larger tank.

The best sheltering plants for hiding fry are Myriophyllum, Nitella, and Ambulia. The fry of live-bearers are comparatively large and should be fed both dry and small live foods several times a day, beginning as soon as they are born.

If you are attempting to breed really fine fishes, or to develop a strain of true quality, you must segregate the young males of live-bearers from the immature females as soon as their sex becomes apparent. Keep each sex in its own tank and watch them develop. If separated when young, they will not have the opportunity to breed indiscriminately. To achieve your goal of quality only the best must be used for breeding. The rest of the young should be sold or discarded. "To achieve the best always breed the best to the best," is a bit of wisdom I learned as a child from my grandfather, who quoted this homily whenever he was "in his cups," a fairly permanent condition, so I heard it *ad nauseum*. It nevertheless makes excellent breeding sense.

THE EGG LAYERS

Egg-laying fishes are often referred to as egg scatterers because of their habit of distributing their eggs when spawning rather than neatly containing them in a specific area. Some of these eggs are adhesive and stick to plant leaves; others are not and fall to the bottom of the tank. Layers of adhesive eggs need lots of room and plenty of plants with fairly wide leaves. Most aquarists remove the female to a special breeding tank when she is ready to be bred and the next day introduce the male. He then chases the female (or vice-versa, according to the species) and fertilization occurs simultaneously with emission of the eggs.

The essentials to success in breeding the egg layers are a well-prepared and well-kept aquarium, plenty of the best live food available as part of the diet, healthy and vigorous breeding stock, soft and acid water, adequate illumination, and a tank flooring of peat instead of sand. Do not allow catfish in the breeding tank or they will eat the fallen eggs.

Watch your breeders carefully: the moment they have completed the spawning process remove them from the breeding tank or they will consume the eggs with all the gusto of a gourmet sampling Beluga caviar. A female egg layer can be ready to spawn every week or two. Some hobbyists place the breeders in the breeding tank after dark on the assumption that breeding will take place the following morning. Sometimes this happens; sometimes it doesn't.

Those egg layers that spawn non-adhesive eggs are another problem. The water in the breeding tank should be fairly shallow and the floor covered with agates or a glass-rod grill. The breeders, who spawn near the top of the tank, have little opportunity to catch the eggs and eat them as they float downward in such shallow water. The eggs falling amid the agates or grill rods are also protected from their voracious parents.

Some fishes, when breeding, engage in strange, energetic gyrations, such as leaping out of the water and wrapping themselves around each other in a ballet of fecundity. Some of the *Rasbora* are community breeders and will not breed unless they are in a crowd. Since these exhibitionists are also egg devourers, like the rest of their X-rated crowd, it is extremely difficult to rescue any of the eggs at all.

Of a less cannibalistic turn, *cichlid* parents both take care of the eggs and young. The eggs are fanned by the parents' fins and the young moved about for protection in their parents' mouths. In their native habitat cichlid parents fight off any fishes that attempt to move into their territory and ferociously protect their fry. They keep their eggs scrupulously clean and eat any that are infertile.

Bubble-nest breeders (the *Anabantids*) build bubble nests on the surface of the water. After spawning, the eggs are floated or blown, by the male, into the bubbles where they hatch. The fry remain in the bubble nest and the male takes care of them, blowing new bubbles for fry that break through. The female should be removed to another tank after the completion of the spawning process because the male will attempt to kill her if she remains. The fry of egg layers are provided with a yolk sac from which they derive nourishment until they are ready to ingest supplied foods.

The *panchax* group of fishes and some of the *top minnows* spawn on the tank surface. Spawning is stretched over a period of approximately ten days at which time the parents should be removed. When hatching occurs, about twelve to sixteen days later, the young must be watched diligently and the larger fry removed to another tank or they will gorge on their smaller siblings. Perhaps by this time, in the full knowledge that life originated in the world's waters, you are beginning to understand where the basic savagery of all creatures has its deep-rooted genesis and understand mankind's losing battle through the centuries against his heritage of violence.

Other *killifishes* (*Cyprinodonts*) spawn at the bottom of the tank and peat should be supplied as a floor for the aquarium. The eggs should be collected with the peat, dried out for from two to four weeks, then placed in soft water to hatch.

Angelfishes sometimes lay their eggs on the aquarium glass, but more often on the large leaves of plants. Angels also fan their eggs with their fins and need a good bit of room if breeding is to be successful. They are cannibalistic toward their young, so the leaf on which the eggs have been deposited should be removed to a fresh tank and treated with 5 percent methylene blue to the gallon to kill fungus spores that might attack the eggs. Gentle aeration should be used on the eggs. Some of the cichlids must be given a flowerpot in which to spawn.

Mouthbreeders engage in a fascinating spawning activity. The female carriers the fertilized eggs in her mouth and throat, keeping fresh water flowing over them by means of a slow, gentle chewing movement of her jaws. The eggs incubate inside her mouth and hatch in about two weeks. The youngsters will then begin to venture forth into their watery world but rush back to safety inside mama's mouth at the first sign of danger. During this whole time the female eats nothing and becomes quite emaciated. About four days after the fry are free-swimming the female must be removed as she might suddenly decide to assuage her appetite with a bit of sea food and begin to devour her own happy brood.

Catfishes breed freely in captivity. These are the *Corydoras,* scavengers that move briskly along the sand at the bottom of the aquarium like animated vacuum cleaners, gulping up food that has dropped to the floor. These rather ugly little fish breed in communities, lay their eggs on the glass of the tank or the leaves of plants, and do not attempt to dine on either eggs or fry. They are evidently not big on fish as food.

Bettas (commonly known as Siamese fighting fish) and some of the *leaf fishes* are bubble-nest builders. Bettas should be kept in slightly acid water at a temperature of from 75 to 85 degrees Fahrenheit. The female Betta should be removed after she has ejected her several hundred eggs or the male will kill her. The tank should be covered with glass to keep the bubbles on the surface from bursting. In forty-eight hours the Betta fry will hatch and the sire will blow them back into the nest. Within approximately seventy-two hours the bubble nest will disappear, the yolk sacs of the young will have been consumed, and the baby Bettas, free swimming, will gather in schools, herded by their proud daddy. At the end of a week the male Betta must be removed because proud daddy becomes hungry daddy and a fish fry sounds like a really prime idea to him.

Rice fishes and *white cloud mountain fishes* do not eat their young which, as you now know, in the watery world of fishes, is unusual. There are all kinds of yummy foods to feed the fry of various sizes. As to the parent fishes, it is best to offer them mostly live food to condition them for their stint in the breeding tank.

Breeding Habits of Reptiles

Reptiles either lay eggs, and are therefore termed oviparous, or give birth to live young. There are some snakes that coil around the eggs aiding in their incubation, but the majority simply lay their eggs and leave them to hatch by themselves. Live-bearing snakes, with very few exceptions, desert their young the moment they are born.

Among the snakes the actual sexual act begins with courtship maneuvers that vary with the different serpent species. These displays are not very animated except for those engaged in by a very limited number of species, the garter snake being one. When the sexual organs of the male and female reptiles touch, copulation follows. Since reptiles lack all emotional response, mating is simply an instinctive gesture to propagate their species.

How Raccoon-Family Animals Breed

Raccoons breed readily in captivity and there are quite a few raccoon ranches where breeders have taken advantage of the beastie's easy breeding habits to produce raccoon pelts for the commercial market. Often pets will not breed, not because they are sterile but because, when they become pets, they frequently do not hibernate and most hibernating animals are ready to breed directly following this period.

Ovulation is dependent upon copulation. If the female is in good condition, left alone and in a quiet place, and if the male is mature, fertile, and put with the female at the proper time, pregnancy should follow. The gestation period is from fifty-eight to sixty days. The male must be removed after the mating takes place, for he will kill the young after they are born. Obviously the male raccoon will never achieve an award as Parent of the Year. The cubs open their eyes from nineteen to twenty-four days after birth and, until they are two months old, do nothing but nurse and sleep. During this time the female should be fed extra vitamins, calcium, milk, and some liver to keep a good supply of rich milk flowing and so help the cubs to be sturdy and fast-growing.

The *coatimundi* also breeds readily in captivity. These intelligent mammals usually whelp from two to four cubs and the breeding procedure mimics exactly that of the raccoon. Breeding pairs of coatis should be about three years of age, though younger specimens have been known to breed without difficulty.

The gestation period of the *lesser panda* or cat bear is ninety days, followed by the birth of a pair of tiny cubs. They remain with the parents during a long period of helpless babyhood until just before the next litter is born. Then they leave the nest for independence and to make their way in the Great World.

Actually very few cat bears, cacomistles, or kinkajous are bred as pets. Neither are most of the other wild creatures that have been given pet status in this book.

Primates are bred in zoos, but not by pet owners, and this is also true of mustelines, viverrines, marsupials, and the creatures that have been given the designation of miscellaneous pets.

Most of the *hoofed herbivores,* other than those species designated as wild, are bred on farms or ranches for meat, milk, hides, and wool, obviously for commercial reasons and not as pets. Horses and their related species are bred for utilitarian purposes, for pleasure, racing, and showing. Very few are bred by their owners as pets.

Some of the *Mustelidae* are also ranch-bred for their precious pelts but not as pet material. Since the breeding of all these creatures, for the reasons mentioned, is not necessary knowledge for the pet owner, it will not be detailed here.

PART
TWO

THE MANY
BREEDS
OF PETS

CHAPTER
9
Canines Large and Small

Canidae

"Dog," according to the dictionary is, "a domestic carnivore (*Canis familiaris*) bred in a great many varieties."

The family *Canidae* also embraces wolves, foxes, jackals, and several kinds of wild dogs, including such interesting species as dingoes, Azura's dog, round-eared dog, short-tailed dog, whistling or bush dog, Cape hunting dog, and raccoon-like dog. Some of these feral canines are quite strange in appearance, looking more like the creatures of archaic lineage that were the progenitors of the canine family than like dogs of today.

Development of the Dog

Long before the simian creature that was to become man crept from the dark, leafy shelter of the trees into the light of specie significance, a small, arboreal carnivore, *Miacis*—common ancestor of both bear and dog—moved stealthily in the dappled shadows cast by the foliage of the giant trees in a primeval time of endless specie birth and death, of endless yeasty stirring, of endless change.

Slowly, almost blindly, as the earth writhed in the agony of birth, specie definition sharpened and nature ponderously shaped new images with living clay and gave them evolutionary direction. Then, about thirty million years ago, give or take a few years, *Cynodictus* came into being. It was not a dog, not yet clearly cut to the canine pattern, but it was a creature sluggishly approaching the specie clarity of the family *Canidae*.

In a direct, but labored, line from *Cynodictus,* about fifteen million years ago, came *Tomarctus,* the prototype canine that was probably the true ancestor of the family *Canidae*. Since the inheritable factors that formed *Tomarctus* were still in a state of flux, various types of canines flowed from its anomalous loins. Of major interest to us are four particular species of canines spawned by *Tomarctus,* for this canine quartette constituted the prototype breeds that form the most important cleavage in canine history and gave the family the basis for all the breeds to come. The first of the four was *Canis familiaris metris-optimae,* from which came the early sheepherding breeds; *Canis familiaris intermedius* produced canines that formed the basis for the hunting, hauling, and toy breeds; *Canis familiaris leineri* was ancestor to the sight hounds; and *Canis familiaris inostranzewi* was progenitor of the large, powerful mastiff-type canines and the early water dogs.

This famous canine foursome were actually not too dissimilar to each other, but they carried in their germ plasm the seeds for variation. Selection for the traits that would mold variety would have to come, but if left to natural selection the only survivors would be the few types that could prosper within the area of a savage and limited environment. So the stage was set for the entrance of man to act as a catalyst to the canine evolutionary process.

Primitive Dogs and Primordial Man

The archaic, true canines were pack animals, and this basic instinct to hunt in packs is still prevalent in our modern dog breeds. Prehistoric man's initial introduction to the canine race that was to become his "best friend" was probably through the roaming hunting packs that tried to run him down as prey.

Undoubedly primitive man, the hunter, the child of violence, also tracked milk-laden bitches to their lairs and stole their tender whelps for food. In those early contacts between Homo and canine it was a case of dog bites man and man bites dog, wherever and whenever possible. As a matter of fact, dogs even today are sold in the marketplace for food in certain Asiatic countries, and we know that some—though not all—of our own American Indians bred dogs to produce fat puppies to eat.

In all probability dogs—injured or too old to hunt, but made bold by hunger—crept by night to the odorous caves of brutish man and carried away the cast-out bones and meat refuse. In due time the fact permeated the dull, slow mentality of Neanderthal man that for many reasons this was a good thing. It rid the cave communities of stench that pinpointed man's dwelling places to his enemies, both two- and four-legged, and it eliminated the flies that swarmed amid offal and bit the young, sometimes causing serious infections. Even today, in India, Africa, Asia, South America, and sections of the European Continent, dogs still perform their age-old role as scavengers.

It is also quite possible that early man kept alive, for the children to play with, one of the wild-dog whelps he brought home for food, and

Early man and his dog. Man and canine have walked side by side for thousands of years, their bond fashioned by a mutual pact of love.

so Stone Age man became the first pet owner. This association was entirely successful because the dog is a social animal that transfers to its human master its loyalty and instinct for submission to the pack leader, and thus develops a responsive and creative relationship with man. So began the domestication of the dog and the partnership between man and dog that was to endure from that incredibly long ago time until our own era—and probably beyond.

The Formation of Breeds

The early feral dog's ability to track and hunt the herbivorous creatures of prehistoric times was recognized by early man, who used it to his own advantage. In this manner the earliest hunting dogs came into focus. Some dogs were better hunters than others and man selected for the chase the animals that were superior. In this manner, he began to fashion the foundations of a utilitarian breed.

Later, in the New Stone Age, man abandoned the economy of the hunter and became a herdsman and farmer (during the Neolithic revolution). With this momentous step forward on the path to social significance he again turned to the dog for aid; the herding canines became the focus of his endeavor. As man drew civilization around himself like a many-colored cloak, hunting became more of a sport than a necessary chore to fill the larder. He added to his arsenal of sporting beasts the great hunting hawks and eagles and hunting cats, such as the cheetahs, but he did not attempt to change these creatures through selective breeding. Only his dogs were close enough to warrant this particular attention.

Mankind's rapport with his canine partners was evinced in his awe and fear of the unknown, of the unexplainable mysteries of life and the nothingness of death. Groping for understanding, he saw in the great withdrawn birds of prey and in the stealthy alien cat creatures the stuff of legends and he linked them with the unknown and worshiped their spirit being. But not so with his dogs. They were too close to him, too much a part of his own basic earthiness to be given godlike status; to man the dog was a friend, a known and welcomed partner in many endeavors, not a god.

Soon large, powerful dogs were selected for pack animals and to guard and protect the families, flocks, and goods of Neolithic man, to wreak havoc among his enemies should he find it necessary to war against neighboring or invading tribes. Smaller dogs evolved to become killers of vermin and to dig into the earth after game that went to ground.

Man shaped the dog to suit his needs and assumed a new role in the process, for he became the first living creature to assume godlike stature as the manipulator of the evolutionary process of a species.

Down through the ages, from that time of beginnings that is buried in the mists of the distant past, man's developing, inquisitive mind led him to ask, "How?" and "Why?" His questions were eventually answered by great men of creative mentality such as Charles Robert Darwin whose books, *The Origin of Species* (1859), and *The Descent of Man* (1872), at last brought civilized man face to face with a feasible theory of the evolution of species and his first real understanding of inheritance.

At approximately the same time that Darwin faced the hate, ridicule, and religious wrath heaped upon him because he dared to link man's origin to the anthropoids and to deny him any special, God-bestowed descent from Olympian heights, Gregor Johann Mendel, a Moravian monk in Brunn (now a part of Czechoslovakia), quietly experimented first with flowers, then white mice, hawkweed, and finally with common garden peas. In 1865, Mendel read to the local scientific society a precise account of his experiments, which he had meticulously recorded over a period of eight years. The society subsequently published Mendel's report in its obscure journal, which was filed away and forgotten— *for thirty-four years.*

Sixteen years after Mendel's death another scientist by chance discovered his great work and gave it to the world. With *Mendel's Theory of Inheritance* a new science was born—the science of *genetics.* With these tools—evolution and genetics—to hand, dog fanciers have fashioned the over one hundred and fifty different pure breeds of dogs known throughout the world today. There are still many wild and basic canines existing in remote parts of the world, feral creatures that man has never favored with his touch of creative genius, animals that have been selected for survival by nature. I have seen a pack of African Cape hunting dogs (*Lycaon pictus*), the sole living survivors of their genus, chasing and harassing a wild female buffalo about to give birth, so that they could feast on the newborn calf. In the jungles of South America I have seen the strange, archaic-looking Slater's Dog (*Atelocynus microtis*), and the primitive bush dog (*Icticyon venaticus*). There are other very primitive feral canines that, though they are contemporaries of man's canine creations, still mirror the progenitors of our modern dogs.

Selecting a Breed

What breed of dog is the right one for you? This is the most important question you must satisfactorily answer. Under the heading The Modern Breeds of Dogs, you will find listed under their specific group category every pure breed available to the prospective pet owner. Read the brief, but comprehensive, profiles of the various breeds, particularly those that are significant to you, so you will know the size of the mature specimens; the coat they carry; which ones need special grooming, clipping, or plucking; what job they were genetically fashioned to perform, and what kind of pet and house dog they will make.

When you have decided what breed best fits your personal needs, read everything you can find that has been written by an authority on that breed. One can be given more stupid misinformation about dogs— or any kind of animal—than on any other known subject.

The Modern Breeds of Dogs

Now that you know how to buy, care for, train, show and, if you care to, breed your dog and the heights to which you can aspire with it, it is time to become familiar with the many breeds from which to select the canine that exactly meets your personal requirements.

The breeds are divided into six groups by the American Kennel Club (AKC), the governing body for dogdom in the United States of America, according to the specific purpose for which they have been molded by man. I have taken the liberty of dividing the Hound Group into two categories—Sight Hounds and Scent Hounds—and on this I insist, since the two kinds of hounds are completely different in type and usage. The groups follow:

GROUP I: SPORTING DOGS

Griffon, Wirehaired Pointing	Spaniel, American Water
Pointer, German Shorthaired	Spaniel, Brittany
Pointer, German Wirehaired	Spaniel, Clumber
Pointer (English)	Spaniel, Cocker (American)
Retriever, Chesapeake Bay	Spaniel, English Cocker
Retriever, Curly-Coated	Spaniel, English Springer
Retriever, Flat-Coated	Spaniel, Field
Retriever, Golden	Spaniel, Irish Water
Retriever, Labrador	Spaniel, Sussex
Setter, English	Spaniel, Welsh Springer
Setter, Gordon	Vizsla
Setter, Irish	Weimaraner

GROUP II: HOUNDS

A. Scent Hounds

Basenji	Deerhound, Scottish
Basset Hound	Greyhound
Beagle	Foxhound, English
Bloodhound	Harrier
Bluetick Coonhound	Norwegian Elkhound
Coonhound, Black & Tan	Otter Hound
Dachshund	Plott Hound (not AKC recognized)
Foxhound, American	Redbone Hound (not AKC recognized)
	Rhodesian Ridgeback
	Treeing Walker (not AKC recognized)

B. Sight Hounds

Afghan Hound	Irish Wolfhound
Borzoi (Russian Wolfhound)	Saluki
	Whippet

GROUP III: WORKING DOGS

Akita
Alaskan Malamute
Belgium Groenendael
Belgium Malinois
Belgium Tervuren
Bernese Mountain Dog
Bouvier des Flandres
Boxer
Briard
Bullmastiff
Collie
Doberman Pinscher
German Shepherd
Giant Schnauzer
Great Dane

Great Pyrenees
Komondor
Kuvasz
Mastiff
Newfoundland
Old English Sheepdog
Puli
Rottweiler
St. Bernard
Samoyed
Schnauzer, Standard
Shetland Sheepdog
Siberian Husky
Welsh Corgi, Cardigan
Welsh Corgi, Pembroke

GROUP IV: TERRIERS

Airedale Terrier
Australian Terrier
Bedlington Terrier
Border Terrier
Bull Terrier
Cairn Terrier
Dandie Dinmont Terrier
Fox Terrier (smooth & wire)
Irish Terrier
Kerry Blue Terrier
Lakeland Terrier

Manchester Terrier
Norwich Terrier
Schnauzer, Miniature
Scottish Terrier
Sealyham Terrier
Skye Terrier
Soft-Coated Wheaten Terrier
Staffordshire Terrier
Welsh Terrier
West Highland White Terrier

GROUP V: TOYS

Affenpinscher
Chihuahua
English Toy Spaniel
Griffon, Brussels
Italian Greyhound
Japanese Spaniel
Maltese
Manchester Terrier (Toy)
Papillon

Pekingese
Pinscher, Miniature
Pomeranian
Poodle (Toy)
Pug
Silky Terrier
Shih Tzu
Yorkshire Terrier

GROUP VI: NON-SPORTING

Bichon Frises   Keeshond
Boston Terrier   Lhasa Apso
Bulldog   Poodle (Miniature)
Chow Chow   Poodle (Standard)
Dalmatian   Schipperke
French Bulldog   Tibetan Terrier

MISCELLANEOUS

Australian Cattle Dog   Cavalier King Charles Spaniel
Australian Kelpie   Ibizan Hound
Australian Shepherd   Miniature Bull Terrier
Bearded Collie   Spinoni Italiano
Border Collie   Staffordshire Bull Terrier

The Sporting Dogs

The first group, Sporting Dogs, is composed of all breeds used to hunt game birds in the water or on dry land. Most of these breeds make delightful pets, are hardy, and are good house dogs.

Pointers are the epitome of the breeds that locate and point their feathered prey. All the pointers are medium to large dogs weighing up to 80 pounds. The *Vizsla,* a solid reddish-gold in color, is the smallest pointing dog, about 24 inches in height and 40 to 60 pounds in weight. Originally a hunting and companion dog of the Magyar hordes that settled in Hungary a thousand years ago, they make excellent pets and family dogs. The Vizsla, Weimeraner, both the wirehaired pointers and the German shorthair pointer have tails cut to about a third of their original length. The pointers, with the exception of the two wirehaired breeds, have close, short coats.

The *German wirehaired* and the *German shorthaired pointers* are much alike except in coat. Their most characteristic color is liver roan. Both make fine pets, companions, house and watch dogs, as well as sporting dogs. In the field they work deliberately and close to the gun, which can be advantageous to the hunter who has slowed down a bit or likes to hunt in a leisurely fashion. If trained correctly, these German Pointing breeds will hunt both fur and feather. I have hunted pheasants behind a wonderful short-hair bitch that sold me completely on the breed as a bird dog, and I remember a crisp autumn day in Florence, Italy, some years ago, watching enviously as a man on a scooter—with a gun strapped to his back, his German shorthair on the vehicle's platform—headed out of the city for a day of sport.

The *pointer* (*English*) is perhaps the most aristocratic of this group. He is a rather aloof, insensate animal who does not make as happy a pet as the other pointers. He usually has a good deal of white in the coat that cloaks his handsome body with liver, black, or orange patches and head markings. In the field he is a streak and will work for anyone. This breed was born, bred, and lives to hunt. At the National Field Trials this breed and the Field Trial English setters are followed on horseback by both judges and spectators. (Both pointers and setters are bred in two separate and distinct types, one for the field and the other for the show ring.)

Stylish, fast, far-ranging and staunch in the field, the English pointer lives for the hunt.

Most European countries have their own native pointers. I have hunted behind Spanish pointers, fashioned generations ago by the aristocratic Hidalgos of Spain, and have watched Portugese and Italian pointers (Spinoni Italiano) work in the countries of their origin, but they are not as lithe and typey in the field as the English pointer. Actually practically all of the sporting breeds were fashioned by genetic factors inherent in the old Spanish pointers and Spanish Land Spaniels. As a matter of fact the word "Spaniel" is derived from the country of this breed's basic origin, Spain.

The *Weimaraner* is nicknamed "The Gray Ghost," which indicates the color of this dog's solid coat. His nose is gray, matching the coat (which is sometimes almost lilac in color), and the eyes are yellowish or light blue-gray. They are intelligent companions, watch dogs and pets and are well liked as a gentleman's shooting dog. In Austria I saw long-coated (Setter-like) Weimeraners and have since judged long coats in F.C.I. (*Fédération Cynogolique Internationale*) shows abroad. These are beautiful animals, their long silky coats evidently the result of a double recessive gene.

Retrievers are breeds that work in water and retrieve shot birds to hand. They, too, are medium-sized breeds with the Chesapeake Bay the largest and most powerful (up to 26 inches and 75 pounds) and the Golden approximately equal in size and power.

The color of the *Chesapeake Bay retriever* varies from a straw color to a dark brown. Unlike pointers, the retrievers are generally not showy or stylish, but they are smart, strong, and willing, and they make good house and pet dogs. The Chesapeake loves and protects the family's children and, since it possesses a rather odd body insensitivity, small tykes can seldom cause it pain.

The *Labrador* is one of the finest of all breeds. It is a superb water dog with a short but dense coat of black, shades of yellow, and occasionally deep brown. Its intelligence and willingness have led it into other utilitarian paths. As a house dog, child's companion, and pet the Labrador is difficult to equal.

The handsomest of the retrievers is the gentle *Golden Retriever*. Its lustrous golden coat is longer than the Labrador's and it is a large-boned, solid, but active, animal and a fine companion and pet.

The *flat-coated retriever,* solid black or liver-colored, and the *curly-coated retriever,* its cloak of crisp curls the same in color as the flat-coated, are not as numerous or popular as the other retrievers. They are, nevertheless, excellent water dogs and intelligent, reliable pets and house dogs.

Setters are all pointing breeds and perform in the field in exactly the same way as the pointers do. They are handsome animals, medium in size (to 27 inches and 75 pounds), dressed in soft, silky coats with long hair called "feathering" on their ears, chest, hind legs, bottom line, and tail. In body shape and head they resemble their cousins, the pointers, with the addition of the setter coat.

The *English setter* is a mild-mannered and sweet dog, adored by the whole family. Coat color is mostly white with ticking (or flecking) of tan, black, lemon, orange, or liver, with corresponding head markings and generally some body patches, though the less of the latter the better. There were originally two distinct strains of English setters, the Laverack and the Llewellyn, but crossing between these two and others has dispersed the purity of the strains. The *Gordon setter,* of Scottish origin, varies in size in different areas but is generally a bit larger, heavier, and coarser than its English cousin. It carries a lustrous coat of black and tan and is steady rather than rapid in the field. Quiet, clean, and gentle, it makes a good pet and house dog. The rich mahogany coat of the *Irish setter* is its badge of distinction. It is not, generally, as "birdy" in the field as the other setters. They make gay and spirited pets, sometimes perhaps a little high-headed and too vivacious, yet they are a gentle and basically sweet breed.

Spaniels are flushing dogs that show great variety in type and size. The term "flushing" indicates that—with one exception, the Brittany—these dogs do not point. Instead they find game birds and flush them out of cover so that they wing up to become targets for the hunter's gun.

The largest of these flushing dogs is the *Irish water spaniel,* a unique breed, solid liver in color and up to 24 inches high with a weight, in larger specimens, of 65 pounds. It is believed that this breed originated through crosses of Spanish root stock and the old Portuguese water dogs called Podengos, brought to Erin by Iberian raiders. This is a hard-working field dog, sturdy and capable of working in very cold water. The Irish seems to possess a sense of humor, a necessary adjunct to its

Harpo Marx topknot and rat tail. The body is covered with tight ringlets of hair and the total appearance is rather comic. One observer remarked that this staunch animal looks much like a Standard Poodle that has been barbered by a mad scientist.

The *Brittany Spaniel,* of French origin, is also unique in that it is the only Spaniel that points game rather than flushing it. About 20 inches high and weighing approximately 40 pounds, these dogs sport a short tail, are square in body shape, and have a head of no great distinction. In color the Brittany is generally dark orange or liver and white and should show no black in its coat. This is a no-nonsense field dog that makes a good pet and house dog.

Two Spaniel breeds that are not very popular and so not in great supply are the *American water* and *field spaniels.* They are similar in size, about 18 inches high and weigh about 45 pounds. The American has a solid liver or dark chocolate closely curled coat; the field spaniel has a flat or slightly waved coat in a variety of colors and combinations. Both make sensible pets.

Of all the Spaniels the *American Cocker* is undoubtedly the most familiar and popular. It is the smallest of the Spaniels (22 to 28 pounds) and its name is derived from its ability in hunting the swift-winged woodcock. Bright-eyed and adaptable, the cocker comes in many colors, solid black, ASCOB (or any solid color other than black) which includes cream, red, black and tan and parti-color. A drawback to pet ownership in this breed is the long, thick, sometimes curly coat that needs a good deal of grooming, clipping, and plucking to keep the cocker type discernible and the dog free of fleas and lice. Earlier cockers were smaller and had the silken coat of the setter and no unwanted hair growth on the head. The larger, heavier-coated cockers of today do not usually project the sweet, amiable character of the earlier dogs.

The *English cocker* is slightly larger than the American breed, up to 17 inches at the shoulder with a weight of 32 pounds, varied in color with solid reds and blue roans most popular. It has a longer muzzle, leaner head, and is slightly higher in the leg than its American counterpart. The breed is coated more like a setter without the difficult-to-groom coat of the American cocker. A fine hunting dog and pet with excellent temperament, it is yet, despite its many virtues, not very popular in the

States, having been unable to dent the popularity of the more showy American cocker.

One of the most handsome and versatile of the sporting breeds is the *English Springer Spaniel*. This 22-inch-high, 55-pound beauty has no peer in the field and is considered a specialist on ringneck pheasant. He carries his short, trimmed tail high and has a medium coat that is longer on ears, chest, underline, and legs. He shows a delightful color contrast in white and liver, or white and black, with an occasional liver roan for accent. The typical springer is a friendly, eager dog that learns quickly and becomes a fine friend and house dog. The *Welsh Springer Spaniel* is much like the English Springer in type but slightly smaller and proportionately longer in body. This is an old breed that is accepted in only one color combination, dark rich red and white. The Welsh is not as showy and dashing as the Springer, but is a fine sporting dog of merry disposition who makes a desirable pet.

The last breeds in the Sporting Group to enjoy our scrutiny are the *Sussex* and the *Clumber spaniels*. The Sussex is long and level with a rather strong, heavy head. It is 35 to 45 pounds in weight and wears a rich golden liver coat. The Sussex was bred in England for a different type of terrain than is found in the United States and, because he is considered too slow in the field, has not found favor here. Actually he is a determined field dog, excellent for upland shooting. The breed frequently gives tongue when on a scent.

The Clumber is the heaviest of the land spaniels and its long, low-slung body gives evidence of a Bassett Hound cross to the old Alpine spaniel in its evolutionary background. Almost all white with sparse lemon or orange markings, the coat of the Clumber is silky, straight, and dense. The head is very broad and heavy and he is slow, methodical, and efficient in the field, the ideal hunting companion for a man past his prime who still likes a day's sport but at a leisurely pace. Unfortunately breeders of this up-to-65-pound Spaniel are difficult to find in America. The Clumber makes a quiet house dog and a safe but unimaginative pet.

In summary, the Sporting Group is composed of varied breeds that, in most instances, make excellent pets and companions. These sterling breeds also offer an added bonus of service to man in the field. This extra consideration can open up a new area of endeavor for the neophyte or add zest to the efforts of the experienced hunter who selects a new breed to accompany him for a day of healthy activity in the out-of-doors.

The Hound Breeds

SCENT HOUNDS

I have divided the Hound category into two sections, Scent Hounds and Sight Hounds. It is my opinion that, except for the fact that both types are hunters of game, there is no other quality they share in common. Though linked through AKC group association, Scent Hounds are in general more closely allied to our first group, Sporting Dogs, than they are to the Sight Hound.

The olfactory senses of the Scent Hounds are almost unbelievable. These sporting canines trail their quarry, generally giving tongue with bell-like voices, and bring their prey to bay either treed or on the ground, holding it there until the hunter joins them. The Greeks used packs of hounds four hundred years before Christ, so we know that these are ancient breeds of canines. By the middle of the sixteenth century hounds were being segregated into classifications based upon size and the game they hunted.

The *Basenji* we will consider first, though the breed is not at all typical of the scent hounds. Basenjis are small, square dogs, slightly larger than a a fox terrier, lightly built, and weighing up to 24 pounds. The breed is of African origin, has prick ears, a short coat, and is barkless. Now that is about as far afield as one can get from a scent hound. In the land of its origin it is asked to retrieve, drive game into nets, find wounded animals, and stalk the reed rats of Africa. Any of these chores could be accomplished by breeds other than a hound and it is my contention that these handsome little dogs are not true hounds. I believe they were bred as house dogs in Ancient Egypt (Pharoan house dogs) and became a general dog-of-all-jobs in the hands of the natives when the mighty Egyptian empire declined.

The *Bassett Hound* is a true scent hound, long in the ears with the sad expression of a bloodhound and a fine houndy, bellowing voice. Long in body and short in leg, these dogs are heavy, muscular, and rather droll in gait, appearance, and character. They look very much like a bloodhound that has been raised under a bureau. My son owned a fine show Bassett—Bullfiddle's Mister Magoo—that was lovable but stubborn, as all Bassetts must be to push their short-legged big bodies through heavy brush. They are hunted on rabbit, hare, and pheasant and have tremendous scenting ability. They are good-natured 50-to-65 pound dogs acceptable in all true hound colors.

Most people are familiar with *beagles*. These small hounds come in two sizes, 13 inch and 15 inch, and are physically akin to small fox-hounds. The same son I mentioned a moment ago also kept a kennel of fine beagles, which we showed, hunted, and ran in field trials. Easy keepers, merry and eager hunters and companions, it is difficult to find a finer pet than a beagle.

Bloodhounds have achieved world-wide renown as man-trailers. Be-cause of this, they have often been branded as vicious. Actually, their name comes from the fact that they were raised by royalty—hence "blooded hounds." They are really large, gentle animals with the finest trailing ability of any known canine. Long in the ear, loose of skin (which allows them to comfortably keep their nose to the ground), these big black-and-tan scenting hounds are not generally good house dogs be-cause they have a tendency to slobber a lot. The bloodhound has genetically influenced the quality of many other hound breeds.

Much like the bloodhound in appearance, the black and tan *coon-hound* is not quite as heavy or wrinkled and is a tough, strong dog that can cover a lot of ground at a good gait without tiring.

The popular, very short-legged and long-bodied *dachshund* is avail-able in two sizes, standard and miniature, and in three coat qualities: smooth, long (like an Irish setter), and wiry (like a wirehaired fox terrier). In color you have your choice of red, the popular black and tan, chocolate and tan, dappled, and several other combinations seldom seen. Again we find a breed in the hound group that doesn't really belong. The Dachshund is more like a terrier than a hound and even in its usage —going to ground after badger and similar game—it mimics the job of the terrier. Dachshunds do make excellent companions, watch dogs, and pets, particularly for small apartments.

English and *American foxhounds* are much alike in basic type and usage, but the English foxhound is a bigger, heavier-boned, breedier-looking (*i.e.* true to the breed) dog, indicating the magic touch of England's master breeders. Americans wanted a lighter-boned dog and bred for it, using English dogs as the breed basis. One of the most noted breeders of American foxhounds in the early days of the breed was George Washington.

The *harrier* is in size and type midway between the foxhound and the beagle. All three of these hounds come from the same basic origin, are close-coated, and clothed in any good hound color. The harrier is occasionally found in a blue-mottled color unique to the breed. Harriers pack well and are specialists in the hunting of hare.

Prick-eared, the picture of a Northern sled dog, the *Norwegian elkhound,* in his gray-brown thick coat, with tail tightly curled over his back, is not at all of hound type and does not really belong in this group. This breed is quite evidently of Northern "spitz" stock and even its voice is completely unhoundlike. It is used in Norway as a big-game hunter of elk. Many of these Northern sled dogs are used by Indians and Eskimos as hunting dogs, but they remain in the Working Group. (Airedales, on the other hand, were often bred and used for hunting big game also, but their status was not changed from terrier to hound.) The elkhound is medium-sized, fearless, devoted to its family and makes a very fine house dog and pet—but it is *not* a hound.

An English favorite, the *otter hound,* is an ancient breed much like a bloodhound, with a heavy, water-resistant, wiry coat, and a natural antipathy for otters. Good-natured and a natural outdoors dog, it does not exactly fit the role of house dog.

The *Rhodesian ridgeback,* also called the African Lion Hound, is distinguished from all other breeds by the ridge of hair that forms a reverse hair-growth pattern along its back. They are solid wheaten-colored, powerful dogs used in Rhodesia and Nyasaland for hunting lions and leopards from horseback. Human hunters ride the horses. The dogs, though intelligent, have never been taught to ride. These are fearless, obedient canines of excellent temperament. They make good pets, companions, and watch dogs. I spent a good deal of time in Africa looking for both the ridgeback, supposedly developed by native Hottentots and Zulus, and the Basenji. The latter breed I never did see, but in Nairobi, Kenya, I finally found a ridgeback that was the companion and watchdog of an East Indian merchant.

Coonhounds are true hounds and most of them are working dogs, running 'coon night after night during the season. Though most Coonhound breeds are not AKC recognized, those we will discuss are pure-bred animals, true-breeding and registered in various hound stud books.
   The finest night hunter, the *Redbone Hound,* is my idea of a great Coonhound. Solid red in color, with a sweet, bawling chant, these dogs show definite evidence of close-up bloodhound ancestry. The *Bluetick Coonhound* varies in size and voice but not in type, all Blueticks being

houndy and heavily ticked. They bawl, bugle, or chop when trailing, according to how they were bred, and they make fine big-game dogs. Several European countries breed similar bluetick hounds. A hound of different coloring and type is the *Plott hound*. Brindle, with a black saddle and a shorter ear than most hounds, this is a tough, strong dog that obviously shows the effect of bloodhound and bullterrier breeding in its genetic background. These hounds are stayers and make excellent big-game hounds as well as coonhounds. The *Treeing Walker* is actually a strain of the American foxhound, bred from dogs that took to night-running raccoons and opossum rather than foxes during the day.

Every civilized country in the world has its native hounds as it does its sheepherding, guard, sporting, working, toy, and greyhound breeds. I will later mention some of those foreign to us but beloved and useful in their own countries. Of course most of the breeds recognized by the AKC, and popular here, are of foreign extraction as are so many of the human citizens of our country. The United States is a very young country in the brotherhood of nations and most canine breeds were well fashioned to specific purpose before we became independent. In the years since that momentous event, we have developed very few breeds of our own.

SIGHT HOUNDS

Sight Hounds are among the oldest breeds of dogs known to man. They were the companions of savage rulers and kings when civilization was born—beside the Pharaohs they watched the building of towering pyramids that proclaimed the infinite might of ancient Egypt. Of all breeds they are the swiftest, for they are the coursing and gaze hounds, using keen vision and racing speed to sight and run down their prey. Generally speaking the Sight Hounds are all greyhounds that were developed with different coats and for different climes.

The *Afghan hound* was a known and valued breed when the Avenue of Rams' Head Sphinxes in Egypt were trundled into line by thousands of sweating slaves to form a passage to the Temple of Karnak in Luxor. These hounds drank from the waters of "Mother" Nile, and at Sinai, the Sacred Place where Jehovah delivered to Moses the Ten Commandments; a scribe, at his master's dictation, wrote of the Afghan Hound, referring to his master's favorite as *cynocephalus* or, "Monkey-faced Hound." The date of this inscription was about 3500 B.C. The Afghan was bred only by and for the nobility as it was unlawful for the common man, in those early days, to own a dog. The breed was used to hunt and run down gazelle, deer, and desert leopards. A strikingly exotic breed, slim and fleet with a long silky coat of a rather odd growth pattern, that comes in a variety of colors, the Afghan has a look of elegance and archaic beauty. These dogs make fine companions and watchdogs but need assiduous grooming to keep them in bloom.

A true aristocrat in the continental manner, the *Borzoi* (Russian wolfhound) was developed from the Laika, an old Russian breed. The tall, elegant Borzoi was the favorite of many of the Czars and never were any of these dogs allowed to fall into the hands of the common classes. With the revolution and the end of White Russian dominance, and during the maniacal purges and abysmal barbarism of the Communist regime, the Borzoi all but became extinct. As a matter of fact the Communists sought out specimens of the breed and annihilated them as symbols of the hated aristocracy. Luckily fine Borzois of the wanted ancient type had reached Britain (and later the United States), so there was a firm genetic basis for continuance of the breed. During my recent visit to Soviet Russia and many other joyless behind-the-iron-curtain satellites the complete absence of dogs on the streets and in the homes was very marked. In Czechoslovakia I was informed by a courageously outspoken former dog fancier that the People's Party frowns on wasting food on dogs. What has happened to the vast, diverse land that is Russia is no fault of the beautiful Borzoi that was, before the coming of communism, used for wolf hunting on the huge estates of the aristocracy. The Borzoi is a moderately affectionate, quiet, very sensitive animal of truly rare beauty. Their hair is very light and, when they shed, it floats into every crevice in the house.

In the halls of great chilly castles the *Scottish deerhound* drowsed as his knightly master entertained noble guests. This was his métier, to hear the song of minstrels, the clash of armor; to view the colorful, shifting pageantry of the Middle Ages and to lead the hunt for the huge, wild stags of the Highlands. Tall and spare in his grizzled-gray wiry coat, this Scotsman is an agile and courageous canine, but gentle, good with all small creatures. Sir Walter Scott paid tribute to his deerhound bitch, calling her "The most perfect creature in Heaven." This is an active breed that likes to run and needs plenty of room in which to do it. It is not an apartment or suburb dweller.

The *Greyhound* is the basic coursing and sight hound type. These speeders can be viewed on dog-racing tracks all over the world. A top racing greyhound can clock up to thirty-seven miles an hour. Originally

The favorite canine of the old Russian aristocracy, the Borzoi is a sight hound and a canine of rare elegance.

used to chase hare, they have been successfully coursed on wolves and coyotes on our Western plains. Almost every country has its own representative of the breed: the Galgo Espanol in Spain, the Magyar Agar of Hungary, the Sloughi of Arabia and the prick-eared Pharaon hound to name a few. I once owned a fawn greyhound that had raced in Australia. He was courageous and sweet with humans but not overly intelligent.

The tallest of all canines is the *Irish wolfhound*. Larger and heavier than the Scottish deerhound, these huge dogs are nevertheless much like the Scotch breed in coat and appearance. There is a record of Irish wolfhounds dating back to Rome in A.D. 391 when seven of the great hounds were sent as a gift to the consul. At that time all Rome ". . . viewed them with wonder." They were the favorite of Irish kings and heard the drunken revelries of puissant Irish knights echo down high stone corridors; their names sung by lisping minstrels and extolled by the storytellers of that wayward age.

By the eighteenth century the wolves of Ireland had been hunted to extinction behind the big hounds, which declined greatly in number and breed purity. Through the efforts and shrewd breeding acumen of a retired English Army officer a generation later, the breed was returned to its pristine type. Standing 36 inches and more at the withers, these animals have a commanding presence and an amiable character. They make excellent guards and house dogs, though they do need room to roam. A small house with a little ground around it just won't do for them.

One of the very ancient canines is the *Saluki,* already an established breed when Alexander the Great invaded India in 320 B.C. I have a colored slide from Greece (part of a fresco that had decorated the later palace of Tiryns, 1300 to 1200 B.C.), depicting a Saluki being led to the hunt by a slave. Ancient hunters rode their chariots to the chase with their hunting hawks and their Salukis, which were used to hunt gazelle, fleetest of all the antelopes. The Saluki is in type similar to the Afghan with which it shares its ancient heritage, but it does not sport the extravagant coat of that breed. Salukis are good pets, companions, and house dogs.

The *whippet,* developed as a racing dog for the British workingman, was originally called a "snap-dog" and is the result of crossing small selected greyhounds with leggy, native terriers. Due to its small size and inexpensive food rations, it became a favorite of working-class sportsmen and a popular racing dog in Lancashire and Yorkshire. The elegance of the Italian greyhound (a toy breed) was bred into the original lines to produce the stylish show whippet of today.

The Working Breeds

Here are the breeds whose service and devotion to mankind is beyond calculable value. Whenever man needs specialized help, there you will find the working dog—guarding the home, family and goods of his master; herding the flocks and driving the herds to market; pulling carts; finding the victims of disaster; fighting crime in the streets; hauling sleds in the frozen wastes of the northland; guiding the blind, and bringing humanity the rare gifts of usefulness and love.

Though some of the working breeds perform in several utilitarian areas, basically they can be segregated into three performance groups: the sled dogs, the herding dogs, and the guard dogs, and in their specific fields of endeavor these canines have no peers.

The *akita* is a large breed of Japanese origin, used in his native land as a hunting, sled, and fighting dog, but mostly as a formidable guard dog. Erect ears, strong muzzle, and a curled over-the-back plumed tail are sure indications of his past relationship to the Northern sled-dog breeds. Akitas are good family dogs, alert, intelligent and rather newly accepted into the AKC family of breeds.

The *Alaskan malamute* is a large, extremely powerful sled dog used specifically to haul heavy freight-laden sleds. It also doubles as a hunting and pack animal. A fine and hardy breed.

The triumvirate of *Belgian sheepdogs, Groenendael, Tervuren,* and *Malinois,* share common ancestry, size, basic structure, temperament, and working abilities. As their name signifies, they are sheepherders, but they also make fine house dogs, guides for the blind, guard dogs, and pets. Prick-eared, alert, medium in size, squarely built, and agile, their medium-length coat is black in the Groenendael and fawn, tipped with black, in the Tervuren. The Malinois is short-haired and fawn in color like the Tervuren.

The *Bernese Mountain Dog* is from the Swiss Alps and is a companion, guard, and draft dog, pulling carts laden with cans of milk or produce to the marketplace. The ancestors of these hardy, intelligent, strong animals came to Switzerland over two thousand years ago with the Roman invaders. Medium in size, black and tan in color, they usually sport white chest markings and make excellent pets and house dogs.

Unless it holds a working title the *Bouvier de Flandre* cannot attain to championship status in the show ring in its native country, Belgium. This is a very sound way to keep a breed's utilitarian abilities intact. Chiefly cattle drovers, these over medium-sized, powerful animals perform other tasks, including guard and draft work. Ears are cropped and erect, tail docked short, and the all-weather coat is rough, tousled, and fawn to black in color. Pepper and salt, and gray and brindle are also accepted colors. Compact and intelligent, the Bouvier is a very worthwhile breed.

A very popular breed, the *Boxer* has been bred to a point close to perfection. He is a medium-sized, square, exceedingly clean-cut, smooth-coated, and balanced dog of German origin. A descendant of the old bull-baiting Bullenbeisser, the Boxer's ears are fashionably cropped and his tail is docked close. The identifying muzzle is short, square, and undershot. In fawn and brindle with a black mask, and usually trimmed with confined white (too much white or all white are disqualifying faults), the Boxer is an alert, fearless animal that makes a good house and guard dog.

The *Briard* is a medium-large dog of French lineage that has found usage as a herding dog, drover, police, guard, and draft dog. It is not very quick to learn, but retains what it has been taught. Briards are quiet, well-mannered animals with semi-erect ears and a hard "goat's coat" that comes in all solid colors but white. *Double dewclaws* are required on each hind leg—an unusual physical trait.

Stocky, powerful, and of upper-middle size, the *bull mastiff* is a smaller edition of the modern mastiff or ancient lineage. Developed by British gamekeepers to eliminate poaching, these muscular dogs are well balanced and indicate tremendous strength in every inch of their muscular bodies. In color they are red, fawn, or brindle with a black mask. These are formidable guard dogs for the home or estate, but lovable and dependable with their human families.

The *collie* has always been a favorite breed and, to most people, the epitome of the true sheepherding dog. This Scotch breed's popularity has been kept green first by the thrilling stories of Albert Payson Terhune and more recently by the adventures of the indomitable Lassie. The long, lean, intelligent head and the profuse coat are hallmarks of this medium-sized breed. Sable and white, tri-color, blue merle and white, and white with markings are the recognized colors. The ears should be semi-pricked (tulip) and the coat composed of long, straight hair. Because of selection limited by breeders to head and coat, you will find many physically unsound animals now in the breed.

The *smooth collie* is judged exactly as the rough-coated version but without, of course, stress on the long coat. A third variety of this sheep-herding breed is the *bearded collie,* which is physically like the rough-coated and smooth-coated varieties but possesses a wiry coat and the tufted eyebrows and beard that go with this type of coat.

Of German origin, the *Doberman pinscher* is one of the most physically superb and statuesque breeds in the working group. Medium large, alert, quick, hard-muscled, and sometimes equipped with the temperamental fire of the terrier, the Doberman's intelligence is one of his many virtues. As a home and family guardian he is superb and his talents spill over into the police- and war-dog area. His tight, gleaming coat can be black, liver-brown (red), or blue with rust red sharply defined markings. Be particular about selecting for amiability and quiet temperament in this breed.

The *German shepherd,* one of the most versatile and intelligent canines ever fashioned by the hand of man was initially a sheepherding breed. Selection was later made for fearlessness and aggressiveness in order to fashion a new role for the breed in police and war work. Now these sensitive animals are also most successful as guides for the blind, avalanche and disaster dogs, and just plain home companions and guards. The German shepherd is a medium-large breed, easily cared for and very close to the feral canine type. Above all else the shepherd craves human companionship and love. Deep, rich coloring is wanted; white dogs are disqualified for showing. The German shepherd is my personal favorite and I have been lucky enough to have owned some truly fine ones, all German imports. I have judged the breed in many parts of the world and have always found them to be the most widely admired and popular of dogs. In the land of its origin a mature specimen is not allowed to achieve honors in the show ring unless it has a complicated training degree (Schutzhund, meaning protection dog). The philosophy behind the Teutonic insistence that adult dogs be fully trained explains why the shepherd, as bred in Germany, is superior as a working dog to those bred in any other part of the globe. Watch out for shyness or toughness when you select one as a pet.

The *Giant Schnauzer* is a hard-working guard and cattle dog that has been bred in two other sizes, standard and miniature. Originating in Bavaria, the breed was fashioned by cattlemen in that section of Germany for their specific purpose. These big Schnauzers can also be trained to be efficient police dogs. They are medium-large in size, robust and powerful, with cropped ears, a docked tail, and a close, wiry coat of

ERNEST H. HART

The German shepherd dog is perhaps the most versatile utility breed ever developed by man.

black, pepper and salt, or black and tan (the last color seldom seen). This is often a high-spirited but reliable breed, in type very much like a wirehaired Doberman.

Another German product, the *Great Dane,* is the most elegant of the giant breeds and ranks with the Irish wolfhound in size. The Dane was originally bred as a boarhound and its genealogy traces back to the early mastiffs. As a matter of fact in its country of origin it was called the German mastiff. The Dane has nobility and character and as a guard dog its size alone is a deterrent to criminals. A fine companion, these big canines can be found in fawn and brindle (black mask preferred with each color), blue (dilute black), black, and the flashy harlequin.

The *Great Pyrenees* is a huge, powerful dog, its heavy white coat lending the illusion of even greater massiveness to its big frame. Majestic and intelligent, the Pyrenees was fashioned to protect the flocks and herds on the rugged mountain slopes of the snow-covered Pyrenees from wolves, bears, and wild dogs, and to watch over the large estates in its native France. When crossed into the Newfoundland breed, the *Landseer Newfoundland* was produced and named for the famous animal artist, Sir Edwin Henry Landseer, who immortalized the black and white breed on canvas. The standard for the Great Pyrenees calls for double dewclaws on the hind legs.

Large, white, heavily coated, the *Komondor* is Hungary's canine guardian of sheep and cattle. For a thousand years they have been the Magyars' guard dogs and were bred solely for their utility. Their unique coat, similar to the poodle's in texture, is often allowed to cord or mat, which leads to a very pungent animal order. This is probably why the Komondor is referred to as a truly, hardy "outdoor" breed. (The plural of Komondor is Komondorok, a piece of information of no great importance.) Another white, fairly large dog, the *Kuvasz,* is closely related to the Komondor, but is in coat texture more like the Great Pyrenees. These are strong, hardy guard dogs of home, flocks, or property.

Of the most ancient lineage, the huge and massive *mastiff* has been the servant of man, probably prior to the beginning of recorded history. The ancient Assyrians used these great dogs both to hunt lions and as war dogs. The errant traveler, Marco Polo, bore witness that Kublai Khan kept mastiffs. Courageous to an extreme, yet docile and above pettiness, these powerful canines need room in which to roam if they are to keep fit. The coat is smooth and in color fawn, apricot, or brindle, with black shading the muzzle and eye area. Select for docility, good temperament, and good physical balance.

The *Newfoundland* is a large water dog of sterling quality as a guard and watchdog, but with a core of gentleness that makes him a particularly safe child's companion. Intelligent and sweet in disposition, they are a big lumbering breed, massive in bone and with a huge head. The coat is dense, rather long, and water resistant. Generally black, there are other color choices in the black and white Landseer Newfoundland and an occasional bronze-colored individual.

The *old English sheepdog* or "Bobtail," has a short tail, bobbed at the first joint, and is a drover not a herding dog. The breed was developed

E·H·HART

*The Italian mastiff is quite often found in various shades of
blue. He is powerful, ungainly, and a formidable antagonist.
Note the wide, fur-trimmed collar typically worn by the breed
on the Continent.*

in the western part of England. Its long hair (which covers the eyes and
takes a good deal of grooming) and its rolling gait are breed characteristics. Intelligent, affectionate, and rather clownish, it is colored always
in some shade of gray, blue or blue-merle, with white markings.

The *Puli* (plural is pulik) shares its genealogy with the two other
Hungarian breeds, the Kuvasz and Komondor. This sheepherder and
drover is smaller than his cousins, with possible genetic ties to the
Tibetan Terrier. The coat can be rusty black, black, and various shades

of gray as well as white. All colors must be solid. Its coat has a tendency to cord, due to its poodle-like texture, and must be frequently groomed to keep it free of matting and odor. Sometimes the puli is born with a short tail, which is acceptable, but the tail must never be cropped. This is not a very prepossessing-looking breed, but it does appear to be the basis for all the "shaggy dog" stories ever told.

The black and tan *Rottweiler* is a medium-large, very powerful black and tan animal. Its ancestors came to Germany with the conquering Roman Legions and the breed found its niche as a guard, draft, and police dog. The Rottweiler is intelligent, strong, dependable, and not excitable.

The *Saint Bernard* is internationally known for its work as a storm and avalanche rescue dog on the dangerous snow-laden heights of the Swiss Alps. There they were bred and trained to this specific chore by the Monks of the Hospice of Saint Bernard. The dogs have an impressive record for rescuing travelers trapped by snow and storm in the St. Bernard Pass. The breed almost became extinct due to a distemper epidemic, but was rejuvenated by crossing into other breeds (notably the Newfoundland and Great Pyrenees). These crosses brought a heavier coat to the breed and today we have the original smooth-coated Saint as well as the rough-coated dog. Medium-large in height but with a huge head, extremely heavy bone structure and very broad throughout, the Saint is one of the heaviest of all breeds. They have a frequent habit of drooling. If a Saint is your choice for a pet, be certain you select from a strain with good temperament. I have judged many who have dispositions a lot less than desirable.

From Siberia's icy wastes comes the *Samoyed,* as snow white as the area of its origin. The Sammy is another of the related Spitz-type Northern sled dogs. Its early ancestors herded caribou and were guards, sled dogs, and household companions to the ancient Samoyed peoples, Sayantsi primitives in the transitional stage between Mongol and Finn. A typical Northern sled dog in type and coat, the Samoyed is good-natured and makes a fine family pet. It has no doggy odor.

A collie in miniature is the *Shetland Sheepdog.* It is a native of the small Shetland Islands where they have small Shetland Ponies, small Shetland sheep, and the small Shetland Sheepdog to herd them. I am happy to report that the people on the island are of normal size. Intelligent, alert, dainty, and agile, these heavily coated little canines make wonderful pets and house dogs. Their coats, of course, need the same rather constant attention you would accord to a collie's coat.

The *Siberian Husky* is a typical Arctic sled dog, smaller and more refined in bone than the malamute. This is the breed generally used in sled racing where the records they have made, despite adverse weather conditions at times, are truly amazing. A thick, soft coat of all colors (with various shades of wolf and silver grays most popular) and an easy reaching (extended) gait are typical of the breed. Frequently the Siberian displays the white or "watch" eyes (both, or one "watch" the other brown). The huskies' handy size, hardiness, and gentle disposition make them fine pets and companions.

Of the three breed sizes, the *Standard Schnauzer* is the prototype dog, an old, basic German breed. Actually the Schnauzer is a terrier in type, used in Germany as a ratter and, therefore, is essentially in the wrong group here. But he is also a good guard dog and companion, facts which give him access to the working group. A strong, square, wire-coated dog of under medium size, his ears are cropped and erect and the tail is docked short. Coat colors are pepper-and-salt and solid black. He is a rather high-spirited dog, but reliable.

The *Welsh corgis,* both *Cardigan* and *Pembroke,* were both bred for the same purpose: cattle drovers and companions. They differ only slightly in type and are similar to breeds of like purpose that are not AKC recognized but which can be found scattered throughout the world. The coats of both Pembroke and Cardigan are dense and medium short. The Cardigan has a long plumed tail and erect ears rounded at the tips, while the Pembroke has a stub tail and pointed ears. The latter variety has generally better type and has a more compact and balanced body. Both varieties are intelligent and make good house and pet dogs.

The Terrier Group

The Latin *terra* means earth, and from that the scrappy, intelligent, courageous canines of the Terrier group have borrowed their basic name. It fits them as does the harsh, wiry coat most of them wear. They came into being and were bred—most of them—in the British Isles, to "go to earth," for their prey are the vast scope of "vermin" or burrowing creatures from voles to foxes. In yet another sense the Latin *terra* can be applied to these plucky tykes, for they are truly earthy creatures that in an earlier day were the only breeds the peasants and common people were allowed to own. Now the many breeds of terriers are plucked, trimmed, and beautified to meet specific standards in the show ring, but underneath the sophisticated veneer they remain feisty, bright-eyed, nervy rascals.

The largest of the terriers is the *Airedale,* one of the best all-purpose breeds in the world. The Airedale is large enough to be effective as a police dog, is a fine big-game hunting breed, a fine water dog, guide for the blind, watch- and house dog. The black and tan wirehaired coat is weather-resistant and he makes the best of companions indoors or out.

From Down Under comes the *Australian terrier,* a small, rather quiet but courageous little fellow who is a wonderful family dog. Erect ears, a whimsical expression, and a harsh tan coat, most often with silver-black or blue-black on the body. Longer than he is high, his tail is three-fifths cropped. The Australian terrier is one of the few terrier breeds not of British origin and is very popular in South America where I have recently been judging.

The *Bedlington terrier* may look like a lamb, but it has the courage of a lion. Like most terriers it is a "varmint" dog, but in its earlier days the Bedlington was used as a pit, or fighting, dog. The coat is rather linty in quality, the tail ratlike, the roached back strong and the mincing gait precise. Colors can be blue, very pale blue, blue and tan, liver and tan, sandy (sometimes with tan), but generally the Bedlington appears to be colored pale gray or just off white. This terrier makes an unusual-looking but excellent pet.

A very old breed the *Border Terrier* will go to ground for fox, otter, or the most savage badger. The wiry coat is waterproof and the stern (tail) is moderately short. Hardy, intelligent, this little 15½-pound terrier is all "guts." Colors are red, blue and tan, grizzle and tan, or wheaten. A good-natured, perky little pet.

The "White Cavalier" was the title bestowed upon the *Bull Terrier* in those days of England's past when the "gentlemen" (the "Bucks" and "Corinthians") wagered heavily on their fighting dogs and the bull terrier was the pit dog supreme. The breed was developed to greater grace and refinement and celebrated in the Richard Harding Davis story, "The Bar Sinister." Despite its early usage, the bullterrier is a friendly breed, but still retains a lack of sensitivity to pain or hurt. Some time ago I painted an oil portrait of the great bitch, Ch. Madame Pompadour of Ernicor, for her owner, breeder Ernest Eberhard, and was fascinated by the bitch's beautifully sculptured musculature. For its size and weight this is one of the most powerful of canines. The breed is pure white, but there is also an accepted colored version that shares exactly the same standard except that it can be any color other than white but must exhibit limited white markings.

The little wire-coated *Cairn terrier* of Scotland was used for fox bolting or worrying the fox from its burrow into the open to face the crofter's gun. The cairn is the smallest of the working terriers, but it is all heart. It is a natural retriever and water dog and will go to ground for any kind of game. It is alert and makes a good watchdog, has small pointed ears, a moderately short tail, and a rather unkempt appearance. It can be any solid color but white.

The *Dandie Dinmont Terrier* is an odd-looking animal, proportionately large in the head, long in body, short in legs (particularly in front), sporting a topknot and a crisp wire coat. The Dandie is generally a rather stubborn little cuss, a fact belied by his big, round, hazel eyes. Coat colors range from lightest to darkest pepper and mustard.

The most familiar of all terriers is the *Fox Terrier*. Handsome, flashy, swaggering, and intelligent, in both the smooth and wire coats, these little dogs are the epitome of the show terrier. Masters of fox-hunt packs bred these courageous little fellows to go to ground and drive the fox from its hole. Smooths in my youth were always seen in circus and vaudeville dog acts. Smart-looking and smart mentally, they make excellent pets, house dogs and alert watchdogs. The wirehaired type needs plucking and grooming to look swank.

The *Irish Terrier* is a game and vivacious solid-colored fellow, wearing a dense wiry coat in red or golden and wheaten red. Up to 27 pounds in weight, the scrappy Irishman is longer in leg and body than the Wire-Haired Fox Terrier. Game, rugged, but affectionate, he offers loyalty and devotion to those he loves.

Also from Ireland comes the *Kerry Blue Terrier,* used on his native heath for hunting small game and birds. Good retrievers and water dogs, they have also been known to be trained to work cattle. The Kerry is playful and friendly with a soft, dense and wavy coat. He is aggressive with other dogs and can hold his own against the best of them, for he is a powerful animal up to 40 pounds in weight with solid, tough muscle.

Born black, the color gradually clears until, when eighteen months of age, the Kerry has attained its adult gray-blue color.

Scrappy and dead game the *Lakeland Terrier* from Cumberland is a handsome, cobby little fellow approximately the size of a Wirehaired Terrier and possessing a rather coarse wiry coat of its own. The coat color is a light wheaten or straw color with blue, gray, black, grizzle, or liver saddle. Gay, friendly, and cocky, the Lakeland makes a good pet.

The *Manchester Terrier* is a modernized version of the old Black and Tan Terrier. These are game vermin dogs that, in an earlier day, were rather quick-tempered and prone to snap when annoyed. Now this unwanted characteristic has been selected against and has been gradually bred out. A dwarf or toy type appeared occasionally in Manchester litters and caught the fancy of some breeders with the result that they were selected for, bred together, and became the Toy Manchester, an exact but tiny replica of the normal-sized Manchester. Smooth-coated in rich black and tan, the head is long and narrow, ears erect and sometimes cropped. The standard variety can weigh up to 22 pounds (but not more), and the Toy Manchester weighs in at between 7 to 12 pounds.

The smallest of the *Schnauzers, the miniature* is, like the standard and giant Schnauzers, of German origin. It is one of the few AKC recognized terriers that did not originate in the British Isles, but was formed by breeding the little Affenpinschers into standard Schnauzer lines, thus combining a toy and a working breed to beget a Terrier. This handsome little tyke is all terrier: sturdy, alert, and active. Cropped ears, a short, cobby body and lots of spunk are characteristics of the breed. They make an intelligent and peppy pet in their wiry salt-and-pepper, black-and-silver, or solid black coats.

The *Norwich Terrier* was selected by the students at Cambridge University, England, in 1880 as the school's mascot. Small but tough and an easy keeper, this is a typical no-nonsense terrier. Rather short in the leg, sporting a hard wiry coat in red, wheaten, black and tan, or grizzle, with an ideal weight of 11 pounds, the Norwich is low, cobby, active, and lovable.

The stout-hearted *Scottish Terrier* has been a favorite over the years. Whimsical, affectionate, and wonderful with children, his courage has earned him the soubriquet, "die-hard." Low-stationed, bewhiskered, with small erect ears and an uncut but short tail, the Scottie wears a wiry coat in iron gray, black, brindle or grizzle, sandy or wheaten. For his size he has heavy bones, is deep in the chest, and up to 22 pounds in weight. This is one of the finest of the terrier breeds.

Sturdy and heavy in substance, the *Sealyham Terrier* is a solid animal, big and strong enough to go to ground for any game. A handmade breed, the Sealyham's low-to-the-ground body carries up to 21 pounds of weight, with short legs but a long skull matching the length of body and a long, powerful, punishing jaw. The breed was developed during the latter part of the nineteenth century by a Captain John Edwardes in Wales and was fashioned for quarrying fox, badger, and otter. The ears hang naturally and the wiry coat comes in all white or with lemon, tan, or badger mirkings on the head and ears. This is a keen, spunky terrier that makes a good companion.

From the Isle of Skye comes the *Skye Terrier*—of very old lineage. Two types were early developed, one with pendant and the other with upright ears. Certainly a canine of odd appearance, its long flowing coat masks the whole body and in movement gives the Skye the appearance of being on wheels. This is a popular breed with all who know him well, for he is alert, dignified, and has an overabundance of courage and character. Long in body and low (approximately 10 inches at the shoulder), he is twice as long as he is high and the hair on his ears floats downward like a waterfall from a central part on the skull and covers the eyes. In color this unique breed is usually seen in dark or light blue, black, gray, fawn, or cream.

The *Soft-Coated Wheaten Terrier* comes to us from Ireland where it fits the category of "sporting" terrier. Loose hairs are caught in the coat so it has the reputation of not shedding. It has no odor, boasts its partisans, and is never noisy. The Wheaten is an old breed in Ireland and was earlier used as the genetic basis for the Kerry Blue and the Irish Terrier. The A.K.C. standard calls for a "hardy, well-balanced sporting terrier covered abundantly with a soft, naturally wavy coat of a good clear wheaten color . . ." Male Wheatens measure 18 to 19 inches at the withers and weigh approximately 35 to 45 pounds, with bitches a bit smaller and lighter. American-bred Wheatens wear a more abundant, straighter coat than their Irish cousins. Puppies are born a dark sable brown and lighten gradually to the true wheaten color when they are a year-and-a-half to two-years old. In all physical features the Wheaten is a moderate dog. As a pet and companion the breed is difficult to surpass.

The *Staffordshire Terrier* is that old and most courageous of breeds, known to dog people earlier in the century as the pit bullterrier. Despite his fancy new name, he is still the toughest, gamest fighting dog ever bred. Like the closely related bullterrier, the Staff is notably insensitive to pain. There is a breed from Staffordshire, England, called the Staffordshire bullterrier that is similar to this breed but slightly smaller. The Staff comes in all colors, but all white or with more than 80 percent white, black and tan, and liver not encouraged.

The *Welsh Terrier* is very much like the Lakeland but slightly larger, and in its black and tan or black, grizzle, and tan coat it could be easily likened to a small Airedale. The Welsh makes a fine house dog and is an easy keeper.

Another terrier from Scotland, the *West Highland White,* is a small trappy and game little tyke in a pure white, rough double coat. About 11 inches at the shoulder, the Westie is a typical terrier in appearance with small, erect, pointed ears. A game but friendly fellow, the Westie makes a very desirable pet.

There is less divergence in the appearance of many of the breeds in the Terrier Group than in those of any of the other groups. And even if there were wider physical differences, the basic typical verve and feisty cockiness of all terriers would advertise their kinship.

The Toy Breeds

The tiny toys of the canine race fill a very real need in our modern culture as companions of the many lonely people who dwell in city apartments and who need something living to love and who themselves need to be loved in return. Blessed with a sturdiness and intelligence not lessened by their small stature, the toy breeds number among their many virtues the pluck and fearlessness worthy of some huge creature of heroic size and fearsome mien.

These little dogs, the toys, prove that items of great value can be wrapped in small packages.

In Germany the name *Affenpinscher* means "monkey terrier" and this toy dog does look somewhat like a monkey but is undoubtedly of basic terrier stock. The breed was useful in helping to fashion the Miniature Schnauzer of the terrier group and is said to have been a progenitor of the Brussels Griffon. The Affenpinscher is sturdy, fearless, and generally quiet. Ears are erect and cropped to a point and the tail is docked. The coat is shaggy and wiry and lends the dog the overall appearance of an unmade bed. Dark, solid colors are most desirable.

The *Chihuahua* epitomizes the toy breeds and is of ancient and singular Mexican heritage. The Chi is indebted for his genetic qualities to the "Techichi" ichi dog, an archaic breed favored by the Toltecs, a race of Indians of rather advanced civilization who were eventually conquered by the warlike Aztecs. The little dog soon gained importance as part of the mystical religious ceremonies and strange mythology of the Aztecs.

The Chi should be well-balanced, alert, quick, compact and saucy. He has erect ears and wears two coats, one smooth and the other long, the latter of soft texture. This 2- to 6-pound toy comes in several colors.

The *English Toy Spaniel,* called the "Comforter" in an earlier time, embraces four color phases, each with a name of its own. The King Charles is black and tan; the Ruby a solid, rich chestnut; the Blenheim red and white; and the Prince Charles is tri-colored in white, black, and tan. All varieties must conform to the single English Toy Spaniel standard. Of ancient origin, the breed was once a sporting spaniel, but selection for small size, cuteness, and pet qualities by the aristocratic fanciers of the breed made of it a "sleeve" or toy dog of from 9 to 12 pounds. The term "sleeve" dog was invented by the Chinese. It referred to a dog small enough to be carried inside the voluminous sleeves typical of the Oriental costume.

Bewhiskered, bizarre, intelligent is the little *Brussels Griffon.* There are three toy Griffons in all: the wirehaired Brussels, the smooth-coated Brabancon and the Belgium. The wirehaired Brussel's coat can be various shades of reddish brown and black, or solid black. The smooth-coated Brabancon wears the same colors, but solid black is taboo. Here is 8 to 10 pounds of a sturdy little terrier-like dog with cropped ears, a stubbed tail, big eyes, and a whiskery muzzle that gives the little sprout a fairly fey appearance.

The slim *Italian Greyhound* is a toy greyhound that has been bred over two thousand years as a pet. Graceful and elegant, there are two weight classes, one up to 8 pounds, the other over 8 pounds. The smaller size is preferred.

A dainty, smart, heavily coated toy, the *Japanese Spaniel* is actually of Chinese origin. Strictly a pet, he is pert, bright, and sensitive. The smaller this little tyke is the better, with normal size averaging about 7 pounds. His coat is silky, profuse, and parti-colored in black and white or red and white.

The tiny *Maltese*—from the island of Malta—is completely enveloped in long, silky, pure white hair that is parted along the back and falls to the floor on either side of the body. The plumed tail is carried up and over the croup and the profuse head hair is generally tied up into two topknots on either side of the central head part. This trustful, lively, but gentle little fellow weighs from 4 to 5 pounds. The coat takes a good deal of care, cleaning, and grooming.

The *Toy Manchester* is a miniature version of its larger brother in the terrier group. See page 199.

The "Butterfly Dog," the pretty *Papillon,* was brought to breed perfection in both France and Belgium. There is a drop-eared variety on the Continent called the "Phalene." A fine-boned true toy, the Papillon is gentle, dainty, and wears a silken coat in parti- or tri-color, white and black, white and sable, white and red or, in the black, white and tan tri-color. The erect ears with their full fringe of hair have the appearance of a butterfly (if you can imagine a hairy butterfly), hence the cognomen "Butterfly Dog."

Ancient dynasties of China celebrated the *Pekingese* as the pet dog supreme. "Lion Dog" was another name used to denote the fantastic courage and combativeness of these heavily coated toys. A massive skull with a very short, broad muzzle, heavy in the chest, medium long in body, bowed forelegs, and an over-the-back tail with profuse feathering describes the Peke.

The Miniature Pinscher should be as much like a very tiny replica of a Doberman pinscher as possible. Slick, sleek, stylish, these clean-cut little dogs are intelligent, alert house dogs and pets, interested in all that takes place in the world around them. The mini-pinscher ranges in weight from 6 to 10 pounds and should be clad in the typical Doberman black and tan, brown or chocolate, or solid red. An easy-to-care-for breed.

With basic wolf-spitz progenitors, the *Pomeranian* has been reduced over the centuries to toy-dog size. It is a compact breed, perky, intelligent and vivacious with a foxy face, the expression aided by upright ears. It has an abundant but fine-haired coat, and the profusely haired tail is held over the back. The breed weight is arbitrarily divided over and under 7 pounds. Practically all colors are permissible, but blacks, browns, blues, and sables must be self-colored and free of white.

The *Toy Poodle* is judged by the same standard as his larger kin, the miniature and the standard. The only difference is in size, accomplished through the introduction of the genetic smallness of the Maltese into lines that produced small Miniatures. See Miniature and Standard Poodles (p. 207).

Once one of the most popular breeds, the *pug* is still a favorite because of his fine qualities. Sturdy and strong, he needs no pampering and his intelligence and no-nonsense attitude is refreshing among toys. Of basic Oriental origin, seamen on Dutch trading vessels brought the pug to Holland from which the breed spread throughout the world. Short-necked, with a pushed-in deeply wrinkled "pug" foreface and rounded, solid skull, these dogs weigh up to 18 pounds and are either colored silver or apricot fawn with a black mask, or are completely black.

From Australia comes the *Silky Terrier*—of terrier type but actually a small house dog that was bred in the city of Sydney as a companion. It is a spunky, smart, low-set, lightly made toy with erect ears, and a medium-long silky coat. The hair on the head is so profuse that it forms a topknot. On the body the coat is parted down the center of the back and colored tan and blue. Silkies can weigh up to 10 pounds and are friendly, lovely pets.

Translated from the Chinese, *Shih Tzu* means "Tibetan Lion Dog," I have been told. These droll, long-haired little toys make absolutely wonderful pets. They are intelligent and quiet and have been described as being, "neither a terrier nor a toy dog." Actually in character and personality they are like a much larger breed. Their wise little pushed-in faces have a distinct charm (and remind me of a shrunken human head). They are arrayed in many single colors and interesting combinations of colors and can weigh up to 18 pounds.

The *Yorkshire terrier* is a modern breed, conceived in England where many of the small native terriers were merged, the specific type judiciously selected from, and the result was the Yorkie. To the Yorkshire as to the toy poodle, genetic smallness was supplied the breed by the Maltese. The Yorkie's straight, silken tresses sweep the ground and tiny colored ribbons hold its head-fall in place. The ears are pricked, the heavily haired tail cropped to medium length, and the glossy coat is dark steel blue from the back of the skull to the tail root, framed by soft tan on all other areas. This is a compact, vigorous little toy dog.

Non-sporting Dogs

Many of the breeds catalogued in this group were canines of specific service before being relegated to a rather meaningless existence in a group that has no true prestige. These are not simply non-sporting dogs, they are also non-working, non-terrier, non-hound, and non-toy dogs. Yet in this category are breeds of character and distinction that are capable of performing many jobs, but are particularly fitted to perform the most noble chore of all—to be just a friend, companion, and confidant of man.

The *Bichon Frises,* rather newly accepted in the AKC family of breeds, were derived from the Maltese in about the fifteenth century. The name, "Bichon" was evidently adopted from "Barbichon" because of the breed's hair quality, which is long and curly like "the coat of a Mongolian goat." All white coloring is preferred and black is a disqualification. Occasionally one finds a bit of tan or gray on the ears. Small but outgoing, the Bichon should exhibit an arrogant, feisty stance.

One of the few native American breeds, the *Boston Terrier* was molded in Massachusetts by controlled crossing of selected bulldogs to the white English terrier. These are smooth-coated, sturdy, short-headed, short-tailed (straight or screw), well-balanced dogs with flashy markings and erect, generally cropped ears. Classes are lightweight—under 15 pounds; middleweight—over 15 and under 20 pounds; heavyweight— over 20 but not exceeding 25 pounds. The ideal color is dark brindle with flashy white trim. Many years ago, when the breed was comparatively young, my dad bred Boston terriers and they were fine, scrappy tykes, muscularly as hard as nails. The breed, through character and bearing, should be in the terrier group.

The *Bulldog* is a prime example of what can happen when a breed used for a particular purpose is pushed through selection to an outer extreme. The ancestor of the modern bulldog was of the old Bullenbeiser breed, used for bull and bear baiting and pit fighting. A rather squat, powerful body was needed as was a pushed-in nose and undershot jaw so that the animal could get a lethal, full-mouthed grip, hang on, and be able to breathe without disturbing the ferocious bite. English breeders, after the era of animal baiting and fighting had passed, bred for extremes of the earlier wanted virtues and the Bulldog is the result. Homely, swaggering like a drunken sailor, the "Sourmug" is a lovable, courageous and (belying his appearance) a sweet companion and pet.

Another native of China, the *Chow Chow,* is evidently of basic sled-dog inheritance and is said to be a good hunting dog. The breed is known in America for its guarding ability and they make excellent watchdogs. The Chow has a distinctly Oriental expression that mirrors its characteristic aloofness with strangers. The head is large and massive with deep-set eyes and a short, broad muzzle. The body is powerful and cobby with extremely heavy bone. Small, rounded upright ears, a blue-black tongue, and a thick stand-off coat in any solid color describes this Chinese gentleman.

The black or liver-spotted *Dalmatian* comes from Dalmatia a province of Austria. In the hands of the nomad European gypsies the breed was accredited with many nationalities and names. In America the Dalmatian has become known as the coach dog and sometimes the fire-house dog. The Dal is a strong, muscular, active dog and its rapport with horses and stables has led to its prominence as a carriage dog. The breed is sometimes a target for liver anomalies. The Dalmatian is an easy keeper and a fine house, family and watchdog as well as being the carriage dog supreme. His striking coloration identifies him from afar.

Small, compact, heavy-boned, the *French bulldog* has erect bat ears and true bulldog strength and muscularity. Fashioned by French breeders from the toy bulldogs of English lace workers who migrated to Normandy for jobs, the distinctive skull and ears that are the hallmark of the Frenchie were molded specifically. Clever and intelligent, he makes an easy-to-care-for house dog, weighing from 22 to 28 pounds and wears a short coat that should be fawn, brindle, white, and brindle and white.

The *Keeshond,* also called the Dutch Barge Dog, was closely associated with the political Patriots in their struggle against the partisans of the Prince of Orange. The breed thus became a living symbol of the philosophy and needs of the common man, a dog of the people. Though brought to prominence at that time of social unrest, the breed had been a Dutch favorite for hundreds of years preceding the latter part of the eighteenth century. Fine pets and house dogs for home or barge they specialize in companionship. Sturdy, compact, hard of flesh, they look quite like a somewhat smaller, foxier-faced edition of the Norwegian Elkhound.

Mysterious Tibet is the birthplace of the *Lhasa Apso,* named in its native country the "Bark Lion Sentinel Dog," which leads one to the conclusion that the language of Tibet is rather strange. The Lhasa is a house dog and companion, up to 11 inches high at the shoulder. Longer than he is tall he wears a heavy, straight coat in golden, sandy, honey, dark grizzle, slate smoke, parti-color, black, white or brown, with golden and tan colors preferred. Darker tips are wanted on the ears and the rather long beard. The hair falls over the eyes and the tail plumes fully over the back. These are gay, easily trained, fine pets, wearing the face of some ancient llama.

The *Poodles* (all three sizes) are the most popular dogs in the United States today. They are gay, active, highly intelligent, and easily trained to do many tasks and do them well. Basically poodles are closely linked to the sporting breeds and in some parts of the world are still used to retrieve water fowl to the gun. Beginning with the largest and most impressive of the three sizes, the standard is over 15 inches at the withers (some I have seen go as tall as 26 inches and more); miniature, over 10 inches and up to 15 inches (both standard and miniature are in the Non-Sporting Group); toy poodle, 10 inches and under. The show standard is similar for all three sizes. The tail is docked but not too short; the head is long, elegant, and well-chiseled; the body should be square and well-muscled. Heavy bone is to be avoided. The dense, profuse coat can be trimmed in any of a number of clips but for exhibition only the "puppy," "continental," and "English Saddle Clip" are acceptable. Any solid color is permissible, but black, white, and silver are favorites. Other colors are chocolate, blue, cream, apricot, champagne, et cetera. The poodle is a fine breed that well deserves its popularity. At the National Show in Bogota, I put a gorgeous black standard bitch to Best in Show and if any dog ever deserved this honor, she certainly did. The care and clipping of a poodle's coat is time-consuming or expensive, depending on whether you do the barbering yourself or have it done for you. The two mature clips are not just effete designs; they were fashioned to protect the joints of water dogs from chill when working in cold water.

In Flemish, *Schipperke* means "Little Skipper," an appropriate name for these black, tailless Belgian barge dogs. Compact, foxy-looking, with erect ears and bright eyes, this is a sharp and lively little fellow that serves as a splendid watchdog and an expert hunter of vermin. The "Skip" can weigh up to 18 pounds and is short, cobby, and well-balanced.

A small breed, the *Tibetan Terrier* is similar to the Lhasa Apso and has been carefully bred in remote Tibet for hundreds of years. These dogs are square and compact with a profuse coat. They can weigh from 18 to 30 pounds. Almost any color is acceptable except chocolate. The heavily feathered tail sometimes has a kink close to the tip. In recent years it seems that there have been quite a few breeds from Tibet added to the roster of acceptable AKC canines. That ancient land of immense silences and snow-laden soaring peaks must indeed be a bow-wow Shangri-la.

Miscellaneous Class

Here we find breeds that are "on trial" so to speak, breeds that have strong sponsorship and may become popular enough to be advanced to recognized status. These breeds can be shown in this class, but are not eligible for points toward an AKC championship, nor can they compete in the variety groups. In other words they may knock at the door, but with no guarantee that the door will open and allow them to enter. This applies only to the United States (including Puerto Rico) where the American Kennel Club is dogdom's governing body. In the rest of the world where canines are bred and registered, and dog shows or exhibitions take place, the Federation Cynologique Internationale (FCI) is the established governing association. Under the jurisdiction of the FCI, the breeds in our Miscellaneous Class—and many more important and worthwhile breeds, not known in the United States, but popular in other parts of the world—are officially recognized and exhibited internationally.*

In Australia several interesting breeds of cattle and sheep dogs have come into being, two of which are listed in our AKC Miscellaneous Class at the moment (*Australian Cattle Dogs* and *Australian Kelpies*). The *Australian shepherd* has become as popular in California as in its native country. Of old-fashioned collie type and coat with blue-merle and white trim preferred in color, the breed often exhibits opaque or

* Editor's Note: Mr. Hart is licensed by the FCI to judge all breeds of dogs throughout the world, and is also a Specialty judge under AKC sanction.

"watcheyes." These sagacious canines are natural guardians and possess a strong, inbred herding instinct. The *Australian Heeler,* weighing about 35 pounds, is a fine cattle and drover dog. Bred from a kelpie-collie-dingo-Dalmatian blending, the short, harsh coat shows a merling or flecking of blue and red. The Australian Kelpie is a working sheep-herding dog bred to type since 1865. It was molded by judicious breeding of small collies (brought to Down Under by Scotch settlers) with the dingo (the native wild dog). The *Barb* is a second kelpie type bred up to 55 pounds in weight and solid black in color. The *Standard Kelpie* is short-coated, weighs about 30 pounds, has erect ears and generally a docked tail. Accepted colors are black and tan, red, chocolate, slate, red and tan, and blue and fawn.

Bearded Collies are the third coat type found in Collies and mentioned in the discussion on Collies. See Working Dogs, Collies, p. 190.

The *border collie* (in the Miscellaneous Class) and the *English shepherd* are much alike in conformation and working ability. Both are superb sheep-herding dogs and have changed little in type from the ancient Roman sheep-herding canines that were their ancestors. The greatest difference between the border and English is in coat color, the English shepherd wearing black and tan with markings akin to a Rottweiler and the border sporting colors similar to those associated with Collies.

The *Cavalier King Charles Spaniel,* a favored pet in England, is a slightly larger and racier edition of the English Toy spaniel. Both breeds share the same coat colors, but the King Charles has a more elongated foreface and a coat more like the larger spaniels. Clean, quiet, but game, these little tykes make fine pets. Tail docking is optional and weight is from 8 to 10 pounds.

The *Ibizan Hound* is found in the Balearic Islands and is a tall, lithe, active canine in the sight hound category. In appearance these large, racy dogs are like prick-eared greyhounds. Red and white are the preferred colors.

Practically a reflection of the normal bullterrier, the *Miniature Bullterrier* loses only in size to his bigger brother. At 14 inches in height and a weight limit of 20 pounds, he shares all the characteristics of the larger bullterrier (see under Terriers, p. 197).

Looking for breed notice in the States, the *Spinone Italiano,* is a staunch, tough, all-purpose gundog that is a descendant of the Spanish pointer and long established in Italy. The Spinone quarters well and is easy to hunt behind. Height up to 24 inches, weight to 75 pounds, he is rather coarse when compared to the normal concept of a pointer and wears a short, wiry coat. In color, the Spinone runs the gamut of pointer and spaniel shades.

This ends the breeds that have achieved, fully or in part, AKC recognition. But there are many unique, interesting and utilitarian breeds in other lands that are available and must be given at least token notice here.

The Mexican *Xoloizcuintle* (yes, the spelling is correct. Ask any old Aztec), hairless dogs that have been used as watchdogs, heating pads (for arthritis and bone aches by the Indians), and as food animals, must be included among these breeds. Some of these dogs still run wild in tropical areas of Mexico. The *Anatolian Sheepdog* is well known in Asia Minor. The *Chinese Fighting Dog* looks somewhat like a very wrinkled and swollen Staffordshire with a ring tail and a weight of about 50 pounds—unique but hideous. The *Eskimo*—once given full AKC recognition but dropped because of a lack of enthusiasm for the breed—is 85 pounds of wolflike power. The *Leonberger* and *Hovawart* of Germany indicate in size and type their Newfoundland and St. Bernard background. The *Toy Fox Terrier,* like the *Spitz* (now called the American Eskimo) are both American-inspired breeds that have been around a long time and have their staunch adherents. The *Dog of Canaan* (as old as Jerusalem) and the scrappy little *Jack Russell Terrier* are two very worthwhile breeds.

The *Pharaoh hound* is a prick-eared greyhound of ancient heritage; a fairly new breed is the *Dogo Argentina,* manufactured from many breeds. These canines look like large, coarse white bullterriers. They are guard dogs, house dogs, and guides for the blind; they are usually white in color. The huge, 130-pound *Tibetan mastiff* more than any other breed mirrors the archaic prototype mastiff. A ferocious watch-and guard dog, the *Italian mastiff* is huge, ungainly, and often found in the favored solid blue color. Portugal has canines in every category of usage, including a *water dog* that seems to share ancestry with the standard poodle; a huge and massive *sheep dog;* a large *cattle dog;* and the *Portuguese Podengos*—hunting and companion dogs that come in three sizes, large, medium, and small. France has developed and refined several scent-hound breeds. In fact most countries have over the years bred and refined their own greyhounds, sheep and herding dogs, spaniels, hounds, pointing breeds, guard dogs, water dogs, small house or toy dogs, and Spitz breeds of various sizes that are related to the Northern sled dogs.

The breeds I have mentioned by name are just a few of the canines native to other climes and countries that I have had the pleasure of judging in dog shows in various parts of the world. Such breeds are extremely interesting to people who are dog-conscious and whose lives have, to some extent, been touched by the dog hobby.

Wild Canines

Wolves, wild dogs, coyotes, jackals, and foxes comprise this group that is well distributed throughout the world. As man lives as a contemporary of the existing primates that shared his origin so the domesticated dog has a parallel existence with the wild canines that came from the same root stock. All animal families attain a frontier where the physiological possibilities are exhausted and when no other variation in any direction is feasible. They have reached a zenith in their evolutionary process. This is the point arrived at now by practically all creatures on earth except, perhaps, man. When this happens, the germ plasm remains static, without change unless mutations develop or a drastic and sudden change occurs in environment, leaving the living organism the choice of changing to fit the new environment if it can—or to succumb.

The germ plasm of early ancestors of man, over a period of millions of years, utilized the ability for change in our species both physically and mentally, for in this area man is unique. Biological evolution gave way to cultural evolution and, because of the growth capacity of man's mental aptitudes and social and cultural attitudes, there seems no end to his possible evolutionary expansion. Due to early man's interest in the contemporary canines, the evolution of many canine breeds was accomplished from the basic feral—and evolutionarily static—stock. Man intervened and accomplished this reversal of natural process through selection for forms and features that fitted his desires. Our ancestors took the living canine flesh and played God, changing and moving canine evolution in various directions resulting in such varied forms as the Great Dane and the tiny Chihuahua, the bulldog, the dachshund, and the greyhound, until it seems almost impossible that these man-made breeds and the wild canines should have shared the same mammalian source, yet they did.

WILD DOGS

Of the true wild dogs there are few that can be domesticated and earn the title of pet. The *Malay wild dogs* or *Asiatic dholes* are certainly not in this category. Actually, though they appear to be canines, they have a different evolution and are quite beyond taming. Of the New World wild canines the *round-eared, Azara's dog,* and the *bush dog* are indigenous to South America and not good pet material under any circumstances. The large *Cape hunting dogs* of Africa are pack hunters that have huge erect ears and harlequin markings on dark gray or olive-colored coats. At a distance they have somewhat the appearance of a hyena. I was told in Africa that, if captured when tiny pups, they become quite tame and act like domesticated dogs.

There are a number of *jackals* in Africa, India, and Asia that look like the larger wild dogs of South America. They generally do not lend themselves readily to domestication.

Japan boasts a small, gray, wild dog that resembles a raccoon and is understandably labeled the *raccoon-like dog.* It is not true that this animal is a less expensive Japanese copy of a fine wild German dog. The raccoon-like dog is said to have been domesticated occasionally.

The *dingo,* Australia's wild dog, was brought to the Island Continent by the early Aborigines (as a domesticated breed, it is thought), and was subsequently allowed to return to the wild. They are the only species of mammalian carnivores in Australia. Reddish to yellow with erect ears, the dingo has been used with domesticated dog breeds to produce some of the native utilitarian canines. If acquired when young, dingoes can be satisfactorily tamed.

FOXES

Foxes are well distributed throughout the world. In North America alone there are over two dozen distinct species. Similar in general form, they vary in size, head shape, color, and ear length, those living in hot climates developing huge ears as vehicles for the loss of body heat. Some species bear coats of great value.

Mutations in the coat color of the common *red fox* of North America have given rise to fox farms where variations designated as the cross fox, silver fox, and black fox are scientifically bred for their pelts. The *gray fox* is also a common form throughout the United States. The *Arctic fox,* indulging in protective coloration, turns white during the

Arctic winter. It also has a blue phase and blue pelts are valuable furs. There are desert species such as the kit fox, and African, South American, and European species of foxes. Unlike wolves, all foxes are solitary

The tiny fennec fox (Fennecus zerda) *from the desert areas of Africa and the Middle East is much sought after as a unique pet.*

hunters, living mainly on small animals and birds. If taken when very young, they can be tamed and as cubs are delightfully playful. When mature, however, they do not all make satisfactory pets.

The species of fox that makes the best pet is the tiny, delightful, huge-eared *fennec fox*. This lovely little creature is a native of Africa and the Middle East. In the wild state, it is a nocturnal hunter. The enormous thin delicate ears are covered with velvety hair, the coat color is reddish-tan, and the pert little inquisitive face is as dainty as the rest of the slim-legged, toylike creature. I have seen fennec foxes wearing jeweled collars—the pampered pets of women of wealth at resorts in France and Spain where the so-called Beautiful People play. The lovely little fennecs were the only truly Beautiful People in view.

WOLVES

Wolves are fascinating animals, particularly the huge *timber wolves* of North America. These are the most highly developed of all the wild canines. Throughout the world there are a number of species and sub-species, differing in habits, size, and coloring, but all are very intelligent and exceedingly adaptable. Wolves hunt in packs under a chosen pack leader and indulge in many social refinements of rank and general community organization. Wolves have been tamed and trained as sled-dog teams and those bred in captivity for generations and selected for temperament and docility have become occasional pets and companions. The character of the individual wolf is the key to its acceptance as pet material. *Coyotes* are lesser wolves and do not have the depth and dignity that make the wolf interesting. In captivity wolves learn to wag their tails and act very much like a domesticated dog. These wild canines have found their way into the folklore and legends of many peoples. To me, the wolf is—as he has been to the plains tribes of our American Indians—a stimulating and highly interesting creature.

With the wolf we reach the end of our discourse on canines. Dogs are truly the pet supreme. Through them we can reach out to new emotional experiences and, in the simple acts of feeding and catering to their needs, discover the pleasure of serving. Dogs have, over the centuries, served mankind in many capacities and I have found exciting moments of pure pleasure working with them. But perhaps the deepest satisfaction that I have realized is to just sit silently and relaxed with my dogs, feeling the wordless rapport that links us as our beings touch in quiet contentment, knowing that we belong to each other.

10

Cats

Felidae

The dictionary tells us that the cat is "a domesticated carnivore, *Felis domestica* (or *F. catus*), widely distributed in a number of breeds"—an extremely trite and uninteresting definition of one of the most fascinating creatures in the world.

Development of the Cat

Since prehistoric times cats (family *Felidae*) have been tamed and have lived with mankind. Those early felines were species of small wild cats, probably taken initially from the nest as tiny kittens, brought back to the caves of early man where they were raised as pets. Today's domestic cat is a descendant of the Cafer or bush cat (*Felis lybica*) of Africa, with a strong infusion of genetic factors from the European wild cat (*Felis sylvestris*).

Aloof, enigmatic, the cat is, like his ancestors and living wild relatives, a solitary silent hunter. Domestication has not changed the hereditary pattern of the feline. It remains (unlike the dog) a completely self-contained, independent creature. Animals are either solitary like the cat or social like the dog. Man differs from all other animals in that he is both solitary and social, displaying in this, as in other directions, his ability to adjust to his environment.

There is a mystique, an aura of alien aloofness, emanating from the cat that has, from the beginning, influenced man and caused him to think of the cat in a sphere of occult reference. A broadening of this philosophy is evident in the writings, sculpture, and frescoes left to us from ancient Egypt, the cradle of civilization. Egyptian priests found something unearthly in the cat, some kinship with their "Other World" of macabre deities. Thus the cat was imbued with religious significance and became sacred, personified in the cat-headed goddess, Bast. Some scholars have thought that the word "puss" is a corruption of the name of the goddess, but in all probability it is simply an onomatopoeic mimicking of the hissing sound made by cats. In that long ago time of the glory that was Egypt's cats reached true domestication and became an integral part of man's household.

Legend and fable became woven into the fabric of feline history, particularly in Persia, Asia, and among the Buddhist monks of Siam and Thailand, where, by selection, special breeds of cats were fashioned by the temple monks to become a part of the religious concept, viewed with veneration and awe by the common people. Certain breeds were held in such esteem that they could traditionally be owned only by the church or the aristocracy. In recent times in Asiatic lands, huge cats of breeds once pampered by the temple priests, but wild for many generations, have been reported prowling in the areas of ruined temples that the living jungle has reclaimed. It is not unusual for feral cats to grow much larger than the size they had reached under domestication, some attaining maximum dimensions of 45 inches and having a body weight of 30 pounds.

The conquering Romans brought the cat from Egypt to Europe. The same feline essence of "strangeness" that affected the peoples of Asia, the Orient, and the Middle East, caused abysmal fear in some Europeans, so they labeled the cat evil, a familiar of witches, warlocks, and sorcerers; a creature to be shunned as a symbol of Satan and black magic. Of course people of good common sense soon realized that cats had more important earthly traits to recommend them. There were found to be most expert as killers of vermin and so were engaged in granaries, grain and food shops, and on ships carrying vital food supplies. Soon they graduated from barn, shop, and ship to the home and there became firmly established as mousers and pets.

The Breeds of Cats

You have a choice of more than thirty breeds of domesticated felines to choose from. Some are long-haired, some short-haired. Most have long tails but not all of them do. Environment, the time you have for pet care, the role you want the cat to play in your life, and your esthetic values and needs are the essentials that must determine the right cat for you.

If you live in the country, you will want a self-reliant animal that you can allow to roam freely. He will keep your barns and storage areas free of rodents yet remain a delightful pet and companion. A grown feline adapts readily to this natural environment. A Maine coon cat or a domestic short-haired cat could be your choice of breeds for a country cat.

Should your abode be a city apartment, a kitten would be best for you, so that you can train him to live happily in the confinement of such an environment.

The long-haired cats are beautiful, but that lovely silky coat that is the essence of their beauty takes time to groom. If you do not have that time, or feel that other interests have priority on your time, select a short-haired cat for your pet.

Consider carefully the use you will make of your cat, the niche you wish it to fill, and select the breed accordingly. If you own a dog, do not be afraid to extend your menage by introducing a cat to the household. To borrow a few words from a friend who uses them to preface every argument, "Where is it written . . ." that a cat and dog cannot live together in harmony? It is people who fight like cats and dogs, not cats and dogs themselves.

The Popular Short-haired Breeds

The *domestic short-haired cat* is the one we generally refer to as the common or "just plain cat" feline. It has always been the most numerous and most favored of cats. Now, however, fanciers consider it a definite breed, have written a standard for it, and it appears under the category of domestic short-haired cat in shows throughout the country. A typical specimen is about 2½ feet long, including its 9-inch tail, with considerable variation in weight up to 21 pounds. Breeders tend to specialize in color types and you have your choice of smokes, silver tabbies, red tabbies, tortoiseshells, and blue-eyed whites.

The *Siamese cat* is the most popular of all the purebred cats. In ancient Siam, these lovely lithe creatures were bred by the temple monks and owned only by priests and the Oriental aristocracy of that archaic era. The svelte, sleek conformation, combined with a very striking color pattern, marks it as the most individualistic of breeds. The Siamese brings to the twentieth century the atmosphere of ancient Egypt when Pharaohs, fanned by giant Nubians, idly watched a thousand sweating slaves toil beneath the blazing sun building the great pyramids that were to be their shrines. The Siamese cat has almond-shaped eyes that are frequently crossed; the tail is often kinked toward its end.

Five color variations are recognized for the Siamese in the United States—the seal point, blue point, chocolate point, red point (a fairly new variety), and lilac or frost point. Siamese kittens are all born white with blue eyes, but, as they mature, their coat changes and the legs,

E·H·HART

*The Siamese cat is one of the most popular of all feline breeds.
This head portrait of a seal-point Siamese gives some indication of the mystique and sleek beauty of this cat.*

ears, tail, and muzzle darken to the point color, lending the breed the
color and markings that so uniquely identify it. There are three other
color-types of Siamese not as well known as the basic colors; the tortie
point, blue-cream point (both a variation that appeared in red-point
breeding), and the albino Siamese, a mutation in the seal-point color.

This fascinating and aristocratic breed has a very detailed standard that judges must follow closely in cat shows. The voice of the Siamese is quite individual. They have strong, distinctive personalities, are exceedingly trainable, and are affectionate pets and companions.

The *Manx cat* is born without even the semblance of a tail, and any Manx kitten that is born with even the shortest of stub tails is not eligible to be exhibited in competition. The lack of a tail as a balancing agent is compensated for by high, broad hindquarters and a peculiar gait that differs from that of other felines. The history of the breed is lost in the swirling fog of long-ago time, but it was evidently developed through selection of the tailless cats that inhabited the Isle of Man. The head of the Manx is large and rather square. The breed can be found in all the colors sported by the domestic short-haired cat.

Of ancient heritage, the *Abyssinian* probably has had a common Egyptian heritage with the Siamese. Unlike most cats, the Abyssinian seems to enjoy water and will spend hours playing with and in it, behavior that indicates descent from some archaic breed that lived close to water. The Abyssinian's distinctive pelt is brown and gray with a reddish undercoat; its guard hairs are ticked or agouti-striped. The overall color effect is of a ruddy brown or a lovely silver with black or brown markings. The eyes of this quiet feline are usually green, yellow, or hazel, and it speaks in a soft, bell-like voice. There is a red Abyssinian that combines reds, browns, and a bit of black into a soft hair harmony. This sensitive, intelligent, dignified breed makes a most excellent pet.

The *Burmese cat* shows evidence of a close genetic tie to the Siamese, which it resembles in both conformation and temperament. The body color is chocolate or a beautiful brown with seal points. Some specimens have solid brown coats without points and hazel eyes rather than the usual yellow, orange, or golden eyes. This is a very popular breed that makes a wonderful pet and companion.

The *Russian Blue* is a comparatively new breed on the cat horizon in the United States. Luckily the coat is blue and not red, or I am sure it would be less welcome and popular. The blue color is evidently a genetic dilution of black that had been selected for from mutations in the home of its origin, northern Russia. This breed is very popular in Scandinavia, the contrast of the plush evenly tinted rich blue pelt and brilliant green eyes being a satisfying combination to fanciers of Northern extraction. The Russian blue is undoubtedly a handsome cat. I saw a few very beautiful specimens in Moscow and Leningrad, and others of equal worth at cat shows here in the States.

The Long-haired Breeds

Long-haired felines are generally rather somnolent creatures and not as feisty as short-hairs. They need a lot of attention, the result of long generations of breeding strictly for beauty. Their coats must be groomed daily and of course they are not to be allowed the freedom of the woods or gardens where they can pick up burrs or mat their gorgeous coats. Not for the Persian the mundane pursuit of rodents. His lot is to rest on silken pillows, disdainfully demanding the homage due his aristocratic stature. Blue Persians have orange and amber eyes. There is also the lovely smoke variety and, the most magnificent of all felines, the silver Persian. The *Persian cat* is an extremely popular, beautiful, sophisticated breed that reflects the touch of master breeders and must conform to a very definite bench-show standard. The breed is said to have originated in Afghanistan, but it has reached its elite peak of perfection over the last two hundred years, both here and in England. The eyes of the Persian are deep copper or blue; occasionally an individual may have an eye of each color. Most Persians today are being bred with a face very similar to that of a Pekingese dog: a rounded skull and head, folds above and between the eyes, and a short, pushed-in nose and muzzle.

A rather rare breed, the *Chinchilla* sports a superb cream coat that forms a delightful contrast to its emerald eyes. These cats make very dependable pets and companions, but, like all long-haired felines, their coats need a good deal of attention.

Excellent temperament marks the *Maine Coon Cat* as a desirable pet. This breed has much less undercoat than the other long-hairs. In Maine, for some rather absurd reason or other, it was thought that this feline was the result of a crossing between the raccoon and the cat, hence the ridiculous name. The breed is prevalent in Maine where it is expert at keeping farm communities free of rodents.

The *Himalayan* is a fairly new addition to the cat roster of breeds. It resembles an elegant, long-haired Siamese and its appearance mirrors its genetic background, for it is the result of a clever blending of the heritable factors of the Persian and the Siamese. The color patterns are

Over two hundred years of selective breeding have fashioned the long-haired Persian into the most sophisticated and beautiful of the domesticated breeds.

identical to those that give uniqueness to the Siamese and, combined with the thick, soft coat of the Persian, the result is a handsome creature that has many admirers.

At one time in the past long-hairs were labeled *Angoras,* but the name was dropped (except for the Turkish Angora) in favor of the all-embracing Persian title. There are two other kinds of cats that are

The Himalayan was synthetically formed by clever breeders who manipulated the genetic qualities of the Persian and the Siamese to produce this very delightful and handsome breed.

named for hair pattern and color rather than being distinct breeds: the *Calico Cat*—a name derived from a designed cloth, calico, that was originally of East Indian manufacture—is a multi-colored cat of black, orange, and white. This feline usually possesses green eyes and is almost always female. Evidently the calico marking is a sex-linked characteristic. The *Tortoiseshell* is also a color manifestation rather than a breed. It can display clear and distinct spots of red, black, and white and, if it carries the tabby gene, will exhibit striping. The tabby striping so prevalent in the domestic cat has been acquired honestly from one of its known ancestors, the *African bush cat* (*Felis Lybica*), which is a tabby with hair fashioned to color by the banded or agouti stripes.

Of the newer breeds of cats the lovely long-haired *Balinese* is gaining quick popularity in the United States as is the *Birman* cat, a breed popular in France, England, Germany, and Sweden. *Havana Browns* (not to be confused with rabbits of the same name) are solid-colored shorthairs of a rich brown color so deep and even as to appear black at a distance. *Egyptian Maus* come in several attractive colors, including bronze, silver, smoke, and spotted. *Korats* are a new breed of Thai ancestry (new to the United States that is), and the *Rex* is the result of a coat mutation that has resulted in the pelage becoming wavy, tight, and curled. It is caused by a double recessive; a single breeding to any normal-coated cat results in kittens with normal pelts, but they carry the recessive gene for the sparse crinkled coat. I personally do not find the Rex a very attractive breed. Novel, yes, but not beautiful. *Turkish Angoras* are comely long-haired felines that are building a good following in the U.S.

Miscellaneous Breeds

The following breeds are relatively new and have not, as yet, acquired wide acceptance. Though they are experimental breeds, they are approved for registration in most cat associations. At the moment the list embraces nine new breeds, an appropriate number for cats: *Somalis, Tonkinese, Scottish Folds, Lavenders, Bombays, Chartreux, Polydactyls* (possessing extra digits), *Ragdolls* and *Leopard Cats*. If you are interested in something new, exotic, and exciting in a feline pet, you might find just what your heart desires in one of these breeds. *Cats* magazine, published in Washington, Pennsylvania, carries advertisements for all or almost all of the known breeds.

The most prominent cat registration organizations are the American Cat Association (America's oldest registry); the American Cat Fanciers' Association; National Cat Fanciers' Association, Inc., United Cat Fanciers' Federation; Cat Fanciers' Federation; Cat Fanciers; The Cat Fanciers' Association, Inc.; Crown Cat Fanciers' Federation; The International Independent Cat Council; and the Canadian Cat Association.

Wild Cats

People at times attempt to make pets of wild—often dangerous—animals. Some of the wild cats head the list in this category. It is a form of "Machismo" or "Chutzpa," I suppose, to tame, train, and make a friendly pet of a species of animal that is labeled a dangerous wild beast. Just between us I have also heard this tendency characterized by individuals who work with wild cats as plain egotistical stupidity. But it can also come under the heading of courage or a desire to attain dominance over a creature considered savage. In some cases, if the opportunity is present, it can be a challenge to an individual who sincerely wants to find an area of understanding between himself and a wild beast.

Throughout the ages men have kept dangerous creatures as pets so they could boast about their achievement and feed their bloated egos. There are no dearth of such people today: they have a feral cat's teeth and claws removed and eventually turn the animal over to a zoo where it must be kept in solitary confinement because it no longer has its natural weapons of defense. Those who treat a wild creature in such a cavalier manner should be open to legal action. I have been told by curators of zoos that when they hear of someone in their area possessing a jaguar, a bear, or any of the so-called wild creatures, they know that sooner or later the animal will be brought to them as a "gift." Not one person in many thousands is physically, psychically, or mentally equipped to own and deal with a wild pet—particularly a feral cat.

I am not going to list the larger cats because, though in some instances they have been trained and possibly tamed, they cannot legitimately be labeled pets. Those I will mention here have had, to my knowledge, some history of association with man in the role of pets.

The *African bush cat* (*Felis Lybica*) looks very much like a tabby and is also similar in color and markings to the *European wild cat*. It was a blending of the inheritable factors of both these progenitors that produced the domestic cat. Both the African bush and the European wild cats were domesticated by early humans on both continents.

A very handsome feral cat, the *Ocelot* (*Felis pardata*) is, in appearance, similar to a miniature jaguar. It has rather wide distribution in the American tropics, particularly Mexico. The ocelot weighs up to 40 pounds and is a nocturnal hunter. Frequently tamed and trained as pets, they tend to become dangerous when they reach maturity. There are several related species, one of which, the *giant ocelot* (*Felis chibigouavou*) of South America, is too large to be recommended as a pet, some species reaching the size of the smaller jaguars of nothern Mexico. The *Margay* (*Felis tigrina*) is a smaller cat, sometimes called a tiger cat, and is much like an ocelot but more spotted than banded in pattern.

The *Caracal* or *desert lynx* (*Felis caracal*) is a reddish-fawn, short-haired cat with large black ears that bear sweeping tufts at their tips, an ornament which some zoologists claim puts the caracal in the same category as the lynx of North America. The caracal, lithe and graceful, stands up to 18 inches high at the shoulder and is widely distributed

The tawny Caracal (Felis caracal), *often named the Persian lynx because of its tufted ears, is a bit larger than a fox and can be trained as a hunting cat.*

throughout the savannah and semi-desert areas of Africa, Southwest Asia, and eastward to the United Provinces of India. Though an accomplished nocturnal hunter and killer, the caracal is easily tamed and, when caught as a very young kitten, makes an interesting pet. In India caracals were trained and used for sporting hunts. One such "sport" involved releasing a pair of the cats at a flock of ground-feeding pigeons. Each cat would strike down as many pigeons as possible before the flock became alarmed and took flight.

Caracals in the wild state hunt young antelopes, rodents, monkeys, wild fowl, and snakes of many kinds. There have been melanistic (black) specimens of this interesting cat recorded.

Golden Cats (*Felis aurata*) are red-brown or gray-brown forest cats that stand about 16 inches high at the shoulders. They are quiet, solitary, nocturnal felines, rarely seen in their native habitat, the jungles of the Dark Continent. Black spots adorn the insides of their legs and their under-bellies. In Kenya I saw a golden cat that was owned and had been domesticated by a Masai Forest Ranger. It was a nice pet, differing little in deportment from any domestic cat.

A strongly marked spotted cat, the *Marbled Cat* (*Felis marmorata*) is similar to the spotted cats of tropical Asia; all spotted felines are similar to the New World ocelots. The marbled is a bit longer than the domestic cat. There have been reports of its domestication throughout its habitat which extends from India to Malaya. Another small cat that inhabits the deserts of southwestern Asia is nocturnal, pale buff in color, and is called the *Arabian sand cat*. It is similar in appearance to the domestic tabby, but from all reports is savage and unmanageable.

The *Serval* (*Felis serval*) is also a spotted cat of good size, standing approximately 18 to 20 inches high at the shoulders. Its habitat is East Africa where its pelt is prized as a mantle by black tribal chiefs. The tawny-yellow base color of the coat is well spotted, with black bands running across the back. Its forelimbs are proportionately rather long, causing the back to slope downward toward the rear. The Serval is quite fast afoot, running down its prey as does the cheetah. The serval's tail is only about a foot long. When caught as tiny kittens, servals have been domesticated and sometimes trained as hunting cats.

The *Cheetah* (*Acinonyx jubatus*) is considered one of the "big cats." This status is not achieved by size alone but through the position the animal takes when crouching with its feet in front of its body. Cheetahs

Long-legged and slim, the Cheetah (Acinonyx jubatus) *is as fast afoot as he appears to be. These handsome hunting cats can be tamed and trained.*

attain a height of about 3 feet and weigh over 100 pounds. They are, to my mind, truly beautiful cats: long, slender, lithe, exhibiting small black spots on a tawny background. Their running speed is phenomenal—officially clocked at over 70 miles per hour. You will note that scientifically the cheetah is classified differently from other cats because it is not a true cat but has some doglike characteristics. For instance, cheetahs cannot retract their claws, which are blunt, more like the toenails of a canine than a feline.

As a captive, even when caught at maturity, the cheetah becomes very tame. Also called the *hunting leopard,* these handsome creatures are found in East Africa, though at one time they also inhabited India where they were trained as hunting cats by Indian potentates. In the sixteenth century more than a thousand cheetahs were kept for the chase by the Emperor Akbar. These big cats make affectionate and playful (but expensive) pets and can easily be trained to a collar and leash. Some years ago *Field and Stream* magazine made a film, showing cheetahs that had been trained as hunting and water dogs retrieving to hand ducks shot in water. Since the birth of civilization, cheetahs have been kept as pets and hunting felines, in the latter capacity often in conjunction with hunting hawks and eagles. In the plains country of Uganda I saw a female with two cubs. They showed no fear of me and continued their playing even though I managed to get quite close to them. But, a word of caution here: cheetahs are creatures of the chase so, should you ever be fortunate enough to possess one, never run away from it in play. The result could be disastrous.

The *Cougar* (*Felis concolor*)—or puma, panther, mountain lion, call it what you will—is not nearly as savage in captivity as the other big cats. In zoos they are considered quiet and good-natured; their kits, if raised by hand in a home, become very tame. I have known several people who have hand-raised young cougars and successfully fashioned them into acceptable pets that were leash-broken and loved to ride in the car with their owners. No matter how bad the neighborhood in which they had to park, these people were never afraid that their car would be "ripped off" in their absence. Like all of the wild cats, cougars generally become neurotically attached to one or two people in their human family and become frantic if left alone or in the care of a stranger. As a result people who own animals in the "wild" category do not frequently indulge in vacations away from home.

In reading books about human-animal association in the wild, such as *Born Free, A Lifetime with Lions,* et cetera, one may get the impression that lions and other big cats are easy to live with—that is, if you can accept the constant odor of big-cat urine. But—not so. These are wild, basically savage beasts that cannot by any stretch of the imagination be considered pets. What this literature does make obvious is how an occasional human (that one in many thousands) can find rapport with feral, dangerous animals in the creatures' own environment where they are not confined and their freedom is not taken away from them. I am well aware that stories of this type are dream-inducing, but it is best that they remain in the realm of fancy. The reality could be a rude and possibly perilous awakening.

CHAPTER

11

Birds

Aves

Our dictionary tells us that a bird is "Any of the *Aves,* a class of warm-blooded vertebrates having a body more or less completely covered with feathers, and forelimbs so modified as to form wings by means of which most species fly."

Man has, from the dawn of time, envied those feathered creatures that spurn the earth and fly upward toward the heavens on swinging wings, for he has ever dreamed of finding that freedom for himself—to fly, to shed earthly burdens and wing toward the sun, to be "as free as a bird." Early man looked upon the larger birds with awe and in his slow and reaching mind wove fancies and myths around them, for to spurn the binding earth and fly like the winged creatures was to him incomprehensible.

So through the ages man looked to the birds and dreamed of emulating them. Leonardo da Vinci, a man of brilliance in many fields and an artist of scope, allowed his searching mind to embrace the problem of flight and became obsessed with the desire to fly. He built mechanical wings to lift humans into the air, but alas, even his rare intelligence could not find the answer to the riddle of flight. Many men over the centuries thought they had solved the ultimate mystery—only to crash to ignominy and failure. Now, with the technology and scientific skills of the twentieth century, man at last flies—but not like birds.

Development of Birds

In 1859, in Bavaria, a skeleton was found of a creature said to be the 138-million-year-old link between reptiles and birds. Anthropologists agree that the bird developed from a tree-climbing lizard-like reptile, that during millions of years of evolutionary change, scales became feathers, tails disappeared, and wings developed. Lizards and birds have many characteristics in common. Both species lay eggs, the embryological development of both is parallel, including the production of the egg tooth which drops off after being used by the embryo to break out of the shell. Diurnal lizards and birds also share the same keenness of sight. Birds give visual evidence of at least one connection with their reptilian ancestry—the scales they wear on their feet and legs. The descent of birds from reptiles evolved through creatures like the extinct *Archaeopteryx,* which existed during the Jurassic period but retained the reptilian teeth. It had three digits on the forelimbs, the long tail of the reptile, but had a body covering of feathers—and the unique ability to fly. Thus the gorgeously feathered creatures that delight the eye and, in some instances, fill the world with song, are directly linked with the horrendous dinosaurs (from the Greek, meaning "terrible lizards") that made the Mesozoic and early Jurassic eras unending ages of nightmare.

Ornithologists recognize approximately forty thousand kinds of birds that are cataloged into twenty-nine living orders. Distribution of each category is universal. There are also six fossil orders. Ornithology, incidentally, is the branch of zoology that focuses on birds; aviculture is the rearing and keeping of birds as a hobby. Aware of the scientific findings made by ornithologists, some aviculturists, using these studies as well as their own acumen, have been instrumental in preventing the extinction of quite a few bird species when their domains have become untenable due to the advance of civilization.

Three-quarters of all known birds are gathered into one huge group scientifically labeled *passerine,* or *perching birds. The Passerinus,* though they vary greatly in coloration, habits, and shape, are similar in one specific and all-important detail—their feet are fashioned to clutch branches, locking in a grip that cannot be released until the bird leans forward to hop, or to fly. Insessorial, or perching birds, feed on injurious insects and weed seeds to a great extent and so have economic value. Many of these birds—such as mynahs, canaries, toucans, finches, and so forth—also make excellent pets with unique talents. Others are familiar to everyone who has ever seen a bird—and who hasn't? These are the crows, blue jays, sparrows, robins, and cardinals. All of them are *passerines.*

Birds display almost unbelievable variations in color, size, shape, and flying ability. All varieties exhibit aspects not found in other animal species. They possess two feather coats: the contour feathers, which are the visible ones, and the soft down feathers, which are close to the body and covered by the contour cloak. The beaks and feet of birds reflect their adaptation to environment and specific habits of feeding. The wings are, of course, modified arms and forelimbs, adapted to the bird's manner of movement—flight. Size varies fantastically from the tiny hummingbirds, some of which are scarcely larger than a bee, to the ostrich, the largest contemporary bird, a creature that can reach a height of 8 feet and can weigh as much as 340 pounds.

The Breeds of Birds

Are you interested in falconry, eager to train a bird to hunt and enable you to thrill to the sport of ancient kings? Or are you looking for a bird that is easily fed and housed and not much trouble to care for? Do you want a songbird that will fill the house with music? Perhaps you desire to breed birds for exhibition or to experience the heady excitement to be found in competition. You may be looking forward to owning one of the larger psittacine birds and training it to talk. Birds are marvelous creatures, delightful and wonderful pets, that can bring you many hours of sheer pleasure.

Parrot-Family Birds (family *Psittacidae*)

Throughout the ages, whenever and wherever the golden wand of civilization has touched man, parrots and other psittacine birds have been tamed and kept as pets. Ancient, powerful Rome, trampling the known world under the mailed feet of its victorious legions, and classic Greece, decadent, languid, dissolving in its own philosophical sophistry, knew the value of the pet parrot as a vehicle to wile away empty hours or to bring interest and happiness to a household. China and India, old in the ways of civilized man when other cultures were just emerging from the abyss of savagery, kept parrots and other birds as ornamental pets. Merchant galleys, braving capricious nature and the legendary monsters of the seven seas, brought spice, goods, and psittacine birds to Europe from Africa and other exotic coasts. And in the cloudy heights of Machu Pichu in the towering Andes the Incas kept macaws and wove from their glowing feathers the colorful cloaks of chiefs.

Today parrot-family birds are owned and cherished throughout the world as pets without peers. Unfortunately the only psittacine bird known in this country in modern times—the Carolina conure—is now extinct, the victim of the abysmal stupidity of farmers who considered it a pest and slaughtered the species. All psittacine birds not bred here must therefore be imported. Unfortunately, because of government bans related to psittacosis (or ornithosis), a disease that can affect a wide variety of bird species, the importation of psittacine birds is difficult and the prices of parrots quite high. But the pleasure the parrot owner will derive from his pet is certainly beyond price.

Technically the order of parrots is composed of many categories with a host of different types of birds. Scientifically the order of parrots is tagged *Psittaciformes* and all members have certain shared characteristics: strong hooked beaks, mallet-shaped tongues, two hind toes, and two toes in front. The evolutionary process formed the *Psittaciformes'* feet, strong legs, and beaks to enable them to climb in trees rather than hop from branch to branch in the manner of most birds. Parrots are mainly vegetarian, though their tastes are wide. They possess rather harsh voices and varying talent for vocal mimicry.

The terms *parrakeet* and *lorikeet* will be applied here generally to slender, long-tailed parrot-family birds; *parrot* and *lory* will be indicative of short-tailed birds. Size is not important to these categories as some lorikeets are actually larger than lories and not infrequently we find certain parrakeets that are bigger than some of the smaller parrots. Incidentally you should be aware of the fact that birds that have been pets are very seldom useful as breeders, preferring the company of humans rather than their own kind.

THE BUDGERIGAR (*MELOPSITTACUS UNDULATUS*)

I have selected the *budgerigar* for pride of place because it surpasses any other bird in popularity and in the number owned as pets and breeders. It is, of all birds, the most mutable. It is lovely in its feathered cloak of many colors, is easy to breed, and is easily taught tricks and speech. About 7 inches long in the wild state, or 9 inches in length for the gorgeous exhibition birds, the millions of these little birds owned as pets or kept as breeders now probably exceeds the population of wild budgies that still inhabit the Australian continent that is their original habitat. The budgerigar is also called the shell parrakeet, zebra parrakeet, or just plain parrakeet.

As a pet the budgerigar has no peer. Unfailingly good-humored, easily tamed and trained, and able to mimic the human voice and acquire an amazing vocabulary, this delightful pet well deserves its huge popularity. As an exhibition bird, it is also most desirable. One of the budgerigar's main attractions is the host of colors and patterns from which you can choose when buying a pet. There is the basic green, rich and brilliant in three shades; the gorgeous blues, also in three shades; the violets, cinnamons, yellows, pieds, grays, gray greens, albinos, graywings, fallows and a host of other colors and shades. There is also the opaline, a pattern mutation, and the yellow-face, which appears in the blue series. The one color not represented in the budgie's wide color range is red, except for the wash of this color over cobalt blue that results in the beautiful violet shade.

E.H.HART

The most popular and mutable of the hook-beak birds is the small but delightful budgerigar (Melopsittacus undulatus), *a bird of many virtues and very few faults.*

Purchase your pet budgie from a breeder or a pet shop and buy only a male chick. Unlike humans, male budgies are the talkers in their family. The age of the bird can be estimated by the bars of dark-colored feathers that cover the brow of the youngster and lend him the name "Bar-head." If this area is clear of barring in a normal bird, then it is not a youngster but has already gone through its three-month molt. Large, dark eyes with no outside rim around them; and pink feet and legs are also indications of youth. Older normal birds *usually* have gray legs and feet.

The sex of a budgerigar can be determined by the color of its cere, which is the hard, horny growth with nostril openings just above its beak. The normal baby male budgie's cere is a painful pink that gradually becomes dark blue as it matures. The hen has a blue-white cere, almost like mother-of-pearl, that becomes tan and then nut-brown with maturity.

Should you become so enamored of these charming creatures that you decide to breed them, purchase several pairs of breeders from a reputable aviary. Try to get virgin stock about a year old and do not choose too great a variety of colors, so that it will be relatively easy to switch mates if you have to and still know approximately what colors you will find in the nest. Join the American Budgerigar Society (ABS) which will issue you a band number to identify the chicks. Colored family bands that are open at the sides can also be purchased, allowing you to know immediately by the band color what family any bird is from. Your pairs should be in breeding condition before being bred, the cocks strutting and feisty with deep blue ceres, the hens bright-eyed with deep brown ceres. Budgerigars will seldom breed unless several are paired and put into separate breeding cages at the same time. Breeding cages should be stacked so the birds are close and can hear each other as they begin their courting.

The act of mating should take place within a few days if the pairs are ready. The hen will begin peeking through the hole into the nest box and finally begin to pop in and out. The male will make overtures, strutting as all males do, bird or human. Soon the hen will squat on the perch, raise her tail, and the cock will mount her, balance and "tread" her, comsummating their tryst. The hen will stay inside the nest box for increasingly longer periods. Her stool becomes quite loose and large and then she begins laying, one egg every other day until the clutch is completed. In eighteen days after the first egg is laid the clutch, generally about five eggs, will begin to hatch.

The chicks are tiny embryonic mites of pink flesh but grow rapidly and should be banded with the closed ABS band when they are from five to seven days old. During the thirty to thirty-five days they remain in the nest they will be fed on "crop milk," a rich colostrum-like substance that contains (you hope) all the dietary necessities.

Once the chicks begin to feed themselves, they can be removed from the breeding cage and put into a baby cage. Meanwhile the hen should have started a new nest of eggs. Flights as large as possible should be constructed for the older birds when not breeding.

I have really just touched on the subject of budgerigar breeding. Of one thing I am sure—breeding budgerigars is one of the most absorbing and interesting hobbies you could possibly find. In fact the budgerigar fancy has become more of a cult than a hobby and I have given this delightful little psittacine so much space because of its tremendous importance to aviculture.

THE COCKATIEL (*NYMPHICUS HOLLANDICUS*)

Next to the budgerigar the *cockatiel* is the most popular pet of the parrot family. It too is a native of Australia and one of the most gentle and affectionate of all birds. Cockatiels are not expensive. Normal birds are selling for about $35 at this time and rare ones (whites or albinos, yellows and pieds) for from $75 to $200. They are good whistlers and fair talkers, and as companions are unexcelled.

To be sure of getting the precious pet you anticipate, buy a young one, preferably a male just out of the nest. Or purchase one that has been hand fed. You will have to pay a bit more for one of these specially raised youngsters, but they are well worth the extra money because they make gentler pets, more tractable to training. With a little patience your pet will very soon be finger-tamed and showing its affection for you in no uncertain manner. I have had a lovely dark-eyed albino hen for several years. She has never been much of a talker, but is a wonderful pet. She likes to have breakfast with us and will spend hours sitting on my wife's shoulder, whistling and rubbing her head softly against my spouse's cheek.

The cockatiel is unique in the parrot family in that it is the only example of its genus and is thought to be the evolutionary link between parrakeets and cockatoos. Today there are several mutations in cockatiels: the albino (all white with a yellow crest and orange cheek patch), and the pied cockatiel, which has the normal gray base color but is theatrically splashed with large white areas are the most available. Some albinos have almost black eyes (actually a deep plum color), and some are almost completely shaded in a rich sunlit yellow. The pieds can be very attractive and unique in appearance. The normal cockatiel is colored with various shades of gray with orange cheek patches, a yellow-white face, and a white splash on the wings. The identifying crest is high, delicate, and bright yellow.

Cockatiels are bred much like budgerigars, but the nest boxes must be larger to accommodate their bigger size. They need small flights as breeding boves. Generally the cockatiel takes best to colony or group breeding rather than being separated into pairs as is the custom with budgies.

Cockatiels are genuinely lovely birds that are the best of companions and pets. If you like parrot-type birds, I can sincerely recommend this wonderful feathered friend from Down Under.

THE LARGER PARROTS

The parrot that has the reputation of being the best talker of all the psittacines is the *African gray,* a statement which could engender a lot of argumentative talk from owners of other parrot species, particularly those who have parrots of the Amazon family.

The African gray is a lovely soft gray color with a bright red tail and a black bill. The color combination is quiet but pleasing. The bird seems a bit long in the neck to be perfectly balanced. The African gray parrot is about 13 inches long, vivacious, intelligent, and makes a delightful pet. At the moment this parrot is priced at about $400.

South America makes up for the dearth of parrot-birds in North America, the *Amazon parrot* family being one of the largest of the order of parrots. There are fifty different species and subspecies that range in length from 8 to 21 inches. The Amazons make excellent household pets and companions if trained when young. I have seen many of them (as well as other parrots and macaws) given their liberty on large estates, parks, rancheros, and farms in South and Central America and they are very tame and approachable.

Because of the great number of parrot-type birds I will concentrate only on those that are the most popular and available.

The *Mexican Double Yellow Head* is a highly popular breed with a reputation as a marvelous pet and an excellent talker. The yellow head is about 15 inches long, becomes rather massive with maturity, and is mostly green with a yellow head, red on the shoulder and tail feathers, and some slight bit of red and blue in the wings.

The *Yellow-Naped Amazon,* also from Mexico, is easily trained to do tricks and is a consistently good pet and talker. This parrot is certainly one of the most affectionate and lovable of the whole family if properly raised and trained. It is a bit larger than the double yellow head and somewhat more expensive. It is a massive, strong bird with a large, impressive head, a deep green color with a band of yellow over the nape of the neck and an area of the same color over the beak. There is some red and blue in the flight feathers.

The *Panama Amazon* and the *Yellow-Fronted Amazon* are closely alike in appearance. The Panama is an excellent talker and is a slightly darker shade of green than the yellow-naped and the yellow-fronted. The latter, also a good talker, is about 14 inches long.

Lesser Amazons that make fine pets and are available in the United States are the *Green-Cheeked* (very pretty but rather noisy, about 13 inches long), *Finsch's* (a very reliable pet about 13 inches long, also called the Lilac-Crowned Amazon), the *Spectacled Amazon* (small and a screecher, too noisy to be a good pet) and the *Yellow-Cheeked Amazon,* popular, available, attractive, and a good pet and talker. It is also a talented and recommended parrot if handled correctly. A Mexican native.

The large *Blue-Crowned Amazon* is a very good talker and an outstanding pet, strikingly colored with a large blue head. The body is green, tinted with blue, and it wears blue and red in the flight feathers. At the moment this parrot is unfortunately not readily available.

A truly beautiful parrot, the *Cuban Amazon* is of varied colors, including white, pink, slate, and maroon. Other Amazons that must be mentioned here are the handsome *Versicolor,* the *Yellow-Crowned, Dufresne's, Red-Vented, Maximilian's Parrot, White-Crowned Parrot, Bronze-Winged, Dusky Parrot,* and a host of others that make excellent pets but are rather rare.

MACAWS

Only a limited number of these large flamboyant birds are generally available. Macaws are long-lived, hardy, highly intelligent, playful, and good talkers. They make impressive, truly excellent pets, but be careful while in the process of taming and training them. Their powerful beaks can inflict a painful bite. (I tell you this as a voice of experience.) Near Canima Falls in the Venezuelan jungle several scarlet macaws flew over me through the tangle of rich green foliage of the jungle's roof, squawking vigorously at my invasion of their domain. While eating breakfast the next morning I coaxed down from the trees a pair of these beauties that had been curiously watching my every move. Eventually they sidled up to the bread and bacon I put down for them. In just a very few minutes they became so bold, practically snatching at the food in my hands, that I found it necessary to shoo them away.

Because of their large size, the bigger psittacines generally prefer to walk or climb, using feet and beak, or to remain contentedly on their perches rather than make the effort to fly.

The *Blue and Gold Macaw* and the *Scarlet Macaw* are the two most popular and readily available of these feathered giants. The blue and gold (or yellow) is particularly beautiful, the iridescent quality of its deep cerulean blue back and wings, complemented by the rich yellow breast, lend it a unique loveliness. This bird is more expensive than the vivid scarlet with its cobalt blue flight feathers and large flecks of yellow on the wings and back in contrast to the brilliant red of the rest of its body. Both are intelligent, inquisitive, often good talkers, and always excellent pets. The scarlet often reaches a length of about 3 feet, making it the largest psittacine bird in the world.

As I write this, my lovely blue and gold macaw, "Macho" and my scarlet, "Coco" sit watching me type, indulging in an occasional slurring remark about my ability to describe adequately their glowing beauty. They were a gift to me from my very good friend, Señor German Garcia y Garcia, whose TV show, "Animalania" is one of the most popular TV entertainments in Bogota, Colombia.

The *Green-Winged Macaw* is quite similar to the scarlet. The red is slightly deeper in color and the wings are green. Tiny red feathers form lines on the bare area of the face, which is unlined in the scarlet. All three of these macaws are now selling for up to $1000 in the United States. In South America they can be bought in the native bird markets for from $25 to $50 (about 1500 pesos), and if bought from Indians who bring young ones out of the jungle, the price would be about $10.

The *Military Macaw* is large but not as outgoing in character as the macaws just mentioned. Because of this and the fact that its comparatively dull coat of green does not begin to match the vivid glory of its peers, the military macaw has lost out at the popularity polls. Due to its large size, however, it is still a very impressive bird.

The most magnificent of all macaws, the *Hyacinthine* (or Hyacinth) is big in the beak and the body, and is solidly colored in deep blue with a brilliant sheen. These very hardy and gorgeous creatures are rare, commanding a very high price. Both the *Glaucous* and *Lear's macaws* are rather smaller versions of the beautiful Hyacinthine, not as brilliant in color but equally rare. All macaws are very long lived—fifty to sixty years not being uncommon.

There are several smaller less impressive and less available macaws of which the *Yellow-naped* and *Severe macaws* are very rare dwarf varieties. The *Spix* and *Noble macaws* are small and rare as are several other dwarf species.

The Military Macaw (Ara militaris) *is not as popular as the more brilliantly colored macaws but like them shares large size and trainability.*

COCKATOOS (FAMILY *KAKATOEINAE*)

All the macaws are from the New World—Mexico, Central America, and South America—but the cockatoos are native to Australia, and are mostly birds of medium to large size (12 to almost 30 inches). Unlike other parrots, these extraordinary birds are never green in color. Cockatoos bloom in captivity, are very hardy, active, extremely intelligent, and live to ripe old ages, some authorities claim in excess of a hundred years. Such birds have been known to become family heirlooms, serving as pets and companions to three generations of humans whose fondling they always adore.

All cockatoos flaunt decorative crests of various kinds. They are generally very comic characters that are entertaining to observe. It is quite possible that these lovely creatures, which learn so quickly and are such intelligent birds, are one step upward on the psittacine evolutionary ladder. It is too bad that their cost is so high as to put them beyond the reach of most fanciers.

The *Great Sulphur-crested cockatoo* is the most popular and available of this fine family of birds. It is about 20 inches long, snow white, with a yellow pointed erectile crest, and a black beak. This is a large, robust bird, a satisfactory breeder; hardy, adaptable, and very intelligent. Add to this list of admirable qualities the sulphur-crested's undeniably great beauty and there is nothing else one could want in a pet bird.

Like all cockatoos the sulphur-crested boasts of an unusual type of feather not duplicated by other birds. It has waxy filaments, very fine in texture, which constantly supply to the body feathers a chalk-like substance that cleans and keeps them spotless.

Cockatoos are good talkers and many are actually larger than the big macaws, for the giant macaws have very long tails while the cockatoo's is short and square. For instance, if the palm cockatoo, that reaches a length of 30 inches, sported the long tail of the macaw, it would be a much longer bird than the largest of the macaws.

The *Rose-breasted cockatoo* is perhaps the second most popular of this breed. About 17 inches long, it sports a soft gray color on the tail feathers, and back, wings and underparts are a delicate pastel pink. Not flamboyant in color, yet this beautiful bird is undoubtedly one of the most exquisite feathered creatures in the world. Gentle, amusing, and affectionate pets, the rose-breasted is a fair talker and a fairly easy breeder.

The third favorite of the family is *Leadbeater's cockatoo*. This very friendly bird is also one of the most strikingly beautiful with head, neck underwing coverts, and breast a subtle salmon pink, and the wings, tail, and back startling white. The curling crest is banded with yellow enclosed on both sides by a band of red; the tip of the crest is white. Leadbeater's is an excellent aviary bird, a free breeder, fine mimic, and

From the island continent of Australia comes the Great Sulphur-crested cockatoo (Kakatoe galerita galarita), *a large and long-lived bird of the family* Psittacidae. *Of the many cockatoos the sulphur-crested is the most popular.*

whistler. It is friendly, and makes a wonderful pet. It attains a length of about 16 inches.

The huge *Palm Cockatoo* is black with a very large head. Like the beginning of dawn after a moonless night, his feathers show a hint of gray. These are impressive, gentle, loving birds, but are quite rare. The *Red-Tailed Black* or *Bansian Cockatoo* is even larger than the palm, in fact the largest of the genus—a veritable mammoth black. Gray-tipped feathers on the chest relieve the funereal appearance and the tail bears a band of deep scarlet for accent. The very largest, attaining a length of up to 31 inches, come from New Guinea. There are several other basically black species and subspecies of cockatoos all quite rare.

The *Gang-Gang Cockatoo* is a rare oddity in the family due to the scarlet head topped by a loose curly crest. The basic body color is light gray, the feathers tipped by a lighter gray margin. The *Blue-Eyed Cockatoo* makes an intelligent and docile pet. Crest feathers are rounded at the tip and the bare skin that surrounds the eyes is blue in color. A smaller version of the greater sulphur-crested is the *Lesser Sulphur-Crested Cockatoo*. This bird and its five subspecies, because of their lesser size, are sometimes referred to as apartment-sized cockatoos. *Ducorps Cockatoo, Philippine, Umbrella-Crested* and *Bare-Eyed Cockatoos* are all available at times. The bare-eyed is considered one of the most intelligent of a talented family.

The *Caiques* are a genus of about five species, only two of which have any great importance—the *White-Bellied Caique* and the *Black-Headed Caique*. All caiques are short-tailed, small, stout, and generally unusually colored. They have a roguish sense of humor and make great little pets. The Indians of South America will attest to that. These little parrots were at first eaten by the Indians, but when they found that they made such wonderful pets, they decided that you can't have your caique and eat it too. Thus ends this valuable bit of Indian lore.

Among a host of parrots from various parts of the world the *Yellow-Bellied Senegal* (native to Africa) is well liked in Europe and is also available and not too expensive in the United States. Young Senegals have gray eyes and are easy to train. There are three varieties.

From Madagascar comes the *Greater Vasa Parrot,* a rather large bird, fully 20 inches long, that is good pet material. It is rather dull in color and not often seen in pet shops or aviaries. *Electus parrots* are extremely beautiful in a multiplicity of brilliant colors. The hens are rather shy, but the cocks make excellent pets and can be taught to talk. These vivid parrots from the Australasian Islands are easily bred.

The *Philippine Green Parrot* is also a popular, readily available pet.

There are several subspecies. The *Dwarf Panama, Thick-Billed, Song parrot,* and the unusual *Pesquet's parrot,* a large and heavy bird with a small hawklike head, are all less-well-known parrots and rather rarely found here.

There are fourteen races of the genus *Pionus,* all natives of South America and all under a foot in length. Quiet in voice and movement, they all make lovely, affectionate pets. Their coloring is never brilliant, but it is subtly beautiful when closely examined. The *Blue-Headed parrot* (also called the *Red-vented parrot*) is the best known with its rich blue head and neck, and red tail coverts and vent. I bought one of these fine parrots in the bird section of the Indian market at Giradot, high in the mountains of Colombia, South America. It was a perfectly charming pet.

PARRAKEETS

Some of the most popular psittacines are birds of this genus. The greater number wear feather cloaks of soft green. All have long, slender tails and a band of color like a silken scarf around their throats. This is a tremendously large genus of gorgeous birds, shimmering in pastel colors. Generally parrakeets are not noted for their talking ability, but there are exceptions to this rule as there are to all rules and the lovely little budgerigar is a classic example.

The *Indian Ringneck parrakeet* is a slender, graceful subtly colored bird about 17 inches long. The ringneck is also available and not unduly expensive. It is a very desirable psittacine with its classic beauty and balance and loving temperament. A wonderful pet and companion, the ringneck will master a bit of conversation to please its owner. Easily bred, ringneck mutations have appeared in blue and Lutino (sex-linked yellow) and I don't doubt that canny breeders will eventually produce many more mutations and, through inbreeding, introduce great color variety to the species. Ringnecks do not mature before two to three years of age—a slight drawback to greater popularity. In India these birds are favored over all others as pets.

The *African Ringneck* and the *Alexandrine parrakeet* greatly mirror the ringneck's type and personality. The Alexandrine is the largest—about 20 inches long—parrakeet. Since ancient days these wonderful, large parrakeets have been kept as pets. There are several other races of ringnecks rarer than those to which you have been introduced.

An exceedingly attractive bird, the *Mustache parrakeet* is also from India, and there are some other races (types) that enjoy different habitats. The *Plum Head* is easily bred and quite beautiful. The *Crimson-Winged* is one of the very lovely parrakeets that originate in

Australia, the home of many fantastically colored parrakeets. There are several other species of crimson-winged parrakeets from other parts of the globe.

Australia also gives us the brilliant *King parrakeet*. Majestic in its scarlet hood, with accompanying black, blue, green, and orange carefully distributed, it is a gorgeous bird. The king shares its domain with the *Barraband* or *Superb Parrakeet,* and the *Rock Pebbler*.

In my opinion there are no more beautiful birds in the world than some of the Australia Rosella parakeets. As an added inducement to hobbyists, they are quiet and possess a musical whistle.

The *Crimson, Adelaide, Yellow, Green, Red, Blue* and *Princess Alexandra parrakeets* are so dazzling in color as to be beyond the mundane words that could be used for description. *Barnard's parrakeet* is a broadtail that is a fair talker and makes a fine pet. There are several excellent *Blue-Bonnet parrakeets* from Australia that flaunt elegant color combinations and share their habitat with the *Redrump parrakeet,* a charming bird, though not as brilliantly colored as his peers. A favorite is the *Many-colored parrakeet,* handsome and not expensive. The superbly hued *Hooded parrakeet* is rather rare.

The genus *Neophema* is a group of parrakeets, commonly called *grass parrakeets*. They are generally rather small and they vary in color, some displaying brilliant plumage and others fairly dull feathering.

The charming but not excitingly hued *Elegant parrakeet* of Australia is a very well-liked bird and so is the *Splendid* or *Scarlet-Crested parrakeet* whose radiant coloration defies description. The *Turquoisine* is a very beautiful and charming bird while *Bourke's parrakeet* is one of the largest of the Neophema.

The *Quaker parrakeet* (genus *Myiopsitta*) is a South American bird and one of the few parrakeets that builds a nest. The *Bee Bee parrakeet,* often referred to as a dwarf parrot, is popular and a fine pet. A very abundant species (and subspecies) of parrakeets is known as *Hanging parrakeets* or *Loriquets*. These very desirable little birds are rare in the States and have been described by aviculturists as "the jewels of the tropics," but many other feathered creatures have deservedly been likened to jewels.

There are a multicolored multitude of other parrakeets, but they are mostly rare and seldom seen in this country, so we'll skip them and hope that someday they will be more available, giving us greater scope in selecting a pet psittacine. But as in a huge Continental menu of gourmet delicacies, there are so many splendid members of the family already available perhaps more would only lead to confusion.

Three unusual subfamilies of parrots are represented by the *Owl*

Parrot of New Zealand, a nocturnal bird that has the appearance of an owl rather than a parrot, an acceptable reason for its descriptive name. The *Kaka (or brown) parrakeet* is a neighbor of the owl and is rather dull in color. The *Kea Parrot* inhabits the white-capped mountainous regions of New Zealand and has been called a sheep killer, a rather ridiculous accusation when one considers the average size of this parrot and the fact that the brushlike tongue indicates that at least part of its diet is nectar. Keas are said to be highly intelligent and to make very fine pets and companions.

There is a group of very tiny *pigmy parrots,* smaller than the smallest finches, boasting six species and about double that number of subspecies. These tiny creatures are exceedingly rare. Their habitat is the Solomon Islands and New Guinea.

LORIES AND LORIKEETS

This is an exceedingly interesting group of psittacines, energetic, acrobatic, very amusing birds that make intensely affectionate and intelligent pets. They have in common brush-tipped tongues that lap up (in a catlike fashion) the nectar that is part of their diet. Lories have short, broad tails while the lorikeets, usually smaller than the lories, flaunt long pointed tails. Like vain women (or men, to prove that I am not a chauvinistic bird), both spend a good deal of their time preening, posing, and bathing. These charming members of the parrot family run the gamut in size and in color from very plain Jane to extravagant elegance.

Swainson's Blue Mountain lorikeet is one of the most spectacular of the lories, readily available, cheerful, and endlessly amusing. They are most affectionate pets and companions. In color they rival an artist's palette with a brilliant violet head, orange beak, shades of sparkling green on the body and a radiant red and yellow chest shading into deep violet. Add some black, blue, and more yellow, all with a bright sheen, and you have the utterly dazzling Swainson's lorikeet. To add abundance to a good thing, there are over twenty subspecies much like the original.

The brilliant red *Cardinal lory* is well named and popular. It is an amusing and active bird and a delightful pet. Another available and splendid lory that displays a dazzling combination of colors with a wealth of scintillating crimson is the *Chattering lory.* It is available and has a comic sense that makes it a truly amusing pet. The *Red-Quilled* and *Red-Fronted lories* are fairly large and both come from the area of Geelvink Bay. There are also several species of black, dull red, and green lories (of the genus *Chalcopsitta,* as are the red-quilled and red-fronted lories), but these are dull in color and quite rare.

Quiet in color and sometimes called the *Plain lory,* the *Perfect lory* is almost 11 inches long and makes a cute pet. The *Blue-Crowned lory* is very common in Samoa. The *Purple-Capped* and the ten members of its genus are among the most flamboyantly hued birds known. Most of the body feathers are a flaming red and the color does not fade with domestication as it so often does in other species.

Similar to the Blue Mountain and just as radiant is the *Red-Collared lorikeet. Forsten's lorikeet* is also very like the Blue Mountain but not as readily available. The *Jobi lory* is a true beauty as brilliantly painted as the *Black-Capped lory,* and *Stella's lorikeet* is a delightful, rare and lovely little creature.

Lorilets or *Fig Parrots* are quiet, small, mostly green-colored birds that are extremely fascinating, but very rare.

CONURES
Conures are much like macaws and have long, slender silhouettes, large heads and beaks, and long tails. Though not approaching the size of the larger macaws, many of the conures are of greater size than some of the dwarf macaws. Conures make very affectionate pets and can be found in this capacity in the huts of many South American Indians. They can be taught to talk fairly well and have the capacity to make a good deal of noise, so when you select one, try to find a quiet individual.

The *Jenday Conure* is the most popular conure in the United States. Jendays make fairly good talkers and are excellent breeders. About 10 inches long, they are clothed in golden yellow, red, green, blue, and black, patterned into vibrant splendor. It makes a good pet if obtained when young and trained. The Jenday's habitat is eastern Brazil.

The *Halfmoon,* or *Petz' Conure,* is generally called a dwarf parrot and is a popular pet in the United States. It makes an admirable pet, living up to its popularity. The *Nanday conure,* also very well liked, can become an admirable pet, but is not very expert as a talker.

There are quite a few species of green conures of which the largest is named, believe it or not, the *Green conure. Finsch's* is another green conure. The *Cherry-Headed* is a rather large (13 inches long) and attractive green conure with a cherry-colored head, which is what one would expect. The *Aztec* is much like the Petz' or Halfmoon conures in color. The most attractive of its genus, the *White-Eared conure* is vivid in its aesthetic pattern of hunter green, deep maroons, blue with a spendidly barred chest. There are a great many other conures, but they are rare and not generally available to aviculturists or pet seekers in the United States.

LOVEBIRDS

Lovebirds are miniature parrots, the largest specimens never attaining a length of more than 7 inches. All wild lovebirds share the same basic habitat—Africa. There are nine separate species. All are hardy little tykes, and many are easy breeders. They live long and as pets are talented and amusing if tamed when young. They will also learn to talk and can be taught any number of cute tricks. Purchase one or two that have just been weaned and are eating well and they will tame and train quickly. I must warn you, though, that many of these little darlings are extremely pugnacious and quarrelsome with other birds as well as members of their own species.

The *Peach-Faced Lovebird* is the most popular of this family, probably because it is readily available, inexpensive, and easily bred. These are extremely interesting, colorful, intelligent little birds and become fine pets if tamed when young. They are particularly fascinating to aviculturists because they are highly mutable, several mutations in color having appeared in aviary-bred birds in the past decade.

I have several of these delightful birds that I am breeding. Most all of the Lovebirds are quite difficult to sex correctly.

The very comely *Black-Masked Lovebird* is available, easily bred, and rivals the peach-face in popularity. A mutation, the *Blue-Masked Lovebird,* is also well liked in the United States. Both make excellent pets.

Also very popular is *Fischer's Lovebird.* Exquisitely colored, the head is brilliant orange-red and green, with blue, and blue-gray body colors providing a cool contrast to the hot head hue. The *Nyassaland Lovebird* is small, exceedingly pretty and is known for its very pleasant personality. These little beauties are not at all pugnacious and they never bite.

The remaining members of the lovebird family are rare and not as colorful and lovely as those discussed above.

PARROLETS

All parrolets have their original habitat in South America. They are the New World's answer to the African lovebirds and are even tinier. They are not very highly regarded as pets because they are more difficult to tame and train, not as diversified in color, or as easily bred as other species. Therefore I will not indulge in a lengthy discourse in their behalf. I will simply say they exist and, should you happen to own one or plan to purchase one, I am sure you will enjoy it and find a good deal of satisfaction and pleasure in your association.

Finches (family *Fringillidae*)

The dictionary tells us that finches are: "Any of numerous small passerine birds of the family *Fringillidae,* including the buntings, sparrows, crossbills, linnets, grosbeaks, et cetera, most of which have heavy, conical, seed-cracking bills."

The bare bones of the dictionary's reference do not even begin to tell the finch story. There are such a multitude of these dazzling little living gems called finches that in describing them one becomes trapped in one's own rhetoric. Tiny, exquisite, seldom exceeding 15 inches in length, they run the full gamut of color combinations, shapes, sizes, and personality variations. These birds for all seasons and tastes are sometimes called hard-bills because they are mainly seed eaters. By far the greatest number of these dazzling creatures are originally from Australia.

There are some finches that are not emblazoned with color, but those that are, are so elegantly radiant that their beauty seems to embrace the whole finch family. As with most birds, the cocks are the more colorful, the hens being much more drab. That is Mother Nature's way of protecting them from harm when they are nesting and assuring the next generation a chance to reach maturity and attain their destiny as progenitors of their race.

Finches also played an important role in man's understanding of his own origin, for it was only after analyzing the thirteen species of Galapagos finches that Charles Darwin began to evolve his theory of evolution. Darwin studied these finch species in the Galapagos and concluded that they stemmed from a basic Finch-type. From that type each species then specialized and adapted different exploring life-styles necessary to compete, and so spread over a larger area, their ability to survive as a race. Canaries, of course, are the best-known of all the finches, though not native to the Galapagos.

CANARIES (*SERINUS CANARIUS*)

That marvelous virtuoso of song, the canary, developed from the wild canary, a rather drably tinted olive-green singing finch. Canaries are undoubtedly the best known and foremost of all finches, generally thought of as a special species divorced from all other birds. The canary and the budgerigar are by far the most popular cage birds in the world and so, as with the budgerigar, I must give this songster fuller coverage than any of the other finches.

These wonderful little birds were not the first of their kind to be kept in cages as pets, but they certainly were the easiest to care for and no other species can match their lyric song. They have been desirable cage birds for about five hundred years, for it was about that long ago that a Spanish trading ship bound for Africa ran aground one fateful night on the rocky coast of the Canary Islands. The shipwrecked sailors—with typical Latin zest—became much taken with the small green finches that inhabited the Island and filled it with glad madrigals. The seamen cleverly fashioned small cages from reeds and managed to capture some of the sweet-singing birds. When the men were finally rescued, they gave thanks to God and took their operatic pets back to Spain with them. Canaries are still the best-liked birds in España and any bright morning, in any Spanish town or city, you will see their cages hanging outside next to the house door or on flower-filled ornamental balconies and hear their trilling greeting to the Iberian sun and the new day.

Canaries are recognized everywhere as the "kings of songsters" and they thrive as domesticated cage birds. Through selective breeding the yellow canary was produced and in due time, and through the expertise of master breeders, many colors and varied types followed. The cock bird is the singer in this family, so be sure you purchase a male if you want a singing pet.

Basically there are two classes of canaries, those bred exclusively for their song, and those bred for type. Type canaries are also generally good singers in the open-beaked, *chopper* category. The *Roller canary* has a soft song of beautifully modulated notes called rolls or tours. The finest specimens sing flute notes, bass, smooth hollow rolls, deep bubbling water tours, glucke, schlockel, and bell tours. From some of the names of the musical passages, it is obvious that many of the finest rollers were developed by the master breeders of Germany. Familiar names such as Hartz Mountain and St. Andreasburg indicate that strains of canaries originated in those specific places. Actually the Germans produced the first fine rollers, but excellent singers were bred in many other European countries.

Choppers are rather loud open-beak singers, a style many people like. Many of the large canaries that are type-bred are fine choppers. The chopper song does not have the beauty or subtlety of the roller's aria and the notes are not as varied or rich. Developed in the United States the *American Singer canary* is a truly fine songster, combining the best notes and passages of both the roller and the chopper. Some very fine rollers are bred in the British Isles, notably the *Glucke rollers* whose song is rich, lovely and of greater variety than the *Seiferts,* another well-liked type of roller. The best rollers sing upon command and those entered in contests are trained to burst into song immediately upon facing the judge. They are awarded points for each musical tour.

In a time long past I bred canaries, crossing some of the hens with handsome Siberian goldfinches to produce lovely but infertile "mules" with a song that was a delightful blend of wild bird and controlled canary passages. I also bred the strange *Scotch Fancy canary* (now practically extinct), the *Yorkshire* and *St. Andreasburg* rollers. I was quite young then and I look back rather nostalgically to those days of complete immersion in the care, breeding, and training of my canaries as an interesting and self-satisfying interval that added something of immeasurable value to my youthful mental and emotional growth.

I urge any who are interested in purchasing a canary as a pet to first visit some earnest breeders who exhibit at shows and, after inspecting the birds, really listen to the amazing song virtuosity of a good roller. Then visit some bird shows, watch the judging, and listen to the good talk of experienced bird men. Only then will you be qualified to bring at least a minimum of good sense to the selection of your pet canary.

From Germany, Switzerland, Italy, Belgium, and Holland came the early rollers and other singing canaries. The large, stately type birds were generally developed in the British Isles. To the United States goes the credit for producing the already mentioned *American Singer* and the highest development of the *Red-Factor canary.*

The *Dutch Frill* is a rather strange type canary, clothed in loose feathers that give the bird the appearance of an unmade bed. The *Norwich Plainhead* is a large, strong, chubby bird bred in a variety of colors. Because of its size, it needs a comparatively large cage. It is a fearless bird that can be handled and taught a variety of tricks and it is also a good, open-beaked chopper. The *Crested Norwich* is a mirror image of the Plainhead in type, color, character, and song, but it sports a full, round head-crest. Crested birds must never be color-fed.

The *American Singer* is the result of shrewd crossing of rollers to Border Fancy canaries and generations of selection to stabilize type and song. These are beautiful, talented birds of great quality and popularity. The *Yorkshire,* large, tall, and slender, originated in Yorkshire, England. Bold, showy birds, they are choppers and bred in just about every canary color available. A *Miniature Yorkshire* is also bred.

Developed in the British Isles, the *Border Fancy* is the most in demand of British canary breeds. Not as large as the Norwich, but similar in type, it has deep coloring and is a fine show bird. Its song is a nice chopper effect and it can be purchased in all of the popular colors. The

Gloucester canary also originated in Berlin and is close in type to the Border Fancy except that it is crested. It has a nice chopper song and, though a fairly recent breed, is becoming very popular.

The *Scots Fancy* is a large, slender bird with a very odd outline: it holds its head and neck down with its shoulders humped upward giving it a hump-backed appearance in profile. This Quasimodo of the canary family is from Scotland and is mostly seen in buff and yellow shades. The *London Fancy* is a large breed from England, noted for balanced and evenly marked feathering, but seldom seen these days. The *Lizard canary* on the back and shoulders boasts scalloped feather markings that resemble scales, hence the name. They are bred in two colors, gold and silver, and are very comely.

COLOR-BRED CANARIES

The *Red-Factor canary* is a modern development and is the most popular color phase of any that has preceded it. Red Factors can be found in deep red-orange, apricot, pink, copper and red-bronze. These are natural colors that have been bred in, *not* the result of color-feeding. The factor was originally produced through fertile offspring of a Venezuelan siskin and a Border Fancy canary hen. The red color was passed on in succeeding backcross-to-canary generations of breeding. Selection has fashioned the Red Factor into a type breed that, enhanced by its lovely song, will remain always at the peak of popularity. Crosses between Red-Factor and Border canaries are made to improve Red-Factor type.

Frosted canaries have a light veil of white chastely covering the basic ground color of the feathering, which lends them a "frosted" appearance. The Frosted Red-Factor canary is of better type than the non-frosted and is closer to the true and brilliant red color that is desired. When Frosted is bred to Frosted, unwanted snaky-headed, light-colored birds are produced, so it is an axiom among breeders that a Frosted must always be bred to a non-frosted canary.

The *Dimorphic Hen* is a distinctive bird, dressed in pure white with faint markings of pale red. The coloring is very delicate and this canary is evidently a mutation in the red-factor series. Dimorphic Hens with their virginal aura, are extremely valuable in red-factor breedings and also in the red-hooded siskin cross. *Dimorphic Cocks* resemble the hens, but are generally much more richly colored. Both the hens and cocks are definitely and visually frosted. There is also a rare *Pink canary* found occasionally in both frosted and non-frosted varieties, and genetically related to Dimorphic canaries.

A new group of canaries labeled *Dilutes* are finding devotees. This group is the result of a simple, recessive dilute factor that reduces the normal dark colors to pastel shades. These canaries are sometimes called Agate canaries. There has always been with us, of course, the normal pure yellow canary, the basic wild green color (somewhat modified), and the handsome Cinnamon.

Color-feeding is indulged in by some canary breeders. Due to the feather structure of the canary, color derived from ingested food can tint the bird. Color-fed birds are allowed to be exhibited in England in certain classes.

There is no finer, more easily cared for pet than a canary. It will give you a maximum of pleasure for a minimum of care and fill your house with song.

GOLDFINCHES AND SISKINS

These are the real songsters among our feathered friends. The much-loved and admired canary, discussed at length at the beginning of this section on finches, is the most celebrated member of this group. Careful attention to the diet of these little minstrels will pay melodious dividends. Canary song food with extra niger seed and a grated hard-boiled egg supplement with a pinch of vitamin powder will keep these finches in excellent voice and feather.

The *British (or European) Goldfinch* is a delightful bird and an extremely desirable pet. The *Siberian Goldfinch* is an intelligent and very beautiful bird that is not as available today as it used to be. Bred to a canary, the Siberian produces lovely "mules" with a delightful singing range. The *European Siskin* is another well-liked finch that is also used for canary hybridization. The stunning color and pattern of the *Colombian Black Siskin* and the *Venezuelan Black-Hooded Red Siskin* make them prized additions to any aviary. They also make delightful pet birds. The *Green Singing Finch* and the *Yellow-Eyed Canary* are both sweet songsters, very similar in type and very pretty.

The true *wild canary* of the Canary Islands, Madeira, and the Azores is the basic genetic stock from which the drastically changed domestic canary evolved. In color the wild canary is a smooth olive green. The *Serins,* closely related to the wild canary, can be included in this family of finches. They are not distinguished in color but possess a sweet song.

There are several *warbling finches* and *seedeaters* that are generally larger than most finches and unlike them in both diet and appearance. They are not great avicultural favorites.

GRASS FINCHES

Unfortunately many of these and other finch species cannot legally be shipped from Australia, the land of their birth, or owned by fanciers

Color mutations are rife in the popular Zebra Finch (Peophila castanotis), *giving fanciers a wide choice in hues and patterns.*

in this country. But fortunately some of the species that come under this heading can be—and have been—bred in the United States from imported birds and so are sometimes available.

To me one of the most exquisite creatures on land, sea, or in the air is the splendid *Lady Gould finch* of Australia. There are three different varieties, which is certainly an abundance of a good thing, the Black-Headed, Red-Headed, and Yellow-Headed. The coloring is definitely divided and appears to be brilliant, smooth lacquer that has been deli-

E·H·HART

The Cutthroat Finch (Amandina fasciata) *is another well-liked species of the widely variegated family of finches.*

cately poured by a master hand. From the same Island Continent comes another beauty, the *Parson finch,* which breeds easily in captivity.

The *Grass finches* of Australia, including the Lady Gould and Parson finches, are a magnificent and very popular group of finches. Others are the *Shafttail* and the *Masked Finches,* the *White-eared,* the *Fire finch* (very aggressive toward other birds, but very lovely), the *Plumhead, Painted,* and *Fire-tailed finch.*

Of all the Grass finches the *Zebra finch* is the most popular and the

most available. Easy to breed and feed, the zebra matures early and has
produced several interesting mutations in color. Today one can find
White Zebras, Silver (a dilute), *Pale Grays, Pieds, Penguins, Blues,
Fawns, Cinnamons* and *Creams.* They are inexpensive, can be finger-
tamed, and make excellent pets.

PARROT FINCHES

This is a very beautiful group of finches, but they are also very rare,
very expensive and extremely shy. They panic easily and are difficult to
approach. Being extremely rapid on the wing, they can easily injure or
kill themselves when frightened. I feel that there are too many draw-
backs to owning these lovely birds to recommend them as pets or companions.

MANNIKINS

Very hardy, numerous, available, and inexpensive, the mannikins are
not, as a rule, as brilliant in color as most of the popular finches. Mannikins do, however, exhibit great variation in genetic characteristics and
are generally heavier in body with heavier but shorter heads than most
of the waxbills (see p. 257). Mannikins, whydahs, weavers and waxbills (Ploceidae) all belong to a very large family of small, brightly
hued birds distributed throughout the Old World. The handsome, intriguing mannikin makes a very desirable pet.

The *Society Finch* is as much in demand as the zebra finch. Society
finches are about as inexpensive and available. There is a crested form
with the crest very much like that of a canary. Color varies radically so
that seldom will you find two exactly alike. There are white societies,
cinnamon, dark and chocolate brown. If whites are inbred, they produce
blind chicks.

The *Pictorella* (also *Pectoral* and *Pectoralis*) is one of the most
radiant of the Australia mannikins. It is sweet in temperament and
makes a lovely pet. As a breeding bird it is not entirely successful.
Keep your Pictorella where it is dry, since dampness can cause respiratory troubles.

Australia also sends us the *Chestnut-Breasted mannikin,* a very lovely
finch but only fair in the breeding pen. This pretty mannikin makes an
ideal pet. The last of the Australian mannikins to be recorded here is
the *Yellow-Rumped,* rather drab in color and not much in demand.

The *Spice Finch* of India is available, inexpensive and is a hardy, well-
liked mannikin. There are a trio of desirable finches that are listed in
England as mannikins but known in the United States as nuns. These

popular little birds, the *Black-Hooded, Tri-Colored* and *White-Headed nuns* are generally available. Other mannikins are rare and expensive.

WAXBILLS

Two of the waxbills come from India, one from Australia and twenty-five from Africa. These tiny feathered charmers are usually not vividly hued, but harmonious patterns and aesthetic color contrasts make them very pretty birds. Most are both well liked and available.

The *Tiger Finch* (also called the Indian strawberry finch) is a favorite due to its attractiveness, availability, and inexpensiveness. It makes a lovely cage bird and pet, but is, for the aviculturist, a rather difficult bird to breed.

Other pleasing waxbills are the *African Fire Finch,* a very calm, happy, and easily bred species. There are several different fire finches, some quite beautiful and also rare except for the *Lavender Fire Finch* (or *lavender waxbill*), a popular, inexpensive, hardy finch. Fire finches are sometimes allowed to fly free, but seldom stray far from their aviaries. There are also a series of anatomically colored finches such as the *Blue-Capped, Red-Eared, Crimson-Rumped, Orange-Cheeked, Black-Crowned, Orange-Winged, Red-Faced,* and *Gold Breasted waxbills.*

The *Cordon Bleu* is certainly one of the most exquisite of all finches in its scintillating feathered cloak of lustrous sky blue. Inexpensive, not rare, peaceful, this very beautiful little bird wears its high popularity with extreme grace. Breeding success has been rather erratic.

WHYDAHS

These strange birds of the Dark Continent are the true Jekyll and Hydes of the bird world. In full plumage during the breeding season most whydahs are exotically lovely, but the males in their seasonal molt become colorless and drab, and lose the long decorative tails that are the identifying feature of most whydahs. These interesting pets are easy keepers. The tail feathers of some whydahs grow so long that if these appendages become wet the bird cannot fly.

The *Paradise Whydah* is the most favored of the species because of the long (often as long as 14 inches), elegant tail feathers it displays when in full feather. The paradise is an easy keeper, generally available and not too highly priced.

Other popular whydahs include the *Pintail,* attractive and available; the *Broad-Tailed,* not easily found; *Jackson's Whydah,* handsome, flamboyant but rare and expensive; the *Red-Collared, Red-Shouldered, Red-Naped,* as well as a host of others not readily found here. If you can find a specimen of the spectacular (and fairly expensive) *Giant Whydah,* you will have acquired a real avicultural prize. These stunning creatures are comparatively large in body with long, flowing tails, are very hardy and peaceful, and make elegant pets.

WEAVERS

This is a very large family of prized, gregarious finches. They are hardy, long-lived (about twelve years) and easy to care for. As pets they are difficult to finger-tame because of their innate shyness, which also causes them to panic when kept in small cages.

The *Orange Weaver* is the most wanted of this family because it is pretty, available, and inexpensive. Other popular varieties of weavers are the *Half-Masked,* frequently available; the *Napoleon,* almost as much in demand as the orange weaver; the *Red-Billed,* a hardy but aggressive bird; and several other kinds of weavers not often imported.

Miscellaneous Finches and Other Birds

There are several attractive Cuban finches, and the splendid *Black-Crested Finch,* the cock displaying a long, black head-crest of delicate feathers. Among the South American birds of this family the *Saffron Finch* is quite popular. Saffrons are prolific breeders and wear a feather cloak of glowing, lustrous golden-yellow.

Java Ricebirds (or *temple birds*) are very well-liked finches. Only the canary and budgerigar outnumber the Java as a household pet. Their feathering is smoothly textured with sharply contrasting colors. They are easy keepers and need only a seed diet to stay in condition.

There are three color varieties of Java rice finches, the *Gray Java,* the *White* (*Albino*) *Java,* and the *Pied* (*or calico*) *Java Ricebird.* The departure from the normal gray coloring is due to color mutation. If they are aviary bred, not captured wild, all the varieties are excellent breeders. Finger-tamed Java ricebirds make delightful pets.

There are a number of attractive European finches of which the *European Bullfinch* is an avicultural favorite. Black feathers contrasting with soft gray and rosy pink made it a most comely bird. The *Chaffinch* is subdued in color and quiet in character. The *European Linnet* is rather plain in color, but sings a sweet song and is used by canary breeders to produce splendid singing hybrids. A rather larger, strong-bodied finch, the *European Greenfinch,* is a soft, smoothly shaded bird that is hardy, a good breeder, but rather aggressive. The *Brambling Finch* is very hardy and an attractive bird that needs little care, but is also quite aggressive. There are two *Redpolls* that are seldom seen in this country.

CARDINALS

Cardinals are charming, brilliantly colored birds that make admirable pets. The most dazzling of all male cardinals has got to be the *Virginia Cardinal* and its similarly crested subspecies. Velvety rich, deep scarlet with small accents of black, this beautiful bird can be seen all over the country during warm weather.

The popular *Pope Cardinal* (lacking in crest) and the vivid *Brazilian Crested Cardinal* are both handsome birds, the Brazilian very much in demand as a cage bird and pet. It has been bred here but, like all cardinals, is susceptible to cold. The Brazilian Crested is a large, highly active bird that makes a lively companion. There are several other varieties of cardinals, but they are rare and seldom seen here. Both *grosbeaks* and *hawfinches* are not in very great demand, perhaps because the most outstanding of these birds are not readily available in America.

SOFT-BILLS AND JAY THRUSHES

The most-in-demand member of the *soft-bill* family is the *Peking Nightingale*. These lovely, lively birds are hardy, in good supply, and not expensive. Their song, when at its best, is truly splendid. Related species include the exquisite *Silver-Eared Mesia,* the beautiful *Black-Headed Sibia,* and the active little *Blue-Winged Siva.*

The several kinds of *Jay thrushes* in the family of babblers are not scarce and make entertaining pets.

BULBULS, WAXWINGS AND FLYCATCHERS

The *Bulbuls* of Asia, Africa, and Malaysia, and the *Fairy bluebirds* are not generally available, though they are most delightful birds. Bulbuls are extremely popular in the Orient because they are so easily tamed and many are fine songsters. In the wild they are gregarious when on their own—but prone to join together to attack their enemies. Like so many of our contemporary birds, their courage is amazing. There are a trio of waxwings, of which the *Cedar waxwing* is most familiar. *Flycatchers* must be mentioned even though they are rare because the *Paradise flycatcher* is credited with being one of the most beautiful birds in the world, joining the multitude that share this sobriquet.

TROGONS

The fabulous *Quetzal,* finest of the *trogons,* is a splendid, calm and easily trained bird with an interesting history. The quetzal was revered by the ancient Aztecs as a sacred bird. Today it is the national bird of Guatemala. This iridescent green and brilliant red beauty makes a really

superb pet. The finest specimens of these noble birds that I have ever
seen were in the aviaries of a commercial animal dealer in Costa Rica.

The *Cuban trogon* is rather easy to acquire. It too is truly elegant in
its glistening, vari-colored metallic cloak of feathers. Although not as
large as the quetzal and, like all Trogons, delicate and difficult to feed,
once acclimated the Cuban trogon will do well. They are worth every
bit of time necessary to bring them to acceptance of a new environment.
Of the really exotic soft-bills the Trogons are certainly among the most
desirable.

THRUSHES

This is a tremendous family of birds with quite a number of very
lovely active members that exist in many parts of the globe. They are
known to aviculturists for their lilting song and their propensity, when
correctly handled, to become tame and precious pets.

The *Hermit Thrush,* the *Wood Thrush,* and the *European Song Thrush*
are all splendid additions to any aviary. The most popular and coveted
of all thrushes is the *Shama* whose thrilling song matches the charm of
its personality. The *Duyal* and the *Dama* are both very comely and desirable thrushes. Our own very familiar *American Robin* is of this family
as are the *European Blackbird,* the *Gray-Winged Blackbird* and the
Black Robin of South America. The last-named bird is easily trained,
becomes a wonderful pet and, when in good voice, is one of the outstanding songsters in the bird world.

There is a very rare bird called the *Jewel Thrush* that is actually an
extremely elegant Pitta rather than a true Thrush, but I list it here because of its name. A migratory bird of great brilliance in plumage, it is,
like all Pittas, difficult to find. There are many Pittas from many tropical
countries and all are rarities in the North American avicultural world.

NIGHTINGALES, MOCKINGBIRDS AND LARKS

The *Nightingale* has been known from ancient times for the lovely
quality of its song. It was a pet and cage bird in Babylon; down through
the ages it has never lost its attractiveness to man. The *European Nightingale* is softly colored and sings splendidly. The *Thrush Nightingale* is
also from Europe, while the *Orange-Billed Nightingale* inhabits central and northern South America and has somewhat richer coloration.

Mockingbirds sing loudly and clearly. Though some are rather shy,
they will train well once you have gained their confidence. The *Mexican
Blue Mockingbird* is one of the most desirable of the species. In color
it is a dusky blue; there are several subspecies quite similar in size,

song, and color. Most of us are acquainted with the *Common Mocking-bird,* which we welcome for his song and his ability to consume large quantities of harmful insects. He is a citizen of the New World and is a gifted singer and mimic. There are several New World mockingbirds, one of which, the *Colombian Mockingbird,* is particularly available.

Skylarks and meadowlarks are also familiar to most of us. They are sweet and cheerful little feathered creatures with a trilling, piping song that has brought a measure of peace and serenity to the hearts of many a man and maid walking the fields on a sunny summer day.

BIRDS OF PARADISE

"By their names shall ye know them." *Birds of Paradise:* what else could they be other than the most exotic, ethereal creatures clothed in feathers? So sublime are the ornamental feathers of these fantastic birds that they were almost brought to the point of extinction through savage man's egotistical need to adorn himself with their plumes. Later a similar fate again almost overtook these gorgeous creatures when sophisticated women used the elegant plumage to decorate their hats in a vain attempt to borrow for themselves some of the eternal beauty of the bird of paradise.

There are many species and subspecies of birds of paradise. All are now protected from the onslaughts of man and a repetition of the slaughter that has twice put the species in jeopardy. Yet these sublime creatures are still rare—perhaps it is better so, for paradise should ever be dearly bought and not within the reach of man. I have seen three birds of paradise that have been hand-tamed, that were truly magnificent pets. One of the three was actually a related species, a Satin Bower-bird.

Other Birds That Talk

Birds that can be taught to talk have always intrigued mankind, perhaps because he considers the ability to talk, to convey thoughts and desires through speech, his by divine right, or a reward for his struggle through evolution. Yet man inevitably takes great delight in the birds that mindlessly mimic speech.

In the ability to mimic human speech certainly the *Greater Indian Hill Mynah Bird* is without peer. It learns speech with amazing facility, including speech patterns, specific enunciation, and even dialectal overtones. There are many other mynahs but none as popular, or as available, and as quick to learn to talk as the Greater Hill Mynah. If you are fortunate enough to own a mynah bird, remember that the shadowy jungle is their natural habitat, so do not hang the cage of your pet mynah in the sun. Always provide him with an abundance of shade.

The common but sagacious *crow* and *American Raven* make ideal pets and can be taught to talk. So can *rooks* which, when tamed, seem to have a marvelous sense of humor. The brilliantly iridescent *European Starlings,* with tutoring, will also learn to mimic human speech but not with the insouciance of some of the other talking birds. There is an *Indian House Crow* that is said to make a charming pet and that can learn to mimic word sounds quite well.

A Host of Other Birds

There are so many birds of all colors, all sizes, for all men and women, and for all climates that there seems no end to them. Pigeons will be given their own section as will the keen-eyed, voracious birds of prey, for they are distinct and popular birds that fill specific purposes for man. But there are still all the common *magpies* and *jays,* the *starlings* and *orioles, troupials* and *blackbirds, tits* and *nuthatches* (a wonderful pet, the *Japanese Tumbler* is of this family); the radiant *tanagers, sunbirds* and *honeycreepers* that feed on nectar; the fascinating and brilliant *cocks of the rock, bell birds,* and the tiny *hummingbirds* whom Audubon so poetically described as "glittering fragments of the rainbow." There are *ibis, woodpeckers, hornbills, kingfishers* and *toucans.* The last-named fascinating birds are such wonderfully droll pets that I must tell you a bit more about them.

Toucans are easily tamed and trained and their huge flamboyant beaks are rather thin shells that cannot inflict a dire wound. They have wonderful personalities and make completely satisfying pets. To become thoroughly and quickly tamed they should be acquired when young; then they become exceedingly affectionate, demanding attention and reciprocal affection. Their antics are constantly interesting and charmingly comic. All toucans are found in the American tropics.

The *Sulphur-Breasted Toucan* is readily available and the cost is increasing all the time. *Cuvier's Toucan* is usually a bit easier to train than the sulphur-breasted. Larger and more uncommon is *Swainson's Toucan,* which has green eyes and flaunts a huge beak of deep yellow, black, and red. My preference among the toucans is the *Toco,* a large and naturally friendly bird of splendid color. Though not readily found, the Toco is well worth searching for. Other toucans are very scarce in this country.

Flaunting a huge and colorful beak, Swainson's Toucan (Ramphastos swainsonii) *makes a droll and interesting pet.*

Trumpeters make first-rate pets and when shown affection by their owners make sounds that mimic the contented chuckling of a happy human. These strange, endearing South American birds adore being petted and made much of and can't seem to get enough loving from their human family. In their native land trumpeters are sometimes utilized as guardians of poultry flocks. These flightless birds are a single genus with three species and several subspecies. Their devotion to their master is unique in the world of aviculture, more closely akin to the affection one would expect from a dog than from a bird.

There is no color quite like the red that clothes the *Scarlet Ibis*. Have you ever seen a flock of these dazzling birds wheeling against the blue and white background of a tropical sky? I sat in a rowboat in the Caroni Swamp, on the outskirts of Port of Spain, Trinidad, and watched the Scarlet Ibis approach in huge flocks, flashing like living rubies in the rays of the setting sun, passing overhead to their nesting grounds in trees along the river.

Penguins are familiar to everyone because of their unique appearance and habits. They are flightless and their natural habitat is the cold waters of Antarctica. There are about twelve recognized species of penguins, some very large, others descending in size to birds with the body size of a pheasant. Though some species travel a good deal farther South than the Arctic Circle, most penguins do not thrive well in any place other than frigid areas. I list them here because friends of mine have a *Humboldt Penguin* pet, proof that there are always exceptions to the rules. They live in a very temperate climate, yet the bird seems quite content and happy. This little fellow is an impish pet that constantly begs for affection, attention—and fish fillets.

Many of the birds you have read about in this section seem to be of similar size and shape, but their diversity of song and brilliant color sets them apart and individualizes them. It is wonderful to have so many lovely feathered creatures within our reach should we want them as pets to gladden our homes with their songs and chatter. And it is still more wonderful to be aware of those native to our area, with bright colors and charming voices that reach out to us to make any day somehow a little brighter and happier.

Pigeons (family *Columbidae*)

Pigeons are the descendants of the wild rock dove (*Columbia Livia*) of Europe and Asia. Ornithologists list all domestic pigeons under the one title, *Columbia livia domestica,* but beside the domestic pigeon there are wild pigeons and doves in many areas of the world. In fact there are more than eight hundred forms listed scientifically under one family, *Columbidae,* and divided into three subfamilies, the fruit pigeons

(*Tretoninae*), seed-eating pigeons (*Columbinae*), and the crowned pigeons (*Gourinae*).

Fruit Pigeons are generally brilliantly colored, almost completely arboreal, and found in tropical and subtropical sections of the Old World, Australia, the East Indies, the Philippines, New Guinea, Celebes, and Sulu Archipelago, and the Malay Peninsula.

Doves along with the common pigeon, are included in the subfamily of seed-eating pigeons. These birds, of more terrestrial habits than the fruit eaters, are a very large group. Specimens can be found in most parts of the globe, including Australia, home of the many kinds of handsome bronze-winged pigeons.

The giants of these wild pigeons are the crowned pigeons, found only in the area of New Guinea. Some of them are equal in size and weight to a small turkey. In Caracas, Venezuela, I saw several specimens of a huge pigeon in pet shops. These were not wild pigeons. They were domesticated and looked exactly like an ordinary pigeon except for their size, which was larger than that of a very big chicken. They were called simply *Palomas Gigantis,* and were probably a very large local breed of runt pigeon.

Long before the Christian era, pigeons were used to send messages, living carriers of airmail that changed the course of history, began and ended wars, caused empires that had endured for ages to crumble, or bore sweet tidings of love and birth. In the book of Genesis we find that a dove brought Noah the news of dry land; Greco-Roman literature informs us that pigeons were bred and kept as pets and couriers in those ancient times. As late as the First World War airborne doves, eternal symbols of peace, ironically winged above the rending sounds of ravished battlefields to bring messages of victory or defeat. Through the long centuries pigeons have been used by man as couriers, as pets, and even as food. Here is a creature whose service to man has literally known no bounds.

There are more than three hundred domesticated breeds of fancy pigeons in a fantastic variety of colors, sizes, flying abilities, conformation and feather growth. Certainly a high tribute to mankind's ability to shape living creatures to his own needs, through the selection of genetic factors.

Today pigeons are raised as a hobby or for food. The racing pigeon provides for young, old, or middle-aged one of the finest hobbies that can be found. Throughout most of the civilized world, no matter where you may travel, you will find avid fanciers and racing homer clubs. In some areas purses and betting have changed the hobby from a sport to a much more intense form of competition. Races in the Northeast United States have brought as much as $10,000 to the winning loft. As a result of this kind of invigorating competition, more people throughout the world raise and race racing homers than any other known breed of pigeon.

The classes for show birds are Old Cocks, Old Hens, Young Cocks and Young Hens. In the larger shows, particularly for the more popular breeds of fancy pigeons, classes are also provided for Yearling Cocks and Yearling Hens. Exhibitions are important to the pigeon fancy. Only at the shows can fanciers compare the quality of their birds with others and assess their own ability as breeders. Without shows there would not be standards toward which the breeders could strive and to which their birds should conform. Without standards there would be no reason for the great pigeon variety that men of imagination and genetic skill have found interest in fashioning.

DOMESTICATED BREEDS OF PIGEONS

Wild *Rock pigeons* domesticate easily and are frequently crossed with domestic pigeons. The wild rock and its crosses are the familiar pigeons one sees in all parts of the world, descending in flocks in parks to be fed by tourists and people who make a fetish of feeding these birds.

The *Racing Homer,* of all pigeons where performance is the one essential, is the most in demand. Color, size, and type have little importance where the racing homer is concerned. The two essentials demanded by breeders and fanciers are that the bird, when released, returns to the home loft with the greatest rapidity and upon reaching home traps without delay. The *Miniature American Crest* is a chunky, pretty pigeon, peak-crested and not widely bred. The greatest concentration of fanciers and breeders is in New Jersey. The *American Domestic Flight Pigeon* and the *Modern Show Flight Pigeon* are bred almost exclusively in the New York State area.

Antwerps were originally racing pigeons, but are now an ornamental breed, frequently seen in European shows, but seldom here. This is also true of the *Archangels* and *Bagdads.* The *Syrian Bagdad,* however, does have a small but loyal group of fanciers in the United States. *Dragoons* were once flyers, but now are show birds. The *Barbs* have a limited but enthusiastic nucleus of fanciers in this country and so too have the *Damascenes.* The *Carneau,* of Belgian and French origin, is a utility breed that is a favorite in North America and widely exhibited. *English Carriers* have their hobbyists here and are probably the most popular pigeon breed in England.

The *Fantail* is an ancient, unique breed much in demand as a show pigeon in America. The lovely *Indian Fantail* is also popular here. *Syrian* and *Thai Fantails* do not have many devotees in this country. *Frillbacks* are an interesting breed, displaying curls or frilled feathers on the back and outer wing coverts. Both *Frillbacks* and *Helmets* have small groups of interested fanciers in this country.

The *Giant Homer* is a well-liked pigeon bred for exhibition and food production (squabs). There are many other families of homers popular in the various countries of Europe but not in America. The *American Show Racer* is basically a racing bird, but its ability as a flyer has taken second place to its potential as a show-ring competitor. The *Hungarian Pigeon* has always been quite popular with American fanciers since its introduction here just before the turn of the century. The strikingly marked *Lahore Pigeon* that probably originated in Persia is becoming increasingly well liked here.

A pigeon of utilitarian value is the large and handsome Giant Homer. This is a fairly recent breed that was developed in the United States.

The *Ice Pigeon* has a limited group of appreciative fanciers in America and so does the *Jacobin,* a "feather" breed with a hood, mane, and frontal chain that forms a feathery circle completely masking the head and face of the bird like a muff. *King Pigeons* originated as a breed in this country. Like the giant homer they are a dual-purpose breed—one of the most popular pigeons for show and squab production in the United States. *Mondains* hold this same position in Spain and France where the *French Mondain* is as popular as the King for show and meat production. There is also an *American White Swiss Mondain* that has its advocates here.

A rather unique pigeon is the *Thai Laugher,* which is bred and selected for vocal qualities rather than the other qualities that pigeon breeds are generally selected for. The laugher is thought to have originated in the vicinity of Mecca. A gentle breed, it emits cooing sounds that mimic human laughter. The laugher makes a fine pet—if you can accept being constantly laughed at. Erect, long-necked, the slim *English Magpie* and the *Maltese* pigeons are exhibited here but not widely bred. For more than twenty-five years the *Modena*—an ancient breed that had its origin in Italy—has been a most popular breed in this country. The *Mookie* from India, and the *Nun,* bred here only for exhibition purposes, have aroused the interest of a small group of fanciers in America.

A very well-liked breed here is the *Oriental Frill.* Of Turkish origin, it is beautifully laced and has an interesting, unique head shape. The various *Owl Pigeons* are archaic, rather small breeds from Asia that are somewhat, but not wildly, popular here. The *African Owl* is one of the smallest of all pigeons. Some of the owl breeds have crests and beak formations like the Oriental frill.

Of the many breeds of Pouter Pigeons few are bred or shown in any great number in the United States, although the *Pigmy pouter* has found rather wide acceptance here since 1920. In Spain, where breeds known as *Thieving pouters* are fashionable, a regulated and highly organized sport has been fashioned around the flying activity of these pigeons. A hen is released and then a number of cock birds belonging to different owners and breeders are sent after her. The cock that entices the hen to follow him to his loft is the winner. Rather a typical Spanish sport, romantic, gay, and uninhibited.

Runts are giant pigeons that were one of the first breeds to be introduced to the United States. They have since been brought to an apogee of development in the *American Giant Runt.* The name gives one pause; it is like calling a breed of animals or birds "the smallest giants in the world." Monks are bred here, but have never become widely accepted. *Strassers* are fairly popular as a dual-purpose breed and the *Swallow pigeons* have their fanciers here, the best-liked being the *Crested Hairy Swallow,* brought here in the nineteenth century. Most of the wide range of *Trumpeter pigeons* are very rare in the United States and only a very few are raised here.

THE FLYING BREEDS

There are a vast number of pigeons listed under this heading—all are birds that perform in the air. The flying categories are: *tumbling* (a very large group of which some varieties are bred here), *pack-flying* and *high-flying.*

Birmingham rollers perform backward somersaults in an unbroken sequence. They are highly popular show birds in the U.S. The *English Long-faced Tumbler* is also held in high esteem here, as is the *Ancient Tumbler. Flying Tipplers,* bred in England for astonishing flying endurance (up to twenty hours of continual flight) are well liked in this country. The *Stettin Tumbler,* which doesn't tumble and is actually an exhibition bird, also has its admirers in the United States, while in New Jersey and New York the *Moorhead Tumbler* is rather well liked.

An interesting breed, the *Turbit,* has always had its avid followers in America. It is an exhibition bird that is somewhat similar to the Owl pigeon. *Silkies* or *Lace Pigeons* are the result of a genetic feather mutation and are most admired in the *fantail varieties.*

The breeds listed here are those that are being bred and exhibited and can be bought as pets in this country. One can of course find other breeds to select from, but not in such great abundance. Certainly anyone interested in acquiring a pigeon as a pet has a vast choice, and, should he enter into breeding, squab raising, or exhibiting pigeons, it cannot help but bring great interest and enrichment to his life.

WILD PIGEONS AND DOVES

Earlier (p. 264) I named the three subfamilies under which were listed the wild pigeons and doves. I gave them rather short shrift in the opening paragraphs of this section, simply because the prospective pet owner has so many beautiful and interesting breeds of domesticated, man-made breeds from which to select. But I cannot completely ignore the wild birds of this species because they too are interesting and have value as pets. Before I name some of these birds you should be aware of the fact that there is no difference between pigeons and doves. Generally smaller birds of the species are called doves.

Fantail Pigeons have long been favorites with fanciers who breed and exhibit fancy and exotic species.

Fruit pigeons are found in the tropical and subtropical regions of the Old World. The *Pin-tailed Fruit Pigeon* and the *Wedge-Tailed Fruit Pigeon* are both found in the lower Himalayan areas. Others are from Africa, but the most colorful make their habitat in Australia and the East Indies. The *Black-chinned, Painted, Superb Bronzed, Orange-naped,* and *Blue-Tailed fruit pigeons* are all lovely in color and make nice pets.

Seed-Eating Pigeons include the typical pigeons and numerous other pigeons commonly called doves. This group is more terrestrial than the fruit pigeons. The *Blue Rock Dove* is the wild ancestor of our domestic pigeon. The *European Wood Pigeon,* the *Bare-eyed, Splendid* (a very beautiful seedeater), are not native to America, but the *Mourning, Gray*

Ground, Eastern Ground doves and the *Red-tailed, Red-billed,* and *White-crowned pigeons* are. There are also in this family many so-called turtledoves from Europe, Africa, and Japan. Included in this category is the well-known *European Turtledove,* and kin to all seedeaters are a large variety of *Bronze-wing Pigeons* including a great number of handsome, brilliant-winged species. *Quail-Doves* and a large sub-family of *Bustard-Pigeons* must also be added to this category.

In the *Crowned Pigeon* subfamily we find six forms of giant birds, all found near the New Guinea area, all ground feeders. Some of these pigeons are equal to a small turkey in size and weight.

Birds of Prey (order *Falconiformes*)

Eagles, hawks, vultures and owls are all predacious birds. These great-winged, diurnal creatures are the feathered royalty of the infinite skies. Primitive types of these beaked and taloned carnivores existed at the dawn of the Cenozoic era, thirty-six million years ago.

When man began to build his civilization, he was awed by the majesty and unbridled ferocity of these kings of the air; legends about them, born in the mists of time, were woven into the richly colored tapestry of mankind's early history and religions.

Within the crumbling walls of Machu Picchu, high in the thin-aired reaches of the mighty Andes Mountains, I saw carved stone bas-reliefs of the great Andean Condors that the proud Incas worshiped as Gods of the World Above the Earth. And in a spectacular kind of bullfighting that had religious overtones they tethered the birds to the backs of bulls. But, being sacred to that vanished Indian race, the condors were set free, unharmed, once the ceremonies were over.

On the walls of Egyptian temples and tombs at Luxor and in the Valley of the Kings, in heat that seemed to dry the very marrow in one's bones, I have studied the carvings and paintings of Horus, the Falcon-Headed God, protector of the dead, and seen the bas-reliefs depicting the activity of the Vulture Goddess, Mut. The priests and people of that land where civilization was born believed every Egyptian had three souls, and that two of them were represented by bird forms. In ancient Babylon and Assyria people prayed to an eagle-headed, winged demi-god, and a golden eagle screamed his scorn of all things earthbound as he flew over silent Mount Sinai where Moses received the Covenants of the Lord. This noble bird symbolized the strength and protection of the Lord on the awesome day when the Lord spoke to Moses, His voice a thunder in the Heavens and the earth. He said:

Ye have seen what I did unto the Egyptians, and
   how I bore you on eagles' wings, and brought
   you unto myself.
Now, therefore, if ye will obey my voice indeed, and
   keep my covenant,
then ye shall be a peculiar treasure unto me above
   all people:

                                              Exodus 19: 4–6

Classical Greek mythology brought into focus Zeus, god of the sky,
and his companion eagle, the only bird that dwelt on fabled Mount
Olympus. The Romans had a similar mythological god whose familiar
was an eagle, but in Roman legend the name of the god was Jove. In
more modern times the thunderbird, a part of the folk belief of some
Western Indian tribes in America, was depicted as a huge raptorial
bird that produced the thunder, lightning, and rain. In the Amerindian's
metaphysical philosophy the eagle is the symbol of expression of the
Great Spirit.

Owls were an early symbol of wisdom, perhaps because they looked
so solemn, as though communing with their inner being. Ravens and
crows, because of their funereal lack of color and their voices, were
thought of as birds of ill omen. It has ever been the large birds of prey,
the conquerors of the vast upper silences, that enriched the legends,
mythology, and religions of man throughout history.

Falconry

The dog, the cat, the eagle and the hawk—all these man has used in
the pursuit of game, but falconry has been the most emotional, ecstati-
cally thrilling, and fiercely stimulating method of hunting ever devised.
Throughout the ages of man royal hunters have used the large raptors
in the chase. Falconry had become a regulated sport in Central Asia
before 2000 B.C.; Alexander the Great, as early as 1700 B.C., rode afield
with his falcons; and the sport flourished in England where it was introduced by the Saxon kings who were avid falconers and who brought
with them their fierce Gyrfalcons, captured by the Saxons from the
brawling, marauding Vikings, who were themselves keen falconers. At
one time in medieval history falcons were so highly prized that they
were used as a monetary means of exchange.

When knighthood was in flower, falconry was a sign of social status,
dictated by the breed of bird the falconer flew. A falcon on a man's fist,

a merlin on my lady's glove, were symbols of the rank of my lord and lady and a part of the opulent, gaudy pageantry of that long-ago era of gallantry. The mighty emperor rode forth on his gaily adorned stallion with his hooded golden eagle on his fist; a king carried a spirited gyrfalcon; a prince a bold peregrine falcon; and a clerk a male sparrow hawk as a pet, not as a hunter, for only the females of the predacious birds are used for the hunt. The females are the largest and the fiercest of this clan of birds of prey. Pets can be—and have been—made of all the raptors, but to make a pet of the largest species' rapacious females takes a special kind of skill and daring and requires intense dedication.

The young are not best for taming and training as with other birds. When these predators are taken from the nest as young downy chicks for training, they become pets, losing the killer instinct so necessary for falconry. They must be captured when grown or almost fully mature, and then trained, if they are to be the fierce, savage predators they are meant to be. They must be kept sharp, honed to a fine savagery, and fed just enough to stay at hunting weight (yarak). Pet predatory birds must be fed much more food to keep them content and moribund. A lot of patience goes into the often dangerous work of training a hunting bird and tragically, trained raptors die fairly early from accidents and disease when in captivity.

The art of falconry was put into words on the printed page in a fantastic volume *De Arte Vernandi Cum Avibus* that took thirty years to complete. It was written by the brilliant, learned Emperor Frederick II, a passionate scholar who was also a devotee of the art of falconry. Frederick was the grandson of the famous Barbarossa, himself a rabid falconer.

The furnishings and accouterments described in Frederick's great tome are still in use by the fraternity of falconers throughout the world; I should say those still left in the twentieth century.

The raptor (bird of prey) is controlled by two narrow strips of leather called *jesses,* one end attached to each powerful leg and the other to a short leash. Bells of silver or brass are sometimes used to adorn the jesses. Over the raptor's fierce head a *hood* is adjusted to blind it and keep it quiet. Often this hood is decorated with a few colorful feathers jutting upward from the center like a proud crest. The hood, or blinder, is necessary during the early training or *manning* (handling by man) to help the bird become accustomed to its master and domestic environment. The *lure* or dummy prey, used in later training, is a leather sheath sometimes feathered on the outside and stuffed with raw meat inside. The *gloved fist* is a glove, made of heavy leather for hawks and of thick, reinforced buffalo hide for eagles. By holding the jesses between the fingers of the gloved hand the falconer controls his bird, which is kept hooded and fed pieces of raw meat while the falconer pets and vocally cajoles her until she gives every evidence of being docile and tame enough to begin working. When the tamed, trained bird is released from the falconer's fist to fly game, the jesses remain attached to her legs but the hood, of course, is removed. Though it is not a hard-and-fast rule, generally the long-winged falcon is used for open country and the shorter-winged hawk for hunting wooded areas.

THE BERKUT GOLDEN EAGLE

Of all the fierce and mighty birds of prey, the savage *Berkut golden eagle* is without a peer. This huge eagle was hawked as early as 689 B.C. by a great Chinese Emperor. Saladin (Yusuf ibn Ayyub), the Sultan of Egypt and Syria in the twelfth century—who captured Jerusalem and brilliantly opposed the armies of the Crusaders—flew a wing of Berkuts against the Crusaders, wreaking havoc among their ranks. It is said that Saladin and his arch opponent Richard Coeur de Lion (Richard I, King of England) would halt hostilities between their vast armies so they could, with their attendants, engage in friendly, chivalrous competition with their favorite Berkuts.

These almost priceless birds were the aerial hunters of Ghengis Khan, Kublai Khan, and the early Czars of Russia. They were flown at ferocious Asiatic wolves, bears and deer; and a cast (two eagles) have been flown successfully against such dangerous adversaries as the savage snow leopard of the high snow-capped Himalayan mountains of Central Asia, the clouded leopard of Southeastern Asia, and even so dangerous a beast as the monstrous Manchurian tiger.

These fabulous eagles are capable of an air speed of one hundred and twenty miles an hour when diving at their prey for the kill. They are still flown in China, Tibet, and in the Kirgis steppes of the Soviet Union by the Khans of the mountain Mongol Tribes. The Berkuts of the Khans are generally both hooded and sealed (their eyelids sewn together) until they are ready to be flown by their primitive masters, who consider them killers that are trainable but not tamable or trustworthy. The hunting method used by these tribesmen involves starving the Berkut and then flying her at prey, making her eager to hunt and kill so she can eat to alleviate her gnawing hunger. At 25 pounds in weight, a wingspread of over 9 feet, and talons like great razor-sharp steel scimitars, these majestic birds are a match for any man. They are said to live in the wild for over one hundred years and to range over a hundred miles of territory each day when hunting to feed their brood.

Of the many raptors the mighty Golden Eagle (Aquilar chrysaetos) *knows no peer. Fierce and magnificent, the savage Berkut golden eagle is the aristocrat of the species and was flown as early as 689* B.C.

OTHER HUNTING EAGLES

The *Golden Eagles* of America (*Aquila chrysaëtos*) are slightly smaller than the Berkut, but are still formidable birds of prey. To have manned and trained one to falconry is a rewarding feat. There are about six subspecies of this handsome predator in America. Like all the raptors their sight is phenomenal. These are birds of the high mountains and, in common with all eagles and hawks, the golden eagle has talons and claws of tremendous power. The *Tawny Eagle* and the magnificent *Verreaux Eagle,* both inhabiting Africa, are close relatives of the golden eagle.

The *Bald Eagle* (*Haliæetus leucocephalus*), used as the emblem of the United States, is one of the group of handsome, powerful sea eagles. The Alaskan form of this noble predator is exceptionally large and powerful. The bald eagle, like all sea eagles, feeds on fish. *Steller's Sea Eagle,* a heavy-beaked black-and-white giant is one of the largest members of the eagle family. I have heard of sea eagles being flown at migrating salmon, sturgeon, and other large fish, but this is not legitimate falconry and the fish-eating eagles are seldom trained or kept except as exhibits in zoos.

Harpy eagles (*Thrasaetus harpyia*) range from Mexico to the Argentine. These are large, fierce, spectacular birds with an erectile crest and punishingly great grasping power in their claws. They feed on monkeys and sloths. Because of the crest that gives the bird the appearance of having hair, coupled with its ravenously ferocious attacks on bands of large monkeys, this raptor was given the name of the harpy from Greek Mythology, that ravenous monster with a woman's head and a bird's body. *Hawk Eagles* (or *Crested Eagles*) are fiery, noble raptors much like the harpy eagle. The *Martial Eagle* and the *Crowned Eagle,* both from the Dark Continent, are large, fast-flying savage birds. The Philippines is noted for its *Monkey-Eating Eagle,* a large, powerful ferocious, fearless monkey-hunting bird and one of the biggest raptors in the world.

FALCONS (FAMILY *FALCONIDAE*)

In this group of handsome, savage predacious birds we find the raptors most often used in the art of falconry. The flight of these birds is a thing of unsurpassed beauty. Their ocular prowess is beyond compare, and their appetite for the stirring ferocity of the hunt is never satiated.

First must be listed the *Gyrfalcon* (also *gerfalcon*) (*Falco rusticolus*) of Norway, Iceland, and Greenland. The great gyrfalcon, the largest and most strikingly beautiful of all the falcons, is unexcelled in the sport of falconry. This swift, bold bird of prey has always been the favorite of kings. The *Peregrine Falcon,* most commonly used in Europe, is considered the most versatile as well as the most perfect hunter among the raptors. It was widely used by nobility and rode to the field on the fists of princes, dukes, earls, and barons.

The *Duck Hawk* (*Falco peregrinus anatum*), a much-sought-after raptor in America, is the counterpart of the peregrine falcon. It is known by falconers for its audacity and speed in flight. *Saker falcons* are large, excellent hunting birds. *Merlin's, Sparrow hawks* and *Goshawks* all can be, and have been, trained to falconry. *Eleanor's*

Falcon and the *Laggar Falcon* of India are both excellent hunters of quail. The *Laughing Falcon* of the South American rain forest preys on snakes and lizards.

Proudly beautiful, the Gyrfalcon (Falco rusticolus absoletus) *from the lands of ice and snow, was the favorite of kings. The illustration depicts a young bird not yet in mature plumage.*

Cooper's hawk (*Accipiter cooperii*) is swift in flight and is a fierce hunter, while the *Eastern Red-Tailed Hawk* is one of the true buzzards and is often called the hen hawk. These latter birds are tractable in temperament. There are many *hawks* and *kites, goshawks, kestrals* and *ospreys,* predatory birds that range in size from the tiny pygmy falcons of Indonesia and Malaya to the gaint Berkut and Monkey-Eating eagles. *Old World kestrals,* brave and easily trained, were often kept as pets by children and servants in medieval times. The true *buzzards,* represented here by the *Eastern red-tailed hawk* and generally called hawks in the United States, are, like the Old World kestrals, gentle, excellent pet material. There are more than seventy-five forms of these lovely birds. Many of the smaller species of hawks make fine pets, but the larger species are truly a handful.

CONDORS AND VULTURES (FAMILY *CATHARTIDAE*)

It may seem strange to find vultures listed as pets, but I have a friend who has a private zoo where his vultures wing down to him on call to be petted. They follow him around the compound like the family dogs. He is not the only person who has tamed these huge birds and I know of some that have been trained as hunting birds. Among this group of aerial creatures are some handsome species. All are known for their powerful beaks rather than the strength of their feet and claws. There is little difference in size between the sexes.

Since earliest days these scavengers have been seen by man as symbols of death, for in the wild they are ever present where life ends, and their shadows—cast upon the earth from above—are the winged silhouettes of cloaked death. Vultures are the natural undertakers of the wild, devouring what is left of creatures killed by other predators. In the strange but balanced scheme of things the vultures, pursuing their instinctive way of life, render a distinct service of no little value, especially in the tropics.

On the African plains I caught with my camera a sequence of life and death that is repeated over and over again in the wild places of the world: a wildebeest, brought down by a tawny lioness was feasted upon by the pride—the huntress, her black-maned mate, and two half-grown cubs. At a respectable distance three huge hyenas loped tirelessly in circles around the hub of the pride and their kill, awaiting their turn at the feast; above, limned by the blazing sun of equatorial Africa, vultures floated lazily on outstretched wings, kept aloft by updrafts of warm air. When the lions had eaten their fill and moved away to find respite, the hyenas came in. The vultures wheeled down like silent shadows to share in the feast, only to be harassed by the quarreling hyenas who tore great gobs of dripping meat and bone from the carcass and slunk away. The vultures settled down like a dark cloud, covering the mutilated prey, and a small silver-backed jackal moved hesitantly close, then suddenly darted in to snatch a mouthful of meat, whirl and quickly retreat to avoid the beating wings of the vultures. When the huge predatory birds had finished and, with evident difficulty and a great flapping of wings, lifted their heavy bodies from the earth, nothing was left of the wildebeest but a scattered smudge on the ground that swarms of ants were already busily working to eradicate.

This typical drama of rebirth through death was enacted against a background of huge grazing herds of wildebeests and zebras with the blue and purple twin mountain peaks of Batian and Nelion in the far distance.

The *South American Condor* (*Vultur gryphus*) inhabits the great rugged crags of the awesome Andes. This is the largest predacious flying and land bird in the world, with a maximum wingspread of 14 feet having been reported. The condor possesses a powerful beak with which it can rend large carcasses and seize living game. Revered by the ancient Incas and Aztecs, the redoubtable condor became woven into their legends, mythology, and religion. A close relative of this huge predatory bird—and also larger than any other airborne bird of prey other than its South American kin—is the *California Condor*. Both these huge birds have been trained and tamed. The young of the species remain in the nest for twenty weeks; for ten of those weeks they are flightless juveniles fed by their parents. After the first ten weeks the flight feathers begin to develop. At seven months they begin to learn to fly and forage for themselves. Like the elephant, the largest land animal, these biggest of land birds nest and raise young only in alternate years.

The *King Vulture* is aptly named, for it is large and by far the handsomest of the carrion-eating clan. I was once gifted with a fully mature king vulture, which luckily I was not allowed to take out of South America. Though vultures are classified as birds of prey, they seldom make kills of their own, depending for their sustenance on animals already deceased. The *Bearded Vulture* or European lammergeyer, found in the Alps and east to China, has been accused of swooping down and toppling deer, sheep, and even humans over precipices. This particularly interesting bird is difficult to classify correctly. Some zoologists claim that it could very well be an eagle rather than a vulture. The aggressive *African White-headed Vulture,* the *Egyptian,* the *Black,* and the *Griffon vulture* of Spain, the *Hooded Vulture, Turkey* and *Yellow-headed vultures,* are some of the better known of this family. The heads and necks of these birds are generally devoid of feathers and they are noted for their graceful, soaring flight on wings both broad and long.

OWLS (ORDER *STRIGIFORMES*)

Owls are distinctive predatory birds. They are nocturnal and so blessed with vivid night sight that their maneuverings in the dark seem almost magical. They also see quite well in daylight. These predatory birds possess a zygodactyl foot (two toes forward and two backward), each toe terminating in a sharp, curved claw.

Owls in general have great economic value to farmers, for they kill uncounted numbers of rats that eat, foul, and destroy grains and crops. The female owl is usually larger than the male, a sex characteristic enjoyed by all carnivorous birds other than the vultures. There are two basic families of owls, the barn owls (*Tytonidae*) and the typical owls (*Stigidae*).

Of medium size, the *Barn Owls* lack ear tufts and exhibit a curious feather formation on the head that forms a distinctive facial disk. The most common of this group are the *American Barn owls* and the *White-breasted Barn Owl* of Europe and Africa. The American barn owl can be tamed and given pet status. In this family can be included the *Haitian Barn Owl* and the *Cape Grass Owl* that has its habitat in South Africa.

The *Typical owls* are a large family of many sizes; some of them flaunt on their heads the feather tufts called horns. The larger owls in this group are rather fierce predators, though I have known the *Great Horned Owl,* one of the largest of North American owls, and the huge *Snowy Owl* of the Arctic regions to have been trained to hunt in the manner of a falcon. Incidentally the snowy owl is undeniable proof that owls have excellent daylight vision, for in the Arctic the sun, during certain months, shines all day. If this predacious bird lacked daylight vision, it could not hunt during those months. Obviously the species would starve itself to extinction. I have been told that the *Giant Eagle Owl* of Europe is untamable. It is the largest of all owls, a huge rapacious bird that feeds on rabbits, grouse, and wild creatures of comparable size. I suppose that as soon as this book reaches the public I will receive letters from people who have tamed this great owl. It seems that there has never been a creature, no matter how ferocious and savage, that someone somewhere hasn't challenged, reached out to, and found a level of understanding upon which they could meet in rapport.

In the same typical owl group the *Burrowing owls* are found, a species that understandably lives in burrows in the ground like a rabbit. The *Pygmy owls* are tiny gnomes that are terribly cute and as ferocious as their small stature will allow. Three of the more common forms of pygmy owls are the *Cuban,* the *Trinidad,* and the *Northern Ferruginous,* the latter bird a native of the United States. These small owls can be tamed and will become pets, but they must be handled frequently if you wish them to remain tame and tractable. There are so many worthwhile birds of all kinds that, in my opinion, an owl would not be the best choice for anyone wanting a pet. But each one of us must walk his own path, so if you fervently wish to make a pet of an owl, lots of luck. Just remember to work diligently with him and have patience, for the "wise old owl" is not as wise as his reputation would have us believe he is.

Game Birds

Their group title (Game Birds) designates the nature of their use to man. These are birds that man hunts as a sporting gesture toward those archaic ancestors who hunted to live. No, the twentieth-century man who finds pleasure in a day of hunting birds is not cruel, atavistic, or sadistic. He probably finds his greatest enjoyment in tramping the unspoiled woods, in the scents peculiar to wild growing things, and in the uncluttered pleasurable association with his gundog. The gun, the shooting, is a charismatic thing, the sauce that adds piquancy to the dish.

Though game birds are generally bred in quantity to stock shooting preserves, they are also often kept as pets, individually or in pairs. As a matter of fact there is a small species of tiny quail (button quail) that many breeders of other species of birds (budgerigars, cockatiels, etc.) keep in their large flights to perform the work of janitors—or scavengers if you wish—disposing of seeds and other food that falls to the floor of the flight.

If you are selecting for shooting-preserve stock, look for agility, feathering, size, and wingspan and select only the common well-known species, not exotic types. Hunters prefer the ordinary, familiar game birds, not the way-out kinds because killing them makes the hunter feel slightly guilty. Meat-type birds should be selected for conformation and size. If, however, you are looking for a pet, the most unconventional and radiant species may be your choice.

Game-bird hens produce eggs from early spring to early fall. So mate the hens about one month before production is wanted, using one pheasant cock or mallard cock to five to eight hens, one quail or chukar cock to two to four hens. The hens start producing eggs at the beginning of April, so for maximum egg production breeders use a lighting schedule from April 1 to about October 7, which allows for a gradual increase of light to a peak of twenty hours. Eggs are hatched in incubators and must not be stored more than a few days before incubation. Most game-bird eggs will hatch in from twenty-three to twenty-seven days and need between 65 to 75 percent relative humidity. Feeder and water space requirements are exceedingly important in growing game birds well, and good ventilation and cleanliness are musts for success. Rice hulls and wood shavings are generally recommended for use as litter.

Cannibalism is rife among game birds but control can be accomplished in a variety of ways. First of all, the bird's food should contain an optimal balance of amino acids and salt levels. Secondly, de-beaking can be indulged in. Chicks can be debeaked when one day old with an electric debeaker and the process repeated in six weeks. Both the upper and lower beaks must be squared off about one quarter of the length (measuring from the beak tip). Other methods to control cannibalism include increasing floor space and reducing light intensity and duration.

Pheasants, Quail, Partridges, and *Peafowl* are all of the family *Phasianidae,* a large, complicated group. The New World quails and grouse are the most abundant upland game birds on the North American continent. If properly fed and cared for, they thrive in captivity. Should you desire to begin breeding any of these game birds for commercial use, eggs and chicks should be purchased from a reputable breeder whose stock is healthy, carefully selected and produces well. Breeding birds do best in enclosed housing rather than outdoor accommodations where the environment cannot be controlled. Insulated, fan-ventilated housing results in better breeding performance. For *Chukars* and *Quail* wire flooring is best, but *Pheasants* are best kept in floor pens with litter. *Mallards* and other ducks of similar habits need rock or sloping pens for maximum drainage.

The Breeds of Game Birds

I suppose any bird that is hunted and shot for sport or meat can be listed in the game-bird category. But for our purpose I will name only those birds, hunted or used as pets or ornamental fowl, that can be considered in the basic families of game or fowl-like birds.

GROUSE

Grouse range in size from the *ptarmigan* to the huge *capercaillie* of northern Europe and Asia. They can be distinguished from other fowl-like birds by the feathers that cover the lower legs. The wonderful *sage hen* of our Western prairies is a fine example of this species. Grouse seem to be susceptible to various infections and are, therefore, not usually considered as pet material.

QUAIL

New World quails on the other hand thrive in captivity, make excellent pets and are widely distributed. The *Bob White* is a familiar quail which, in some areas, is loved and protected as a song bird. The *California Quail* is a pretty, crested bird and the *Scaled Quail,* handsome in its blue and gray plumage, adds a decorative motif to the drier sections of our Southwest. Quail eggs, hard-boiled and dipped in a tangy sauce, make delightful hors d'oeuvre and are frequently served in such a manner in the capitals of South America.

Much smaller are the *Old World quails* among which we count the *European, Japanese,* and *Rain* quails of India and Burma. The small but very pretty *Painted Quail* makes a handsome pet. *Button Quail* are quaint little ground birds (mentioned earlier) that are easily frightened and do not like being handled. But when taken young they are easily finger-trained and tamed to be fine pets.

PARTRIDGES

Among the patridges there are a number of handsome species that are popular as game birds. The *European Partridge,* introduced into the United States as the *Hungarian Partridge* is a well-liked game bird. The *Indian Chukar Partridge* is now bred in this country in large quantities to stock preserves. There are the *French, Bamboo, Tree,* and *Red-legged partridges, the Spur Fowl* and the very attractive *Crested Wood Partridge.* The last-named with its crest (only the male is crested), chestnut wings, and green body makes a handsome pet. The *francolins* resemble the partridges in general appearance and habits.

PHEASANTS

Some of the world's most spectacular and superb birds are included in this family that thrives and breeds freely in captivity.

Originally pheasants inhabited Asia and the islands off the Asian coast. Their plumage reflects their exotic origins. Our most popular game bird, the *English Ring-necked Pheasant* is a hybrid resulting from crosses of *Black-necked* and *Chinese ring-necked pheasants* with some small influence from other pheasant sources. The breed was originally produced in Europe.

In the area of truly ornamental fowl the various pheasants know no peers. The *Mongolian, Formosan,* and *Japanese pheasants* are beautiful birds. Length of tail and color patterns differentiate the *Long-tailed pheasants* from the ring-necks. *Elliot's Pheasant* from China is a handsome bird of bright chestnut plumage enhanced by markings of black and white. The splendid *Reeve's Pheasant,* also bred originally in China, sports feathering of gold laced with black and carries a superb 6-foot-long tail. *The Mikado Pheasant,* from the mountains of central Formosa, is much like the Elliot in pattern but iridescent bluish-black replaces the areas of chestnut. The Japanese *Soemmerring's Pheasant* gleams like a just-burnished copper pot with many feathers scalloped in white.

The birds mentioned above conform to our general concept of what a pheasant should be, but there are many rarer forms, frequently so beautiful and strange in conformation that they seem not to be of the same family at all. These extraordinary pheasants make the most wonderful ornamental and pet birds.

Ranking among the most brilliant birds on earth are the *Impeyen* or *Monaul pheasants* with plumage that exhibits an iridescent sheen beyond compare. The glory of their blazing metallic purple, copper, and gleaming green feathering conceals the heaviness of their bodies. Their natural habitat is the high mountains of central Asia. The *Eared pheasants* exhibit long, pointed tufts of feathers on each side of their head, lending them their identifying name. Their tails are feathery and highly ornamental. The *Brown-eared* and the *Blue-eared pheasants* are the most common of this species.

The lovely *Silver Pheasant* is the best known of the *kaleege* group in which the males are generally handsomely marked in black and white that has a silvery cast. There are also in this group *Bel's,* the *White-crested, Horsfield's* the *Black-backed* and *Black-Crested pheasants.*

The *firebacks* are birds of the dense, tropical jungle of the Malay Peninsula and the nearby islands. If bought as pets, they require heated quarters during cold weather. The *Siamese Fireback* is a very attractive bird, clothed in gray, black, bright yellow, and red. The *Maylayan* and *Borneo crested firebacks* are also very handsome pheasants. The *Blue pheasants* are exquisite birds and include the rare *Imperial Pheasant* and the *Swinhoe's* and *Edward's pheasants* of Formosa and Annam.

Closely related are the *Golden* and *Lady Amherst pheasants,* the cock birds of both species noted for their dazzling beauty. The best-known and perhaps most exquisite in his feathered robe of yellow, orange, black, green, and brilliant red, is the *Golden Pheasant* of China seen frequently in the U.S. The Lady Amherst is a bit larger and darker in coloration.

The *Napoleon Peacock Pheasant* is one of the rarest and most comely of pheasants. Peacock pheasants are smaller and more delicate in appearance than others in this large family. The identifying feather "eyes" in the peacocks' trains are carried on the feather tips by the peacock pheasant males. The *Common Peacock Pheasant* and the *Germain Peacock Pheasant* are both lovely birds and frequently available.

The largest of the group, except for the peafowl, are the *Argus pheasants.* The *Great Argus Pheasant* is a truly magnificent bird rivaled only by its close relative, *Rheinhardt's Argus Pheasant,* which is quite a rare species from Annam. The two central tail feathers of these superb pheasants sometimes reach a length of 4 feet.

Peafowl, or *peacocks* as they are commonly called, have long been used as ornamental fowl on large estates and are noted for the magnificent trains of the male during its courtship display. The *Indian* or *Blue Peafowl* (*Pavo cristatus*) is native to India and Ceylon and the habitat of the *Javan* or *Green Peafowl* (*Pavo muticus*) is from Burma and Siam to Java. The *Black-shouldered Peafowl* is a mutation from these two basic forms, and the gorgeous *White Peafowl* is an albinistic form. I suggest that a specimen of the Indian Peacock be selected if the bird is to be used as a pet. The males of the Javan peacocks, particularly those from Burma, are often quite savage and unpredictable.

The *Tragopans* of China and the Himalayas are also of the pheasant family. These are large, powerful mountain-dwelling birds, the males displaying fleshy "horns" and brilliantly colored bibs of skin, which they puff up during courtship.

Although *guineafowl* are interesting birds, I doubt that many have ever been thought of as pets, so I will simply drop a few small but interesting morsels of information about them: They make good watchdogs, just as geese do; they will crossbreed with chickens, but the offspring will be infertile (mules), and the tiny chicks of the guineafowl are called keets. All known 35 forms are found in Africa.

Truth to tell, were I to name and describe every known bird, this book would become so unwieldy it would be a chore to carry or move from place to place and eventually it would become more of a problem than the worst pet you could select from its pages. But there are still other fowl that we must consider in our quest for the best pet for you and we must pursue our almost impossible dream and carry on.

SWANS, GEESE AND DUCKS (ORDER *ANSERIFORMES*)

These birds are all powerful swimmers with short, strong legs, three toes in front joined by a web, and one small hind toe. The legs (tarsi) of geese and swans are reticulated (netlike) and those of the ducks are partially scutellated (scaly). In all, the family *Anatidae* to which these birds belong encompasses 151 species with 96 subspecies, giving us a grand total of 247 different forms. The swans are the largest of the *Anserine* birds and among them are 9 forms and 2 genera. The North American *Trumpeter Swan,* identifiable from all others by its black beak, is the largest of all swans.

Among the familiar *white-plumage swans,* including the just-mentioned trumpeter, we also find the *whistling* and *whooping swans,* the *Mute* and *Bewick's swans.* Two of the most sensational when first found were the *Black Swan* of Australia and Tasmania (now also abundant in New Zealand), and the *Black-necked Swan* of Southern South America and the Falkland Islands, which needs a tropical latitude to prosper. This latter *anserine* carries white feathers on its body, has a black neck, and a red and blue beak. The dazzling black swan is solid velvety brownish-black with wings tipped with gleaming white and a vermilion beak. The wing feathers are gracefully curled, adding to the overall splendor of this lovely bird. These exquisite creatures make beautiful ornaments for a garden lake, their reflections in still water a twofold vision of almost abstract beauty. The splendor of the black swan is rivaled, in my eyes, by the grace and virginal purity of the white swan, which always reminds me of a lithe-limbed, beautiful ballerina.

Everyone knows what a goose is, has seen them on farms, perhaps eaten of their delicious flesh, and maybe has had the dubious honor of having been chased by one. Heads held high, hissing like a barrel of snakes, and rushing at trespassers, geese are dangerous adversaries—the "watchdogs" of many a farm or estate. Next to the swans they are the largest *Anserine* fowl. Not counting the domestic strains, there are about forty kinds of geese thoroughly distributed to most areas of the globe.

Both the domestic and wild species are easily kept and can become good pets, particularly the females; the males can become belligerent and combative with maturity. Some of the wild geese are handsome birds with a stately manner.

The *Canada Goose* of North America is well known as the "wild" goose of our continent, but there are many other geese well worth the trouble of exploring. The *Semipalmated* and the *Spur-winged Goose* of Australia and Africa, respectively, are both worthy of your attention. So are the large *Greater Snow Goose* and the *Graylag Goose* of Asia and northern Europe, the latter generally considered to be the ancestral font from which flowed the genetic tide that fashioned most of our domestic breeds. There are also the *Blue,* the *Bean* and the *Pink-footed Goose* from Russia, the *White-fronted, Hutchin's Goose,* and the small *Cackling Goose* to mention just a few of the many fine wild breeds.

The brants are much like the cackling goose in coloration and size and are divided into three forms: the *American brant,* the *European brant,* and the *Black Brant.*

The upland geese of South America and the Falkland Islands count several handsome species among their number; the *Magellan, Ruddy-headed, Gray-headed, Andean,* and *Barred Upland Goose* included.

There are three prominent breeds of domestic geese, the white *Chinese,* the white *Embden,* and the gray *Toulouse. Pilgrims,* like the Chinese a bit smaller than the others, are also a fairly well-liked domestic breed. If you become enamored of geese and plan to breed them, I must warn you that they are very difficult to sex. If you put a pair together and find that both are laying eggs, you will know that you have made a bit of a mistake. Geese, incidentally, unlike humans, mate for life.

Smaller and more aquatic than geese, many ducks are quite beautiful and the approximately 175 forms that make up the family have almost worldwide distribution. Usually the drake, or male duck, is more brilliantly colored than the female. Birds of this group fall into three general categories; the *Tree ducks,* the *Diving ducks,* and the *Surface-Feeding ducks.*

The most common of our domestic ducks is the *white Pekin.* Caricatured and animated as Disney's Donald Duck, it has stolen the hearts of three generations of Americans and is known throughout the world wherever there is a screen and a projector. The Pekin is both an excellent meat bird and a good pet. Other desirable domestic ducks are the *white Muscovy,* the *mallard, Muscovy,* and *Rouen.*

If you like duck eggs, the best performers in this department are the *Kahki Campbell* and the *Indian Runner*.

The *tree duck,* not to belie its name, likes to perch in trees and in South America is often trained by the Indians to become an amusing pet. The *Black-bellied, Gray-necked, White-faced, Bahama* and *Fulvous tree duck* are all tree perchers. The necks and legs of these ducks are longer than those of many of the other breeds, making this species much like an intermediate between the geese and the ducks. Included in the large group of surface-feeding ducks are some of the most attractive game ducks in North America. The most familiar undoubtedly is the *Mallard* of North America, Europe, and Asia. Close relatives of the decorative mallard are the *Spot-billed, Australian Gray, African Yellow-billed,* both forms of our North American *Black ducks,* and the *Red-legged Black Duck.* The male of the *Comb Duck* species sports a fleshy, ornamental comb (or carbuncle) on his head. Some of the *Sheldrakes* are handsome birds but very quarrelsome. If you select a sheldrake as a pet and have other pets of the family *Anatidae,* it is best not to keep the sheldrake with the others, for in mixed company it will probably cause trouble.

Resembling mallards, but smaller, the *Teals* give us males that are generally colorful and females that are much more mundane in hue. The *Green-winged* and *Blue-winged teals* are commonly seen in North America. In Europe and Asia the *Garganey Teal* is a very similar bird. The *Ringed* and *Brazilian teals* make their home in South America.

Midway between the mallards and the teals in size are the brightly hued *Widgeons* of which there are three known species, the *American widgeon,* the *Chilean widgeon* and the *European widgeon.* Generally conceded to be the most graceful ducks in silhouetted flight are the *Pintails.* The *North American pintail* is a favorite of duck hunters. There are *European* and *Chilean widgeons* and a related pintail species called the *Bahama duck.*

The American *Wood Duck* and the *Mandarin Duck* are two of the most beautiful ornamental species to be found. The males of both are particularly lovely during the breeding season. Then, like many of the other *Anatidaes,* they assume eclipse plumage that scarcely differentiates them from the female of the species. Both these breeds make fine pets.

The last of our duck groups are ungainly birds on land, waddling along like obese matrons at the beach. The hind toe is lobed. They are short and wide in conformation; their bodies are set well ahead of their legs. No landlubbers are these ducks.

The *Canvasback* and the *Redhead ducks* are the most readily distinguishable in this category. Both breeds are native to North America.

The Wood Duck (Aix sponso) *is one of the most beautiful of the family* Anatidae. *Our illustration shows a Wood Duck rising from the lake in the foreground while a pair of Canvasbacks* (Nyroca valisinaria) *enjoys the serenity of the water.*

The Ring-necked Duck is also a native of our country and is the most attractive of the group. Representing the scaups or blue-bills are the *European Scaup,* the *Greater Scaup,* and the *Lesser Scaup.* The latter two are both natives of North America. All scaups are rather drab-colored birds.

The *Tufted* and the *White-eyed ducks* are found in Europe, Asia, and Africa, while the attractive *Rosy-billed Duck* inhabits southern South America.

All these game-type birds make ornamental and handsome pets, but cannot be considered in the same pet category as the songbirds, talking birds, raptors, or psittacine birds with abilities that give pleasure to their owners and place them in a unique niche. Wild turkeys are also considered to be game birds but rather than being good pet material, I think they are fantastic stuffed and roasted, reminding Americans to be thankful for their many blessings on that truly American holiday, Thanksgiving Day.

Ornamental and Domestic Fowl

Jungle fowl, which are closely related to pheasants, are quite comely in color. The *Red Jungle Fowl,* distributed from Kashmir to Java and found in several forms, has the distinction of being the ancestor of our domestic chicken. What horror to think that had this jungle denizen not come into being in the vast and glorious evolutionary plan of species today's world would be barren of Kentucky Fried Chicken parlors. The various jungle fowl families are basically very much alike, yet differ in certain aspects. For instance, the male of the *Javan Jungle Fowl* species varies considerably from the others. Its comb is blue and green in color, is devoid of serrations, and it has but a single throat wattle, while the *Red Jungle Fowl,* the *Ceylon,* and *Sonnerat's Jungle Fowl* all have red combs (the Ceylon's marked with yellow) and all sport double throat wattles. The cock jungle fowl is polygamous and defends his hen harem and territory with beak and spurs.

DOMESTICATED FOWL

Fowl (quoting the dictionary) are: The domestic or barnyard hen or rooster (domestic fowl), a gallinaceous bird (often designated as *Gallus domesticus*) of the pheasant family descended from wild species of Gallus (jungle fowl). And that, I would say, is an accurate definition of a chicken. Strangely enough the earliest usage of domesticated chickens was for religious and sacrificial purposes and the so-called sport of cockfighting. Domestication took place sometime between 3,000 and 2,000 B.C., and before the eating of chicken meat became general these birds were valued for their egg-laying ability. Because of that ability hens became symbols of fertility and due to the elaborate mating displays indulged in by the cock birds, the males became symbols of eroticism as well as of male health and virility.

The modern breeds of *chickens* are divided into two types, the *Asiatic* and the *Mediterranean*. Of the Mediterranean there are thirty-two commercial breeds and twenty-four ornamental. Many of the latter are exceedingly exotic and have reached to such spectacular pinnacles as the *Long-tailed Yokahoma* with the cock birds flaunting tails that stretch to a length of 20 feet. I do not think it necessary to go into a long dissertation about the individual breeds of chickens of which there are a large number both here and in foreign countries. To mention just a few American favorites there are the *Bantams, Rhode Island Reds, White, Barred,* and *Plymouth Rocks, White Leghorns* and *Leghorn crosses, Cornish* and *Cornish crosses,* and *Wyandottes.* More exotic are the *Salmon Faerolle* and the *Auracana,* the chicken that lays colored eggs and is consequently called the Easter Egg Chicken.

Showing fine chickens in classes at the big fairs throughout the country has become highly competitive and is an exciting hobby. The accumulation of ribbons and awards a pet has won is highly rewarding to the fancier.

Feeding Birds

Your pet bird, no matter what species it represents, will not do well unless fed correctly. Most novices, due to a lack of knowledge in this very important area of bird keeping, do not provide the necessary food elements to sustain health, rebuild cells, bring them through their moults, and build up their resistance to disease. Some of the ailments that beset both pet and aviary birds are due to dietary deficiencies.

To feed your bird properly you must understand its physiology. All birds exhibit higher normal body temperatures and breathe with much greater rapidity than other animals. Their metabolic rate is very high and they lack teeth with which to crush, tear or grind their food. They possess crops where their food is crushed so it can be digested. Some birds manufacture "crop milk" with which they feed their young. Due to the fact that most birds fly (there are some that do not) they are creatures of intense activity and constantly burn up a good deal of energy that must be replaced through their food intake.

Many species of birds are seed eaters, which supplies them with an abundance of carbohydrates. But seeds are lacking in proteins and

only a very few contain fats while most have little of the needed vitamins and minerals. The owner must therefore supply his pet with the
necessary elements in which seeds are deficient. Basic additives are
greens, vegetables, fruit, bark (for roughage also missing in the diet),
grit to grind food in the gizzard, cuttlebone or mineral blocks for
calcium, phosphorus and other minerals.

Seed eating birds in the wild state will ingest a variety of hard shelled
seeds (which they shell, eating only the kernel), grasses, vegetation,
berries and fruits, bark for roughage, ripening soft seeds, tree leaf buds,
gravel or sand, and an insect here and there. The bird is eating a
fairly well rounded diet that fulfills most of its needs. Natural selection
weeds out those birds who cannot exist and reproduce their kind on
this diet.

Raptorial birds in the wild find all that is necessary in dietary factors
to survive, grow and reproduce. When a Hawk swoops down upon its
prey like a bolt of feathered lightning and makes its kill, it doesn't
feast on the muscle meat alone. The Hawk eats the entire animal rip-
ping it open and eating the liver, lungs, heart, spleen, stomach and
its contents, the fat-encrusted intestines, and the half-digested vegetation the intestines contain. By consuming the entire animal the Hawk
has ingested a well-rounded diet.

Unlike many other animals birds must have food always at hand
instead of being fed at regular intervals. There is one important point
to remember; do not over-feed your bird with fattening foods and
allow him to become obese. It shortens his life and leads to the formation of fatty tumors. I will list the most popular and available birds,
of which there are many, and the necessary foods they must be fed to
meet all of their dietary needs, the specific foods their species prefer and
must have, and the additives necessary to keep them vigorous and
feracious.

BUDGERIGARS

These delightful psittacines need a basic seed diet of approximately
50 percent canary seed and 50 percent large, white millet. Add about
10 percent hulled oats to this mix. For baby Budgies a mixture of 60
percent canary and 40 percent millet with the oats added is best. A good
quality grit should be supplied and a cuttlebone, mineral block, or both,
clamped inside the cage. Fresh greens should be fed about three times a
week. Dandelion leaves, grass cuttings, clover, celery leaves, carrot
tops, carrots, apples and any other vegetables, fruits or greens the birds
will eat. Wash all greens to float away any harmful sprays that may
have been used for insect control. See that fresh water is always avail-

able in a tube waterer. To the water can be added a few drops of liquid vitamins that are water soluble.

This is a basic diet for Budgerigars that will sustain a pet bird. But if you are breeding Budgerigars and exhibiting them it is *not adequate* because it lacks a sufficient amount of two important factors, protein and fat. To overcome this lack Budgie breeders use many kinds of supplementary foods. I also have my own formula for a supplementary food that will meet all the requirements necessary and will tempt the appetite of my Budgies. I mix together cooked rice, hard boiled eggs, cooked hamburger, dried parsley, tomato juice, celery salt and a pinch of regular salt. I prepare a large quantity and freeze it, allowing only an amount that can be used in about three days to thaw out and be refrigerated. To this base I add milk, a good feeding oil, a bit of vitamin powder and mix the end result with a 30 percent protein game bird food which is composed of tiny pellets just the right size for Budgies.

I feed this mix in a crumbly consistency and once the birds become used to it they prefer it to seeds, particularly if they are feeding chicks. Show birds and breeders keep in beautiful condition and youngsters feather out well and grow rapidly. Chicks brought up on this supplement can't seem to get enough of it. My birds have won many Best In Show and other top awards because I have used the best imports (English) and their finest chicks to breed from, and have fed the proper foods to bring them into breeding condition and the chicks to a maturity that mirrors the full flower of their genetic heritage.

CANARIES

These great little songsters are actually hard-billed *Finches* so they feed on a basic seed diet of 75 percent canary seed, 25 percent rape seed for choppers, with rollers using a higher percentage of rape seed. Canaries also need a mixture of conditioning seeds which consists of equal parts of steel-cut oats, dandelion seeds, teasle, gold of pleasure, maw, flax, thistle and some wild grass seeds. Pet shops often mix and sell this blend in bulk. Feed the conditioning mix about three times a week with a few drops of a good feeding oil mixed in to add to the vitamin value of the mix. Your Canary will also need grain food such as dandelion (leaves and roots), escarole, endive, clover, grass seeding heads, a bit of apple or pear and occasionally a little slice of orange.

If your bird goes off its song or is in a moult, egg food that can be bought already mixed (or which you can make fresh yourself) should be supplied. This same food should be given to breeding birds every day, but for the house pet in good health and singing his heart out two or three feedings of egg food a week is more than adequate. Occasionally a bit of brown or whole wheat bread soaked in milk is relished by your Canary. Be certain your Canary has fresh water always available and a cuttlebone and/or mineral block to nibble on and do *not* allow him to become obese.

COCKATIELS

These wonderful pets require a basic seed diet similar to the Budgerigar but with the important addition of sunflower seeds and some red millet. I also like to feed my Cockatiels a supplement quite similar to that which I feed my Budgerigars. Remember the cuttlebone, greens and fresh water.

SMALL PARROT-FAMILY BIRDS

This category includes *Love Birds, Lineolated* and *Brotogeris, Parrakeets* and birds of the parrot family that are of approximately the same small size. They should be fed the same seed mixture as recommended for Cockatiels except for the addition of peanuts, pumpkin and hemp seeds. A separate container offering the 30 percent protein Game Bird pellets can be offered. Greens, fruit and corn on the cob is also appreciated by these little hook-bills. Fresh water, mineral blocks and a coarser grit than that given to Budgerigars should be supplied. Bread soaked in milk is also relished.

It should be understood that *fresh water, mineral blocks and grit* should be supplied to *all birds* listed.

LARGE PARRAKEETS AND CONURES

Again the basic seeds—canary, millet, oats and sunflower seeds—are used with peanuts, pumpkin and hemp seeds as an everyday food requirement. Fresh fruits of most kinds and a wide variety of vegetables combined with a good supplement and bread soaked in milk provides a good diet.

LARGE PARROTS

Macaws, Cockatoos and other large psitticines come under this title. These larger Parrots should have additional grains added to the basic diet fed to the larger Parrakeets and Conures. Add to the seed mixture dried corn, dried peas, peanuts, dried sweet peppers, and Pigeon food mix. Good pet shops will have all these food elements all ready mixed and ready to feed. The addition of prepared Monkey food biscuits as a supplement is also recommended. My Macaws were always very fond of bananas, papaya, and cooked rice. They also relished bread and milk and, when eating breakfast with us, loved butter, scrambled eggs, bacon, and toast.

A supplement for the big hook-beaks can be the already mentioned monkey biscuits, dog food pellets, or the supplement suggested for Budgerigars but with a little raw meat added. About one third of the diet should consist of vegetables and fruits, according to many aviculturists, though I personally do not think this is necessary with the mixtures and supplements available in the United States. When I lived in South America I did feed more than one third vegetables and fruits because supplements and good seed mixes were not available. If you wish to feed vegetables and fruits the list is long and includes bananas of course, celery stalks, raw and cooked carrots, rice, fresh peas in the pod, carrot and beet tops, dried fruits (dates, figs, raisins, etc.) apple, green and cooked corn on the cob, and just about any other vegetables and fruits available.

FEEDING FINCHES

A basic Finch food mix that can be bought in pet shops along with an insectile mix, greens, fruit and a dietary supplement can be used as a rule-of-thumb diet. The basic mix consists of plain canary seed, small Australian millet, white proso millet and a small amount of oats. As a seed supplement use the same mix recommended for Canaries, fed separately.

So many of the families of Finches need special or supplementary foods to stay healthy and vigorous that I will list them separately. Finches and Softbills do not accept unfamiliar foods readily so it is best to mix any new ration with familiar foods until it is willingly eaten. If you have an older bird who relishes the diet you feed, put him with the new arrival (or arrivals) and he will lead the newcomers to eat the unfamiliar foods.

Lady Goulds should be fed the standard Finch mix with added small yellow Finch millet. Gouldians very much enjoy spray millet and should also be supplied with a separate dish of niger seeds. The same supplement recommended for Budgerigars or a commercially prepared Finch supplement is good for these gorgeous Finches. Also feed lots of fresh greens.

Parson, Grassfinches, and *Zebra Finches* should be fed the same diet as that given to the Lady Gould. *Fire Finches, Star Finches* and *Painted Finches* are given the basic Finch diet but supplemented by meal worms or other live food. If you can persuade these Finches to eat an insectile mixture or a bit of raw hamburger as substitution for live food it will make feeding them much easier.

Parrot Finches are as rare as they are beautiful. One must remember when feeding a Parrot Finch pet to approach quietly and attempt never to startle them as they panic easily. Assuming your pet was acclimated before being purchased, offer him a mixture of hulled oats, canary seed, white proso millet, small red millet, and rice. Fresh ears of corn are relished but must be rationed, and a good insectile mix into which some hamburger is mixed to replace the live food these birds crave. Tempt your pet to also eat some supplement and fresh greens.

All the *Mannikins,* including the popular *Society Finch,* are essentially hardy little fellows and will do very well on the basic Finch mix with supplements, greens and an insectile mix. This group also includes the always available and well liked *Cutthroat Finch* of African extraction. *Waxbills, Weavers,* and *Whydahs* can be fed the same diet as offered to Mannikins. Review the supplement recommended for Budgerigars and add a little hamburger to the insectile mix.

Java Rice Birds can be given the same diet fed to Budgerigars. As hardy as they are popular their diet is simple and they need no fruit or live food to keep them healthy.

The several *Rose Finches, California Linnets,* and *Spanish American Finches* (*Cuban, Piliated* and *Saffron Finches*) should all be offered the same diet that was recommended earlier for Parrakeets with the addition of extra live food (meal worms) or an insectile mix with hamburger.

Meal worms are usually recommended for birds who need live food. They are readily available at the better pet stores and easily fed. But it is my opinion that a commercial insectile mix food, raw hamburger and hard-boiled egg (particularly the yoke) are more easily kept and fed and are a better source of animal protein. If you prefer live foods where they are recommended, meal worms can be raised in your home. White worms are also easily kept and raised for bird feeding. The latter worms can be purchased in large aquarium stores. They are a favorite fish food. Peanut butter can be offered all birds. Some will eat it, others won't, but it is worthwhile to try because it is a highly nutritious food.

Generally speaking *Buntings* should be fed the standard Parrakeet seed mix suggested earlier in this section but with a much greater percentage of canary seed incorporated. Also feed fruits, insectile mix, greens and a supplement that contains meat and eggs. Frequently Buntings will refuse commercial insect mixes and should then be offered meal worms until they have been trained to take the mix.

Bullfinches, Siberians, the *Chaffinches, Linnets, Redpolls, European* and *Brambling Finches* like a great variety of foods. A seed mixture that incorporates both Canary mix and Budgie's seeds, berries, fruit tree buds, and live foods are all relished.

The *European Goldfinch* and the *Siskins* should be fed the Canary mix and song supplement with additions to the seed mix of oat groats, niger and hemp seeds. All *Singing Finches (Green, Yellow-Eyed, Gray, etc.)*, including the *Cape Canary* and the *wild Canary* will thrive on the basic Finch mixture with Canary song food an important adjunct.

For *Cardinals* begin with the basic Parrakeet mix and add sunflower seeds. Mynah Bird pellets should be fed in a separate container. Feed also greens and fruit. *Doves* and *Quails* can be fed the standard Finch seed mix. *Quails* can be offered insectile mix or mealworms in addition.

Softbills and *Jay Thrushes* enjoy a diet designed particularly for Softbills. It is composed of Mynah Bird pellets, dehydrated fruits, meal worms or raw hamburger, peanut butter and available berries. *Pekin Nightingales, Silver Eared Mesias, Blue Winged Sivas,* and *Thrushes,* can all be fed the Softbill diet with an occasional treat of nectar.

The group of birds that include *Bulbuls, Waxwings* and *Flycatchers* do well on the Softbill diet, and we can add also *Mocking Birds* and *Larks* to this category.

All *Trogons* (including the exotic *Quetzals*) and *Jewel Thrushes* eat the basic Softbill diet with a bit more insectivorous foods and raw ground meat. *Robins* and *Blackbirds* should be fed the same diet.

The fabulous *Birds of Paradise* are to be given the standard Softbill diet but with extra raw meat, fruit and insects, some nectar food, and as much of a variety of live food as is possible.

Birds that talk, with those marvelous mimics the *Mynah Birds* certainly listed first, also include the hardy *Crows, Ravens, Jackdaws* and *Rooks*. Mynahs should be fed only commercial Mynah pellets. The rest of the mimics do well on the basic Softbill fare with added scratch corn and a vitamin-mineral powder sprinkled on the seed.

A HOST OF OTHER BIRDS

Lorikeets, Starling Magpies and *Jays* can all be fed Mynah pellets with additional raw meat, fresh fruits and peanut butter. *Orioles, Troupials* and *Nuthatches* should be fed the standard Softbill mixture plus Parrakeet diet and sunflower seeds. *Sunbirds* and *Zosterops* take the Softbill mix plus fruits and nectar. *Tanagers* and *Honeycreepers* should be given Mynah food plus insectile mix, nectar and fresh fruit. *Cocks-of-the-Rock* do best on Mynah pellets, mealworms, and a pastry mixture of bananas, insectile food, grated carrots, boiled rice, grated hard boiled eggs and cooked sweet potato. Roll this mix into small, moist balls and feed. *Bell Birds, Cotingas* and *Umbrella Birds* will all thrive on this same diet.

The more than 300 species of *Hummingbirds* have the highest metabolic rate of all warm blooded creatures. They therefore must eat almost constantly and should be given food rich in the dietary factors that will sustain their terrific activity. At least a dozen fruit flies must be supplied to these tiny birds each day supplemented by a liquid composed of 50 percent cane sugar and 50 percent water colored with red or orange food coloring to attract the bird. Honey is, of course, an excellent nectar food and well liked by Hummingbirds.

Kingfishers and *Hornbills* both do well on the basic Softbill diet, but the *Trumpeter* and the big-beaked *Toucans* should be fed Mynah pellets as a standard diet.

FEEDING PREDATORY BIRDS

This heading embraces *Eagles, Hawks, Vultures* and *Owls*. Diets for captive predacious birds must lean heavily toward meat. The exceptions are the fish-eating diurnal birds of prey such as the *Bald Eagle* and *Steller's Sea Eagle* that should be fed fish.

I have been told by falconers that their haughty birds have a short life span and do not live as long as the same species when incarcerated in zoos. I think that one of the reasons for this is that the falconer's birds are not fed a complete diet. To keep them in lean condition necessary to make them keen to hunt they are very often close to the point of starvation and so have little defense against infection and disease.

Predatory birds should be fed live food whenever possible: mice, rats, rabbits, birds, chickens. When such food is not available raptors must be fed fresh meat. But to supply them with a complete diet Mynah pellets or dog pellets (according to the bird's size) should also be fed. To entice the birds to eat the pellets pour meat juice over the dry food and thoroughly mix in a large quantity of raw hamburger (or fish for the fish eating birds). Reduce the amount of hamburger in the mixture gradually once the birds are eating it until only one third of the total mix is meat and the rest pellets. Birds of prey regurgitate pellets of undigested food and fats so need some roughage in their diets.

FEEDING PIGEONS

Pigeons may be fed a commercial mix or a homemade mixture. The commercial mixtures are excellent and should contain peas, peanuts, hard yellow corn, high protein pellets, hemp and hard red wheat. The formula tag on the bag should indicate that the contents contain no less than twelve percent protein. Dry, prepared foods of this kind can be offered in a self feeder (cafeteria style).

The health grit fed should contain oyster shell, salt, ground bone, limestone, granite grit, hardwood charcoal, and Venetian red 1 percent. This is the formula recommended by the U.S. Department of Agriculture. Always have fresh water available.

FEEDING GAME, DECORATIVE, AND DOMESTIC BIRDS

Game birds, domestic fowl and decorative birds can all be fed on good quality commercial packaged foods. Separate feedings of corn kernels or scratch corn according to the size of the bird is beneficial and keeps them occupied. Rice is also relished by many of these birds. If you wish to give some of the wild-type birds a diet closer to that which they consume in the wild you will find their tastes differ quite a bit. *Woodcock* eat mostly earthworms; *Quail* are, like the Woodcock, members of the group of gallinaceous birds that find food by scratching the ground in search of seeds, worms and insects. *Partridge* eat berries (particularly partridge berries, of course) small nuts, rose hips, grapes and bittersweet drupes. *Doves* feed on grass seed, weed seeds, and waste grain.

Ducks too vary in their epicurean tastes. *Black Ducks,* when near fresh water, will eat roots, water plants, wild rice, grasses, pond weeds and other vegetation. When flying over salt water they will light and eat small clams, mussels, grass and small marine life. Needless to say they are hunted while on fresh water rather than salt for their flesh is tainted by their diet and fishy-tasting duck is no gourmet's delight. *Mallards* thrive on seeds, acorns, water plants, insects, grasshoppers, grains, grasses and small aquatic creatures. *Canvasback Ducks* eat wild celery, wapato ("duck potato") fish and marine life. *Canadian Geese* eat roots, water plants, berries, wild rice, eelgrass and small water plants. In the summer time they also ingest many of the insects that hover near water. The hardy and handsome *Pheasant* eats just about everything including grains, worms, insects, wild plants, seeds and small animal life, embracing such creatures as new-born field mice.

This is a sampling of the appetites of some of the Game Birds and Ducks. Most of these birds when kept as pets or domesticated, decorative fowl, are raised and kept on earth and ponds that will provide them with some of the elements that they feed on in the wild. But it is best to consider this as a plus factor and for their basic diet feed a good commercial food.

Training and Exhibiting Birds

To train a bird you must first tame it, something that can be accomplished only by making the bird completely unafraid of you and at ease in your presence. Some breeders hand-feed baby birds and chicks raised in this manner are worth a premium price. Attempt never to startle the bird, thus triggering its instinctive fear. When you work around your pet—feeding it, changing the water, cleaning the cage— do it slowly and speak quietly to the bird, using its name, while you continue your chores. Never bang utensils or make quick, jerky motions, and always keep your voice low and calm.

The first step in training a bird is to clip the primary wing feathers so that he can't fly (assuming you have brought home an untrained bird). If he gets away from you, he will then be easier to catch. You will also have a psychological advantage for, deprived of his ability to be mobile in his own métier, your pet will be more responsive to your advances. The next step is to put your hand in the bird's cage and just leave it there for ten to fifteen minutes at a time without moving it, meanwhile speaking quietly and soothingly to the bird. What does it matter if your hand goes numb and you feel pins and needles in your wrist and arm! Think only of the future and the wonderful result of this rather painful beginning. After a few days, move your hand very slowly toward the bird, each day a tiny bit closer, until finally you touch the soft down of the breast. This is the beginning: you have made physical contact with your pet. In a day or two more gently move your index finger, stroking the bird very lightly.

You must use your own judgment as to timing and above all be patient. If the bird becomes alarmed at your first touch, retreat a bit and be patient. This is the key word to taming your bird—patience—as it is with all creatures.

Finger-training can be accomplished in a few hours—sometimes even in a few minutes if the bird is just out of the nest. To finger-train you must wait until the bird is on his perch. Then gently, but insistently, press the side of your index finger against the lower part of the body where the legs join the breast. He will be thrown off balance and will, of necessity, step up on your finger. Viola! Your pet is finger-trained. As he steps onto your finger, use his name and say "Up!" In no time at all he will hop onto your finger at the "Up!" command.

The next step is to withdraw your hand slowly from the cage with the bird perched on your finger. If he attempts to fly off your finger, he will fall to the ground because his wings are clipped. This experience will frighten him and he will remain where he has fallen. Go to him, gently urge him to return to your finger, and speak to him quietly. He has now found security on your finger.

Once your pet is finger-trained, make him hop from one finger to another by using the index finger of your other hand. After this, transfer the bird from your finger to your shoulder and let him sit there for a while. Then take him back on your finger. From your finger you can get him to perch anywhere you want him to.

Many birds are completely and utterly spoiled for life by teasing, frequently by youngsters in the house who have not been taught the proper way to treat pets. Do not allow a bird that could become a delightful pet to be transformed into an *enfant gâté* through teasing.

Many birds are fond of having their heads and necks scratched. They react with great enjoyment to such attention. Feed your bird tidbits from your fingers, later allowing him to take food from between your lips when offered. Large psittacines can be tempted by bananas, nuts, carrots, corn on the cob, and graham crackers. Smaller birds like red cherries, small berries, grapes, and mealworms. I do not suggest mealworms as one of the tidbits you offer from your lips.

Birds can become such wonderful pets! I have seen one of our pet budgies play at a peg board for hours with my son when he was a little tyke and bedded with some vague slight fever. The little budgerigar would first pick up a yellow peg, run to the side of the board and drop it off, then back for another one, then change to some other color, both bird and child chatting all the while and finding a wonderful rapport.

By the time the clipped feathers have grown back on your pet's wings, he should be tame enough to be allowed free flight. He will then fly to you and perch on your finger when you hold your finger out and call him to you.

Budgerigars, cockateils, lovebirds, some of the finches and canaries and many of the smaller psittacines are relatively easy to train. The larger psittacines, the macaws and cockatoos, are well able to inflict painful wounds with their large, powerful beaks, yet they too can be trained in the same manner as the smaller birds. The difference is that both of you, bird and owner, are afraid; the bird has the natural fear that all wild creatures have of man, and you are afraid of being badly bitten. One of you must conquer the fear—and it won't be the bird! Its fear is a deeply rooted instinct, so it will have to be you who makes the first move. Be brave, be fearless. Do not flinch or pull your hand back when the bird reaches toward your finger with its big beak. Chances are he is only going to use his beak for balance as he steps decorously on your finger . . . chances are!

For a slightly safer method of training the larger birds use the first steps described previously, then offer the bird tidbits once it becomes used to your hand and has lost its fear of you. Meanwhile make a "T" perch by nailing a round piece of doweling onto a longer handle of the same material in the "T" form. Use this in the manner outlined above for finger-training, except of course the bird steps onto the wooden perch rather than your finger or hand. Later, when he is trained to the stick and completely unafraid of you, you can use your hand.

Remember that a bird kept alone, the single pet, will tame and train much more easily than two or more kept together. Some trainers advocate carrying the bird around the house in its cage with you all day for the first few days, so that when you are reading, eating, watching TV, knitting, or whatever it is you do all day, the bird is always at your elbow and growing more used to your presence every minute.

TRAINING BIRDS TO TALK

There are various methods of teaching those birds labeled "talking birds" to utilize their unique ability to mimic human speech. To begin you must have your pet completely tamed and unafraid of humans. Then, with a good deal of quiet—and sometimes almost desperate patience—begin by repeating the same word or pair of words over and over again. I suggest that one of the first words you train the bird to repeat should be his name.

The bird that makes the best talker is generally one that was young when you got it and that has been hand-raised. Grown birds can also be taught to talk, but it will take much more time and patience. Individuals within species vary greatly in their ability to mimic and in the quality of their voices. Actually almost all the psittacine birds can be trained to talk to some extent, their ability generally limited by the time and patience their trainer lavishes on the chore. Smaller birds have smaller voices. The budgerigar is one of the best talkers and can acquire an amazing vocabulary, but its voice is comparable to its size and one must listen carefully when it talks.

Mynah birds are almost in a class by themselves as talkers, learning rapidly and mimicking the human voice exactly. Among the psittacines budgerigars, yellow-naped Amazons, African grays, Blue fronted Panama, Mexican double yellow heads and the macaws are perhaps the best, though no matter what species you named in any such list you would provoke an argument on the subject with owners of other species. Also don't forget that crows, ravens, rooks, and other birds of like species can also be taught to talk. In a lesser category as talkers are cockatiels, other Amazons, conures, cockatoos, larger parrakeets, magpies, ring-necks and the lesser mynahs, though often an individual of any of these groups will astound you with its mimicking ability.

Begin with the bird's name as suggested earlier, then add another word to the name such as, "Hello, Macho!" or "Hi, Macho!" assuming of course that the bird's name is Macho. One could scarcely hope to get results by calling "Hi, Macho!" to a pet whose name is Fanny. Repeat the words over and over again slowly and carefully in a rather high voice. Many of the smaller talking birds seem to learn with greater rapidity if the trainer is a child or a woman because of the higher tone of their voices. Be very, very patient and always conduct your lessons when and where there are no distractions.

You will find that mynah birds (greater Indian hill mynahs) do not require as much time to teach as the psittacines. I have seen mynahs react to word and whistle sounds, beginning to talk and whistle within a few minutes of a first lesson.

Once the bird learns a few words, advancement is rapid if the trainer works with his pet with the same tenacity as he used in the beginning. A wolf whistle is easily taught to most birds, as are other whistled tunes such as "My dog has fleas." Some trainers advocate working with the bird when the cage is covered and he is in complete darkness on the theory that, with no distractions, the bird will concentrate more deeply on the words you speak and learn with greater rapidity. The reward system is always good. When the bird repeats a word or phrase you have been attempting to teach him, give him a tidbit as a reward.

Another method of training is to use a record. Do not buy the commercial talking-bird records. Cut one yourself. Use the words or phrases (limited to a very few) that you want your bird to learn. Enunciate words and phrases clearly and slowly and repeat them over and over. Play the record close to your pet's cage or stand several times a day—if you can take it.

More advanced training can be accomplished by using sentences or phrases that provoke an answer and make it appear as though you and your bird are actually carrying on a conversation. For instance, you can train your bird to answer the question. "How do you feel today, Popo?" by saying, "With my hands, ha, ha, ha!" Please believe me this is much more humorous when spoken by your bird. To accomplish this, you must evoke a conditioned reflex from your pet. Teach the bird the answering phrase (I won't repeat it) until it is letter-perfect. Then use a key word from the question such as "feel" to trigger the bird's response. Later add the rest of the question with the stress on the key word.

TRAINING THE CANARY

The charm of the canary lies in its wonderful talent as a songster. But to get the most out of your bird you must first purchase one that has a fine natural voice and then tutor it. Even a human opera singer, no matter how great a voice he or she possesses, must be taught to control and enrich his or her vocal endeavors.

Breeders of canaries segregate the rollers from the choppers just after weaning and then begin their training. They are placed in small cages as soon as they complete their baby molt, some breeders actually allowing them to molt out in the training cage. These cages are put in training cabinets with one bird to a cage and during their few weeks of training are kept in the dark except for six fifteen-minute periods spaced out during the day. In the dark they listen to the songs and tentatively try their voices. Often a superb older singer is hung in a cage nearby as a tutor so the youngsters can mimic his quality. You can accomplish this training with your single pet canary by buying a very young bird, keeping him in a small cage during the training period and covering the cage with a piece of black cloth. Hang the cage high and purchase a recording of a very fine singing bird at your pet shop to use to tutor your youngster. Don't forget the six fifteen-minute respites from dark periods for your pet during the day for it is during these lighted inter-ludes that he will burst into song.

TRAINING PIGEONS

There are three specific groups of flying pigeons: the homing pigeon (the racing homer is the best example of this group); high-flying pigeons (the English tippler represents this group); and the tumblers (of which an excellent example is the English Birmingham roller). Homing pigeons return to their lofts across distances in excess of a thousand miles. High-flying pigeons can fly for many hours in endurance or time-flying contests. Tumbling pigeons perform backward somersaults during flight, accomplishing deep rolls.

To train a racing homer it is important that the bird return to his home loft as quickly as possible because he *wants* to, and he must be conditioned by supplying him with a home free from parasites, with good food, clean water, a mate, his own nest, contentment and complete freedom from fear. To make the bird trap (return to the nest) quickly he should not be fed before flying but must be trained to know that food is waiting for him in the home loft upon his return from a flight. Train-ing flights should be from successively longer distances, bringing the bird into the best condition for competitive flying.

Birmingham rollers are the most docile and easiest to train of all pigeons. Fly the roller on an empty stomach and keep him in the loft except when you release him for flight.

To train the tippler to perform, it too should be kept in a closed loft and fed only after flying.

For the neophyte interested in the pigeon fancy I suggest visits to men who have had vast experience in the field. Garner as many opinions as possible on the many facets of the fancy, for almost every fancier has his own successful methods.

EXHIBITING BIRDS

There are a host of bird shows throughout the country, sponsored by various bird clubs and judged by competent authorities. There are an average of approximately six budgerigar shows held each month in various parts of the United States. Many offer classes in exotic birds, which includes just about any species of bird known to aviculture. Exhibitions in England, where there are hordes of rabid fanciers, are even more numerous than here in the United States.

Exotic birds, from tiny hummingbirds to the huge macaws, are exhibited in cages tastefully designed to recreate the natural habitat of the occupant. Many of these exhibits are beautiful, particularly in British bird shows where such displays are considered with the utmost seriousness.

Special cages are used for exhibiting birds at shows. Budgerigar cages must be built and painted to certain American Budgerigar Society (ABS) specifications. Birds must be taught to sit up straight, displaying themselves to best advantage and hopping from one spar to the other when the judge signals with his stick that this is his wish. All birds must conform to a specific standard for their species and there is a point scale for weighing faults and virtues. There are a number of classes that consider age, color phases, and the category of the exhibitor as novice or experienced.

12

Rodents

Rodentia

Rodents range in size from tiny mice to the huge South American capybara that weighs in excess of one hundred pounds when mature. Without any doubt a tremendous number of rodents are kept as pets—and many of them certainly make very fine pets indeed. More than a thousand distinct species of rodents have been catalogued, which gives *Rodentia* the distinction of being the largest order of mammals on this planet both in the number of separate species and the abundance of individuals within specie boundaries.

The uses to which species within this order can be put is also astonishingly numerous. Rabbits, for instance, are bred for pets, for their fur, as exhibition animals, for food, and as laboratory animals. The chinchilla is a very valuable fur producer and also a fine pet. Cavies make exceptionally good pets and in South America are raised for food by the Indians, particularly those Amerindians native to Peru where the cavies run around much as chickens do here. They make a very tasty dish, I might add.

Rodents are distributed throughout the world with the exception of the polar regions, but it is in South America that they reach their peak in diversity of form and size. The smallest number of rodent species is found in Australia and Madagascar. All rodents are characterized by a pair of prominent cutting incisors on both upper and lower jaws. These have constant growth and must be worn down with use or cut to keep from becoming overgown. All rodents are gnawing creatures and in the wild or semi-wild state have no difficulty in finding material on which to gnaw and wear down incisors. Only when kept in captivity or as pets does overgrowth sometimes occur due to a lack of things to nibble on. The incisors then must be manually broken off to normal length.

When the Age of the Dinosaurs came to a close at the end of the Mesozoic period (an enigma to evolutionists) about sixty million years ago, the early small furtive mammal forms took over by sheer force of numbers. Among them were many distinct forms of *Rodentia*. The mighty reptiles had dominated the earth for over one hundred million years—proof of their success as living vertebrate organisms—and supposedly succumbed to racial senescence due to overspecialization. But the theory has been advanced that many of the small, predatory mammals (including the *Rodentia*) hastened the scaly monsters' demise by eating or destroying their eggs. So we see that the rodents have probably been on this earth for a mighty long time. As a matter of record, remains of chinchilla-like rodents called *Megamys* were found in the Argentine in Permian deposits that greatly predate the dawn of man.

The Races of Rodents

Though rabbits and hares resemble the rodents in many physical areas, they are scientifically placed in another order. The main distinction that separates them from rodent recognition is in the formation of the teeth, the rabbit possessing four upper incisors—a large functional pair and a smaller pair behind them—that do not have cutting edges. The movement of the jaws of rabbits and hares during mastication also differs from that of the true rodents, the lower jaw movement being lateral. But since they are commonly thought of as rodents, they will be discussed here under the rodent listing.

RABBITS (*GENUS SYLVILAGUS*)

Rabbits and rodents were probably a meat staple in the larder of early man. Some of our domesticated breeds of rabbits were undoubtedly among the most ancient pets and meat animals known to mankind. Rabbits were discovered in Spain about 1100 B.C. by wayfaring Phoenicians and word of their many attributes spread to other parts of the world.

Of the modern breeds of rabbits, the *New Zealand White,* an albino rabbit, is the best meat, pet, laboratory, and fur rabbit. The *California* is also a good meat and pet animal. The *Silver Marten* has rich, silvery, beautiful fur and is also bred for its meat value. The *Dutch* rabbit has always been a well-liked pet. It is small, attractive, nicely marked and is also a good laboratory rabbit. The *Angora* rabbit is a fancy breed with a long wooly coat and has been bred for its wool. As a pet it takes a lot of care to keep it looking well. The *Belgium Hare* is a lean, racy, alert animal, not meaty enough for the table. *Champagne d'Argents* and *Crème d'Argents* are handsome breeds whose light baby fur changes upon maturity to adult richness. The *Chinchilla* rabbit has fine fur with the chinchilla color. The smallest of the rabbit breeds is the *Polish* rabbit which averages only 2 to 3 pounds upon maturity. The temperament of the Polish is not always placid. The *Satin* rabbit has fur that is soft, shiny, and satiny. Clad in what looks like silver-fox fur is the (guess what?) *Silver Fox* rabbit. The *checkered giant* is interestingly marked and the *Flemish rabbit* (often also called giant) is the largest of them all—a mature one often weighing over 20 pounds. The *Lop* is a rather freakish rabbit with very long lop ears that sometimes will measure as much as 26 inches from tip to tip.

In this day and age when many people look toward independence from rising prices and feel a need to be self-supporting and to grow their own food and staples, the rabbit should come into his own as a source of fine, high-protein meat. Check the proportion of food needed for a rabbit to gain weight against food costs, and you will find that the cost of preparing a rabbit for market is a lot less than preparing a cow. A rabbit is highly economical to produce, is closer to red meat in nutritional values, lower in fats and higher in necessary minerals than other meats. It is also easily digested and exceedingly tasty. Rabbits reproduce well. A 10- to 12-pound doe can produce in excess of thirty 4-pound fryers a year, or 120 pounds or more of meat annually. Percentage wise this is much more by far than a large sow or a range cow can produce in the same length of time. Rabbits take up less space comparatively than other meat animals. Though we are a nation of beef eaters, still over 60 million pounds of domestic rabbit meat is consumed in the United States each year. In Europe a great deal more rabbit meat is eaten than here. Frenchmen enjoy rabbit and Italians consume this flavorful meat to the tune of 115 million pounds annually.

The possession of a rabbit's foot has been a token of good luck for centuries—but not, of course, to the rabbit who supplied the foot.

WILD RABBITS AND HARES

Hares are long-legged, leaping animals, while rabbits are short-legged running creatures, but for some unknown reason some of the wild rabbits are called hares and vice versa. They are closely allied, so it doesn't make too much difference what they are called unless you want to split hairs. These beasties are found all over Africa, Eurasia, and the Americas and have been introduced into New Zealand and Australia.

Hares that are called *jackrabbits* are divided into five distinct groups and are common in the western part of our country. *Arctic* hares are pretty in their various seasonal colors, sometimes almost pure white. There are about six races, all northern in habitat. Recognized by the enormous size of their feet the *Varying hares* range all the way from the northern areas of the United States to Virginia. One species is referred to as the snowshoe rabbit. There are *White-tailed, Black-tailed, White-sided jackrabbits* and many other subspecies. The best-known of the wild rabbits is our familiar little *Cottontail.* These little rascals are found over most of the country. Often young babies, just weaned, can be caught and tamed. They become delightful pets. There are eastern, western and mountain cottontails; brush, marsh, and swamp rabbits and in our southwestern states are found the smallest of all rabbits, the pygmy rabbits, shy little creatures that hide in thick brush.

Sometimes called *Whistling hares* or *Rock rabbits,* the delightful *pikas* or *conies* inhabit Alpine regions of the northern hemisphere. They are tiny, fluffy and in the late spring the females bear three or four miniature babies in their cosy rock caves. They make excellent pets except for the fact that night and day they emit a high-pitched eerie whistle that can drive a comparatively sane man to the edge of madness.

CHINCHILLAS

These handsome little nocturnal rodents are native to the high Andes Mountains in South America and are closely related to agoutis, cavies and viscachas, the latter a burrowing rodent inhabiting the pampas of Paraguay and Argentina. There are two chinchilla varieties—*Chinchilla Brevicaudata,* which is the animal bred mostly in South America for its pelt, and *Chinchilla lanigera* popular with fur breeders in the United States. It is interesting to note that when the two breeds of chinchillas are mated the offspring are sterile (mules). *Brevicaudata* has a large head, small blue ears, a short tail and a larger, chunkier body than *lanigera,* which is a smaller rodent with long ears and a long heavily furred tail. Chinchillas are gregarious, curious, playful, rather vocal and very gentle pets. The males make the best pets because the females are prone to be domineering (and larger than the males). These fine little rodents need a regular, stable environment if they are to be happy. Their fur is valuable, so it is not easy or cheap to purchase a chin as a pet. Your best bet is to visit a chinchilla fur ranch and try to buy a young chinchilla that is badly colored, a mutation, or one that doesn't have the dense, even fur necessary for prime pelting.

These little creatures once thrived in the Andes of Peru and neighboring South American countries, but they were hunted to such an extent for their fur that they were badly decimated and wild chinchillas have found refuge now high in the mountains in northern Chile. They can survive well in altitudes up to 20,000 feet. The Indians of the Andes used the warm, soft fur of these little creatures to make robes for their chieftains. In A.D. 1524, a Spanish conquistador, searching for gold for his Queen, made contact with the Chincha Indians and took one of the precious chinchilla robes back to Spain. He called the rodents whose fur was so beautiful, chinchillas, meaning "little Chincha." From that time on chinchilla became the most precious of furs and the little animals were taken to Europe for breeding. Today in the United States, chinchilla ranching is big business—and has been ever since an American engineer brought eleven chinchillas back from South America with him. He bred his little imports successfully and eventually became a millionaire on the proceeds their pelts brought him.

CAVIES (GUINEA PIGS) (*FAMILY CAVIDAE*)

Cavies are gentle, affectionate little creatures and I have never known one to ever attempt to bite. It is claimed that, other than llamas, cavies were the only animal ever domesticated by the proud Incas of South America. These fine pets seem unusually free of disease and are easily cared for. They live up to seven years and remain, throughout their lives, sweet, affectionate pets. If kept clean, cavies are almost odorless, smelling only faintly of the fresh vegetation they are fed. Another plus for the cavy as a pet is the fact that they are personally one of the cleanest of all animals. These rodents weigh from 34 to 42 ounces and are, upon maturity, approximately 10 inches long—with no external tail. When we lived in Spain on the Costa del Sol, a friend gave us a pair of cavies for pets and called them *Rattas Indios,* or Indian rats.

The various breeds of cavies are identified by the variations in the length and texture of their coats. The long smooth-haired breeds are *Angoras* and *Peruvians. English* and *Bolivian* cavies have short smooth hair; the rough-coated cavies are the *Abyssinians.* In color, cavies have a wide range: there are the solid colors (selfs) in chocolate, red, white, black, tan, blue, silver, golden, cinnamon, orange, lilac, beige, slate, and combinations of these colors. The short, smooth-haired English and Bolivian cavy is a popular pet and is often selected for use in medical research. The Abyssinian has a wiry coat that is ruffled and forms into rosettes, while the Peruvian has long, fine silky hair that parts along the spine and flows down the animal's sides like a waterfall. The agouti (whose hair is banded) provides the basic wild color. Both the *Dutch* and *Himalayan cavies* borrow their names from rabbit breeds with similar markings. Both are very lovely varieties. The *silver* and *golden* cavies are actually Agouti-colored, but the hair is tipped with either silver or gold, respectively. The *Tortoise and White* is patched with red, black, and white squares of equal size and is quite similar to the tortoise-shell feline.

An exhibition cavy should be large, shaped like a brick, and solid in structure. There are classes for cavies in the various stock shows and fairs held throughout our country every year. Breeding toward an ideal and exhibiting your cavies adds an extremely interesting area to cavy keeping. Expose yourself to the thrill of competitive exhibition with your pets. I am certain you will like it.

Other than the common (or uncommon to owners and breeders) cavy, there is another race of these animals called the *Patagonian cavy*. These creatures inhabit the open savannah in Patagonia and, through natural selection to fit their environment, they have, in the course of their evolution, developed long legs and become quite speedy afoot. They look very much like tiny deer. Their tail is a small black dot and they live in self-dug burrows. Like the common cavy they are considered a delicious food staple by the Indians who inhabit the area where these cavies live. They are sometimes caught and tamed by the Indians and make delightful pets.

HAMSTERS

In 1930, near Aleppo, Syria, Professor I. Aharoni of Hebrew University in Jerusalem, discovered a female hamster and her twelve young. This was rather a monumental find, for they were the first golden hamsters to be found in over a century. Two pairs were sent to England and two pairs came to the United States. Within twenty years there were over 100,000 golden hamsters in the United States alone, all from the original pair sent here.

The adult *Syrian Golden Hamster* weighs about 4 ounces and is 7 inches long with a tail about ½ inch long. They have incredibly elastic cheek pouches and look somewhat like little bears with a dense coat of deep, rich golden color and whitish fur clothing their belly. Actually there are three species of hamsters, the giant *Common Hamster* of Europe, found mostly in Germany, are about a foot long and are fierce, untamable beasts. Second is the *Dwarf Hamster,* which seldom grows more than 4 inches long. Neither of these two species proved to be of use as laboratory animals for research, but the *Syrian Golden Hamster* was immediately adopted as an excellent laboratory animal and pet. Hamsters have no odor and are clean. They tame easily and make wonderful pets. Children adore them. In selecting a pet hamster it is best to take a young male. The females are more aggressive and bossy. But you must remember that these little tykes will bite if they are startled or become afraid. So handle them carefully and correctly.

Hamsters have several peculiarities that you should be aware of:

they hoard food, they are nocturnal, and they hibernate in cold weather and estivate (semi-hibernate) sometimes even in warm weather. They have a low normal body temperature and are a mutable species of rodent, probably due to the fact that they are so closely inbred. Large numbers can be raised in small quarters without much danger of disease or of fighting among themselves if a good food supply is always available.

Mutation has produced many new colors in the golden hamster, which have special classes in exhibitions. Show classes were first formed for the hamster in England and a standard was adopted that is also in use here as the official standard for the Syrian golden hamster. Through selective breeding to conform to this standard the heads of hamsters are being shortened and bred to be broader; the eyes are wide-set, bold, and bright; the ears set wide apart; the neck short and the body cobby. Overall good size is wanted. Condition is important in a show specimen. The colors established through canny breeding are the *normal golden hamster, golden agouti, golden fawn, panda, cream, albino, albino with dark points,* and the *banded hamster.* New colors and combinations, as well as mutations in coat quality, have been reported and will undoubtedly be accepted and fixed. When selecting a pet or breeding hamster, look for fully furred ears. Naked ears are a sign that the animal is old and beyond its breeding prime. Also check the belly for beginning skin disease, which is evidenced by a rash in this area. As pets, hamsters are a million laughs. As exhibition animals, they present a challenge to the breeder to develop new and improved strains.

GERBILS

Comparatively new to the pet world is the *Mongolian gerbil.* Unlike many rodent pets the gerbil is *not* nocturnal, so is active all during daylight hours. Gerbils are singularly disease-free, which along with their many other virtues has made them invaluable for scientific research. Another plus is their high tolerance to extremes of heat and cold. Gerbils love to be handled and petted and have excellent temperaments. Families share the household without scrapping and are at home in any world into which they are introduced, so are not prone to nervousness or fright. In appearance they are much like hamsters but smaller. They have a mouse's tail, but one the mouse probably wanted to be rid of because, unlike most tails of mice, the gerbil's tail is covered with soft fur the same color as its body. There is also a strain of red-foot gerbils from India.

Not far from my winter home in Florida, a good friend, the late

The Mongolian gerbil (genus Gerbillus) *is a very popular rodent pet, especially among the little people.*

George Meares, found and worked with all manner of mutations in birds and beasts and had found and fixed several mutations in color and coat quality in gerbils.

MICE

Mice have their advocators all over the world, particularly in big cities where space is at a premium and keeping pets is frowned upon. Mice can be kept under such conditions, for very little room is needed and no one will know they are there. I remember hearing of a very exclusive apartment house in an exceedingly high-priced area of New York City whose socially conscious landlord released white mice on the premises to lend class and swank to the place. I don't know how true that tale is. It was told to me by my friendly neighborhood mouse.

The *white mouse* was the original tame mouse. White strains were developed for laboratory work and after generations of breeding for easy handling (and inbreeding), they were so tame that they became popular as pets. But today there are a host of colors and coat qualities to choose from. Fancy mice can be purchased in solid blue, red, silver, fawn, champagne, dove, lilac, black, chocolate, or mixtures of two or more colors. One can also find mice flaunting wooly, long, wavy-haired coats; *silkies* with long silky hair; *rex-coated* (named after the rabbit of the same coat) with plush, soft coats like velvet; *Astarex* that sport curly plush coats and whiskers of the same quality; *Angora* or *hairless mice* (ugh!); mice from the desert or the highlands; *kangaroo mice; waltzing mice* (these are physical freaks with a hereditary defect), and a large number of wild mice. In the last-named category can be listed various types of *pocket mice,* all very much alike; *grasshopper mice,* which make nice pets and feed on harmful insects; the *harvest mouse,* one of the smallest of mammals, weighing less than ¼ of an ounce and boasting of a partially prehensile tail; *cactus, golden, white-footed, deer, jumping mice,* and the *African jerboas* (also the *Egyptian jerboa*).

It was in Britain that mouse clubs were formed, standards were set for the little beasties, and exhibitions held. Believe it or not, mutations have appeared and, through selection, become varieties that are tailless or curly-tailed. New varieties appear regularly such as *blue fawns, blue reds, black-eyed whites* (not albinos) and *short-eared mice* with very large, round eyes. It is fairly easy to set new mutations because, as everyone knows, mice breed like mice. These little tykes undoubtedly make excellent pets, but they do emit a musty "mouselike" odor that only complete sanitation and spraying can control.

VOLES

Voles, also known as field mice, are the commonest of woods mammals. There are about fifty species in America. They are uncommonly clean little creatures that burrow underground and, at given intervals along their runways, establish communal toilets to keep the rest of the tunnel clean. It is only rumor that these places have "W.C." marked on the walls. Voles are an intermediate species between the lemmings and mice, and like lemmings, if their area becomes too crowded, the complete population will attempt to migrate. Their breeding potential is fantastic, one pair in captivity having produced seventeen litters in one year. They are sexually mature at a very early age (two months). These are adaptable rodents and, if taken when young, make good pets.

RATS

White rats are highly intelligent. I am speaking now of the white rats that have been developed by extreme inbreeding through many generations (in excess of one hundred) for scientific research. Their atavistic fears and ferocity have been selected against and bred out over the years. Rats are nocturnal and should be purchased (preferably from a laboratory) when they have just been weaned. They must be handled

Often called a red mouse, the tiny Bank Vole (Clethrionomys glareolus) *is an appealing little rodent.*

and made much of if they are to be good pets and do well. As a matter of fact many of the large research laboratories employ a man or woman whose job is to make the rounds of the cages petting and gently handling each lab rat. Such helpers are known as gentlers. Feed your pet rat by hand as often as possible and he will tame easily. Sanitation is important to the health of these animals and their health is important to you. You should be able to pick up your tamed pet by curling your hand under and around his middle and lifting him. Beside the white (albino) rats there are many other colors, the result of color mutations, some very attractive such as the *blue, chocolate, black* and *pink-eyed ivory;* the *black Irish rat* which has white feet, vent and tail; solid *black, checkered, red, powder blue, cream, silver, brown,* and the *agouti* color which is close to the wild rat color.

Wild rats, with few exceptions, can never be tamed or become pets. They are too nervous and savage and are also quite often carriers of disease. In this category are the common rat and the Bandicoot Rat of India and Burma, both of which are garbage eaters. There is also a giant *bandicoot rat* nearly 3 feet long. Of the wild rats that have sometimes been tamed we can list the *kangaroo rats,* which are unique physically (they have a huge head and large hind legs) and dwell in the dry, wild country; *rice rats,* which are excellent swimmers; some of the *woods rats,* one of which has an unusual bushy tail; *cotton rats,* the *African giant rat,* and the *South American giant.* In reference to the last-named huge rodent, I have heard of fully grown specimens accepting domestication.

SQUIRRELS

Gray squirrels are everywhere. Friendly little beggars, they are known to every man, woman, and child in the country. There are black or melanistic families found in some of our Northern States. A few years ago, while motoring through Canada, I passed a park abounding with these beautiful black specimens. Just last year, at our Florida home, we found three baby squirrels that my daughter (known here as my daughter, the Spanish scholar) fed and brought up until they were old enough to go it alone. We released them and for several days thereafter they would scamper down from the trees to accept snacks from our fingers. Within a week they no longer needed our watchful care and became one of the gray gang that gambol in the backyard beyond the pool. *Fox squirrels* are the largest of the tree squirrels; the handsomest are the southern species, which appear in gray, black, and buff phases with white ears and nose. The black variety with contrasting white is very striking.

The *Northern Fox squirrel* is brownish in color. A very attractive rodent of this family is the *Tuft-eared squirrel.*

One of the cutest of the group is the *Flying Squirrel* that "flies through the air with the greatest of ease" by stretching the membrane between its front and hind legs. These are small, entirely nocturnal creatures with soft, silky fur and big, shining eyes. Flying squirrels make excellent pets but, being nocturnal, must be caged away from bedroom areas or they will keep you awake all night with their activity. The rain forest of Borneo is the habitat of the *Giant Flying Squirrel,* which is much like our own species but a good deal larger. These creatures can actually bank while in flight, are nocturnal, and very loose in coat. A handsome specimen is the large *Thai Squirrel,* beautifully patterned in reddish chestnut, black, and white. I have seen them in pet shops in the United States offered at a price of $75 each. These handsome rodents belong to the Indo-Malayan family of giant squirrels that are the largest tree squirrels in the world, some species attaining a size comparable to that of the domestic cat. The *Malabar* and *Prevost's squirrels* are also of this group, the latter also called the *German-flag Squirrel* because of its colors. The *Variable* and *Red-bellied squirrels* are species of tree squirrels of tropical America. Most of these creatures are rather small but brightly hued and attractive.

The *Chickaree,* North America's *red squirrel,* is about two-thirds the size of the common gray squirrel. There are two species of red squirrel. One, called the *Douglas Squirrel,* is found from California to British Columbia, while *Tamiasciurus hudsonicus,* ranges from Alaska to New Mexico. These are adaptable little animals that normally make their homes in the deciduous woods and burrow underground. Though diurnal, they can also be found scampering about when the moon is high and its beams bathe the forest in blue light. Pine seeds are their favorite food, but they waste more than they eat. They are also fond of other seeds, nuts, berries, buds, maple syrup, insects, and have even been accused of killing and eating baby rabbits. Like all squirrels, the chickaree engages in a mating chase (don't we all?) and produces two litters a year. There is an unfounded rumor that red squirrels hunt and kill gray squirrels, or viciously chase and castrate them. Don't you believe it! Gray squirrels are much larger than chickarees and I am certain could give a good account of themselves in any encounter. As a matter of fact the two species live together in the same areas in complete harmony.

There are a goodly number of pretty *ground squirrels* of which the *Chipmunk* is the best known. There are two genera of chipmunks, the eastern and the western or *Siberian chipmunk,* which is the smaller and

lighter-colored of the two. The latter has two premolars on each side of
the upper jaw while the eastern chipmunk has only one. They make complicated systems of underground burrows, but do not actually hibernate

The Red Squirrel or Chickaree (Scuirus hudsonius) *is a frequently viewed wild rodent in the woodlands of America.*

as so many rodents do. These little creatures are inveterate hoarders and fill their elastic cheek pouches with nuts and berries to hide. Chipmunks readily become tame and make handsome little pets. Other *ground squirrels* are the fine-looking *Golden-Mantled,* the *Townsend, Antelope, Spotted, Franklin, Richardson* and the *13-lined spermophile. The prairie dog* also belongs to the same family and is closely related to the ground squirrels. Believe it or not the *woodchuck* is actually a large, burrowing ground squirrel.

OTHER RODENTS

The *coypu* is a large aquatic rodent, weighing up to 20 pounds. It bears a valuable pelt that is marketed as *nutria.* Many have escaped from fur farms and established themselves in the wild. Herbivorous and harmless, they can become pets, for they tame easily, but they need an area of water large enough in which to submerge. *Agoutis* are native to Cen-

A giant among rodents, the huge Cabybara (Hydrochoerus capybara), *whose native habitat is South America, readily accepts domestication.*

tral and South America where about a dozen species make their homes in the forests. They are short-eared, almost tailless and have a deerlike appearance, a lustrous coat, and large, expressive eyes. Agoutis tame easily and make interesting pets.

The *capybara* is the world's largest rodent. It looks like a huge cavy, weighs up to 120 pounds and can have a body length of 4 feet. This massive rodent ranges over northern South America east of the Andes Mountains. There is a second species in Panama that is smaller and weighs up to 60 pounds. This creature is called a water pig or water cavy by the Indians of the jungle because of its habit of taking to the water when hunted or frightened. It is extremely aquatic and swims and dives expertly. Despite their size, capybaras are completely defenseless against any kind of predator. Inoffensive, they tame easily and make good-natured pets. But they must have a body of water available at all times or their health is endangered.

Woodchucks, porcupines, and other wild rodents cannot exactly be considered good pet material, though they are inoffensive creatures. There is a *Brazilian Tree Porcupine* that is arboreal and possesses shorter quills than the *Old World* and the *Canadian porcupines.* Uniquely it has a powerful prehensile tail and is native to Central and South America. These rodents are hairless but have a bristling sheath of sharp, short spines. They are inquisitive, intelligent beasts. The Indians claim they make interesting pets but must, of necessity, be handled with extreme caution.

13

Tropical Fishes

Pisces

Life on Earth began in the warm, primeval seas. Thales, a Greek philosopher, was the first man to recognize this. As proof of his theory Thales posited a physiological bond between all creatures and the watery womb of genesis. No living thing can live without water; man's body is 70 percent water, so that element of our ancient origin lingers on even in our very life cells. Since the earliest civilizations mankind has returned to the water to fulfill a basic need for tranquility and beauty. Guided by a tenuous genetical umbilical cord that reaches backward through time to the hoary, turgid waters, and without truly understanding his need, man has built a hobby that transcends all others in variety —the tropical-fish fancy.

It is estimated that there are more than 30,000 species of fish cavorting in the huge areas of water surrounding our continents and in the seas, rivers, lakes, and ponds that partition the land. Comparatively few of this vast finny family are small enough to be kept successfully in the home aquarium, yet the choice of tropicals, fresh water or salt, is so diverse that the hobby remains endlessly exciting and interesting.

One of the most important benefits the hobby offers to its many exponents is the tranquility, the almost soporific serenity that observation of a well-kept tank of tropicals can bring. As a writer and an artist, I am frequently beset by noise, interruptions, deadlines, and other disturbances that are enough to drive a man to drink (a short drive for many of my colleagues), yet in this ulcer-growing atmosphere I can banish the woes by simply sitting in front of a tropical fish tank, mentally joining the denizens in their calm, watery world, and reveling in the hushed beauty of that fairy-tale habitat. Psychologists and psychiatrists often recommend the setting up of tropical-fish tanks in mental institutions for this very reason.

Keeping fish as a hobby probably began during the early Sumerian culture about 5500 B.C. and was recorded by these people on clay tablets that hold the first writing evolved by man. The Romans, at a much later date, kept containers of fish (mullet and moray eels of all things) in decorative fish ponds. And we know that the Chinese domesticated the carp and with true Oriental genius, and through long experimentation and canny selection for small mutations, fashioned the many exotic forms and colors of goldfish.

The word *aquarium* first came into use in England during an exhibition of goldfish and tropicals at the Zoological Society of London. Beginning then, the hobby grew to the immense proportions it has achieved today when over twenty million enthusiasts in the United States alone are fish fans. Because the hobby has become so tremendous in scope, manufacturers in this highly competitive field labor long and frenetically to bring new improved articles of care, husbandry, and food to the hobbyist, thus making the owning and breeding of tropicals, fresh-water and salt, much easier and pleasanter each year. There is one strange and snobbish area to the hobby that you will become aware of the moment you purchase your first guppy—all aquarists constantly use the Latin names for the species of fishes, plants, and even medicines involved. It is a form of ostentatious pomposity that gives greater richness to the ordinary language of fish-keeping.

The Aquarium

Selecting and setting up your aquarium is the first order of business after you have made your choice of its future inhabitants. Inexpensive plastic-framed aquariums can be purchased at minimum prices, but the best aquariums for fresh-water tropicals are stainless-steel-framed. Matching stainless-steel stands can be bought on which to place the aquariums. To obviate contact between salt water and metal, should you desire to keep *marine tropicals,* plastic and full glass tanks are made. Toxic substances lethal to fishes can result from contact of salt water with metal and aquarium cement. The bottom of the aquarium should be of slate or plate glass and for salt-water fishes should be so well fitted that there will be no need for any large amount of aquarium cement.

The cost of your tank in the various categories is predicated upon its size, the larger it is the more it costs. Purchase an aquarium that has the greatest surface area for the volume of water it contains, thus providing the maximum absorption of oxygen from the atmosphere. In a larger tank there is also less variance in temperature and a greater surface area to allow for the escape of carbon dioxide that the fish exhale. Since water is quite heavy, weighing 8.3 pounds per gallon, it follows that a very substantial stand is necessary to support any reasonably sized aquarium plus water, rocks, sand, and fishes.

SETTING UP THE AQUARIUM

Clean your newly acquired aquarium thoroughly with warm (not hot) water and an aquarium germicidal agent. After several rinses in clean water, fill the tank with tap water and allow it to stand for twenty-four hours. Check then for leaks and correct them, if you find any, with a good aquarium cement. Add a commercial water ager to the water and, if necessary, a water softener. There are kits available to check water hardness and a remedy that can be placed in the filter to correct the condition. There are also kits to ascertain acid-alkali balance and chemicals to correct the pH factor.

The gravel you use as the bed or floor of your aquarium should be rather coarse and must be washed several times before placing it in the tank. Gravel of all colors can be purchased, but the color of your fishes are given a more brilliant accent by dark gravel (green, blue, red, black, purple). When buying, figure that you will need to use about 2 pounds of gravel to every gallon of water in the aquarium. Grade the gravel downward from back to front (about 3 inches in the rear to approximately ½ inch at the front of the aquarium). *Rocks* and *Stones,* utilized decoratively, can then be added to the tank floor. Seashells and shell grit should *not* be used in fresh-water aquariums, since they make the water too alkaline, but *can* be used in salt-water aquariums. Buy your rocks in a pet shop and wash and rinse them thoroughly before use. Do *not* use rocks that you have picked up somewhere, for they may discharge into the water toxic elements that will kill your fishes.

All plants should be washed rapidly, soaking for 15 seconds in a salt-water solution (6 teaspoonfuls of salt to a gallon of water) then rinsed completely in fresh water before planting. Large plants are traditionally placed at the back and sides of the tank (Myriophyllum, ambulia, anacharis), smaller plants toward the center. Keep the plants grouped by type with a particularly showy piece in the center at the back of the tank (Echinodorus, Madagascar Sword Plant or lace plant, or Crypto-coryne) and use a horseshoe motif for best visual results. Special tongs can be purchased to make planting easier. Cut back the plant roots to one or two inches before planting for better growth. The plants can be set in trays, but if you use one make certain it is not made of metal.

When all the planting is completed and the rocks and other decorative pieces have been set in place, water can be added to the tank to within 1 inch of the top. Experienced aquarists keep gallon jugs filled with "old" water (water that has stood for twenty-four hours or more and has had time to rid itself of all toxic factors) to replace water that has evaporated or that has been lost in any other way.

AQUARIUM ACCESSORIES

Every tank should have a *thermometer* which should be checked for accuracy against a standard mercury thermometer before being installed in the aquarium. There are several types to choose from, so take your pick. Generally speaking most tropicals find about 75 degrees Fahrenheit a comfortable temperature. A cover made of glass or hardboard to fit snugly atop the tank will keep fishes from jumping out, keep the water warm, and prevent rapid evaporation. The cover should be in two sections with one (in front or on the side) that can be lifted easily for feeding the fishes or servicing the tank.

An *electric heater* is essential for keeping the temperature constant. You will also need a *pump* and *filter* to provide aeration that will allow you to keep in a given area twice the number of fishes that would be safe without aeration. A dip tube will handily vacuum up any "mulm" on the bottom that the pump and filter combination misses. Other accessory pieces of equipment that you can purchase as the need arises are; an *aquarium scraper, filter stem brushes, feed rings, thermostat, clamps,* and a host of other items. You have a wide selection in all these accessories and an elastic price range. Should you see any possibility of expanding to two or more tanks in the future, purchase a good pump that will service several aquariums.

An *aquarium reflector* will bathe the whole tank in luminescence, reflecting and intensifying the beauty and color of the jewel-like tropicals in their watery home. The ultimate joy for the aquarist is to arrive at a complete "balance" between fishes, plant life, and the millions of microscopic organisms that are the tenants of the tank.

HERE COME THE FISHES

Allow the aquarium several days without disturbance before you introduce the *pièce de résistance,* the fishes. This gives the plants time to settle and begin to take root and allows you to check out all the appliances to be sure they are performing capably. You can also make certain the pH of the water is correct and be fairly sure that any fish parasites or disease microorganisms have succumbed without fishes to thrive upon.

Meanwhile, during this time of impatient waiting, you can plan for the number and kind of fishes you will purchase. If it is to be a community tank with a number of different species to give it variety as well as beauty, you must select fishes that can live in harmony with each other. Some fishes are pugnacious—and it is a law of nature that a big fish will eat a smaller fish. This is not actually cannibalism. It is simply Darwin's expressed law of the survival of the fittest. There are so many combinations of fishes that will do well together and fit together esthetically, complementing each other in shape and color, that you would be wise to visit the largest and finest aquarium shop in your area, make selections and substitute choices, and then ask the advice of the shop owner. Chances are good that he will have as much knowledge in the areas that hold your interest as any ichthyologist and rapping with him will lead you to the best selection possible for your aquarium.

Handle the fishes you purchase gently. Lower the receptacle in which you bring them home into the tank and tip it gently, allowing water and fishes to flow into the tank.

Goldfish

Long before the keeping of tropical fishes became a universal hobby, the scientific breeding of goldfishes was an established avocation in China and later in Japan. It is rather difficult to imagine that these beautiful multicolored and strangely shaped fishes have been bred from the prosaic carp. With infinite patience early Oriental scholars and ichthyologists searched for small mutations and through judicious selection produced the many varieties available to us today.

Goldfish have been introduced into temperate waters throughout the world. They are peaceful and possess a wide water-temperature tolerance, but exist best in a temperature range of from 50 to 70 degrees Fahrenheit, and need well-aerated and clean water to keep them healthy. Several years ago, when I was living outside of Malaga, Spain, I stocked a small patio pool with goldfishes. Two days later our maid, Carmina, smilingly informed me that the goldfishes were *muy simpatico* and would allow her to pet them. Knowing Carmina, I was immediately aware that something was fishy. I rushed outside and found all 65 goldfishes on the water's surface gasping for air and the water white with bacteria. Questioning brought forth the information that Carmina had been throwing bread and tidbits into the pool to feed the fishes about every hour. True to their reputation for hardiness, none of the goldfishes suffered any lasting effects from this Spanish hospitality.

China and Japan remain the foremost breeders and developers of fancy varieties of goldfishes. They have produced, through genetic breeding and astute selection, such beautiful and odd goldfishes as the *lionhead, bearded, celestial, telescope, fantail, comet, black moor, pompon, chocolate, shubunken* and a host of other forms. In these varieties they have developed every fin shape you can imagine a fish flaunting, combined with a rainbow of colors from pure white, through yellow-gold, red, silver, blue, to velvet black, and piebald combinations of all these hues.

To the goldfish indubitably goes the honor of introducing to a vast world of avidly awaiting aquarists the hobby of keeping ornamental fishes.

DISEASES AND CARE OF GOLDFISH

The illnesses that affect or infest goldfish are generally parallel to those which trouble other tropical fishes, so please look back to the section on diseases of tropical fish. *Ich, anchor worms* and the *fish louse (Argulus)* must be watched for. Cleanliness and aeration are very important in keeping goldfish healthy and they must also not be overcrowded. About one gallon of water per individual is necessary for small goldfish; medium-sized fishes need approximately two gallons per fish. A good, highly nutritious food made especially for goldfish and containing a balance of necessary vegetable, animal, vitamin, and mineral requirements is available and should be fed. Remember my experience in Spain and feed them sparingly but frequently, and vary their diet. Keep a good mineral-block neutralizer in their water.

The goldfish aquarium should have a floor covering of cleaned gravel to a depth of about 2 inches and it should be generously furnished with plants such as *Sagittaria* and *Vallisneria*. These adaptable fishes are wonderfully decorative outdoor-pool denizens. These pools were used by Chinese and Roman fish enthusiasts thousands of years ago and are now returning as an important extension of the tropical-fish hobby. A cool pool in the right location on your property can become an area of peaceful exotic beauty. If you live in an intemperate climate, sink your pool in the ground so that the water is at least 6 inches below the frost line and your goldfish will weather winter very well. Special filters, pumps, and other accouterments can be purchased that are particularly designed for the goldfish pool.

MARINE TROPICALS

Almost unbelievably beautiful and bizarre, marine tropicals and their aquarium habitat are the most interesting and difficult for the fish hobbyist to keep. It is this very challenge and the esthetic rewards of success that have lured more and more hobbyists to the marine aquarium. There have also been a few rather recent and important developments in the marine-tropical field that have helped to trigger interest. One was the production of a fine synthetic sea salt that makes it unnecessary to have a supply of actual sea water always available. Also a constant supply of the most exotic Marine fishes is being shipped in from Africa and the tropical Pacific in plastic bags to join the coral exotics from Florida, the West Indies, and the tropical areas of the Atlantic Ocean. Add to this a wealth of experience extended to hobbyists by the early marine aquarists in articles and books and a downward range of prices for marine tropicals due to greater avenues of supply and, aside from any esthetic reasons, the elementary basis for the increasing number of salt-water marine hobbyists is obvious.

THE SALT-WATER AQUARIUM

Metal of any kind is anathema to marine tropicals, so it is imperative that all equipment in your salt-water aquarium—and the tank itself—be of non-toxic glass and plastic. Even metal not actually touched by the tank water will hold condensation or spray from jumping fishes and drip into the aquarium causing contamination. In fact salt water draws toxic substances from rubber, cement, and other materials as well as metal.

Place your aquarium in a section of the room where sunlight will bathe it for several hours a day and arrange an accessory lamp for top lighting. Light rays benefit the water biologically by activating the growth of algae. Have a piece of glass cut to fit over the top of the tank to limit evaporation. When you add water to replace that lost by evaporation, remember that the basic salts do not evaporate, so you need only add fresh distilled soft water. It is difficult to maintain the specific gravity of the water necessary in a marine aquarium. Hydrometers should be bought in a pet shop to measure the *water density* (specific gravity), which should be 1.020.

Bottom Filters work well, but should be turned on only for half the day. For the floor of the tank use washed, coarse-grain quartz sand. Colored sand must be tested to make certain that the color is fast. The *aquarium heater* should provide an even temperature of from 75 to 80 degrees Fahrenheit and a *thermostatic* control should be used. A *thermometer* is necessary. I recommend artificial aeration even though it is not entirely necessary.

The best water to use for the marine aquarium is aged tap water. To this add a reliable *marine mix* that contains all the major elements (nineteen) of sea water. The resulting product will provide an ideal media for marine life. Salt water brought directly from the ocean is difficult to transport in the required amount and is almost certain to be contaminated and become foul unless filtered diligently. If you do store natural sea water for use at a later date, filter it thoroughly. As mentioned, it is no longer necessary to use real salt water.

Decorating the salt-water aquarium is a wonderful experience because of the great variety of materials you will have to work with. Coral of all shapes, sizes, and colors; sea fans, hard limestone, igneous rock, fused glass chunks of various colors, and petrified wood can all be used. Remember to thoroughly clean and rinse any object that goes into the tank.

Living plants should be used and, if you wish, some complementary synthetic greenery if it has the look of authenticity. Best of all are the living *sea anemones* and *corals* that can grace the marine tank. Anemones wear rich, flamboyant colors that bring to your aquarium great beauty and a truly natural look that imitates the silent depths of the sea. Other live plants, Merman's Shaving Brush and sea fans lend elegance and grace to the aquarium.

The Species of Exotic Tropical Fishes

FRESH-WATER TROPICALS

To make it relatively easy for you to follow I will list the amazing fresh-water tropicals in groups fashioned by their method of breeding. There are so many tropicals and they are so varied that an intimate identification is necessary or we may become bogged down in a morass of eventually meaningless names. This is not the scientific approach, but it will serve our purposes and interests well.

LIVE-BEARERS (*POECILILDAE*)

We will begin, as most budding aquarists do, with the wonderful live-bearers (live-bearing Tooth-Carps), turning our attention first to that most popular of all fish species, the guppy.

Guppies (*Lebistes reticulatus*) are extremely beautiful fishes, varied in color, with the males vividly iridescent, sporting long, floating tails and dorsal fins of many shapes and colors. These lovely tropicals are hardy viviparous (live-bearing) surface feeders. The females are larger than the males but not as colorful as their brilliant spouses. These gems of the water originated in South America and the West Indies. Their fascination and charm as aquarium fishes is unequaled by any other species. They are easy breeders, produce well, and show frequent mutations. There are any number of different strains, wearing a great variety of colors in body, tails, and dorsals. Crossing the strains often produces new combinations of colors; strains can be inbred without harm to establish new characteristics firmly, so the guppy hobbyist

The most popular of the live bearers, the Guppy (Lebistes reticulatus) *is easily bred and, in fine show strains, produces exceedingly handsome males.*

can often develop a strain unique unto himself. Guppies make superb exhibition fishes and always draw a maximum of attention at fish shows. The varieties have official standards and the judging is quite complex. Though bred by highly qualified professional breeders expressly for exhibition purposes, the guppy can certainly be recommended as the best of all possible tropicals for the complete novice.

Malayan Halfbeaks (*Dermogenys pusillus*) are strange-looking livebearers. They are very aggressive and, like the Siamese fighting fish, are used for sporting contests. These halfbeaks are native to the island waters of Borneo, Thailand, and Singapore. Report has it that they are difficult to breed. They probably enjoy fighting more than loving. Slightly brackish water might help to put them in the mood for romance.

Platies (*Xiphophorus maculatus*) and *Swordtails* (*Xiphophorus helleri*) are peaceful fishes of many colors and they are prolific breeders. Both species are vivid in color and are, like the guppies, live-bearing tooth-carps. The popular swordtails are exceedingly lovely fishes, the male's "sword" a handsome appendage. Easy breeders and keepers, all the platies, including the *Sunset, Mexican Swordtail,* and *Pygmy Swordtail* can be interbred. The latter two species do not actually have swordtails, and they lack the color and beauty of the *Maculatus, Helleri* and *Variatus* (Sunset).

The *Mollies* (*Mollienesia sphenops*), *Sailfin Mollies* (*Mollienisia velifera* and *M. latipinna*) are interesting, easily kept, and very worthwhile. But they are really not a fish for the true novice as they are a bit touchy about their environment. The greatest difference between the two sailfins is in size, *velifera* being the larger with a bigger sailfin. A relatively new and beautiful molly mutation named the *Lyre-tail molly* is a favorite of molly fanciers. In this species of live-bearers the black coloration is like rich velvet.

There are numerous other live-bearers such as *Branner's,* the several species of *Limias, Halfbeaks, Gambusias,* et cetera, but the species I have described here are the most popular by far and certainly very much worth the attention of the aquarist interested in live-bearers of great beauty and ease of keeping.

THE EGG SCATTERERS
We encompass a very large group of tropicals in this overall category, including the *Characidae, Cichlidae, Cyprinidae* and the *Cyprino-*

dontidae. These fishes lay both adhesive and nonadhesive eggs. In a completely matriarchal gesture, the female chases the male during the mating game. The parents, being frugal fishes, will eat all of the eggs they can, so the adults must be removed from the tank immediately after laying takes place.

Characins (Characidae) are some of the most brilliant and popular aquarium tropicals. Characins come in many shapes, sizes, and habits. The group is so huge that the species is often split into numerous families with as many as thirty subfamilies. Most look much like the carps, but sport an adipose fin between the tail and the dorsal fins. The smallest is no more than 1 inch long while the largest characin grows to 5 feet in length. We are concerned with something a bit smaller than the latter fish, so that it will not be necessary to clean the tank in a wet suit and aqualung.

Tetras such as the radiant *Rosy, Rio, Guiana, yellow, blue, black, brass, platinum* and *red* (or flame fish), are a few of the exquisite little living jewels in this family, most of which seem to glow with inner neon lights of a multitude of colors. Other favorites are the *Bloodfin, Glowlight Tetra,* and the most glorious of all the *Cardinal Tetra,* a dream in Technicolor. Other brilliant species in this category that cannot be ignored are the *Featherfin, Garnet, Head- and tail-light, Gold, January, Rummy-nose* and *mourning tetras.*

Characins also rank among their numbers the deadly *Piranhas* of the jungle streams and rivers of South America. These voracious fishes are not, however, allowed to be imported into the United States. The *Spraying Characin, Copeina arnoldi,* the strange *Pencil fish, Hatchetfish,* and the transparent *X-ray fish* are all members of this immense family.

There are over six hundred species of *cichlids (Cichlidae),* a favorite of the tropical-fish hobbyist. The cichlid's body is generally flattened as is the body of the splendid Discus fishes, and the very popular angelfish *(scalare).* The head of the cichlid is well developed with the lower jaw slightly protruding in most species. Their courtship and breeding habits vary, but are always interesting. Except for the many dwarf cichlids most are fairly large.

The *angelfish* is exquisite in its silver and black stripes with trailing, lace-like fins. There is a stripeless variety named the *ghostfish* or *blushing angel* and a velvety melanistic of night *black,* a *veil-tail* and a gorgeous *long-finned angelfish* which is dressed in gossamer fins. (The

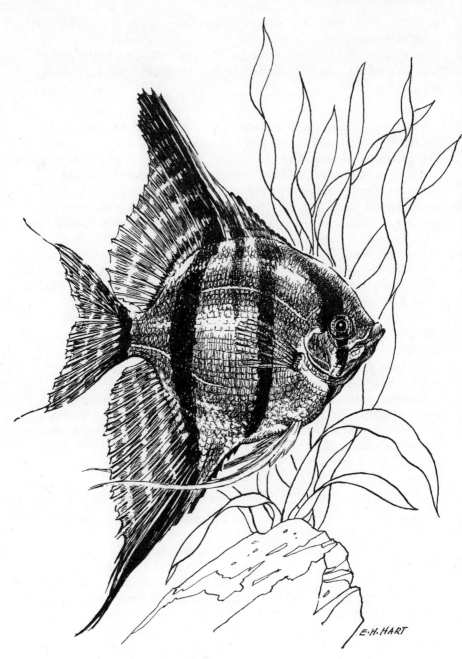

The Angel Fish (Pterophyllum scalare) *is an exquisitely beautiful and most popular cichlid.*

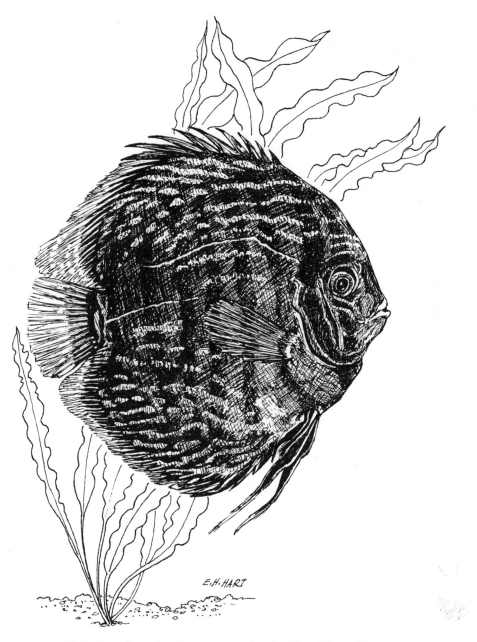

Majestic and a prize for any aquarist, the Blue Discus (Symphysodon aequifasciata Haraldi) *is a difficult-to-breed cichlid.*

latter two are comparatively new mutations.) The lovely *scalare* is a long-time aquarium favorite.

The superb, majestic *Discus* fishes are the answer to an aquarist's prayer. Some of these fishes are large enough to be considered food fishes and are used by the South American Indians as a part of their diet. There are several varieties of Discus fishes and all of them are most impressive.

The most desired of the Discus fishes are the *Half-blue discus* (rather rare), the *Brown* and the *Heckel discus*. The *Firemouths, Keyhole, Flag, Jewel, Brown, Butterfly, Convict, Dolphin, Red (Pompadour), Blunthead, Jack Dempsey* and *Green Discus* are all well known and wanted varieties. Discus fishes are difficult to breed, but aquarists continue to try and occasionally succeed, though not on a steady basis. Specimens of these fine fishes always sell for excellent prices, one of the reasons the hobbyists continue to attempt to breed them.

Other typical cichlids favored by hobbyists are the *Blue Acara,* the *Saddle cichlid,* the *Texas,* and *Pike cichlids,* the *Orange Chromide* and the *Chanchito cichlid.*

MOUTHBREEDERS

These fishes with the bizarre manner of spawn care, are also *Cichlidae;* they are colorful, of true normal cichlid shape (not exaggeratedly flattened like the scalare and Discus), vivacious, and often pugnacious. The females exhibit a baglike throat protrusion. The *Egyptian mouthbreeder* is the most common of these uncommon fishes. The *Nigerian, black-chinned, mozambique,* and *Boulenger* are all mouthbreeders and all make their habitat in the rivers and streams of the Dark Continent.

Barbs are carp-like fishes of the family *Cyprinidae* that grace many an aquarium. This is an abundant family. Generally the barbs are elongated and oval in shape with rather small fins. They are robust and lively. Perhaps the best known of the barbs are the *Tiger, Rosy, Cherry,* and the *Clown barbs,* all colorful and welcome additions to any tank. Other barbs that are well liked are the *Two-Spot, Swamp, Cummings, Dwarf, Banded, Pygmy, Black Ruby* (very colorful), *Half-banded, T-barb, Golden* and *Stoliczkanus barbs.*

Genera of the family *Cyprinidae* also include (among others) the quick and lively *Danios, Brachydanios* and *Rasboras,* all well known and favored aquarium fishes. Add also the *Red-Tailed Shark, Flying*

Barbs, Gobios, Epalzeorphynchus, Bitterling, and a host of other hand-some fishes and you know the reasons this family is so well liked.

The name *danio* was adopted from *"Dhani,"* in the Hindu dialect. These are slender, fast, peaceful fishes, some spotted, as the *leopard danio,* striped as the *Zebra danio* and spotted and striped as the *Spotted danio.*

The *Rasboras,* of which about forty species have been identified, include the *Redrail, Yellowtail, Two-Spot, Red-Line* (almost like a Neon Tet), *Chinese,* and many more with last, but by no means least, the very beautiful and most popular *Rasbora lieteromorpha,* the *Harlequin Fish.*

LABYRINTH FISHES (*ANABANTIDAE*)

A most interesting and splendid family of tropical fishes are the *Anabantidae.* Most of these delightful tropicals at breeding time form a nest of foam bubbles on or near the tank surface, reinforcing the outer coat of the bubbles with an oral-cavity secretion. The nest is often permeated with parts of plants or algae.

The most popular of this family is *Betta splendens,* the Siamese fighting fish, next to the guppy and goldfish probably the most easily recognized of all the tropicals. Ranging in color from cream to red, purple, green and blue, they are, with their exquisite floating tails and fins, certainly one of the most radiantly comely of all fishes. Used as an exhibition fighting fish in Thailand, the betta is seen in the United States in single large brandy snifters—a male, always alone, needing nothing to enhance his fabulous splendor. These bubble-nesters are easy to breed and have as close relatives *Breder's Betta* and the *Slender Betta.*

The *Paradise Fish (Macropodus opercularis)* is also of this family and is another absolute beauty. This fish is very hardy and has been kept successfully in outdoor pools. The males build bubble nests and are easy to breed, but are definitely ferocious. There is a gorgeous Albino strain and also a *Black Paradise* fish.

Anabantids list the *Gouramis* in their family. I have bred *dwarf gouramis* and consider them one of the finest of fishes. They are hardy, peaceful, easy keepers, and particularly lovely in shape and color. Among the gouramis we have the exquisite *Pearl gourami,* gentle, dig-nified, and of good size. Both the dwarf and pearl gouramis are excellent for community tanks. The *Three-spot, Chocolate, Croaking, Thick-lipped, Honey, Opaline* (a mutant), and the ubiquitous *Kissing gourami* are all well worth the aquarist's attention.

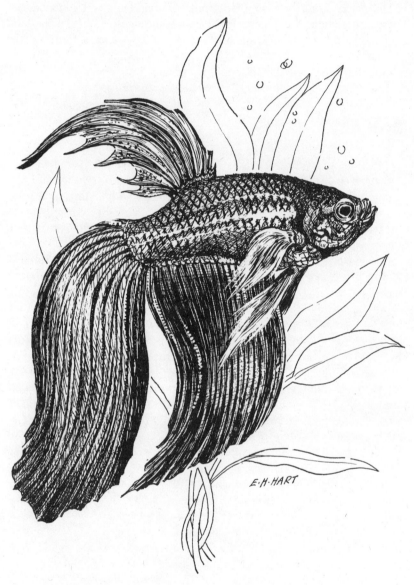

The Siamese Fighting Fish (Betta splendens) *is most admired of the labyrinth fishes. As a display fish the irridescent, flowing-finned males have no peers.*

CYPRINODONTIDAE

This family is composed of the egg-laying *Tooth-carps,* which belong to the order *Microcyprini.* These are rather elongated fishes that never display lateral lines.

The very handsome *Panchax,* the *Lyre-tailed Panchax* and the easily identified *firemouth panchax,* are two of the most beautiful and admired of panchaxes. The *Golden Lyretail, Striped Panchax, Ceylon, Playfair's, blue* and *dwarf* are all under the panchax banner. *Cyprinodontidae* include the many *Aphyosemion, Rivulas,* and *Lampeyes,* the *West African killy* (a superb fish), the *Nigerian Aphyosemion* (gorgeous), and the expensive and radiant *African Fire killy.* All are splendid fishes worthy of the attention of any aquarist.

CAVE FISHES (GENERA *TYPHLOGARRA WIDDOWSONI*)

Some of these unique fishes are of the *Cyprinodontidae* family, but many others belong to unrelated orders and families. They have in common the fact that they spend their lives in underground caves and, in the stygian darkness of their habitat, have no need for vision. They have little or no skin pigment and are scaleless or almost scaleless. The fry are often born with eyes that atrophy as the fishes grow until they completely lose sight.

There are thirty-two known species of *cave fishes* that live in an environment practically devoid of enemies and generally with an abundant supply of food. Living blindly in this environment, the purpose of the body's lateral line comes into focus: it compensates for sight loss by detecting vibration and pressure changes in the water. This, in turn, registers the existence of objects at a distance. Many of these cave fishes have lips and barbels abundantly supplied with taste buds, which allow them to keep in touch with their immediate environment.

The breeding habits of these interesting fishes vary greatly. Some are live-bearers, some egg-layers. There are seasons when food, though generally plentiful, becomes scarce and the fishes have to fast for a period of time. It has been theorized that by not growing eye tissue there is a saving in energy which carries the cave fishes through their infrequent periods of food deprivation. The idea is one over which to ponder.

CATFISH

This is an immensely large and varied group of fishes, that includes the *European catfish,* or *welsh,* that grows to 9 feet or more in Central and Eastern Europe and western Asian rivers, and the small, rather comical *Corydoras* that grace the tanks of many aquarists. An interest-

ing sidelight on these fishes is their role in one of America's newest
industries, *catfish farming*. The catfish utilized in this farming are the
ordinary ones fished for as food in ponds and streams, particularly
throughout the southern part of the country. Ponds are prepared and
stocked; with correct husbandry and management 2,000 pounds or
more of marketable food fish can be grown per acre.

Corydoras (*family Callichthyidae*) are quaint little bottom feeders
that constantly hustle around the floor of the tank cleaning up food that
has settled on the sand or gravel. They are undemanding fishes and are
free breeders but during breeding must be supplied with cooler water
than most tropicals. Though not colorful, many of these small Cats are
prettily banded or spotted. Among the most attractive are the *Black-
top,* the *Aeneus catfish* (most popular), the *Banded, Tail-spot, Skunk,
Dwarf, Whiptail, Myers', Cochu's, Elegant, Leopard* (very well liked),
Bandit, Light-spot (distinctly marked), *Spotted, Peppered* (also an albino variety), *Network* (attractively patterned), and the *U-numbered
Catfish.*

Loaches, (*Acanthophthalmus—family Cobitidae*) are elongated and
interesting scavengers that share with the cats the chore of tank cleaning. These are generally banded or adorned with a body pattern of
black markings. Favorites among aquarists are the *Coolie loach, Half-
banded* and *Long-nosed* loaches.

For today's aquarists the eggs of fishes with long incubation periods
can be mailed to and from any part of the world, which makes it easy
for enthusiasts to acquire fishes that are not frequently available in
their own areas. This is a wonderful advantage, for the·cult of "Tropical Fish Keepers" is more widespread than most people realize. All
have their colorful aquaria. Look around and you will see well-cared-
for aquariums in hospitals, in the offices of architects, doctors and
dentists; in cellars, restaurants, apartments, and a multitude of other
locales. This is the "Secret Brotherhood" of tropical-fish enthusiasts,
a kind of benign and fishy coterie that has reached out benevolent
tentacles, invaded every segment of our social structure, and given
all of mankind an area in which to find a universal dialogue.

Species of Marine Tropicals

There are in the oceans and seas throughout the world, thousands
of fishes that are undoubtedly suitable for the marine aquarium, but we
are concerned here only with the limited number of beautiful specimens that are available to the salt-water hobbyist.

A few years ago I was invited to judge a big specialty dog show in

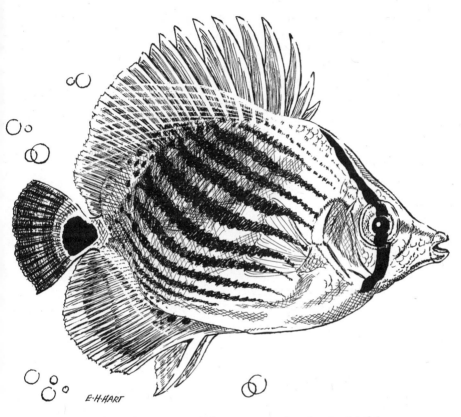

The Chaetodon *is one of the many regal and colorful fishes that can be acquired by the salt-water aquarist.*

Barbados and then go on to Trinidad to lecture and do a survey of the island's dogs for the local club. On the way to Haiti from Trinidad my wife and I flew Arawak Air Lines to the rather undeveloped island of Tobago to visit Buccoo Reef in the Caribbean. A native boatman took us to the reef where, in swimsuits, sneakers, and underwater goggles, we slipped over the side of the boat. Guided by our boatman, we entered a veritable fairyland where gorgeous tropical marine fishes of every size and brilliant color were darting about amid bright-hued coral, waving anemones and sea fans. It was a strangely eerie experience, as though in the underwater silence I had suddenly been reduced in size and become an inhabitant of a huge marine aquarium wherein dwelt the most extraordinary, exquisite, and fantastic fishes in the world.

Marine Angelfishes are generally fairly large and always exceedingly handsome. Some of the angelfishes are called *butterfly fishes,* but the latter belong to a different family, which leads to some confusion. The angelfishes and butterfly fishes together number more than 150 species. They can be found in shallow seas and estuaries and are usually neither aggressive nor afraid. The wide range of dazzling colors and intricate patterns worn by these splendid fishes seems unending.

The *French angelfish* (*Pomacanthus paru*), velvet black, patterned with hot yellow and sporting a bright blue pectoral fin, is both bizarre in shape and gorgeous in color. Other fantastic angels are the *Bluering* found in American waters, *Tricolor, Imperial, Koran, Cortes, Vermiculated, Rock Beauty,* and the *Queen.*

Very elegant *butterfly fishes* (discus-shaped much like the angelfishes) are the *Four-eyed, Long-Nosed, Townsend's* (gold, edged with brilliant blue), the *Morpho* (dazzling blue striped with black and bearing an orange tail); *Coral, White Collar, Orange, Reef, Banded,* and several more, all completely superb fishes. In describing these myriad fishes one runs out of adequate adjectives. Actually their beauty is indescribable; they must be seen to be believed.

The *Moorish Idol* is stately and much desired by marine aquarists. So are the *Batfishes* (*Platax pinnatus*) with a black body edged in scarlet, and *Platax orbicularis.* These fishes become *wonderful pets,* recognizing the aquarist, eating out of his hand, and indicating that they want to be fondled and stroked—an amazing display of affection for a fish. These are not the proverbial "cold fish."

The popular *Sailfin Tang* (silver with heavy black stripes) and the *Yellow Tang* are discus-shaped. They are examples of the family *Acanthuridae* and are also called *surgeonfishes.* They are very beautiful. The *Clown Fish,* or sea anemone fish, colorfully clothed in orange with three white bands, live in a symbiotic relationship among the tentacles of poisonous sea anemones.

Triggerfish (*family Balistidae*) can be identified through their lack of ventral fins. Instead of a first dorsal fin they possess spines that look like the trigger of a gun, hence their name. The most popular and colorful of the triggerfishes is the *Queen* (or *oldwife*).

A very interesting group of marine tropicals are the *Trunkfishes* (family *Ostraciidae*). Baked in the hard shell that covers them, these are delicious food fish, a unique taste-treat for seafood addicts.

There are *Scats, Lamb fishes, Hawkfish, wrasse,* and several *anemone fishes, hogfishes, Dascyllus, drumfishes,* and an oceanful of other marine tropicals that will add interest to any salt-water aquarium. The *Sticklebacks* can be kept in the marine tank and *Monodactylus argenteus* and the *Scat* (*Scatophagus Argus*) can both be kept in either salt-water or fresh-water aquariums.

I must not forget the *Sergeant Major* and the species of *Lion* or *Scorpion* fishes, very dangerous fishes that can inflict extremely painful wounds with their deadly porcupine-like spines. There are the not-yet-mentioned *Sea Horses,* which are well-liked and interesting pets, and the *Pipefishes* (there are both fresh- and salt-water species) which can be fed and cared for in the same identical fashion as the sea horses. They even breed alike in that the male has a pouch in which the young are carried. *Lophiocharon horridus* is so strange in shape and color that it doesn't even look like a fish.

SEA ANEMONES

"Flowers of the sea" will form a sympathetic rapport with the fish in the aquarium. Anemone is adapted from the Greek word meaning "wind." The smaller reef species of anemones particularly will live in symbiosis with other species. Anemones are in fact sea animals and fulfill the didactic rules for animals in that they have simple organs, ingest solid foods, and are capable of locomotion. In higher animals, patterns and colors have utilitarian purpose, but in the sea anemones patterns and colors appear as pure art forms.

To complete the aura of the world's waters within the confines of the aquarium one can judiciously add other creatures such as shrimp, hermit crabs, snails, colored tube worms and any other pacific denizens of the deep that one may fancy.

The marine aquarium is a delightful adeventure, bringing into one's home a tiny bit of exotic seas, of the mysterious and still unknown depths, the unexplored planet within our planet; that colorful, adventurous place of sunken galleons and Lost Atlantis, which may someday be mankind's salvation, yielding the food and sustenance that a crowded earth no longer can produce.

14

Reptiles of the World

Snakes (order *Squamata*)

The reptiles in existence today are divided into four orders: the *Squamata* (lizards and snakes) *Crocodilia* (crocodiles, caiman, alligators), the *Testudinata* (turtles and tortoises) and the *Rhynchocephalia* (an ancient order with but one living example, the Tuatera or Sphenodon). There are hundreds of species of snakes that vary in size from the six giant species—the largest of which are the monstrous 30-foot or more and over 300-pound Indian pythons and the South American anacondas—to tiny burrowing snakes no bigger than small worms.

Snakes have come to be symbols of evil, no doubt through reference to them in the Bible where, even at the beginning of symbolic biblical genesis, the Serpent was the villain. During the evolution of man great, silent, deadly snakes undoubtedly took their toll of the small, early primates that gradually but inevitably became man's bestial ancestors. Perhaps for this reason a vestigial fear remains in the human mind. There is no doubt that in most people, even those who have never seen a snake, there exists a residual and abysmal fear of reptiles.

Nonvenomous reptiles are certainly useful in helping to rid the world of many rodents that destroy grain and other foodstuffs, and harbor dread diseases. There are also nonvenomous snakes that kill and consume venomous reptiles. So the snake is not really a villain; in fact he has an economic value to our society. As pets, however, snakes leave something to be desired, for they are not capable of feeling a strong emotional response toward a human being. They will seek the warmth of the human body and will accept handling from the human who feeds and tends them. They cannot, of course, be trained as can most creatures (other than fishes) that have attained pet status.

But if you do not expect to find rapport or affection between yourself and your pet snake, if you derive pleasure from caring for and handling them, and if you are enthralled by some of their beautiful rhythmic body patterns, then you are a true snake hobbyist and should pay no attention to the opinion of others who cannot achieve your height of interest. Or if you are fascinated by snakes as a different life-form and eager to study their behavior patterns and perhaps find a way to reach out to them in an attempt to arrive at some manner of understanding, I'm with you and applaud your efforts. Certainly many people do keep snakes as pets.

I will not list or give attention to the venomous snakes, even though they exert upon many people a rather dread psychotic fascination. They certainly do not qualify as pets and anyone who keeps them for other than professional reasons is a candidate for the "funny farm." I am certain that herpetologists will agree with me.

We know that mankind has found religious significance in the serpent, perhaps fostered by the awe that is a part of religious mystique. Throughout early religious history, particularly in the Eastern religions of the Hindus, Moslems, and Buddhists, snake myths abound. Snake cults are as old as man and as new as tomorrow; you will generally find that this kind of cult was founded on superstitious ignorance and was akin to the basic fear most people have of serpents. Through the science of herpetology, and the efforts of reptile hobbyists whose sincere, sympathetic, and objective study of their charges have shed new light on our knowledge of snakes and their habits, superstition and baseless fear may be eliminated.

Before delving into the various elements of snake care, there are some hard-core facts about snakes that you should be aware of, that will eliminate false ideas and beliefs about them and bring you to a better understanding of these much-maligned creatures.

Snakes are not cold-blooded (*poikilothermic*). They take heat from their surroundings, but are not able to absorb warmth and store it in their bodies as we do. This is why reptiles enjoy sunning themselves.

You cannot recognize a poisonous snake by its head shape, or any other outward physical sign. *Viperine snakes* have triangular heads, but so do many nonvenomous reptiles. The family of deadly snakes, containing the cobras, mambas, coral snakes and their lethal allies, all have narrow heads, as do most typically harmless snakes.

Snakes are not "slimy." They are dry to the touch; in many instances their scales look and feel like enameled metal. They do not have the capacity to hypnotize, mesmerize, or "charm" their prey.

They do not cover their prey with saliva before ingesting. They generally swallow their prey head first.

The tongue of a serpent is not a "sting"; it is a sensitive smelling device. The tongue "licks" odors from the air and transfers them to a section on the roof of the mouth (Jacobson's organ) where smells are analyzed and catalogued.

Snakes have no voice, so make no vocal noises—a fact that most people have never even thought about.

The age of a rattlesnake cannot be told by the number of its rattles. Nor do they *always* rattle when about to strike. Babies of this family do not play with their rattles; some adult snakes believe in "strike first and rattle later."

Tropical countries, contrary to popular belief, do *not* have a corner on poisonous snakes.

Other interesting information about snakes includes the facts that they can engage in four modes of locomotion, and that all snakes—not just those that are known as water reptiles—can and will swim should the occasion arise.

Varieties of Nonpoisonous Snakes

Let us examine the larger reptiles first—the boas and pythons. These varieties are all constrictors that kill their prey by wrapping it in their coils and squeezing or constricting. Actually boas are New World reptiles with only a few, physically small Old World species. The big snakes of the African and Asian tropics are *pythons,* found only in the Old World. Of the large snakes there are six species that can be considered as being in the category of true giant snakes: the *anaconda, boa constrictor, African rock python, Indian python, reticulated python* and the *amethystine python.*

These huge creatures share certain interesting characteristics. They are the only large terrestrial creatures that lack a vocal apparatus; the only sound they produce is the characteristic hiss. Lacking external ears, they do not hear well. They have limited vision and, for perception of the world around them, depend mostly on their organs of smell, including their highly sensitive tongue. They are all at home in the water and swim expertly even though only the anaconda really lives in or around water constantly. They have a transparent eye covering that is completely watertight. No other land animal of approximately similar size can swallow pieces of food almost equal to their own bulk. Because these large reptiles can consume creatures the size of deer and large swine weighing hundreds of pounds, they can, in a single meal, consume as much as five hundred times their energy needs for a day.

Because of this amazing facility these snakes can subsequently fast for well over a year without any other food intake.

The *water boa,* or *anaconda* (*Eunectes murinus*) of the Amazon and Orinoco basins is the most aquatic of boas. It is also the largest of all snakes, though this statement is often argued. The name of this giant is said to have been derived from an Amerindian tribe, the Indian words *anai* meaning elephant and *kolra* for killer. In my humble opinion this is stretching things a bit far, since an Amazonian Indian would never have seen an elephant and wouldn't know one from a large hole in the ground. It is, though, quite conceivable that the name was conferred upon the large Indian rock python by natives of that country. A widely accepted measurement of 37½ feet is a great deal less than the 62-foot-long anaconda claimed to have been killed by the eminent South American explorer, Colonel Fawcett.

I can well understand how exaggeration of size can occur from a sighting of one of these huge *Boidae.* I once saw one in the Amazon jungle of Peru, on the Manati River in Yagua Indian country, and to me it looked as big as an ancient dinosaur. It was close enough for me to smell it (or think I did). Upon sane consideration, I believe this snake was probably no more than 16 to 18 feet long, but the circumference (they are very thick-bodied) made it appear much larger.

There are several Boa subspecies in the Guianas, Trinidad, and Paraguay. Olive green in color, with large round black spots along their length, these giant reptiles usually hunt their prey at the water's edge, grabbing their quarry as it drinks and dragging it underwater until it drowns. Sometimes Boas hunt on land, dropping from trees onto their victims, which consist of birds, small mammals, rodents, deer, peccaries, capybara, fish, and even turtles and caiman. Wrapping their coils around their prey, the boas tighten the coils each time the animal exhales until it dies of suffocation, not from being squashed by the boa.

South American Indians enjoy many myths and legends about anacondas. The Taruma Indians proudly claim to be descendants of the giant snakes. Anacondas, like all other boas, are viviparous, having from 20 to 100 young born early in the year. Each baby is about 3 feet long and, when young, can be tamed to become pets. When these boas begin to reach full growth, they can and should no longer be given pet status.

All the giant boas and pythons are lethargic snakes. They need very little exercise and so can be kept in relatively small cages, with sufficient height so they can climb upward and, of course, with water for the anaconda. Individuals of up to 3 feet in length should be fed about 3 live mice a week, with the number increasing as the snake grows. Giant serpents over 3 feet long will readily accept live chickens for a meal.

The second largest snake (some say the largest of all) is the *reticulated* or *Regal python* (*Python reticulatus*) of Burma, Indo-China, the Malay Peninsula and surrounding Islands. This python, with an authenticated record measurement of 33 feet in length, is more slender than the anaconda. In Greek mythology the python was a monstrous serpent slain by Apollo near Delphi. It is strikingly marked in dark

E. H. HART

Patterned like a rare oriental rug, the magnificent Regal Python (Python reticulatus) *is a constrictor that reaches tremendous size.*

brown and yellow, the pattern much like that of an Oriental rug. Youngsters of most all the boas and pythons are quite beautiful in their body design and make handsome pets. Like the anaconda, this Python is much too big to be considered a pet when it reaches maturity.

The *Black-tailed python* (*Python molurus*) is not quite as large as the reticulated, its maximum length not exceeding 22 feet. It also becomes tamer and is more easily handled in captivity than the Regal. There is a paler-hued black-tailed variety inhabiting the western area of India that becomes very tame when handled properly. This species is often used by snake charmers in the entertainment field.

The *African Rock python* is about the same size as its Indian relative and, like all of the large pythons, is beautifully mottled throughout the considerable length of its body.

Inhabiting Australia, the Moluccas and New Guinea, the *Amethystine python* is another large, handsomely patterned snake that is one of the giant six.

The last of the "big six" is the *Boa Constrictor* of South America, the snake that has the dubious honor of being the second largest New World serpent. There are three species that are very much alike—all inferior in size to the anaconda, all reaching a maximum length of not more than 15 feet. These boas boast particularly interesting markings and color and, if taken when young, make nice pets. Half-grown mice make excellent food for young boas that gradually work up to rats, pigeons, and finally rabbits. I have heard that some boas are used as watchdogs in South American homes, but so far this interesting concept in home protection has remained just a rumor. I have not been able to track down a single authenticated usage of a snake in this capacity.

There are also smaller pythons, such as the *ball python* that seldom grows beyond 4 feet long, is thick-bodied, and is rather timid. The *Green Tree boa,* is in color, a very pretty green with crossbars of white. It grows to be approximately 5 to 6 feet in overall length. Most boas are arboreal, but there are several *small ground boas* about 2 feet long that inhabit Cuba and the western section of the United States, particularly the Pacific region. One in particular, the *rubber boa,* of silvery gray color, is a very gentle snake and makes an ideal pet.

The *Paradise Tree Snake* of Borneo has the unique ability to glide through the air for a distance of up to 40 feet. Because of this strange capability, it does not make a particularly good pet.

The *Bull Snake* of our own Great Plains is a powerful constrictor that is commonly about 8 feet long. It feeds in the wild on Spermophiles or ground squirrels and other grain-devouring creatures. The temperament of these reptiles varies greatly; some become quickly tamed, others remain wild. In color they sport a straw-colored body base upon which are distributed large reddish patches along the spinal area. If you can find one that is mild-tempered, you will have an excellent reptile pet. It is easily cared for because the bull snake can be fed six hen's eggs a week without any other food and yet remain in very good health. *Pine snakes* also display very erratic temperaments. Both these reptiles deserve protection because their eating habits make them economically valuable to farmers.

The often-seen *Black Snake* grows to a length of 6 feet and is very active and fast. As a matter of fact it can outrun a man. I have seen many of the big reptiles in the Connecticut woods, but have never been attacked by one. If I had been, I would guarantee that the species would immediately have lost its reputation of being able to outrun a man! Because of their legendary speed they are sometimes called the *black racer*. This snake is too high strung to make a good amiable pet. A close relative to the black snake is the *Coachwhip snake*. Slender and about 8 feet long, it is not as slim as the *Whip snakes* of the southwest United States or the extremely fast gliding *Desert Racer* of the same region.

The largest nonvenomous snake of North America is the *Indigo,* a very handsome tractable species, so docile and easily tamed that it is a favorite of collectors and hobbyists. This lustrous, blue-black beauty is hardy, easily cared for, and will reach a mature length of about 8 feet. These snakes make terrific pets.

The *Rat Snakes* form a genus of large, handsome North American reptiles, all of them very strong constrictors. The *Corn Snake* has been named the most beautiful of all large North American snakes. In the Florida Everglades this species will attain a length of over 7 feet. The *Pilot Black Snake* is closely related to the rat snakes and is often mistaken for the black racer. The handsomely colored *Red Rat Snake,* superb in pattern and hue, is a superior mouse and rat killer. India's

Rat Snake is a very large reptile that grows to a mature length of 10 feet and has great speed of movement.

The *King Snakes* are particularly interesting. They deliberately seek out other snakes, including the most venomous species, engage them in battle, kill and eat them. They are probably, inch for inch, the most powerful of all constrictors and seem to be immune to any form of reptile venom. As savage and cannibalistic as they are with their own kind, they are completely docile toward humans and enjoy great popularity as pets. Of the king snake genus is the *Milk Snake*. Because of its habit of prowling barns in search of mice, this reptile garnered the fallacious reputation of stealing milk from cows.

The *Hog-nosed Snake* or *Hissing Adder* is a perfectly harmless serpent with a much-maligned reputation. It has the appearance of a venomous reptile and acts exactly like one, puffing up, hissing and striking, its thick, yard-long body swaying like a cobra's, but it seldom, if ever, attempts to bite. It will also writhe on the ground as though mortally wounded, then flop over and play dead. These snakes can be picked up without fear and soon become docile pets. I found one of these bluffers in the woods in Southington, Connecticut. It was reared up in my path hissing, weaving, and puffing out its cobra-like hood. I walked over to it and picked it up, intending to give it to my son for the Boy Scout museum and zoo. As I lifted it from the ground, the snake struck—but with the wrong end. In its fright at being handled it defecated all over the front of my shirt and trousers. This species eats mostly toads and will become a completely amiable pet.

A very delicately colored and attractive group of snakes is represented by the *Eastern Ring-necked Snake*. These pretty serpents have a ring of brilliant orange, yellow, or red around their neck. A lovely little red-banded reptile of the Southeast is the *Scarlet Snake*. It is rather rare and a prize in any hobbyist's collection. The *Green Snake* is another highly regarded reptile that *never bites,* even when initially handled. It is entirely insectivorous, subsisting on spiders, hairless caterpillars, and crickets. It must be fed several insects each day. The green snake makes a wonderful serpent to house in the community terrarium because it will not molest other creatures such as frogs, lizards, or newts. This serpent makes a perfectly marvelous pet.

Undoubtedly the *Garter Snake* is the most familiar reptile in this country. It is extremely adaptable and will subsist nicely on frogs and earthworms. Though it varies in color, the garter snake is generally striped on the body and quite slender. Garter snakes' teeth are very small and, even though they bite fiercely when first captured, they can't do much damage. Within a short time they become very worthy pets. They can be conditioned to eat raw beef cut into narrow strips and an occasional bit of fish. The *Ribbon Snake* is closely related to the garter snake, but is much more aquatic. There are about a dozen species of *water snakes,* one of which is constantly being mistaken for the very lethal water moccasin. These creatures will fight hard to keep from being captured. They also have the ability to discharge a very noxious liquid from their anal glands. I would not recommend them as pets.

There is a very large group of interesting snakes called Colubridae, members of which inhabit all the continents. They possess short,

The most commonly seen of all snakes in the United States is the Garter Snake (Thamnophis sirtalis). *If handled correctly they can become fine reptile pets.*

grooved fangs at the rear of the upper jaw and are appropriately called *Rear-fanged snakes*. Few of them are dangerous to man, but they are not to be considered in the pet category.

There are many other species of snakes from other parts of the world, particularly from tropical zones, that can be tamed and that can become fine serpent pets, but those I have named are the most readily available to hobbyists and herpetologists in this country. Snakes are very much misunderstood creatures and, though the rumor that you collect or own snakes as pets might make certain of your acquaintances look at you askance, be strong and persevere. You are entitled to your hobby and you and I know that snakes can be fun.

Lizards, Turtles, and Such

Like many humans who indulge in ancestral pride because of progenitors' accomplishments—good, bad, or colored by time to assume heroic proportions—the reptiles we will now discuss certainly have the right to such ancestor worship. But they do not think, reason, or remember, so the world is spared the boredom of "Dinosaur Day" or "Reptile Culture" studies.

It is true, however, that many millions of years before the Roman Legions tramped the civilized world beneath their iron-shod sandals, great Saurians shook the ground with their roars and ruled a forming, plastic, miasmic earth with mindless ferocity and sheer force of size. The remnants of those fantastic reptilian monsters, that for countless millions of years were monarchs of this planet, exist in the crocodilia, lizards and turtles of today that are, with few exceptions, poor imitations of the archaic, dominant giants of the Mesozoic, Jurassic, and Cretaceous periods.

CROCODILIANS (ORDER *CROCODILIA*)

There are about two dozen species of *Crocodilia*. I give them recognition here simply because hundreds of baby Crocodilia are purchased as pets each year by ill-advised people. I do not consider them to be truly in the pet realm, for within a short time after purchase their growth elevates them to the category of dangerous animals. They must then be given to zoos or released in woodland ponds. The latter solution is what one would expect from the misguided individuals who bought them in the first place. Young crocs mimic closely the life-style of mature specimens.

Commonly sold as a baby alligator, this young Spectacled Caiman (Crocodylus fuscus) *inhabits the American tropics.*

LIZARDS (ORDER *SQUAMATA*)

This is a huge family of *Sauria* that exhibit wide diversification in size, habits, color, and form. The big *Monitor Lizards* of the Old World (*Varanus*) include the 10-feet-long, 300-pound *Komodo monitor* or "Dragon," the *Giant Australian Lizard* and about two dozen other species of Monitors distributed throughout the tropical areas of the Old World. The Giant Lizards are not in the pet category. Indeed, a Komodo monitor is big enough to make a pet out of you . . . until he becomes hungry.

The largest of the New World lizards are the tropical iguanas.

The South American *Iguana* is a spectacular creature that grows to be 6 feet long. It is arboreal and feasts on leaves, fruits, and bird's eggs. The *Rhinoceros Iguana* of Haiti is a bulky lizard with one or two prominent horns on its snout; a slow-moving, truly grotesque creature. Most

A seaweed-eating Iguana, the colorful Marine Lizard (Amblyrhynchus cristatus) *inhabits Hood Island, one of the Galapagos Islands.*

of the lizards make good pets, but they are rather dull, quiet, and, in many cases, move no faster than a slow-motion movie.

Other large iguanas can be found in Mexico, Central America, Cuba, and the Bahamas. In the Galapagos Islands there lives a large *Land Iguana* and an extraordinary *Marine Iguana,* the only known lizard with maritime habits, though the monitor lizard of Borneo is known to have the ability to swim like a fish. The marine iguana subsists mostly on seaweeds. In Mexico and South America, iguanas are eaten by humans who say the flesh is tasty. I have often seen peons, at the side of the road in Mexico, selling live iguanas for human food. Borneo boasts of a *Flying Lizard,* quite a unique adaptation for a true reptile.

Iguanas are large; some are quite active and need very roomy accommodations with tree forms on which to climb. They must be kept warm and given plenty of water. Feed them lettuce, celery leaves, bananas, berries and other plant material and fruits. In a park in Toluca, Mexico, I met a hobbyist who was walking his pet, a 4-foot iguana, wearing a small harness with an attached leash.

Next in size to the iguanas is the *Tegu* of South America. Stout, powerful, and reaching a length of 4 feet, these are swift creatures that raid tropical poultry yards to dine on small chickens. They are voracious and bold and will not hesitate to leap at a man's hand to bite it. The *Racerunner* of the Southern United States is a much smaller, prettier example of the *Teiidae.* They inhabit dry, sandy places and are very fast afoot. For housing, provide a floor of sand, a couple of small, growing cacti, and a piece of rough, dried bark. A dish of water will attract this lizard and he will drink from it.

A very interesting lizard is the *Glass "Snake."* This fellow obviously looks like a snake, most of the family *Anguidae* being limbless. Lizards generally have fragile tails that break off easily if touched or bitten. But the tail of the glass "snake" is ridiculous, one tiny touch and it shatters into myriad shards.

One of the most handsome lizards in the United States is the *Collared lizard,* delicately colored and lovely in pattern. It inhabits the rocky plains of our great West. Fine, dry sand and plenty of warmth will help this lizard to be healthy and hardy. The colored lizard is oviparous; its eggs incubate for several weeks. Feed insects and, on occasion, some clover or dandelion blossoms. Keep these fellows to themselves as they have exhibited cannibalistic tendencies.

Skinks do not make good pets because of their innate shyness. In the terrarium they constantly hide and rarely are you able to really see them. The obvious answer to this conduct will not work because the skink, if deprived of his concealing facilities, will not do well and he will eventually die. The scalation of these little creatures is exceedingly smooth and polished. Skinks eat all kinds of insects and an occasional meal of raw, beaten eggs and raw meat, scraped or finely ground, is relished. Many varieties of lizards other than skinks enjoy this latter combination of food. *Plated lizards* are somewhat like skinks in type. In captivity they are the most hardy of all lizards and will thrive in a plain, glass-fronted exhibition cage or tank. Like the skink, the plated will drink from a shallow water receptacle. The plated also likes to have a small house in which to retire and plenty of flies to eat.

Chuckwallas are quite large, maturing at about 15 inches. They are completely herbivorous, so are easily supplied with food. They need a temperature of from 85 to 100 degrees Fahrenheit and their quarters must be well-lighted, roomy, and dry. They eat sparingly and prefer flower blossoms and greens. From Europe comes a popular lizard, the *Green Iguana,* a very pretty, docile insectivore, which makes a very fine pet. There is also a little-known family of lizards, *Amphisbaena* or *Worm Lizards* of which there are over a hundred species. These strange burrowing creatures grow from 1 to 2 feet in length; they lack limbs and so look exactly like worms. The head and tail are almost identical and their main source of food is insects and their larvae. Many of the *Amphisbaenids* live in the nests of ants and termites, a custom which has led the South American Indians to think that they are cared for by the ants, so they call them "ant kings." Since they are generally found underground and both ends are similar, they make very poor pets because, even when you catch a glimpse of them, you never know whether they are coming or going.

The *Geckos* are a large family of lizards of myriad varieties in both the Old and New worlds. They display extremely fine scalation and adhesive toe pads but are not noted for striking color or pattern combinations. Geckos are jungle creatures and need a warm, moist environment. They should be fed a variety of insects.

One of the most prevalent lizard pets of all is the American *Chameleon* or *Anole* (*Anolis carolinensis*). If you live in a tropical or semi-tropical climate, the anole is no stranger to you. Near our home in Florida they exist by the thousands, frequently coming into the house. These little chameleons are very typical lizards in form, are extremely fast-moving and are wonderful climbers and jumpers. Sucker-like discs on the bottom of each toe enables them to climb even a sheet of sheer glass with evident ease. They are capable of changing in color from dull gray-brown to bright green with a whitish underbody. There are a host of closely allied species—over three hundred—some almost black with white dots, some striped and ridged along the back like tiny dinosaurs, and others pale tan. Males have an obvious gular fold or "dewlap" under the neck (in large specimens the size of a nickel), which can be distended at will. These little lizards make excellent pets. They are insectivorous and like warmth and broad-leaved plants on which to climb about. Sprinkle fresh water on the plant leaves for them to drink and feed each lizard from three to six live insects the size of a mealworm per day. These are the lizards sold at circuses by hawkers whose spiel encourages you to imagine that the anole will change to any color—even Scotch plaid.

There are about eighty species of the *Chameleon,* most droll of all the lizard clan. Among the great legions of lizards none attain to such grotesquerie of form or strangeness in habits as is exhibited by these gargoyle creatures. They seem to live in a different time scale of excessive slow motion. Periodically they shed their skin as does a snake and are mostly arboreal. The tail of the chameleon is prehensile, as is a monkey's, and the eyes are huge and bulging, each capable of movement independent of the other. The toes are joined so that the feet are like a pair of tongs giving them a tenacious grip. They resemble the opposing grasping digits of a primate. The chameleon lives up to his name, for he can change color at will. It possesses a highly extensible tongue that is longer than its head and body combined and can be shot out with amazing speed—in direct contrast to the incredible slowness of all its other physical movements. This lizard catches its insect food by flicking out its sticky tongue in the same manner as an Anteater.

The *African Chameleon* is noted for its quick and marked color changes. There is a *Common Chameleon,* a *Giant Chameleon* that attains a length of 2 feet, a *Dwarf Chameleon* and the interesting *Jackson's Chameleon* that wears a pair of horns. Some of the dwarf types measure less than 2 inches long. Many of these creatures live at heights above 9,000 feet. Some chameleons are oviparous and others bear their young alive. These bizarre lizards make excellent pets if you are an individual of vast patience.

The only known *poisonous lizards,* both of the New World, are the *Gila Monster* and the closely allied species of the same genus, the *Beaded Lizard.* These two dangerous reptiles form a family by themselves. They are easy to keep and interesting to study, but because they are lethal creatures carrying a viscid poison as toxic as the venom of the poisonous snakes, I do not consider them in the category of pets and I advise you not to either.

The lizards are an attractive and interesting group of reptiles. They are generally cosmopolitan in distribution and can perform many amazing feats, from skimming over water to swimming like a fish, from changing color to sailing through the air, and catching insects with a tongue like an anteater's. But of most interest, to me at any rate, is the fact that they are the present-day relatives of the mighty saurians that, in the dim, vast reaches of time, were the living kings of our planet.

TURTLES AND TORTOISES (ORDER *TESTUDINATA*)

Of the almost 250 kinds of shell-encased creatures, 55 distinct species reside in the United States and its waters. They are, because of their protective shells, unique among vertebrate animals. They are also the longest-lived of the reptiles, surpassing even the crocodilians in life expectancy. All the species produce their young from eggs. The term *turtle* is commonly used to designate the aquatic kinds of *Testudinata,* while those species that are land creatures are called *tortoises.* Some of the larger aquatic turtles are frequently named terrapins and are shipped to markets in large numbers, for their meat is delicious and much desired by gourmets. The *Diamond-back Terrapin* is known for the delicate taste of its flesh. It prefers salt marshes as its habitat, which for a terrapin, is a unique selection of environment.

The *Alligator Snapping Turtle,* an ugly, savage brute weighing close to 100 pounds, can inflict serious wounds. The *Common Snapping Turtle* is no beauty either. It can be found all over North America, and weighs up to 40 pounds. This snapper is also bad news in the biting department and is particularly unpopular with fish and young water fowl. These two turtles are the villains of the turtle clan and naturally neither of them can be recommended as pets. In fact they should be religiously avoided unless you wish to trap them for their food value. I have eaten snapping-turtle stew and must report that it is a flavorful dish.

Throughout the United States turtles abound. There are the *Common Musk Turtle,* the *Mud Turtle,* and the popular and attractive *Painted Turtle* with an upper shell that sports vermilion and yellow patches. Of all the *chelonians* the most wanted and easily adaptable as pets are the *Wood Turtles.* Their sculptured shells with concentric projections and their brick-red legs and neck quickly identify them. They become tame rapidly and will beg for food from their owner. The *Spotted Turtle* is a close relative, but is more aquatic.

Box Turtles live only on land and are easily recognized by their high domed shells. The plastron (ventral section of shell) of the box turtle is hinged so that it closes tightly against the carapace, the dorsal or top part of the shell, creating a tightly sealed shell box into which it can seal itself completely from outer danger. These are aggressive creatures and the males battle viciously to proclaim their dominance. The *Eastern Box Tortoise* is terrestrial and seen often in the woods. *Box Turtles* seem to be quite intelligent and are rugged individualists in their eating habits, some preferring raw meat and fish while others will consume nothing but vegetables or fruit. It is not necessary to supply turtles with water. They obtain all that they need in liquids from the food they ingest.

Giant Tortoises reaching a weight of over 500 pounds once flourished on oceanic islands. But ship masters had them killed for food for their sailors, and turtle-oil hunters, wild dogs, and pigs rapidly diminished their numbers. Smaller tortoises such as the *South American Tortoise,* the *Leopard, Star* and *Hingeback Tortoise* of Africa and the *Gopher Tortoise* of the United States still flourish. The gopher, probably the best-known of the tortoises, makes an excellent pet.

The Soft-Shell Turtles represent a family of several species that occur in both North America and the Old World. Strictly aquatic, they can be found in slow-flowing rivers. These critters have formidable knifelike jaws that can deliver a vicious bite, which immediately lifts them from the pet category. They can attain a length of almost two feet.

There are less than a dozen known species of *Marine Turtles* and they are the largest members of the order, one species reaching the impressive weight of 1,000 pounds. These are not pet material either, since you would have to supply them with a small ocean in which to live. The valuable tortoise shell of commerce comes from the *Hawk's-bill Turtle* of this group.

Frogs, Toads, Salamanders, and Newts
(class *Amphibia*)

I can remember—and I am sure you can too—the thrill of watching tadpoles grow from tiny fishlike things to creatures with formative legs and finally into recognizable frogs. It is even more fun to start with the eggs, watch them hatch and see the youngsters go through their amazing transformation.

Basically there are three orders of amphibians, the *Salientia,* which includes *frogs and toads;* the *Caudate* which includes *salamanders and newts;* and the *Apoda,* which are wormlike tropical amphibians of little interest to us.

FROGS AND TOADS

There are about fifteen hundred kinds of amphibians that range in size from tiny frogs no bigger than a nickel to huge African giant frogs that can—and do—swallow a fully grown rat. In North America there are two major families of frogs: the *Tree Frogs (Hylidae)* and the *True Frogs (Ranidae).* The tree frogs are generally small, dainty, and long-legged and are themselves divided into *Tree Frogs (Hyla), Chorus Frogs (Pseudacris),* and *Cricket Frogs (Acris).*

Green Frogs and *Bull Frogs* take all of two years to become mature, but the more common varieties take only one season, and toads emerge from their aquatic habitat in from two to three months. Toad's eggs will produce swimming polliwogs in from four to five days, while frog's eggs won't produce young for two weeks.

Among the more attractive frogs of the United States are the *Leopard, Wood, Pickerel, Green, Southern Tree,* and *Green Tree.* Everyone is familiar with the big *Bullfrog* and to the list we must add the *Spring Peeper* (harbinger of spring), the *Mountain Chorus Frog* and the *Gray Tree Toad.* Frogs have many enemies in the wild and they find it rather difficult to stay alive. Snakes, fish, birds, mammals and even large aquatic bugs, all take their toll. Man also hunts the large bullfrogs for their meaty legs, which are a true delicacy.

Some of the handsomest of the tropical frogs are the *Dominican* and the *Painted Frog,* the latter as large as our American bullfrog. The huge *Horned Frog* of Brazil swallows mice whole and can—and will—inflict a painful bite with its strong jaws if you attempt to handle it. It is the only frog that will do that sort of thing. Cross it off your list as a possible pet.

Another South American species is the *Surinam Toad.* Flat of body and fairly large, it is completely aquatic. Its breeding habits are unique in that the male pushes the eggs into small craters in the back of the female where the tadpoles eventually hatch. The *Smooth-clawed Toad*

The Southern Leopard Frog is a tiny, colorful denizen of America's woodlands.

(called a frog as well) of Africa is strictly aquatic in its habitat. Also in Africa there is a *Giant African Pixie Frog* that dines on snakes— rather a nice switch.

The *Marine Toad* of South America grows to huge size, but the arboreal *White's Tree Toad* of Australia is tiny and utters loud cries. The *Haitian Tree Toad* is another of the huge species. This big fellow emits a skin secretion that burns human skin like acid. Needless to say it cannot be enthusiastically recommended as a pet. In this same negative category are the tiny, jewel-like South American *Poison Frogs* that boast a deadly skin poison. Together with other lethal materials it is utilized by the South American Indians to make poison for their arrows and blow-gun darts.

SALAMANDERS AND NEWTS (ORDER *CAUDATA*)

There are about 150 known kinds of these scaleless, clawless, tailed amphibians, and there are more species of salamanders in North and Central America than in all the rest of the world. Quite a few of the *Caudata* look much like lizards, but they can readily be separated one from the other if we remember that lizards are reptiles and possess a scale-like skin, while salamanders and newts have a scaleless body covering. Some of the species that occur in the United States are very brightly colored; some are aquatic and some partly aquatic. With only two exceptions, they are rather small creatures. But in China and Japan there are two kinds of salamanders that attain a length of 5 feet and that, friends, is an awful lot of salamander! These huge creatures are said to have a life-span of from forty to fifty years.

Salamanders (and newts which are of the same order) begin life as tadpoles that quickly develop legs and lungs and then crawl out of the water seeking air. These amphibians are truly interesting, exhibiting a great deal of diversity in their breeding habits and gill-stage life. They are well worth the time of the hobbyist—especially the young hobbyist.

The *Tiger Salamander* has a wide habitat range that extends over most of North America and into Mexico. It is about 6 inches long and has yellow markings. In some localities it breeds while still in the aquatic form. In the larval stage it is called axolotl in Mexico and exhibits stalk-like gills.

The *Spotted Salamander* has the appearance of a stout-bodied, scaleless lizard and can be found in boglike deep woods where it hides under loose bark and stones. In color it somewhat resembles the tiger salamander, its blue-gray base color relieved by bright yellow spots.

The *Eastern Newt* is very common in this country, inhabiting lakes and ponds in many locales. It goes through a rather strange intermediate stage in which it leaves the water that is its natural habitat, and wanders in the damp woods. During that time it turns a bright red color, very different from its normal hue of olive-brown with red side dots.

There are several amphibians in America that look like eels but are instead closely related to the salamanders. These creatures, called *Mud Eels,* burrow in the mud and have minute, completely useless fore and rear limbs. Odd creatures, these are vastly interesting. If kept in an aquarium or terrarium, they need fairly deep water with some rocks and plants and with plenty of mud on the bottom.

You can appreciate, from a perusal of the myriad types of reptiles and amphibians, including snakes, lizards, turtles, frogs, and salamanders, that there is a vast number of extremely interesting forms from which a pet can be selected and kept in a small space without much trouble. With the exception of most of the snakes, they can be easily fed and cared for.

15
Primates in General

Primates

Mimicking man anatomically and physiologically, the primates have for centuries held the office of pets in the homes of civilized and semi-civilized peoples. Without doubt the knowledge that sometime in the vastness of dim bygone ages we shared a common ancestry accounts for the fascination we experience today when modern man and a lesser primate meet. We must admit that, given the only two choices offered us of man's beginning, the anthropological, rather than the theological explanation of human genesis, seems more sound from the scientific point of view.

Perhaps the popularity of primates as pets is hidden in some exciting premonition that we may sometime, someday, see something of ourselves mirrored in the eyes of the primate pet—two creatures of the highest level of animal life on this planet, branches of a basic ancestry, each questing and, in some instances, possibly finding in the other a kinship, a uniting of some small archaic core of inner being that is the same.

Development of the Primates

During the Paleocene age, about sixty-five million years ago, small, agile arboreal creatures flicked through the giant trees of the steaming hot rain forests. These small, shy mammals were tree shrews, the progenitors of the large family of primates. Some of the shrews remained the same, not progressing along an evolutionary path, and they are the tree shrews living in Madagascar today. Others changed, evolved by the time of the Oligocene period (approximately forty million years ago) into a new kind of mammal which was structurally part shrew and part lemur.

Gradually the lemur came into focus in its species purity and it too has changed little from its archaic ancestors. But again, some of these early lemurs did change, mutations, accompanied by natural selection, aiding in the evolutionary process. Due also to an inborn curiosity inherited from its tree shrew ancestors and the development of a grasping hand to better fit its arboreal habitat, plus brachiation (a method of locomotion by swinging through the trees), the true primates began to evolve. Perhaps the strangest of all lemurs is the way-out aye-aye, a rare lemur with some rodent characteristics that still exists in the forests of Madagascar in this century and makes a delightful pet if one can be found.

Most of the lemur-like creatures (*Prosimians*) disappeared except in South East Africa and Madagascar, which was, in those early days when the earth was young, a part of the Dark Continent. When the land bridge that connected Madagascar to Africa disappeared, the lemurs, not confronted with any serious enemies, flourished in Madagascar and developed into a variety of different forms. One giant lemur, the size of a chimpanzee, came into being, but before our modern day became extinct. A group of lemur-like mammals did survive in Africa, India, Indo-China, and Ceylon. These creatures, the *Lorisoids,* are even more primitive than the Madagascar true lemurs. The *Lorisoids* include the *Slow Loris,* the *Slender Loris,* the *Galagos* and the *Pottos.*

Closer to the true primates than the lemurs is the little *Tarsius* of Borneo and the Philippines. In its evolutionary process and its relationship to man, this tiny creature occupies an important niche, for it has been asserted by some distinguished anthropologists and anatomists that man descended from early specimens of the Tarsius. Anthropological finds indicate that during the Eocene age over twenty variations of the species Tarsius were in existence, but today there is only one species and that one is so similar to the fossil Tarsius it is evident that this mammal (named the most ancient living mammal) has survived millions of years on earth with very little physical change.

Some Facts About Primates

From the prosimians we move to the *half-monkeys,* then to *true monkeys, baboons, apes* and finally *man.* With a few notable exceptions most of the simians can be tamed, trained and catalogued as pets. But the True Monkeys are much too intelligent to be treated as anything less than a child when they are relegated to pet status. Monkeys cry, sob, become sexually excited, and indulge in numerous emotional and psychological crises. They speak to each other and their owners in a language that is compounded of both sounds and elaborate movements,

One of the most interesting of the Lemurs, the Sifika is a handsome rascal, walks upright like a man when on the ground, and is a renowned jumper.

signs, and gestures. It was probably in this identical manner that our early cave-man ancestors communicated. I often wonder if some of the proprimates and primates, as well as other creatures, might not make use of some supersonic sounds during communication.

Like human children, primates create trouble because of their intense inquisitiveness and intelligence and, like children, they must be disciplined if they are to become successful household pets. As a matter of fact no more mischievous and destructive pets can be found than monkeys. But, as with children, you must be just in your discipline and not suppress their natural intellectual curiosity and mental reactions. Toys should be supplied them. If you give them large, hard dog biscuits to chew on, they will aid in keeping the monkey's teeth and gums healthy and help alleviate their basic instinct to bite.

The obvious sexuality of primates is a basic part of their social behavior. In the wild, in primate colonies and bands, sexuality constitutes a form of acknowledged obeisance to the dominant male. In the role of a pet a primate will often indicate its love for its owner through subtle sexual gestures. The pet monkey does not generally indulge in overt perversions such as we see taking place among incarcerated primate colonies in zoos. When many primates are caged together with no true freedom or relief from boredom they, like human prisoners, develop a talent for perversion.

The act of reciprocal grooming is also a very ancient form of primate behavior and probably the most archaic indication of instinctive social contact. Feminine readers should remember this the next time they visit their hairdresser. They are reaching back in time to the earliest form of social intercourse.

Though practically all the primates can become good pets, some of the larger monkeys can be formidably dangerous opponents, using hands, feet, and sometimes tails to grasp with and huge (often 3- to 4-inch) canine teeth with which to bite and tear. The speed with which they can launch an attack is extraordinary. Some species of pet primates (and some individuals) are not always reliable and can suddenly turn savage. To make a pet of a primate one must have complete rapport with it as well as a knowledge of primate behavior. If you manage to achieve this and have selected the right species and individual, these human-like creatures can become the most delightful of pets, droll, interesting, and a constant source of wonder. Once friendship and trust have been established perhaps, in time, you will find it possible to reach out to your pet and touch its unique and capricious inner being.

Present-Day Primates

The scope of this mammalian order is larger, embracing a dozen families—one of which is man, the most dangerous and destructive mammal known—and about five hundred species and subspecies. The anthropoid apes, the highest forms of wild primates, are much larger in size than the lower primates and are tailless like man.

The tree shrews, prosimians, monkeys, apes, and man all have highly developed clavicles (collar bones), which are necessary to articulate the upper limbs away from the body. Birds possess clavicles and so do other mammals, but dogs, cats, horses, and other four-footed creatures that use a different mode of locomotion do not have, or need, this part of the skeletal structure. Most of the primates are confined to tropical latitudes with the exception of a few species of Old World macaques, inhabitants of the northern Asiatic regions where there is seasonal winter weather and snow.

Other mammals, relying mostly on scent and hearing to identify their world, are color-blind and restricted to values that range between dark and light. The primates, however, *do* see color, for they rely upon sight for identification rather than their olfactory ability and so have developed binocular vision. Because of their ability to see color, some of the primates, notably the drills and mandrills, have, through evolution, developed patches of vivid color, which identify them to other members of the primate order.

Many of the very interesting species of New World primates have prehensile tails, but the Old World monkeys, though often displaying long and handsome rear appendages, use them, since they are not prehensile, only for balance, not grasping. The eating habits of the primates vary as does their desirability as pets and their hardiness when given pet status. New World monkeys are generally rather delicate when kept in zoological collections but, if properly fed and cared for, can do well as individual pets. Unfortunately, the young primate which you buy as a pet was probably brought to a trading center on the edge of some jungle by a native who acquired it by shooting the little one's mother and taking the tiny monkey from the dead parent's breast. Baby monkeys that are bred in zoos never reach the pet market.

Please remember that many of the primates can be dangerous, and some that are excellent pets when young can become unsafe when they mature.

TREE SHREWS

Since these small creatures were the forerunners of the primate, we will deal with them first. They were once (as the ground shrews are) classified with the insectivores, but when the tree shrews' role in the evolution of the Lemuroids was ascertained, they were graduated to a loftier position.

There are a number of species of *tree shrews* in various parts of the world, but mostly concentrated in the far-flung Orient. A placid animal with a great deal of inquisitiveness, tree shrews have been mistaken for, and described as, squirrels with elongated muzzles—a description as close as one can get. Due to their delightful character, tree shrews make interesting and unique pets, but they are not often available commercially, so few people have had the opportunity to adopt one of these little creatures.

LEMURS

Lemurs are the lowest grouping of the primates, the proprimates or half monkeys. For many millions of years lemurs were the principal primates on this planet and roamed over most of it. But by the end of the Eocene epoch they had been replaced—or more likely killed or driven away—by the developing and highly competitive true monkeys. Retreating to survive, the lemurs found sanctuary in Southeast Africa, in particular a large land mass that jutted out into the Indian Ocean. Eventually the ocean swirled in, due to earthquakes and natural upheavals, and separated the land mass that is Madagascar from the main body of the Dark Continent, thus forming an island paradise where, without competition, the lemurs prospered, multiplied, and diversified.

Today there are about twenty-five different species of Lemurs that vary greatly in physical aspect and size, though some of them are so little changed from their ancestors of sixty million years ago that they are like living fossils. This is the quality that to me makes these creatures so utterly fascinating. Imagine having a living fossil for a pet, to study and attempt to fathom its status in this, the sophisticated twentieth century, to reach out to your pet across the centuries and so to touch the living, ancient past.

Lemurs have sharp claws instead of nails on the index toes of their hind feet; the rest of their digits have nails. They have the ability to grasp strongly with their hands, a necessary attribute inherited from their ancestors the shrews. Their mentalities, like those of all proprimates, are much less advanced than those of the true monkeys. The two front incisors in the lemur's lower jaw jut forward and are used as a grooming tool. Some lemurs can leap amazing distances from a standstill, and in any direction. As pets they have one drawback—they are difficult to housebreak.

The tiniest of all lemurs, the *Mouse Lemur,* weighs about an ounce and a half and is the smallest living primate. Its little head is delicately formed with a doglike snout from which sprout tactile whiskers like those of a cat. Their sense of smell is well developed and they appear to be rather intelligent. The *Mongoose Lemur* makes a very desirable pet. This lemur is a very active, arboreal creature, extremely gentle and good-natured. The largest and handsomest of the proprimates is the *Ruffed Lemur.* It can grow to 4 feet in length and sports a long, silky black and white coat. The ruffed is partly nocturnal. Quite similar to the ruffed is the *Black and Red Lemur,* the difference being mainly one of coloration. There are also black lemurs and brown lemurs, the latter similar in color to the mongoose lemur. Both black and brown lemurs are much alike. Basic colors often vary so much in individuals that no two lemurs are colored exactly alike.

Other than the tiny mouse lemur there are *Dwarf Lemurs, Hairy-eared, Gray, Snub-nosed, Spotted* and *Lesser Mouse,* all belonging to the same family. The latter two are nocturnal.

The *Ring-tailed lemurs* are about the same size as brown lemurs and very much like them except for more distinctive facial markings and decisive rings on their long, handsomely furred tails. These are pretty creatures and easily tamed when acquired young. They are generally considered to be cleaner in their habits than most of the other lemurs, but they are inclined to be high-strung. *The Woolly lemur* has rather large feet and is completely arboreal, nocturnal, and solitary.

The *Indri Lemur* is an interesting species that lives in the volcanic mountains of "The Island at the End of the Earth." They are about 2 feet high and proportioned somewhat like a human, a fact made more obvious by their small 2-inch tail. Indri lemurs are beautifully patterned in black and white fur. They roam the forests of their native Madagascar in family groups. If taken when young, they become excellent and unique pets. Much like the Indri, the *Sifaka Lemur* (or monkey), with a body about 3 feet high and a long tail, is also handsome and a renowned jumper. Its face is flat and its appearance is much like that of a spider monkey or a gibbon. In its arboreal habitat it leaps from limb to limb with consummate grace; on the ground it walks upright like a man but with generally greater dignity. The sifaka is also beautifully patterned like the Indri. These creatures have fantastic vision and also a well-developed olfactory sense. All their fingers but one have nails like a human's. The exception (the second toe of each hind foot) has a claw with which they scratch themselves, clean their ears, and perform other rites of toiletry. The sifaka lemur can become a most interesting pet.

Perhaps the most interesting of all the lemurs is the *Aye-Aye.* There was evidently a time, during the very early divergence and specialization of animals, when for one specific animal species there was an evolutionary choice of becoming either a proprimate or a rodent. As time passed the two evolutionary lines separated and specialized. One line became the creatures we call lemurs; the other evolved into the mutitudinous family of rodents. The creature that millions of years ago was the fountainhead from which flowed those two diverse animal forms was almost exactly like the extraordinary, cat-size, living aye-aye.

The aye-aye is like a creature that has become stuck in a crack in time and has not, in 65 million years, changed or made up its evolutionary mind which to be—lemur or rodent. This nocturnal creature has typical rodent teeth with chisel-like front incisors that never cease growing. The aye-aye has a long, thick tail and primate hands and feet, but with claws on its strange, long, thin fingers; only the big toe has the typical primate nail. It is absolutely fearless. Truly here is a living fossil. Though these droll creatures are very rare, I saw one in Africa that had been brought from Madagascar as a baby. It was an unbelievably strange and unusual pet.

THE LORISOIDS

Found in Africa, India, Indo-China and Ceylon, the Lorisoids are possibly more primitive than the lemurs. There are two main groups, the *Galagos* and the *lorises,* both usually smaller than the lemurs. These small, cute creatures are big-eyed nocturnals and any of them, if you can find one, will make a marvelous pet. These tremendously interesting proprimates have a strange habit of urinating on their hands to give them a better grip as they swing through their arboreal habitat. How fortunate it is that our circus acrobats have long ago discovered the effectiveness of resin.

The Galagos of Africa are long-tailed and furry. They have large thin ears, pointed muzzles, and generally big bugeyes. They have a tendency to hang upside down from a horizontal bar or branch.

The tiny, attractive *Demidorff's Bush Baby* (a dwarf bush baby) is a sweet-natured, diminutive proprimate about the size of the mouse lemur. From a completely relaxed position in the palm of your hand this creature can suddenly leap 12 feet in any direction. But they do make cute and gentle pets. The *Bush-tailed Bush Baby* is the largest of the Galagos, with a body about the size of an opossum's, clothed in a very woolly coat. They, too, are great leapers, but when on the ground their form of locomotion is a hop like a kangaroo's. There are about a dozen races of the *Great Galagos* and all are very gentle creatures that adore being petted and fondled. In Africa I was told that the natives capture these proprimates by luring them at night to small containers of an alcoholic beverage called palm wine. The bush babies drink the wine, become inebriated, and are then easily captured. The idea of a bombed bush baby almost boggles the mind! Dr. Geoffrey H. Bourne also mentions this method of capture in his excellent book, *Primate Odyssey.* I have never heard of any of the Galagos biting a human—a statement that will surely bring some denials. But I will go out on a limb with the Galagos and state that they make excellent, gentle pets.

The *Lorises,* a group of rather small, tailless, slow-moving creatures that live in southern India, Ceylon, Asia, Maylasia, and Africa, are the *Slow Loris, Slender Loris,* the *Potto,* and the *Angwantibo.* Large, owl-like eyes indicate the nocturnal habits of the Lorisoids. All are completely arboreal and exhibit on the second toe of the rear foot the same claw as the lemurs and Galagos. Both the thumbs and the big toes are widely opposed and their index fingers are very short. Perhaps because of their bizarre appearance many strange tales have been told about these gentle creatures.

The *Slow Loris* is about the size of a kitten and moves with all the speed and vim of a slow-motion movie. There seems to be a variety of species that occur in various colors, color patterns, and sizes. Their coats are long and woolly and they are very mild, passive creatures. The *Slender Loris* is small, less than a pound in weight and moves with great deliberation. It is, in appearance, exactly what its descriptive name would indicate . . . a slender edition of the slow loris. This small and appealing animal makes an excellent pet.

Another tremendously interesting Lorisoid is the *Potto* from Africa. This fine little fellow has a reputation in Europe, and to some extent in America, as a uniquely interesting pet. The potto is also sometimes colloquially referred to as the honey bear, bush or tree bear. The honey bear connotation leads to confusion because this is also the common name used for the kinkajou (*Poto flavus*), another delightful pet of the raccoon family that looks very much like a proprimate.

The Potto moves even more slowly than the other Lorisoids. Unlike any other mammal, sharp bare spurs of the neck vertebrae of this pro-primate uniquely protrude through the skin in what is evidently a defensive mechanism.

A rare relative of the potto, the *Angwantibo,* about 10 inches long, is smaller than the potto, has a longer muzzle, and slightly smaller eyes set closer together. Two subspecies exist that exhibit a slightly different pelage hue. Thick fur of a beautiful golden sheen is evidently responsible for the alternate designation of golden potto. Unlike the potto, this prosimian proves the exception to the Lorisoid rule by being quite active and agile. The pendadactyl, or five-fingered, hand, exhibited by the primate family has reached an out-of-this-world development in this quiet little creature. Nocturnal, mild and passive, angwantibos make strange but fascinating pets.

The golden-coated Potto (Perodicticus potto) *is a nocturnal Lorisoid whose vernacular and highly descriptive name in Africa is "Softly-softly."*

A Lorisoid that resembles the Potto but is smaller is the Ang-wantibo (Arctocebus aureus), *which possesses unusual digital development.*

The proprimates certainly form an interesting and unique group of creatures. Now I want to introduce you to the strangest of them all: the *Tarsier,* a native of Indonesia and the Philippines. The present-day tarsier is the last of the species *Tarsius* and has survived millions of years without any discernible change. I know that I have used the connotation before, but I must again say that this is another of those living fossils, for indeed it is.

The tarsier looks like a dwarf version of a prehistoric creature born in the imagination of Hollywood makeup men in a horror-movie studio. It is small—no larger than a squirrel—has big eyes, a long tail with a flange of fur on both sides toward the tip—somewhat like a furred arrow—and strange, batlike hands and feet. During the Eocene era, fifty million years ago, there were many kinds of Tarsius in North America, but only this one species remains today. Though it is a pro-primate, it is not a lemur. It occupies a species niche of its own. It well deserves its title of the "oldest living mammal on earth." How fortunate that such small and rather gentle creatures have survived the dangers and holocausts of the years rather than the monstrous Mesozoic reptilian nightmares that ate themselves into oblivion when the world was young.

Tarsiers make excellent pets. They become close to their owners and are easily seduced by kindness. One of their cutest tricks is, when agitated, to clench their tiny fists, stand up on their hind legs, and go through the motions of boxing. They are easily tamed even when mature and enjoy being petted and made much of, reciprocating by kissing their owner's cheek.

New World Monkeys

The monkeys of tropical America were isolated from Europe, Africa, and Asia—as were the Magdalenian peoples we call Indians—by the closing of the Bering Sea bridge that separated the Americas from other continents. Subsequent ice ages pushed the monkeys south, seeking the tropical habitat necessary to their survival. In Central and South America they found the needed environment and prospered.

These American primates differ from those found in other parts of the world in that they have an extra premolar. Most of them have prehensile tails, but lack cheek pouches and buttock callosities, the latter an attribute in a monkey that is to become a pet. All the Central and South American monkeys are forest dwellers. They are fewer in number and generally smaller than the Old World monkeys; their young seem to grow more rapidly and reach maturity earlier.

MARMOSETS

The tiny *Marmosets* are primitive but lovable little creatures, one of the species being the smallest of all monkeys. To prove the exception to the rule their long, heavily furred tails are *not* prehensile. They have thick soft coats and are oddly droll little creatures, possessing a nail on their big toes but claws on the rest of their digits. They are members of a group of monkeys called *Hapalines* and the different species vary in coat, color patterns, and facial appearance. Most primates, including humans, do not as a rule have multiple births, but the marmoset does, usually giving birth to twins. Though marmosets are gentle, they can inflict a painful bite if not properly handled.

Pygmy Marmosets are, obviously, very small, attractive, and move with great agility. Like most of the marmoset tribe they have for centuries been tamed by the South American Indians. In the fifteenth and sixteenth centuries a number of these tiny primates were brought back to Europe by Spanish and Portuguese conquistadors. Their popularity spread throughout the continent and many of the noble ladies of France, Spain and Portugal kept marmosets as pets.

Often sold by pet shops, the *Common Marmoset* is a quick and long-reaching leaper. The *Cotton-Headed* or *Pinche Marmoset,* sporting decorative tufts of white hair, the *White-Headed,* and *Geoffrey's Marmosets* are all related Hapalines.

There is another group of *Hapalines* called *Tamarins.* The marmosets of this specific type include the *Black Tamarins,* rather vicious little beasts that seldom can be tamed and so, unlike the other marmosets, are not recommended pet material. The *Mustached, Bald-headed, Red-handed* (orange hands and feet), *Maned* (or Golden Lion), *Titi Tamarins* and *Goeldi's Marmoset* are all part of the tamarin clan. Added to the list are the *White-eared* and *White-lipped* marmosets, both of them marmosets and quaint creatures. The *Golden Lion,* when in full coat, is reputed to possess the most exquisitely colored pelt of any mammal, with hair that is actually an iridescent gold.

OTHER PRIMITIVE PRIMATES

There is a group of somewhat primitive primates that have not quite made it scientifically as true monkeys but are closer to this desirable state than the marmosets. I suppose we could call these primates born losers, for not only do they miss true monkey status, but they don't even look like monkeys to the discerning observer. They do possess interesting species names however, *Sakawinkis, Bearded Sakis, Uakaris, Douroucoulis,* and the *Squirrel Monkey,* the only one of the whole group that looks like a real monkey. None of these half-monkeys have prehensile tails. Many of them are quite delicate unless given special care.

Owl monkeys is another name for the *Douroucoulis.* They are small, with thick, soft fur and the large eyes of all nocturnal creatures. They produce twin babies like their kin, the marmosets, and are sometimes called night monkeys.

Sakawinkis have longer, coarser fur than the Douroucoulis, and are about equal to them in size. They are very agile and run along branches on their hind legs like human tightrope walkers.

The *Cacajao* or *Uakari* have completely bare heads and plaintive faces that are normally pink but become scarlet when the animal becomes mad or excited. They have short tails or none at all, uneven body pelts and they move rather deliberately. The *Bald Uakari* is tailless, has a hairless head, and sits slumped over so that it looks like a tired old man with the world's woes on his shoulders. *Uakaris* have punishing canine teeth that can inflict a deep bite, yet they make excellent pets if acquired when young—and if you can forget their appearance, for these creatures are a good deal less than handsome. As a matter of fact they look as though they had spent their lives taking ugly pills.

In apearance every bit a true monkey, the *Squirrel Monkey* is a charming, active little character that has no relationship, genetically or physically, to the squirrel or rodent family. These half-monkeys are sweet and affectionate, making excellent pets. Being very gentle and easy keepers, they are popular in the pet market and are always available. Squirrel monkeys can be bought for about $100, weigh about a pound when fully mature, and are used by the thousands for medical research.

True New World Primates

New World monkeys are the highest order of primate in the Americas, possessing well-developed mentalities. They have prehensile tails that are like a fifth hand. With the exception of the *Howler Monkey*—with a raucous voice, large canine teeth, and an unfriendly disposition that does not give him a high rating in the pet category—the majority of South American monkeys are socially very acceptable. Both the *Howler* and the *Spider Monkey* are quite large, ranking in this respect with the larger African and Asiatic primates. Though highly intelligent, the New World monkeys with their prehensile tails were so suited to an arboreal existence that they never developed specialized hands and feet and so failed to produce a primate of ape quality, size, and specialization.

Of all the New World monkeys the *Woolly* is one of my favorites. It has thick pelage, in color from silver-gray to chocolate brown or black, and is very intelligent, quite clean, and as a pet cannot be surpassed among the New World species. Affectionate and ever ready to please, it is quiet and becomes attached to its owner. At maturity its body is about 2 feet high and very sturdy. It has a black, round appealing face. This monkey exhibits very emotional responses to various situations and seems to have a language or method of communication of its own. The one fault I find with woolly monkeys is that they positively demand all of one's attention and want to be cuddled and petted constantly or they pout and sulk.

Portrait of Sally, a Spider Monkey (Ateles ater), *a very special friend of the author.*

Spider Monkeys are another of my particular favorites. They walk upright much of the time and will grasp your hand and stroll along next to you like a child. Their faces are highly expressive and their tails are like a fifth limb. Like the gibbons they resemble physically, they are fantastic brachiators, their grace and swiftness in arboreal flight a thing to marvel at. The dexterous spider is a real swinger. The coat color of spiders varies greatly from black to almost gold and is not necessarily solid throughout. Most of these we see are black. I also admire the way their head hair grows forward in the modern manner. I have heard that these monkeys sometimes have dangerous tempers, but the few that I have had contact with were completely amiable, comical, quaint, and gentle. If selecting a spider for a pet, attempt to find one with a stable temperament.

The *capuchin* is the monkey most commonly seen in captivity—for several very good reasons: it is an exceedingly gentle and responsive monkey, and its intelligence is said to be equal to that of a chimpanzee. The name capuchin is derived from the head markings, which resemble the pointed cowl (or capuche) worn by Franciscan monks. This delightful monkey is one of the few primates that can make rhythmic paint scribbles, manifesting an inner need for expression. Capuchins can be purchased for about $175. They do not become sulky or mean when mature and I would, without hesitation, list them at the top of the ladder as pets.

Old World Monkeys

Much more widely distributed than the New World monkeys, Old World primates do not have prehensile tails, but most do have elastic cheek pouches for storing food temporarily. Distribution of Old World monkeys is much broader than that of primates of the New World. These monkeys can be found in Africa, Asia, Malaysia, Japan, eastward to the Celebes and even to the Rock of Gibraltar. The number of monkey species in Africa and Asia alone is tremendously large, so let us forthwith examine this branch of our family tree for those primates that can be considered good pet material.

MACAQUES

We will begin with the Macaques, a very large family with at least two well-known species. I must caution you relative to macaques in general: many of them, when young, make great pets, easily tamed and very amusing, but as they grow older tend to become savage and dangerous. These monkeys are usually hardy and long-lived.

A quartette of Simian V.I.Ps.: (1) a Japanese Macaque
(Macaca fuscata); *(2) a Douc Langur* (sub-family Colo-
binae); *(3) a gentle Colobus primate* (Colobus polykomos);
and (4) a Patas Monkey (Erythrocebus patas).

The *Barbary ape* is perhaps the best known to international tourists
of all the macaques. It is the only primate that lives in Europe, on the
Rock of Gibraltar where a small colony's welfare is diligently guarded
by the British Army, aided by a civil fund allowance. This odd patronage
is due to a superstition that if the "apes" died out or left the Rock,

Britain would lose sovereignty over Gibraltar. I am surprised that Spain has not long ago sent monkeynappers under cover of night to spirit these macaques away. Despite the name, predicated upon the fact that apes are tailless, these Barbary primates are monkeys, not apes, and they do sport a very short tail. They are also the only macaques found in Africa (which lies just across the strait from Gibraltar). All the other macaques are Asiatic monkeys. The "apes" were probably introduced to Gibraltar by the Moors during their early invasion of Spain, for it is known that they kept monkeys as pets. The Barbary "apes" are fairly large, strong monkeys. I have fed them by hand on Gibraltar and they are quite pushy, showing no fear at all of humans.

Other macaques are the *Tcheli Monkey* of northern China, a relative of the *Japanese Macaque;* the *Java Monkey* of Asia and Malaysia, a very amusing pet that is easily taught when young; the *Bonnet* and the *Toque Monkeys* of India; the *Pig-tailed Macaque* with a tiny, curled appendage; and the *Red Stump-tail Macaque,* which is considered untrustworthy when adult.

Macaques have true economic value because of the tasks they can be taught to perform. *Pig-tailed macaques* are often kept by Thai farmers and trained to run up coconut trees. There they twist the fruit loose to fall to the ground and so be collected by the farmer. Macaques are also used for picking tea and picking peppers. These monkeys, in Malaya, have been educated by botanists to collect certain species of plants, and some Thai banks, believe it or not, use them to detect counterfeit coins. When fully trained (which takes from one and a half to two years), "bank monkeys are worth many thousands of dollars"—and you may take that statement any way you wish. If you find a macaque behind the teller's window in your bank, I suggest a hasty withdrawal.

Japanese Macaques are an extremely interesting tribe. They can exist in an area of changing seasons and, with heavy winter snow, they will grow a thick coat to insulate them from the cold. These are the monkeys made famous by the statue of three monkeys visually expressing the Buddhist philosophy: "See no evil, hear no evil, speak no evil." Isolated colonies have been closely studied by Japanese scientists, who have found that these remarkable monkeys have developed new traits such as the ability to swim with ease, and to wash food (sweet potatoes) before eating. These Japanese macaques have little fear of man and, though aggressive, can be trained and tamed successfully.

The macaques of the Celebes Islands near Australia, the *Moor Macaque* and the *Celebes Black Ape* have good dispositions and can become excellent pets if correctly trained when young. The *Long-Tailed*

Macaque (*or Wanderoo*) of India—handsome in its long black or chocolate coat with areas of silver, and sporting a lion-like tassel at the tip of its tail—is vicious in the wild, but several noted authorities declare that, if taken when young, cared for and reared alone, the wanderoo makes a gentle and intelligent pet. These monkeys are rather rare and are, therefore, relatively expensive to purchase.

The most numerous and visible of the macaques is the *Rhesus Monkey* from India. Mature males of this species attain the largest size of all monkeys. These are intelligent primates and many have lived in close contact with man in India where large troops of them frequent cities and are allowed to roam unmolested. Research using rhesus monkeys has resulted in a number of scientific discoveries that have been of great benefit to mankind. Rhesus monkeys make good, smart pets, but become untrustworthy with sexual maturity, which occurs at the age of about three years. Sometimes, like other macaques, if obtained when tiny babies, brought up sympathetically by someone who has a rapport with animals, and kept as the sole pet in the household, a rhesus, particularly a female, will remain sweet and gentle even when mature.

LANGURS

This is a tribe of beautiful monkeys that are at home in India. They are generally catalogued with the leaf-eating primates. Of this group the *Hanuman* (*or Entellus*) *Monkeys* are held sacred by the Hindus and are never touched or scolded. As a result these intelligent primates have become so bold that they plunder fields, bazaars, and temples. *Hanumans,* also called sacred monkeys, are a familiar sight around old Hindu temples.

The *Himalayan Langur* prefers cold to hot climates and ranges to altitudes in excess of 12,000 feet in the high Himalayas. *Capped Langurs, Silver, Banded Leaf* and *Douc Langurs* are favorite specimens of this clan. The douc langur is particularly beautiful in color and an exceptionally appealing monkey. It is about 2 feet high with the slim langur silhouette, thick, glossy fur in several patterns and combinations of colors, including yellow, gray, brown, black, white, and chestnut. The markings are decisive and the colors bright.

The langurs are fascinating primates and, like most of the wild-animal species, make fine pets if their education is begun when they are young.

GUENONS

This is the largest genus in the primate family. Including the subspecies there are more than sixty individual species of Guenons. They are sturdy and, on the whole, the most brightly colored of all monkeys. Guenons were popular pets of the early Egyptians, who also used them as items of barter and as gifts to VIPs. In the wild state Guenons generally inhabit the tropical areas of Africa south of the Sahara and the Atlas Mountains. Africa is a monkey paradise and primates from the Dark Continent, in many instances, are the most brilliantly colored and patterned of all the many families of these manlike creatures.

The *Green Monkey* is not as colorful as some guenons, but it is typical in its hardiness and activity. It is an attractive monkey and the most commonly imported of the guenons. A representative type of green monkey frequently seen in this country in pet shops, is the *Vervet*. On the Masai-Mara preserve in Kenya, Africa, I had an interesting tête-à-tête with a band of wild vervets that ended a bit disastrously. I was staying at Keekorak Lodge for a few days to photograph and sketch the wildlife that came to a large waterhole just beyond the lodge. Going in to breakfast one morning, I noticed a band of vervets watching me. On impulse, after I had breakfasted, I brought several pieces of toast outside with me and made offering gestures to the vervet band. After about fifteen minutes they came close enough to snatch pieces from my hands and within ten minutes more I had them all over me, on my lap and shoulders, females with babies, young stock and yearling males. One large, aggressive male that was evidently the alpha, or dominant, male and lord of the group, stood upright in front of me with arm and hand outstretched, arrogantly demanding his share. When the toast had disappeared, I had a bit of a job brushing the monkeys off me without getting nipped. The epilogue occurred the next morning.

Two elderly women, members of a group staying at the lodge, were walking some distance in front of me toward the lodge dining room when the same band of vervets came down from the trees, marched up to the two women, and made it evident that they had arrived for their breakfast toast. The big alpha male came very close and made his demands insolently.

The two women had, by this time, become rather alarmed and began to back away, trying to evade the confrontation. But the big male vervet was not to be denied in this cavalier manner in his own territory. Angrily he rushed in, grabbed the leg of one of the women and sunk his teeth in her calf. He then stalked haughtily away, calling his band to him and leaving a hysterical woman behind.

The lady was badly bitten, the monkey's large canine teeth having driven in deeply. She insisted upon being flown out to a hospital immediately, but there was no nearby place where even a very small plane could set down. The group's guide was at his wit's end when my wife, who luckily is a registered nurse, stepped in, cleansed, medicated, and bandaged the wound, administered anti-this-and-that, aspirin, and good advice and soothed the woman. I, of course, kept out of sight, for I felt I had brought the plague of vervets down upon us with my breakfast toast.

Mona Monkeys are pretty primates, aggressive but also very playful. They were probably named by Moors who adopted the Spanish word for monkey, *Mona.* The largest and handsomest of the guenons are the *Diana* monkeys. There are two color varieties of Dianas and, due to the inordinate amount of grooming indulged in by these primates, their coats are always clean and glossy. When youngsters, they make delightfully intelligent pets, but upon maturity some Dianas lose their ability to respond to human affection.

Mustached Monkeys, White-nosed, Sykes, Hamlyn's and the *Huassar* or *Patas Monkeys* are all Guenons. The patas or Huassars have been given several names and are also known as *Military, Ground, Red* or *Dancing* monkeys, this last because of their quaint habit of jumping straight up and down in what appears to be a dance step. Whatever you choose to call them, they have adapted to an existence on the ground rather than an arboreal one, though they do climb, rest, and sleep in the trees. Both the patas and a related species, the *Nisnas,* make wonderful pets that can be toilet-trained, taught to walk on a leash, sit in a high chair and eat with a spoon. They are the most evenly tempered of pets. *Hamlyn's Owl Guenon* is a strange-looking creature when mature, its face like something dreamed up by a mad sculptor.

De Brazza Monkeys are also quite odd in appearance, but are beautifully colored and marked. They are excellent swimmers, fast afoot, and make exceptionally handsome pets. I have seen these monkeys filling their roles as amiable pets in lodges owned by natives and rangers in Kenya, Uganda, and Tanzania. Like all primates, they must be tamed and trained when young, and never teased if they are to remain gentle and lovable.

Dianas borrow their name from an ancient legend. The white crescent of hair on their foreheads is supposed to be the crescent symbol of Diana, the Moon Goddess.

COLOBUS OR GUEREZA MONKEYS

These are large, handsome, very agile primates, commonly called *Colobus Monkeys.* Their black and white pelage is silky, thick, and luxuriantly flowing to such an extent that pelts of this primate are the "monkey furs" used commercially. Their value and use for women's coats and trimming resulted in a "slaughter of the innocents," but was finally brought to a halt before the species became extinct. These monkeys are thrice remarkable in that they eat only leaves and twigs, possess a stomach divided into compartments like that of ruminants, and have no thumbs. The young are born all white and are really cute little creatures. Colobus monkeys were highly valued as pets by the Romans, probably because in temperament they are generally different from most monkeys, even mature males being quiet and gentle. There is also a smaller species of different coloring, the *Red Colobus,* and in Zanzibar there exists a distinct race named *Kirk's Red Colobus.*

MANGABEYS

Mangabeys are large monkeys, active, hardy, and sporting long tails. They have mobile, expressive faces and "talk" a great deal. There are several species of mangabeys of which two, the *Sooty* and the *White-collared* are most frequently seen. The latter is also called the *Cherry-head* because it wears a bright red head crown. These primates are agreeable and respond eagerly to handling and training. A monkey very similar to the mangabey was probably the ancestor of the baboons.

BABOONS

In ancient Egypt, baboons were kept as pets and even worshiped by some religious cults. In the famous Valley of the Kings in Thebes, there is a large monkey cemetery where many baboons, pets of the nobility and the royal family, are buried. The *Mandrills, Drills,* and *Gelada* baboons are weird, hideous and by most authorities are rated highly dangerous animals not to be considered as pets. Yet other pundits claim baboons are gentle and easy to handle. I would say that these powerful creatures, with their long vicious canine teeth, cannot be catalogued as true pets. Distribution of the baboon (*Cercopithecidae*) family is confined to Africa; the *Chacma* generally confined to eastern and southern Africa, the *Yellow* to central Africa, the *Guinea* to west-central Africa, and the *Doguera* baboon from Kenya to Ethiopia. Both the drills and mandrills are from West Africa, the gelada baboon roams *Ethiopia,* and the hamadryas can be found to the north in Arabia, Egypt, Somalia, and the Sudan.

The largest of the species, the *Chacma baboon,* is not as savage as it appears. It is intelligent and in the mature state, is frequently seen performing in animal acts on the Continent. In ancient times, particularly in Egypt, baboons, probably of this species, were trained for all manner of tasks from catching fish and serving wine to piling wood and herding sheep. So many tales are told of the trainability of baboons that it would seem they could be interesting and manageable pets—if one discards the more formidable and vicious species, and remembers that they possess canine teeth that are tiger-like, and are extremely powerful beasts that *can be* very dangerous. Baboons and other species of monkeys, are not for the casual pet owner.

Anthropologists give considerable attention to the baboons because they are primates that left the trees for a life upon the ground just as the monkey-like primates that were our ancestors courageously did. Through studies of the problems baboons face in sustaining life and reproducing their species, some clues to the life-style of the earliest humanoids might be gleaned.

THE GREAT APES

We are all, I am sure, aware of the intelligence and trainability of *Chimpanzees*. For the first few years of their lives (up to six or seven) they make excellent pets, being extremely intelligent, playful, and trustworthy. When reaching toward maturity, their dispositions change and, when mature, they become savage and dangerous.

Orangutans ("Men of the Woods" in Malayan) are almost completely arboreal and, when young, are quite gentle, intelligent, trainable, and affectionate. They are considered to be more gentle upon maturity than the other two great apes. But, since they can reach a weight in excess of 200 pounds and are tremendously powerful anthropoids, I think we can rule them out of the cuddly pet department.

Young *gorillas* are affectionate when small, but unfortunately they grow up to be big gorillas and of course cannot be considered as pets.

The only ape, therefore, that can be considered of pet caliber is the *Gibbon* of eastern India, Asia, and the Malay Peninsula. The gibbon is considered a "lesser ape" because it is inferior in size to the "great apes," and has been placed in a family by itself. The species can be found in the islands of Malaysia, the Malay Peninsula, and southeast Asia. Of the several species of gibbons the *Siamang Gibbon,* thought to be a link between the true gibbons and the great apes, cannot be recommended as a pet. This species is surly, vicious, and unmanageable. But the several other kinds of gibbons, the dark or light phases, are valued household pets in the homes of many Indonesians, Thais, and Burmese. These people claim that pet gibbons are docile, intelligent, and basically gentle creatures even though some authorities insist that mature gibbons are aggressive and dangerous.

There is no doubt that these slim, handsome apes are fabulous brachiators. To watch them glide through the treetops with the ease and grace of falling leaves is a lesson in the abstract beauty of motion. In

A fabulous brachiator, the Gibbon (genus Hylobates) *is named a lesser ape due to its size.*

Burma there is a legend that gibbons are disappointed lovers whose souls have taken a new form. A pretty thought that leaves me profoundly unmoved, for I shudder to think of the many future lives I might spend reincarnated as a gibbon.

Man can learn a great deal about himself from a study of his fellow primates. Luckily scientists in this area of inquiry have been able to make the Federal Government understand this—an amazing accomplishment in itself—and several centers for primate study and research have been established, funded by government dollars. Major contributions in medical research and human behavior patterns have already been made and many more important contributions to medicine and man's understanding of himself, his past, present, and future, through the study of his fellow primates, are yet to come.

16

The Raccoon Family

Procyonidae

The family *Procyonidae* is a delightful group of interesting and intelligent mammals that share an evolutionary heritage with both bears and canines. An ancestor of the family *Ursidae,* which embraces all the species of bears, and of the family *Canidae,* or canines, was a primitive carnivorous, arboreal creature called Miacis that stalked his small prey in the tree heights of the steaming jungles of the Eocene period some forty million years ago. It took all of twenty million years before a mutation occurred in the yet not completely delineated wild canine family that produced the ancestral *Procyonidae.* From this creature evolved the modern forms. The family name Procyonidae means animals that came before (*pro*) the dogs (*cyon*) from the Greek word *kyon* (meaning dog).

During the evolutionary process, as the *Procyonidae* adapted to different climates and conditions, selection and mutation took place over a span of twenty million years (from the first mutation) varying form to fit environment. So the several species of the family developed: the *raccoon,* the *coatimundi,* the *cacomistle,* the *kinkajou,* the *lesser panda,* and the *giant panda.*

I will not dwell on the latter despite its fascination as a species, since it is unlikely that a specimen will ever come into your possession. Even if it did, it would not be pet material, for the giant panda reaches a 200-pound maturity weight.

Of interest is the fact that the feet of all *Procyonidae* are plantigrade, or flat to the ground from hock to toes when in motion, in the same manner as those of the primates and bears, a residual reminder of archaic *Ursidae* influence.

THE RACCOON (*PROCYON LOTOR*)

Here is one of the most adaptable and intelligent of mammals, characteristics that have enabled the raccoon to live side by side with man,

A creature of the night, the Raccoon (Procyon lotor) *has made his habitat side by side with man's. This masked mammal is smart and adaptable.*

prosper and increase despite slaughter by hunters and the crowding of suburban civilization. The raccoon's appetite is indeed catholic and it is at home on land, in water, and in the trees.

The habitat of the raccoon extends throughout the North American continent and parts of Central America. It has 40 teeth and clever, delicate, sensitive hands that it utilizes with astonishing dexterity to feel, hold, and manipulate objects in and out of water. The word *lotor* means "washer," but the raccoon actually does not wash its food; it "feels" it in the water. As a matter of fact it feels everything and should have been named "feeler" rather than washer. Feeling and climbing are the two habits to which the raccoon is addicted.

Raccoons are highly intelligent creatures and possess excellent memories. They have a keen sense of smell and good vision, especially night vision. Being nocturnal they are color-blind. There are many sub-species and color variations. The *Crab-eating Raccoon* of Central and South America is one of the best-known subspecies. The pelt of this 'coon is quite short and sleek with the result that the animal appears to be slimmer physically than the northern raccoon. This, however, is probably an illusion due to the pelage. Color variations range from pure black melanistic specimens to snow-white albinos (pink-eyed and brown-eyed). Between these color poles we find yellow, cinnamon (quite rare), buff, red, chocolate, silver-tipped and the natural gray-colored raccoons with the black highwayman's mask.

The average weight of a mature raccoon is about 13 pounds, but 18 to 20 pound 'coons are not unusual and I have heard of 'coons weighing as much as 35 pounds. In my misbegotten youth I indulged in some 'coon hunting in Connecticut and Maine with my very good friends and neighbors, Dr. Leon F. Whitney, an authority on the raccoon, and his son Dr. George D. Whitney. The largest 'coon I ever remember taking weighed 24 pounds. When skinned out, the pelt looked as big as a bear's. Raccoons are hunted at night behind several hounds who pick up the scent and trail the 'coons. The best 'coon dogs are always a topic for lengthy argument, but so far as I am concerned my vote goes to the redbone hound.

When we hunted in Maine, we would usually examine the 'coon care-fully in the flashlight's beam after it was treed and if it appeared to be young, vigorous, large, and deep in color, one of us would climb the tree, capture it in a burlap bag and take the creature back to Connecticut when we finished our hunting vacation. It would be ear-tagged and then released to produce superior raccoons in our native state.

Raccoons are immensely inquisitive animals, fascinated by anything new, an indication of the high order of their intelligence. As pets, they are definitely individuals, showing wide differences in character and temperament. Like cats, they are independent and, like monkeys, they can wreak havoc in a room if left unsupervised. During the winter months in cold climates they go into semi-hibernation for about a month to six weeks. Some make good pets and others don't, so it is up to you to select for a pet a youngster that is affectionate, docile, and sweet.

THE COATIMUNDI (*NASUA NARICA*)

The *Coati* belongs to a group closely related to the raccoon. South America is the coatis' habitat and I have seen several related species, including a very handsome, deep-chestnut-colored coati, in Colombia. The *Ring-Tailed Coati* and the *White-Nosed Coati* are the most readily available in the United States. The ring-tailed, most typical of the coatis, has body, legs, and feet like a raccoon, but its ringed tail is longer and not as heavily furred. Its head, particularly the muzzle, is elongated, with the muzzle being a sensitive, rather concave, attentuated, and flexible appendage. Very interesting beasties, they are arboreal, social, diurnal and, like the raccoon, omnivorous. These colorful animals seem particularly docile and make fine pets. I have even petted some that have not been frequently handled and played with and they have never attempted to bite. Coatis from the Bogota area in the mountains, at a height of over 8,600 feet, are immune to dampness and chilly weather and are quite hardy. All coatis are sensitive to odors and become excited over scents that please them. Probably the scientific name *Nasua* comes from this characteristic as it literally means "the nosey one."

Coatis are extremely intelligent and easily leash- and collar-broken if taken when young. In South America they often assume the stature of pets and, in some instances, are preferred above primate pets, which they greatly resemble in their ability to get into mischief. Their general docility can be fairly well assessed by an experience I had with a young coati that wandered into our jungle camp on the Amazon. He never exhibited the slightest inclination to bite and after a few days of feeding would jump up into my lap and fall fast asleep. Individuals, of course, vary in temperament and disposition as they do in all animal groups, including man.

THE LESSER PANDA OR CAT BEAR (*AILURUS FULGENS*)

These beautiful, appealing animals are also called the fox-cat, Himalayan raccoon, fire-fox and red panda. They are the original panda and the only living relative of the black and white giant panda of western China. Both of the pandas are distinct enough to be classed in their own family (*Ailuridae*) and both live on a part of the globe remote from the other species of the raccoon family. Nevertheless, all share common ancestry and so the cat bear is placed among the *Procyonidae*. The lesser panda's body is covered with rich chestnut-colored, woolly fur; the tail is ringed in black. Its muzzle and cheeks are white with a dark stripe from the eyes to the mouth corners. The underbody and limbs of the lesser panda are black.

The cat bear does not possess the dexterous front paws of the raccoon or coati. Instead its feet are bear-like and it boasts long claws that are partially retractile. This interesting creature is about the size of a large cat with a long, furred-out tail similar to the appendage of a raccoon. The habitat of the arboreal cat bear is in the mountain forests of Upper Burma, Szechwan, Yunnan, Sikkim, and Nepal, at altitudes of from 7,000 to 12,000 feet. It is a nocturnal animal and spends its days sleep-

ing in the trees. Cat bears walk with rather an awkward gait, for, like
the bear and raccoon, its hind feet are plantigrade and rather oversized
for its bodily dimensions. Like most nocturnals, it eats in the early
morning and in the evening, feeding on leaves, buds, bamboo shoots,
and fruit on the ground, with an occasional sly raid on a native village
to steal milk, butter, and eggs. Though its teeth have much the same
pattern as the true carnivore, the cat bear does not eat meat.

THE KINKAJOU (*POTOS FLAVUS*)

This very gentle raccoon-family creature is one of the most popular
pets of all the *Procyonidae.* It is arboreal, nocturnal and inhabits the
New World's tropical forests. Though its Latin name, *Potos caudivol-
vulus,* would indicate relationship to the potto of Africa, it is a true
Procyonidae, while the potto is a *lemuroid.*

The kinkajou lives in South America, Central America, and Mexico
and is a valued pet in these areas. Its silken coat is tannish-brown and
it looks like a little Teddy bear with expressive eyes. Like a New World
primate rather than a raccoon-family mammal, it boasts a prehensile
tail. About the size of a cat when fully grown, the kinkajou is extremely
docile, gentle, and affectionate, and can be a trouble-free pet in a small
apartment.

Like the raccoon and coati the kinkajou's front paws have exceptional
dexterity. Because of that and its prehensile tail, it is often thought to be
a monkey or lemur. With good care and lots of affection, your pet
kinkajou will give you years of pleasure and charming companionship.
It is not at all mischievous or destructive as are its relatives the raccoon
and coati. On the contrary, it is quiet and cuddlesome. Psychologically
the kinkajou is as emotional as a monkey, though not as high strung
or frenetic. It can be emotionally affected by changes in its environment,
food, or method of handling.

The kinkajou is nicknamed "honey-bear" because of its predilection
for honey. Other then this its tastes are wide-ranging, its feeding habits
being similar to those of the raccoon and coati.

THE CACOMISTLE OR RING-TAILED CAT
(*BASSARISCUS ASTUTUS*)

The *Cacomistle* is a New World *Procyonidae* found mostly in Mexico
where it was also called the cacomixle and cacomixtle by the early
Aztecs. It is smaller than the raccoon with a sharper muzzle and a longer
tail. It is carnivorous, nocturnal, arboreal, and much shyer and more
elusive than the raccoon. The coat of this little beast is rich orange-
brown and glistens with a golden sheen when the animal is in full, healthy

The Cacomistle (Bassariscus astutus) *is also often called the Ring-tailed cat for a very obvious reason.*

coat. The tail is quite long—much more than half the creature's length —and between the seven broad, white bands is very dark in color. The cacomistle builds a permanent nest between rocks or in holes in the trees and hunts small animals by night, tree snails and frogs being edible favorites with green nuts for dessert. If you are lucky and are able to acquire a tiny baby from the usual litter of four that are born in the late spring, it can be easily tamed and trained to be a nice pet.

17

Hoofed Mammals

Bovidae

Considered the most impressive orders of mammals, the even-toed and odd-toed hoofed animals are composed of almost two dozen distinct families, the tallest being the 17-feet-tall giraffes and the tiniest being the dik-diks (Guenther's dik-dik), which are not larger than a rabbit. I will select carefully from among this mammalian order for certainly, as pets, we can eliminate giraffes, bison, camels, hippopotami, rhinoceroses and elephants. Tarzan and Sabu may have their huge, wild pets, but we must draw the line somewhere within rational boundaries.

Undoubtedly in Tibet Yaks have become pets. As riding and pack animals they have made it possible for men to inhabit the wild, bleak, inhospitable mountains of Tibet and Turkestan. Indeed, without the yak, I am certain we who live in a more mellow climate would have been robbed of the famous story and motion picture *Shangrila*. The gayal of north India has also been domesticated, and certainly some of those dark, handsome, white-stockinged buffalo have become pets of the families who own them. They are rather beyond our reach, however, and all other wild cattle are savage creatures without pet status. Occasionally, on farms, calves and sometimes even adult cattle can be called pets. Generally speaking bulls of all species are dangerous.

SHEEP (GENUS *OVIS*)

Goats, lambs and sheep have often become pets and there are many species to choose from. In Barbados a type of sheep peculiar to that small island—tan with dark markings and to the eye more goat-like than sheep-like—often become pets of the natives. During lambing time, particularly when multiple births occur, many ewes will forsake one of the lambs, which is then taken into the house by the farmer, given a bed near the stove, and hand-fed with a baby's bottle by the farmer's family. Such orphaned animals often become pets.

Many of the great wild sheep of foreign lands (as well as our own *bighorn sheep*) are princes of the heights and considered trophies par excellence by the sporting fraternity. But they are savage lords of the untamed peaks, not to be domesticated or petted. Of the wild sheep perhaps only the handsome *aoudad* (*Barbary wild sheep*) can be assigned the pet title. They differ from other sheep in being devoid of scent-secreting glands on the face.

GOATS (GENUS *CAPRA*)

Only the domestic varieties of goats make good pets. The kids are particularly vivacious and humorous pets. Wild goats—such as the *Siberian Ibex,* the *Markhor* of Asia and the *Himalayan Tahr*—are too rare and capricious in temperament to be labeled pets even if available. They inhabit some of the most dangerous terrain known to man. The *Rocky Mountain Goat* and the *Chamois* are goat-antelopes and the chamois is a species of the type that includes the *Gorals* and *Serows* of Asia. The *Nubian Goat,* with its Roman-nosed profile and pendulous ears, is an interesting species and makes a fine pet.

A "Grade" goat has one parent purebred and the other of unknown ancestry. Of the better-known breeds, Nubian, Toggenburgs, Alpines (*Swiss and French varieties*) and the new and popular *La Mancha* goats —which are docile, have a very sweet temperament and Goat-wise reach the impossible dream—are all candidates for pet status. Some bucks are dangerous during the mating season and I am sure you've heard someone accused of "smelling like a goat." The phrase is not entirely without substance for buck goats are quite odorous. So there you have two basic reasons to choose a female goat as a pet. As an added bonus the female goat gives milk.

Goats have been associated with Devil worship over the centuries. The powerful canvases of Francisco Goya in the Prado Museum in Madrid lend visual strength to this dark and medieval concept.

ANTELOPE AND DEER

Antelope and deer, generally speaking, do not make good pets despite the universal appeal of Bambi. The adults are dangerous, the antlered bucks particularly so, and even the females can do considerable damage with their slashing front hoofs. Ancient, ancestral deer had tusks but no antlers; and today, in China and Korea, there exist herbivorous mammals of such archaic type—the *Chinese Water Deer* and the *Nuntjak*—that they too grow long tusks, reaching below the bottom jawline. The males do not have antlers, but can do considerable damage with their strong tusks. The Chinese water deer is also unique in that it can give birth to as many as seven fawns at a time, a veritable litter. It is scientifically assumed that as the deer developed antlers, the need for tusks for defense and attack lessened, until in the advanced evolutionary types the tusks disappeared and only the antlers remained.

If you insist upon making a pet of an antelope, Africa teems with some of the most beautiful animals of this family. The largest of the antelopes, the *Eland,* is being bred experimentally in Africa as a meat animal and has become quite domesticated. It can reach a weight of over 1,500 pounds. Most of the antelopes are large, shy, and wild. They should be considered strictly game and trophy animals. Luckily they are protected in the many reserves and preserves in Africa. The most familiar of the African species are the *hartebeest, gnu, oryx, Greater kudu, bongo, sable antelope, impala,* the *Sititungas* and the *waterbucks.* Asia shelters the *saiga, black buck,* and *chiru.* The *pronghorned antelope* of our own plains country is not an antelope at all. I truly cannot think of one of these creatures that, when mature, would make a reasonably good pet—not even the females.

The *deer* are a very large family (*Cervidae*) unique among hoofed animals in that the males bear antlers (head weapons) and the females do not. An exception to this rule is the *Caribou* (*reindeer*), for both sexes bear antlers. The *Alaskan Moose* is the largest of the New World deer, followed by the *American Elk* or *wapiti,* then the *Woodland Caribou.* *Moose* and *elk* are not in the pet domain, but caribou have been domesticated and trained as riding, and sleigh animals just as has the horse. The caribou is also used for food, milk, and hides. Economically it is extremely valuable to Laplanders and other far northern peoples who, in all probability, could not exist in their inhospitable environment without their reindeer herds. Undoubtedly pets can be made of caribou, but they can only exist in a specific environment that is devoid of heat and humidity.

Virginia Deer furnished valuable food and buckskin clothing to the early American pioneers and so have historical significance. They are also remarkably able to hold their own, despite civilization's constant encroachment and the large numbers shot by hunters during the open deer season. The Bucks (males) of this species are particularly dangerous, but this is also true of *Mule, Colombian Black-tailed, Florida,* the *Central* and *South American Marsh* and *Pampas* deer and the many deer species of Europe, Asia, and India. If you must have a deer for a pet, select a *female* and get it *young,* for females are much less dangerous than the bucks.

There is a light in the darkness of pet deer owning. There are three species that are generally so docile in temperament that even the bucks make excellent pets. Because of their docility they are also ideal for park herds and ornamental deer on large estates.

The *European Red Deer* is a fine, showy abundant species in the parks and preserves of Europe, particularly in the British Isles. This species each year grows a huge rack of antlers that often weigh over 20

One of the few breeds of deer that are trustworthy, the handsome Fallow Deer (Dama dama) *is represented in our illustration by a yearling doe.*

pounds. These antlers are covered by a coating of skin called "velvet" comprised of a complex of blood vessels. The velvet is subsequently rubbed off, leaving the bare bone of the antlers. Later the rack is shed and the process repeats itself, timed so that at the rutting (mating) season the stag's antlers are at the peak of their proficiency as weapons.

The *Fallow Deer* is another docile and popular *Cervidae* whose habitat is spread throughout the world. Albino specimens are not uncommon in medium-sized herds. The extinct *Giant Irish Elk* was actually an archaic fallow deer that prospered during the latter Ice Age. It stood over 6 feet high at the shoulders with an antler spread exceeding 11 feet! These fallow deer themselves are beautiful creatures with antlers that flare out into a broad plate of bone (palmate).

The last of our triumvirate of docile deer, the *axis deer,* is one of the handsomest of its family. Basically of Asiatic origin, it has a reddish coat liberally and vividly marked with large white spots. It is said to be a particularly healthy species and is valued for this asset as well as its sweet character.

There are several species of very tiny deer, gazelles, and Duikers that make cute, interesting pets if available and if acquired when young. The *Chevrotain* or *Mouse Deer* of India is about the size of a jackrabbit, is hornless, and is completely defenseless against the many predators of its world. Delicate in the extreme, the young are tiny beyond belief. The *Dorcas Gazelle* of Egypt is dainty, delicate, and slender. The smallest of the African antelopes, the *Duikers,* are widely distributed and rarely grow as tall as 2 feet at the shoulders. These little herbivores are all slender-legged, pretty, and active. In Africa we also find the true pygmies of the hoofed mammals, the tiny, rabbit-sized Dik-diks. These elegant deer make rare pets.

LLAMAS (FAMILY *CAMELIDAE*)

We can skip the *giraffes,* though they become very docile in captivity, and the *camels,* those marvelous ships of the desert that are invaluable beasts of burden and make it possible for man to travel through the sun-blasted nothingness of the great deserts, terrain impossible to navigate without them. Wonderful as the camels are at this important task, they have dispositions that leave a lot to be desired.

We come then to the members of the camel family that live in South America, the *Llama, Alpaca, Guanaco,* and *Vicuna.* I have seen many specimens of this group of llama-type animals in the high Andes. The *guanaco* is the wild and basic breed from which the others originated. The llama is the largest of the four and has been used as a beast of burden by the Indians since the time of the ancient Incas. The alpaca is smaller than the llama, and bred for its abundant wool. The vicuna is more slender still and the only member not blessed with a luxuriant pelage. The young of all four animals make good pets and llamas and alpacas, even when grown, are docile and easily manageable. Like their cousins, the camels, these animals have a nasty habit of spitting at anyone who annoys them, but unlike the camels they learn to control this tendency and exhibit it very infrequently.

SWINE (FAMILY *SUIDAE*)

Piglets are cute, smart, and often become pets on farms. When fully grown, the larger boars can be dangerous. But youngsters can be trained to a harness and leash and the female of the species, when trained early, remains tame. Pigs are not dirty animals. If given a dirty environment, they will be dirty; given a clean environment with good food—not slop —they will be as clean as any other animal.

Wild Swine of all kinds can be rated as among the most dangerous animals in the world. By no means can they be considered in the pet category. Recently a friend of mine in South America, who has a small private zoo, found it necessary to execute a *White-lipped Peccary* he owned because it was killing his rabbits and attacking the capybaras and any other animal it could reach. We dined on wild boar—a tasty dish indeed. The exception to the recriminating statement above is the wild *Red River Hog* of Africa's forests. Grotesque, long-faced, its ugly head adorned with tufted ears, these Swine are handsomely colored in rust, black, and white. They are said to be easily tamed and make interesting pets. The famous Dr. Albert Schweitzer kept one as a pet at his clinic in Africa for many years. He did not, however, win the Nobel Peace Prize in 1952 for making peace with this wild hog.

Swine were first domesticated in China in about 4900 B.C. and were brought to America by Christopher Columbus. Some of the species in this family attain huge size and it is not uncommon to hear of boars that weigh over 1,000 pounds. Females and youngsters of most of the domestic varieties make intelligent and interesting pets. A female is called a gilt and a castrated boar is a barrow. There is a large selection from among the domesticated species of swine in size, color, and disposition.

TAPIRS (FAMILY *TAPIRIDAE*)

There are four species of tapirs distributed in tropical America and one specie, the *Malay Tapir,* inhabits the Malay Peninsula and Sumatra. Actually the tapir is an odd-toed hoofed animal and belongs in that category. But the species is inevitably thought of by the layman as being a close relative of the swine. Because of this and the fact that the following odd-toed hoofed animal section will concentrate on the family *Equidae,* I have listed the tapirs here. These creatures are not very different from their ancestors of prehistoric times. They are stolid and good-natured. They are fond of water and swim well. Because of their docile and placid temperaments, combined with their stupidity, they make good but dull pets. The *Giant Tapir* is the largest of the species; and the *Woolly Tapir,* covered with reddish hair, is perhaps the most interesting of a dull lot. *Dow's* and the smaller *South American Tapir* are New World beasts. The mobile, elongated snout of these creatures is typical of the family. During the Miocene period about twenty-five million years ago, tapirs roamed large areas of the globe, but they are most abundant now in South America where their flesh is highly prized by both the jungle Amerindians and the prowling jaguar or El Tigre of the New World tropical jungles.

Odd-toed Hoofed Animals (order *Perissodactyla*)

Most people are aware that the equine race was initially quite small and possessed multiple toes which, in the long course of evolution (sixty million years), eventually became one toe, or hoof, borne by an herbivorous animal that had also gained great size during its evolutionary period. Evidently the ancestors of the horse died out in the Americas before men came to these shores across the neck of land that later became the Bering Strait. When the waters rushed in, separating this continent from Asia, the Magdalenian peoples who had crossed over from Asia were isolated from the rest of the world. It was not until the conquistadors, those men of incomparable courage, boldness, and cruelty, came to these shores that the equine race was reintroduced to the Americas. During the conquest and rape of the great tribes of Amerindians by the small but arrogant bands of conquistadors, some of the mounts of the Spaniards and Portuguese explorers escaped. On the vast plains of our country, they prospered, reproduced prodigiously and, through capture and taming as mounts, added a vividly new chapter to the fantastic saga of the American aboriginal that the befuddled Italian seaman, Columbus, named Indians.

The true wild horse that was the basic ancestor of the many breeds of equines evolved in central Asia. These basic horses, the *Mongolian* or *Prjevalsky Wild Horse,* still exist in the archaic form and can be found on exhibition in most of the larger zoos. They are fairly small, bay-colored with a dark dorsal stripe and erect mane. Upper Paleolithic man often painstakingly drew these horses on the walls of caves as he groped toward artistic expression. Wild horses of very similar type were common during the last Ice Age. The *Tarpan,* another primitive and ancestral equine, became extinct about a century ago. By selection over the centuries man established the initial breeds to suit his needs; from the early Persian mounts came the *Arabian* and *Barb* families, the genetic material from which all the various subsequent equine breeds were fashioned.

The riding of a horse has been an accomplishment of man for only about five thousand years. It is an indication of man's uniqueness, of his creative mentality that he should presume to think that such a thing could be accomplished. It is also indicative of the philosophy of the human being that life is, in the last analysis, an adventure in learning.

The Breeds of Odd-toed Hoofed Animals (family *Equidae*)

For our purpose we can eliminate the several species of *zebras* from discussion, since these sensationally striped African equines are erratic in temperament and usually too savage to be considered as having pet status. The wild *Onager* of Persia, the *Abyssinian Wild Ass of Africa* (one of seven wild-ass species) and the *Tibetan Wild Ass,* all are quite untamable. The *Mongolian Wild Horse* has better temperament, but is too rare to be easily obtainable.

The *onager,* a *wild ass,* was probably caught, tamed, and trained by emerging civilizations—such as the Sumerian—at the head of the Persian Gulf (between 3600 to 2400 B.C.). Early Persian equines were probably developed from the tarpan and the *Mongolian Wild Horse* that inhabited the Gobi Desert. Crossbreeding of selected stock undoubtedly produced new equine genetic material which, through selection from changing types, formed by small mutations and natural environmental selection, eventually produced the basic breeds from which came the many kinds of horses we know today.

BURROS

The use of the patient *Burro* as a beast of burden is as old as civilization itself. In many parts of the world the poor people depend upon these wonderful little animals to help them in the labors that feed, clothe, and shelter them and their families. I have seen burros in all sections of the globe so loaded down that the beast itself could only be distinguished by four tiny hoofs and a nodding, rabbit-eared head. Unassuming, patient as Job, plodding onward, I do not think that there is another animal on the face of the earth that has given as much to man—

The Onager (Equus hemionus) *was domesticated by the Su-merians, who formed the first great human civilization. Sym-bolically, behind the grazing Onager stands the figure of a Sumerian house god.*

The only existing wild species of equine, the Mongolian Wild Horse (Equus przewalskii), *also called the Przewalski Horse, is a living replica of the wild horses prevalent during the Ice Age.*

kind as the lowly burro. There is a *Midget Burro,* an incredibly small, comical replica of the normal-sized beast, that is sold purely as a pet. Both midget- and normal-sized burros fill their roles admirably.

HORSES

There are a number of horse breeds of great quality and utilitarian value that have developed in all parts of the world. A moment ago I glanced up from my typewriter, looked out the window, and saw a

Chibcha Indian riding past on a fine *Criolla*—a proud, lively native horse of rocking-chair gait—developed in South America. Portugal has its *Lusitano,* bred on beautiful government rancheros from basic Iberian, Arabian, and English thoroughbred stock. Of similar conformation are the Spanish *Andalusian horses* of pure Iberian ancestry. Both the *Lusitano* and *Andalusian* are of surpassing beauty and intelligence and possessed of staunch temperament. They are trained to haute école and used in the bull rings of Spain and Portugal by the rejoneadors, who, on horseback, fight the savage Andalusian bulls in a demonstration of unrivaled control and horsemanship. In the face of the complete mastery of the mount that is seen in these bull-ring demonstrations, it is astonishing to realize that the riding of the equine species by man is less than five thousand years old. It is still more amazing when one is aware that the act of riding a horse is unnatural for a human.

The *Arabian* and the *Barb,* both of basic Asiatic origin, were the original stock from which trace the races of light horses we know today. The romance of the Arabian has been told in song and story throughout the ages. The beauty of this species is unequaled in the equine world. The Arabian has the ability to engender beauty and improvement in any other horse breed into which his genetic qualities are blended. I have seen Arabian horses raced on the Bierut race course and ridden recklessly in wildly savage tribal displays by Moroccan desert tribesmen. Always the Arabian's delicate but fiery beauty was heart-stopping.

The English *Thoroughbred* is also a basic type that is used for improvement and is found in the background of many other equine breeds. The Irish Thoroughbred is of the same stock. From the Thoroughbred come the true track horses, animals of tremendous speed and power that make the best of hunters and jumpers. Polo ponies and racing quarter horses are also by-products of the genetic worth of the Thoroughbred. These horses owe their great hearts and courage directly to their Arabian and Barb ancestors, though they do not have the fantastic stamina or ability to travel unbelievable distances that is possessed by the Arabian.

The *Standardbred* is an American equine developed for sulky racing that began as a farmer's sport at stock fairs and now rivals Thoroughbred racing as a sport. The Standardbred can be either a trotter or pacer and is the product of judicious crossing of early Morgan horse stock and English Thoroughbreds (specifically the superb early

The aristocratic racing horse of today is the Thoroughbred, formed initially by English breeders from genetic material lent by the beautiful Arabian horses of the desert crossed with fine native mares.

Thoroughbred, Messenger). A great Standardbred racing horse, Dan Patch, so caught the hearts and imaginations of the American public that he stands beside the famous Thoroughbred, Man O'War, in equine recognition and popularity.

A blend of several major breeds produced our *American saddle horse*. This is the show horse supreme in three- and five-gaited classes, a most noble and handsome equine, bred for gait quality, beauty, and riding pleasure. In any show ring in the country when the Saddlebred classes are in session and the call comes from the judge to "Rack on," you will be treated to one of the most thrilling exhibitions of equine movement you have ever seen.

The *Tennessee Walker* is a Southern creation like mint juleps and magnolia blossoms, boasting a genetic background similar to that of the Saddlebred, but with selection made for the very special, long-striding, rhythmic walking gait and rocking-chair canter that are the breed's trademarks. A true show and pleasure mount, the Tennessee Walker is the kind of horse you want when spending a full day in the saddle. The Walker is blessed with a docile and pleasant temperament.

Another fine, truly American-made equine is the *Morgan Horse.* Developed from the breeding of one great horse, Justin Morgan (said to have come from Arabian and Barb Breeding, a claim never really proven), this breed is justly popular as a show and general riding mount of endurance and beauty. The Morgan Horse farm outside of Middlebury, Vermont, is one of that state's outstanding attractions.

Bred in the West as a cattleman's horse, the *American Quarter Horse* is another equine product this country can be proud of. The quarter horse is medium-sized, but exeremely muscular and powerful and has excellent character and temperament. Prominent in the background breeding was a great stud horse named Steel Dust—hence in the early days of the breed development quarter horses were called *Steel Dust Horses.* Bred to work cattle, they can "stop on a dime and give you change," but their name, Quarter Horse, comes from the fact that for a quarter of a mile or under they are probably the fastest equines in the world. Many short-distance Thoroughbreds have been bred into quarter-horse stock to produce fast quarter-mile racehorses. The breed also makes agile polo ponies.

Other well-liked horses are *Palominos, Appaloosas, Paints,* or *Pintos* and *Indian Ponies.* They all have their own registries and standards, but with the exception of the last-named breed, are color phases rather than breeds. The golden *Palominos* are quite beautiful and popular as parade horses. Appaloosas show a correlation between the odd color patterns of the breed and certain physical traits. This was the breed that the Nez Pierce Indians rode when, under the leadership of their chief, Quanah Parker, they showed their heels to the U.S. Cavalry in their tragic attempt to reach Canada and freedom. *Pintos* have always been

ERNEST H. HART

A color variation, the Appaloosa, because of correlation between the mutant color and certain physical virtues, became a breed well liked by the American Indians, particularly the Nez Percé.

well liked by our plains Indians because of the horse's colors and patterns. The *Indian ponies* are basically of the old stock that escaped from the conquistadors and populated our southwest savannah country. Some years ago, on an isolated mesa in the West, a group of *midget horses* was found, their loss of size evidently due to inbreeding and natural selection for smallness to fit their limited terrain. *Hackney horses* and *ponies* are stylish show animals of great beauty and stunning gait that are bred and trained to harness. I have also known of at least two hackneys that became famous jumpers.

Mules are the hybrid offspring of an ass (jack) and a female horse (mare) as mentioned previously. They are noted for their ability to work long hours under trying conditions, with heavy loads. They are famous for their stamina, stuborness, and sometimes meanness. Many horsemen claim that mules make excellent riding animals and fancy mules have been bred in attractive colors (palomino, chestnut, et cetera) and with excellent conformation for this purpose. The *jackass* itself is an exceedingly strong, tenacious equine, but fractious and generally not easily handled.

Of the pony breeds the best-known are the *Shetland* and *Welsh ponies,* both excellent breeds with usually steady temperament. These small equines can be broken to saddle and harness and make excellent utility animals and pets. Crosses to Arabians and other breeds will produce jumpers and hunters for the small fry. The Chincoteague ponies that run wild on Chincoteague Island, off the coast of Virginia, are annually rounded up and some brought to the mainland for sale. When gentled and trained, they make excellent riding and driving animals and pets.

The horse, developed by man into a faithful servant, has also played a major and dramatic role in the development of human racial stock. Genetic drift became much more rapid and widespread when tribes became horse-borne and rode, raided, and conquered in areas far from their own, thus blending racial qualities and genetic characteristics to form new races with new needs and mental vistas. So the horse became woven into the fabric of mankind's genetic tapestry as a vehicle of human change and racial expansion, making it unique in the realm of animal-human relationship.

18

Mustelines

Mustelidae

The large, and varied family *Mustelidae* has worldwide distribution and no dearth of familiar species. Many of its members are among the most valuable fur bearers known. All the mustelines are carnivorous. Characteristically their footprints show five distinct toes; they also feature the presence of musk glands on each upper thigh near the base of the tail, an anomaly brought to its fullest expression in the defense mechanism of the skunk.

Though both the badger and otter are inoffensive creatures, and there has recently been a definite drift toward pet status for the ferret, I personally do not think of mustelines—other than the constantly maligned skunk and the domesticated ferret—as being pet material. Most of the mustelines are savage predators and vicious killers, but have economic value because the bulk of their prey are destructive rodents, and because their pelts bring a premium price in the marketplace.

FERRETS (*MUSTELA NIGRIPES*)

The dictionary tells us that *ferrets* are "a domesticated, albinistic, red-eyed form of the polecat . . .", which is rather an obtuse description. I remember when I was young, a man came knocking at the door of our home, carrying a small cage in which were two gimlet-eyed ferrets. He was a "ferret man" and he wanted to know if we had rats in the walls of our house and could use his services. Curious to see what his services consisted of and what role the animals in the hand-cage played in the performance of his work, I followed him from house to house until he found one where his talents were needed. It happened to be the home of a boy with whom I went to school. I watched and listened with fascination when my friend's mother admitted to having rats in the walls and cellar (in later years I found that her son had "bats in his belfry") and the ferret man prepared to render his services. First he searched for and found the holes through which the rats entered and left the house and carefully blocked all but one of them. Then he released the pair of ferrets in the remaining hole. The squealing and rushing around through the walls was horribly fascinating. Later, when all was quiet, the ferret man called his charges to him, put them, bloodied and bloated, back into their cage, collected his fee, and went on his way. The experiment, as you can see, etched itself on my young mind, never to be forgotten.

The wild *black-footed ferret* (M. Nigripes) inhabits the plains of our middle west.

BADGERS (*TAXIDEA TAXUS*) (AMERICAN)

Badgers have strong, 2- to 3-foot bodies, short but powerful legs, and short tails. They resemble bears because they walk on the soles of their feet, like a bear, and with that animal's rolling gait. These are very shy, nocturnal creatures, so wary that they are seldom seen. Of the several varieties the best-known are the *European Badger* (*Meles meles*) ranging all across Europe and Asia, and the *American Badger,* distributed from central United States to Saskatchewan. China has its own version of this musteline called the *Hog Badger*.

Badgers are found throughout Britain where they do not hibernate but are active all winter. They are inoffensive animals, but with their strength and powerful claws, jaws, and teeth, they can inflict grave wounds on any opponent. They live in setts (underground burrows), which they supply constantly with fresh bedding. They also dig latrines within about 20 yards of the sett, justifying the description of them as being clean and fastidious animals.

Boar and sow badgers (male and female) mate for life and the development of the embryos takes place about five months after mating, an interesting example of delayed implantation.

OTTERS (*LUTRA CANADENSIS*)

These are *Mustelidae* family animals, valued for their relatively short but lustrous fur, that have adjusted to an aquatic existence. Species of otters inhabit the greater part of North America, Europe, Asia, Africa, and South America. They are active intelligent creatures, lithe and strong, with webbed feet and fairly long tails that are partially flattened laterally.

Otters emit a rather strong odor similar to that of a wet dog. As protection from the brutal cold of Arctic waters where some of them are to be found during their long, and typical journeys, they possess a thick layer of fat under their pelts. Known for their agility in the water, where they perform incredible ballets, otters are also swift on land. They are extremely playful creatures and frequently construct steep slides from land to water, down which several of them will toboggan on their underbodies for hours at a time like kids in a play park. They make very good pets if acquired when young.

There is also a large-sized species of otter that frequents salt water and has the ludicrous habit of floating on its back with its dinner on its stomach, as though laid out on a table.

SKUNKS (*MEPHITIS MEPHITIS*)

The last of the family *Mustelidae* to be discussed is the one that makes the best pet—the *Skunk*. This much-misunderstood and vilified animal in its glossy black and white coat and full-feathered tail is a beautiful, affectionate creature. It is clean, quiet and inoffensive, never fractious; always nonaggressive, they do not attract members of the opposite sex, and shed sparsely only once each year. Skunks are also excellent mousers, rivaling and even surpassing most cats at this worthwhile occupation.

Skunks acquired a reputation for being obnoxious due to their ability to spray at their enemies the strong musk from their anal glands. Granted the stuff isn't attar of roses, the spraying is nevertheless the only way the skunk can avoid extinction in the wild. Skunks are lovers not fighters and they have no other means of defense. I don't imagine their sense of smell is very highly developed; if it were, they couldn't live with themselves and any kind of family life would be ridiculous.

When I was a youngster and fortunate enough to know someone who had found a litter of baby skunks in the Connecticut woods, I weaseled one out of him. We would hold a baby skunk head down between our legs, with a piece of glass between the kit and the upper parts of our body (just in case). Then, with a sharp knife, we would cut a shallow X into the hind leg with the center of the X exactly at the opening of the scent gland. When the cut healed, which it did in a very short time, the scar tissue formed a seal over the scent gland, closing it forever. Even though forever is a long, long time, I would advise you not to depend on this method. Infection could occur or scar tissue rip open. It is best to leave the excision of the musk glands to your veterinarian. Once the glands are completely removed, you never need worry again. But remember this—if your kit is descented, never turn him lose to roam for any reason, for without his scent glands he is at the mercy of any animal who sees him as prey.

Much maligned, the Skunk (Mephitis mephitis) *is a fine mouser and makes a wonderful pet once his scent glands are removed.*

WEASELS, SABLES, MINK, FISHERS, MARTENS, AND WOLVERINES

None of these mustelines are good pet material, so we will give them only token recognition. All are vicious killers. They have been hunted and trapped for their pelts to a point that for most creatures would result in extinction, but these mustelines are swift and crafty and so seem to hold their own. The American Wolverine (*Gule luseus*) is a powerful, heavily muscled, sagacious, and fearless villain that raids traplines in the Far North and wantonly destroys the larders and caches of the fur trappers. This animal is much too tough and dangerous to be considered pet material.

So we come to the end of our section on mustelines, having seen that of all the many species that form this interesting family, only "the three mustelines" (with an apology to Alexandre Dumas)—the skunk, the ferret, and the otter—have real pet potential.

19

Viverrines (family *Viverridae*)

Viverridae

Palm cats, civets, genets, mongooses (not mongeese or gise), the Binturonga, and Meerkats are all of the family *Viverridae*. Actually many of them are barred from importation into the United States. But they do occasionally turn up at an animal dealer's and over the years some of them have achieved pet status with a scattering of individuals. Therefore, in a book of this kind, they cannot be completely ignored.

Most of these animals have elongated bodies, sharp muzzles, and long tails. Their evolutionary background is interesting in that they are related through ancestral ties to both the weasels (family *Mustelidae*) and the cats (family *Felidae*).

The viverrines are an Old World family largely inhabiting the Indo-Malayan and African regions, Madagascar, and southern China. Some of these creatures are particularly attractive and intelligent and have been tamed and fashioned into worthwhile pets on their native soil.

CIVETS (*CIVETTICTIS CIVETTA*) (AFRICAN)

There are fifteen species of *civets* or *civet cats* and little is known of some such as the *fanaloka, Fossa, Owstons,* and the *otter civet.* But the *African* and *Indian civets,* large and small, have been used for centuries to produce a musk utilized in the manufacture of very delicate Oriental perfumes for milady, and so are well-known animals. The word "civet" is derived from the Arabic and is applied to the scent obtained from these animals. Civets are nocturnal, solitary and, in the wild, feed mostly on small animals, some fruit, roots, and tubers. They are rather short-legged and about the overall size of a large cat, weighing from 15 to 25 pounds. They sport a ringed tail and their head is similar to a raccoon's in appearance. The body of the civet is marked with a profusion of black spots and stripes on a grayish-fur background. The

The African Civet (Civettictis civetta), *a viverrine, secretes a glandular substance that is used in the manufacture of certain perfumes.*

African and the large Indian civets are about the same size and share general appearance and habits with the small Indian civet.

In Ethiopia these animals are kept in captivity and the musk is removed from the glands near the reproductive organs several times a week. Tons of this commodity (with the consistency of honey and composed of fats and oils) is exported from Africa every year. The perfume used by King Solomon came from Ethiopia, attesting to the antiquity of the industry. Shakespeare, through the voice of Claudio in "Much Ado About Nothing," makes us aware of his knowledge of the civet's contribution to the making of sweet-smelling scents when Claudio remarks "The sweet youth's in love" when said youth sprinkles himself with civet.

Despite the long years of handling civets for their glandular products, little is known of their life history because they have never been bred in captivity. They are, however, easily caught, easily fed, and not very aggressive, so they tame readily and quickly if caught when young.

They do exude a strong, sweetish odor that is offensive to most people. If you have lost your olfactory sense or have chronic hay fever, this might be the pet for you. Of course I don't imagine cocktail or dinner parties at your home would be entirely successful.

The *Binturong* or *Bear Cat* (*Arctictis binturong*) is the largest of the viverrines. It too is of the civet family. It has a coarse, but luxuriant, coat of dark gray and black and is heavy in body. Arboreal, it is found from southeastern Asia to the Malayan Islands, particularly in Borneo's rain forest. The binturong walks like a bear but in body somewhat resembles a Persian cat, hence its name bear cat. The binturong is an amiable animal and can become a highly interesting pet. Its tail is prehensile.

PALM CATS, GENETS, AND MEERKATS

A group of civets called *Palm Cats,* smaller than the binturong but larger than the smaller Viverrines, are found in the Indo-Malayan region. They have exceedingly long tails and solid body colors, generally yellow, gray, or chestnut. The *Two-Spotted Palm Cat* and the *Rusty-Spotted Genet,* both of Africa, boast of over a dozen allied species, all strikingly marked with bands and blotches. Small, sharp-snouted, they make a practice of destroying the nests of rats and mice. They are readily tamed even when mature, becoming family pets and, as rodent catchers, surpassing cats by a wide margin.

Very closely related to the genets, but with heavier bodies and shorter tails, the *Meerkats* of Africa are somewhat similar in appearance to the mongooses and, like them, are not allowed to be imported into this country. Meerkats destroy rodents, the young of poisonous snakes, and birds of all kinds. If they were not barred from importation, some pet specimens might get loose and breed and—particularly in sections such as Florida—thrive to such an extent that they would become a menace to all wild birds, poultry, and small animals that are ecologically important. Meerkats are easily tamed and I have seen several that had become house pets in Africa.

MONGOOSES

There are many species of *Mongooses* ranging through Asia, Malaysia, China, and Africa and they are all much alike in appearance and habits, but differ slightly in size. The Indian Mongoose, immortalized in Kipling's *Jungle Book* as Rikki-tikki-tavi, was given heroic stature as a killer of the deadly, huge, hooded cobra of India, though

Also a viverrine, the Indian Mongoose (Herpestes edwardsii)
is generally thought of as a killer of deadly snakes. This inter-
esting mammal was immortalized in Kipling's famous "Jungle
Book."

the Indian Mongoose is really not any more proficient in this department than the African species. The mongoose attains its largest size
in Africa. It feeds, in any habitat, upon rodents, reptiles, and birds.
Again we have a member of the family *Viverridae* that is barred from
importation to the United States to prevent accidental introduction of
the species to the environment through escape from captivity.

The Mongoose was brought to the West Indies and Pacific Islands to eliminate the deadly *fer-de-lance* (a venomous reptile), rats, and other destructive and dangerous pests. Instead mongooses played havoc with small reptiles, benevolent rodents, and native birds of economic value, destroying the natural balance and affecting the fauna drastically. The mongooses were afraid of the fer-de-lance, a much swifter-striking reptile than the cobra and so did little to effect elimination of this deadly snake. In fact the mongooses bred prolifically and became greater pests than any of the creatures they had been imported to control or eliminate. They became bounty animals in a desperate but unsuccessful bid to reduce their numbers.

Man, in his arrogant wisdom, often accelerates the ecological replacement of one species by another by introducing an alien genus to a particular environment . . . and often lives to regret that he ever had such a bright idea.

Incidentally, before condemnation of the mongoose reaches a zenith in your mind, remember that their failures have been due to man's muddling and meddling. Let me assure you that these animals are highly intelligent and can be tamed to become interesting, valuable pets.

CHAPTER
20
Marsupials

Marsupialia

Do you know what a marsupial is? Well, don't fret if you don't. Many people have no idea of what they are and even the marsupials themselves are never quite certain as to their identity.

To keep the record straight, marsupials are viviparous, but non-placental mammals most of which carry a marsupium, or pouch that contains mammary glands. As we explore this branch of the mammalian class you will learn more of the physical idiosyncrasies of these strange creatures.

Australia, the island continent and the basic habitat of most marsupials, was isolated from the changing flow of evolution that was occurring in other parts of the primeval world for over sixty-nine million years. As a result, the animal life that formed on the Down Under island is unlike any other, except for a small overflow of animals that touched neighboring Tasmania, New Guinea, and North and tropical America. The only animal found in Australia that is not a marsupial is the dog-like dingo, which is said to have been brought to that country by the aborigines who were the first human inhabitants, having come to Australia from some other part of the world. No humans, or dogs, or any other normal creatures evolved upon that soil; only the marsupials are native, a race of creatures more closely linked to life's beginning on this planet than any other living mammalian group.

This ancient order of mammals is much older than the placental, or true, mammals that superseded it in areas other than Australia. In remote prehistoric time, as nature fumbled blindly to create myriad animal shapes upon the earth, pouched animals were widely distributed in a variety of forms. But in the intense struggle of species survival the pouched, marsupial-type creatures become expendable because they could not compete with the true mammals. And they only survived in significant numbers in this area of the world when it broke away from the larger land masses and became isolated. Cut off from the intense competitive struggle, and with only their own kind as competition, marsupials flourished and, having no reason to change, maintained an evolutionary stagnation. Not only did they remain inert physically, they also failed to develop mentally toward competitive sharpness.

These strange animals, in all their forms and sizes, differ from all other creatures in that the young are born while still embryonic. The females are provided with an abdominal pouch (the marsupium already mentioned), to which the blind, tiny, babies make their instinctive way immediately after birth. They attach themselves to the teats within the pouch and there they may remain for several months or until grown and active enough to be less than easy prey. The young are so incredibly small that the babies of a 6-foot kangaroo are no larger than just-born mice, and the babes of more normal-sized marsupials are often smaller than insect larvae.

Perhaps the strangest thing about these very odd creatures is the intriguing way in which, in all their bizarre forms, they tend to mimic other species of mammals to which they have absolutely no relationship. Witness the fact that there are marsupial "bears," "cats," "moles," "mice," "wolves," "anteaters," squirrels," et cetera, each a modification in form filling an environmental niche occupied by a mammal of similar appearance in other sections of the globe.

The unique mimicry of other, unrelated mammalian forms that the order *Marsupialia* display would lead one to theorize that after eons of testing living material, of selecting and discarding within given boundaries, the process of evolution can be successful and fundamentally workable only with a limited number of basic mammalian forms.

Perhaps before the great land mass that is now the Australian continent broke away and became solitary, the marsupials gradually developed physical similarity to the mammalian creatures with which they were attempting unsuccessfully to compete. Inevitably this pathetic mimicry was doomed to failure, for it was the mammalian brain, the ability to react swiftly to stress situations, the intensity of the will to survive through genetic pliability—not their physical properties per se— that gave the mammals dominance in their world. And it was these values that the marsupials lacked. Only when their habitat became isolated, forming a sanctuary, were these strange beasts, dressed in their partial masquerade, saved for the future.

Perhaps this is true, perhaps not. But I have heard no better argument to explain the phenomenon.

OPOSSUMS

Our own *Common* (or *Virginia*) *Opossum* (*Didelphis virginiana*) looks very much like a giant rat but has many more teeth. This dental peculiarity possessed by many marsupials is also a typical physical departure from the norm. The opossum also has a prehensile tail, so is arboreal, and the big toe is thumb-like and widely opposed. These extremely interesting American marsupials are slow-moving, generally light gray in color and their acrobatic tail is ratlike. Prolific breeders, they produce as many as eighteen young at a time; but since there are only thirteen nipples in the opossum's pouch, any youngsters in excess of that

The Opossum (Didelphis virginiana) *of the United States has a prehensile tail and is a prolific breeder. It is America's example of the marsupial.*

number die immediately. This marsupial has little defense against enemies and, when frightened, it will "play possum," which has been thought a clever trick to confound an attacker. We now know that the poor creature actually goes into shock.

Some years ago my son and I found a pair of young opossums and took them home. They soon learned to scamper up and down a vertically held rope, hang by their tails from our fingers and sit on my son's shoulders, showing their innumerable teeth and making contented little hissing sounds. They became wonderful pets.

The *Murine* or *Mouse Opossum* is the smallest of the Central and South American marsupials. It is a cute tropical mammal. There are several genera in Australia that are sometimes called opossums but are usually designated as *Phalangers*. These creatures are much more active and indubitably more handsome than the opossums of the New World. They have woolly coats and long, luxuriantly furred tails, and range in size from that of a normal mammalian squirrel to a small European fox.

With its pouch out of sight in the rear, the *Marsupial Mouse* is in appearance much like our common mouse. If taken when young, these marsupials make nice pets, but mature specimens are ferocious little beasties that eat snakes, snails, and anything else that doesn't eat them first.

The squirrel types ape real squirrels so well that they could be mistaken for these rodents. Several species have skin folds between front and hind legs just as do our flying squirrels. The *Flying Phalanger* (*Petaurus sciureus*), prevalent in eastern Australia, makes an interesting pet.

The *Brush-tailed Opossum* (*Trichosaurus vulpecula*), also known as the *Vulpine Opossum* or *Foxlike Opossum,* is about 2 feet long, about the size of a red fox with a foxlike face. Its diet consists of buds, blossoms, other vegetation, and occasionally bird's eggs. These arboreal prehensile-tailed marsupials probably fill the niche in the marsupial social order that the monkeys hold in more normal animal communities in the wild. The brush-tail is found all over Australia and Tasmania. Introduced into New Zealand in 1858, it has thrived there. Like the American opossum it is a versatile creature and can live in close proximity to man. The brush-tail has a thick woolly coat; its tail is also thickly furred but with a nude patch toward the tip like the tails of our New World primates. These attractive creatures seem utterly indifferent

Another Marsupial from "Down Under," the Brush-tailed Opossum (Trichosaurus vulpecula) *is a typical example of this ancient order of mammals.*

to humans when mature, although if acquired when young, they make very delightful pets.

Their enemies are eagles, dingoes, the huge monitor lizards (Goanna), and man. The aborigines eat them and the white man hunts them for their pelts. Each year approximately one million are trapped for their fur and another million destroyed under an Australian bounty system. But despite these population inroads and the fact that the brush-tail gives birth to only one baby (weighing about $\frac{1}{15}$ of an ounce compared to the dam's mature weight of 10 pounds), this marsupial continues to thrive. Lately its appetite for mistletoe—which it clears from the flowering gum trees that produce nectar for the honey industry—has brought it favorable attention as having economic value to the country.

THE FLYING MOUSE

Eastern Australia also harbors the *Flying Mouse* (*Acrobates pygmaeu*s), which, like its neighbor the flying phalanger, sports dilatable planes of skin that enable it to take long, flight-like leaps. Hair at the end of its tail gives that appendage a feather-like quality and is the reason for this little marsupial's second name the *Feather-tailed Mouse*. These odd little creatures make unique pets.

THE WOMBAT

The *Wombat* (*Vombatus hirsutus*) is so much like the woodchuck (which it mimics) that it even lives partly underground and has teeth much like a rodent's. It is, however, larger than a woodchuck, and, because of its body shape, the pouch is not very obvious. These creatures are enormously strong and are not recommended as pets, though I have heard that folks in the "outback" do occasionally tame them. It is tailless, long-lived, nocturnal and herbivorous.

THE KOALA

One of the most attractive of Australia's marsupials is the cute, cuddlesome, and solitary little *koala* (*Phascolarctus cinereus*) called the native "bear." The word "koala" is aboriginal and means "no drink," describing succinctly the fact that the koala, once weaned, never again drinks anything but dew from leaves. Incidentally, many of the eucalyptus leaves it ingests are poisonous to other animals. Koalas look exactly like soft, cuddly Teddy bears and are generally docile, amusing, but rather stupid as pets. Young koalas can be trained to be good companions but, despite their innocuous snuggly appearance, mature wild specimens will bite and claw if handled roughly. These little

A native of Australia and, of course, a marsupial, the Koala Bear (Phascolarctus cinereus) *looks like a Teddy bear.*

marsupials have one tiny baby every two years. An interesting fact is that koalas are capable of raising their arms above their shoulders, a physical feat which they, as mammals, share only with the primates and man.

THE MARSUPIAL "CAT"

The native marsupial *"cat"* carries the parallel mimicry to the bitter end, endowing these Dasyurops with carnivorous appetites. The several "cat" species appear very much like small felines. The handsomest is the shiny black, white-spotted *Viverrine Cat (Dasyurops masculatus)*. Unlike our common domestic cats, these ersatz marsupial felines are said to be rather unintelligent, but when taken young, they make strikingly attractive pets.

BANDICOOTS

There are nineteen species of *Bandicoots* and they are all over Australia, Tasmania, and New Guinea. They are ratlike in appearance with long pointed muzzles and naked ears; their size varies between that of a rat and a rabbit. They have sharp claws and the second and third hind toes are joined by a skin section shaped like a mitten. The *Pig-footed Bandicoot (family Peramelidae)* has lost its first toe, but the fourth toe compensates by being quite large and bearing a big claw. The resultant gait of this creature is that of an individual more punchy than pouchy. Bandicoot diets vary, some being carnivorous and others herbivorous. Some of the larger specimens are good hunters and ratters. The pouch that protects their young opens backwards between the hind legs. The bandcoot's pelage is highly prized and they have been slaughtered for their pelts to the point where they can almost be considered a vanishing species. Young bandicoots make easily tamed pets.

A cute little codger called the *Rabbit-eared Bandicoot* lives in burrows and spends its time digging for insects, particularly termites, which it devours by the thousands. They are also known as *Bilbys (Thylacomys)*, and are, like all bandicoots, nocturnal. There are two species of these bizarre, comical animals with long, pointed ears, bushy tails, and pinkish fur. They can become good pets and can be taught to eat food more readily available than termites.

THE TASMANIAN WOLF

The *Tasmanian "Wolf" (Thylacinus cynocephalus)* and the *Tasmanian Devil (Sarcophilus herrisii)* are powerful flesh-eating, pouched marsupials that are too savage to be considered pet material.

KANGAROOS

The large *Kangaroos* can also be dangerous and consequently are ruled out of pet status even though they are seen in circuses as boxing opponents for clowns. The moderately smaller kangaroos, commonly called *Wailabies,* make excellent pets. Many of them are attractively patterned. There is even a genus of kangaroo (*Dendrolagus Iumholtzi*) that is arboreal.

THE DUCKBILL

The *Duckbill* or *Platypus* I am sure you will never acquire as a pet because they are much too rare. But these semi-aquatic creatures are certainly bizarre with their broad duck bill, muskrat pelt, webbed feet, and flattened beaver type tail.

The marsupials are undoubtedly interesting creatures that—whenever we seriously consider them—take us on the long journey back through millions of years to the beginning of life on earth. It was a time when, among the teeming mammalian species, fighting desperately for recognition and specie immortality, many found survival impossible. How lucky it is that isolated Australia gave sanctuary to the marsupials so that they could survive to intrigue and astonish us today.

21

Insect Pets

Insecta

There are more insects in the world than any other living creatures. Over 600,000 species have been identified and entomologists claim that there may be millions more yet to be discovered and classified. Insects are everywhere (in case you haven't noticed), some destructive, some beneficial to mankind. Some of us think of insects as crawly things that should be stepped on; others know that many insects are numbered among those creatures necessary for the preservation of an ecological balance. Many of these tiny creatures are food staples for animals and other insects. Bees make honey, so useful and so delicious to the palates of countless people. And ants are the ultimate scavengers, cleaning up the last fleshy remnants left by the procession of carnivores.

Insects are found everywhere. They were the first forms of substantial life to crawl the earth. They have been here for more than two hundred million years and will, presumably, remain as the last life forms on a dying earth.

Insects, like the sea crustaceans to which they are related, have their vulnerable bodies encased in an exterior skeleton. The body is composed of a head, thorax, and abdomen, and each of these segments has a pair of jointed legs, giving the insect a total of six legs. There are a few insects that are devoid of wings. Some have only a single pair attached to the thorax, but the vast majority of these tiny creatures sometime during their life process possess two pairs of wings. Sex differences are not often discernible and really don't make a whale of a lot of difference except to another insect.

ANTS (FAMILY *FORMICIDAE*)

"Look to the ant, thou sluggard." Good advice, for these most active and numerous of all insects are diligent in their labors. Fifteen thousand species, subspecies and varieties of ants have so far been

classified, a tribute to their ability to find, consume and digest a great variety of food. Ants have few natural enemies. They are preyed upon by some mammals, parasitic insects, and plants, but their most deadly adversaries are other ants, just as man's worst enemy is man. Most ants can bite. Some can sting and inject into the wound they make a formic acid that paralyzes or kills other insects and irritates human skin.

Ants are among the most intelligent of the "lower" orders of living creatures and are the most highly developed of all social insects. You can purchase commercially made ant farms, small replicas of colonies, with a glass front through which you can watch the ants in their various activities.

Teeming human cities contain hospitals, playgrounds, nurseries, cemeteries, beauty parlors, paved roads, and tunnels. All these existed in the formicary (ant hill) long before man was introduced to the evolutionary scene. Ants that are builders, carpenters, masons, and farmers, as well as miners, nurses, policemen, servants, soldiers, and undertakers, swarm over and in the ant hill, each going about its specific business. An ant colony is composed of a queen, a great number of underdeveloped females called workers, and, in late fall or early summer, male ants. Most young queens and males have wings, but not all. The three groups—queens, workers, males—are called castes (from the "caste" system of Oriental countries). This is a basic form of ant colony, though there are numerous exceptions to this presentation. Working females show tremendous variation from huge soldiers to minute minims.

On a certain perfect spring or summer day the ritual occurs that guarantees the continuation of the species. The young queen and males are escorted to the surface where they spread their wings and perform an aerial dance of romance and love. They mate and return to earth, where the queen sheds her wings and begins to lay her eggs, while the poor groom—abandoned, deserted, his love gone—dies of starvation. What a pretty tale of love!

One hears that the lion is the king of the African jungle and the jaguar or the monstrous anaconda is the ruler of the Amazon jungle. Not so. The ant is the true king of the jungle. *Driver ants* of tropical Africa and Asia and the *army,* or *legionary ants* of South America are the jungle's most ferocious creatures. They kill all living things in their path and the stench of rotten meat warns the remaining jungle denizens of the ants' approach. When they are on the march, even elephants flee in panic before their uncountable numbers.

Many stories about ants have become classics. As an instrument of ecology they have been imported into many countries to rid crops of other insect destroyers. In Africa the natives sometimes hold the edges of wounds together with the mandibles of ants, using them as a sort of surgical clamp. In South America the Amerindians eat ants. I have been told that they taste very much like bacon when fried. . . . I have been told. . . . Chocolate-covered ants are sold in this country in some gourmet shops—but not to me!

I will mention *bees* merely in passing, for the scientific breeding of bees to produce honey assigns them to the field of commerce rather than the pet realm, and anyone who has ever been stung by a bee will agree that there must be a better choice for a pet. *Wasps* are also interesting to study, but they cannot be classified as pets.

WALKING STICKS
Walking sticks (family *Phasmidae*) are large, wingless insects that can become pets. They are rather like the mantis, but their legs are all of the same length. The male of the species is smaller than the female and their principal foods are cherry-, oak-, walnut-, and locust-tree leaves. Their protective form and coloring mimics small sticks and branches. The young, hatched from scattered eggs, are similar to the adults, but as they grow, they cast their outer skin several times.

MANTISES
Introduced in America more than fifty years ago from China and Europe, the *Mantises* (family *Mantidae*) make odd but interesting insect pets. These large carnivorous orthopteroid insects are voracious predators which, in their savagery, will dine on their own kind. After the act of mating has been consummated, in the fall of the year, the female may turn upon her consort and kill and devour him, an act that in my humble opinion is carrying women's lib a bit too far. The young mantids hatched from within a hard, brownish foam, are similar in shape to the parents but light yellow in color. Eggs found by the hobbyist can be brought indoors and hatched. Mantises grow by shedding their skins and pumping air into their bodies, literally blowing themselves up to a larger size. You can keep mantises in a vivarium, but each must have its own compartment or they will eat each other. A piece of banana in the vivarium will attract flies for your pet's dinner. The flies will also lay eggs in the fruit, producing aphids for the mantids to eat. Water sprinkled on plants in the vivarium will supply the mantis with liquid refreshment.

There is a wide assortment of mantises throughout the world. All have protective coloring. There is one species that uses orchids as a base of operations from which to find its prey. It is colored like any pink or violet orchid and is quite a beautiful insect.

Due to the position of its eyes a mantis can look backwards as well as forwards.

FIREFLIES

Do you remember when you were young and on summer nights, perhaps while camping out, you captured fireflies in a jar and brought them back to your tent? What memories this brings back of callow youth and innocence. In fact I was not even aware in those days that fireflies (family *Lampryridae*) are actually soft-bodied beetles, not flies at all, and that there are many species to be found, especially in the tropics. Both larvae and adults feed on other small insects. How the strange fatty tissue that produces the "cold" light in the last segment of a firefly's body works was for a long time a scientific puzzle.

BEETLES

Scarab Beetles (*Coleoptera*), held sacred by the ancient Egyptians, form a tremendous family of over thirty thousand species. Some of these beetles are beautifully colored and all are completely harmless, even the huge savage-appearing *Rhinoceros* and *Ox Beetles*. *Stag* and *Horn beetles* are also related to the scarab beetles. The huge mandibles of the stag beetle look like antlers, hence the name. Other handsome beetles you might consider for your collection are the *Caterpillar Hunter,* the *Tiger Beetle* and the odd *Click Beetle.*

The best-known of the various beetles are the *Ladybird beetles* of the family *Coccinellidae*. In the Middle Ages these valued little beetles were dedicated to the Virgin and to this day are called ladybirds or ladybugs. They are valued because of their propensity, in both adult and larvae states, for feeding on damaging aphids. They are distributed all over the world and there are approximately 350 species of this colorful beetle in this country alone. Ladybugs, imported from other parts of the world, once saved the citrus industry in California when a scale threatened to destroy the groves.

BUTTERFLIES AND MOTHS

The most attractive, largest and most familiar of insects are the *butterflies* (*Lepidoptera*) and *moths* of the same order. The *Lepidoptera* go through four stages of development from egg to larva (caterpillar), to pupa, to adult. Butterflies usually take to the air during the day, while the moths are night-flyers. When at rest, the two hold their wings differently and the antennae of the butterfly ends in a knob, while that

of the moth has no knob and is usually feathery. These winged creatures can be taught to rest upon your hand or finger and certainly no
other pet presents such delicate and colorful beauty.

Among the most attractive of the butterflies are the common *Mon-
archs* and *Viceroys,* the gorgeous *Banded Purple, Red-Spotted Purple,
Mourning Cloak,* and the handsome *Swallowtails,* including the *Giant,
Tiger* and *Zebra.* Some of the moths are also highly attractive. The
Ailanthus Silk Moth, imported originally from China, and the *Cecropia
Moth* are both handsome specimens as is also the *Polyphemus Moth.*
But the most exquisite of this species is the *Luna Moth* with its sweeping
swallowtails and radiant light green coloration. Unfortunately the life-
span of the *Lepidoptera* is short. It is of extreme interest for the hobbyist
to find a *Lepidoptera* in its caterpillar stage, put it in a small cage with
a leafy branch, watch it as it forms its pupa or cocoon and then, eventually, see the fairy-like and radiant butterfly emerge in all its full-blown
beauty.

We generally think of insects as being pests rather than pets, and, to
be quite honest, they generally are. But they do fit into the ecological
picture and many of them prey upon other more destructive insects.

Sometimes one collects insects without having any desire to do so, and
when this occurs, there is only one solution—immediate elimination via
louse, bedbug, flea, or tick powders and sprays.

Collecting insects for pets or to form a colony is not very difficult,
because they are everywhere in the air, in the water, and on and under
the ground. Some are creatures of the night, others appear in daylight,
but always they are there. So, if insect pets are your bag, then go to it
with my blessing and the exhilarating knowledge that a whole wide world
of selection is at your doorstep.

22

Miscellaneous Pets

There are a group of strange creatures of various families that have reached tentative but definite status as pets. These creatures are occasionally found in pet shops or at animal dealers and I include them here because I know of dealers who have sold them and people who have bought them for pets.

SPIDERS (ORDER *ARANEAE*)

Spiders are eight-legged, predacious, insect-like arachnids, and many of them spin webs that serve as traps for their live prey. There are, of course, a huge number of spiders, but we will be concerned here with only two allied species, the *Tarantula* and the *Bird-Eating Spider,* which is also a type of tarantula. Both of these spiders are sold and bought as pets. I don't know why, but I know they are. Frankly my first impulse when I see a tarantula is to say, "Arrrggghhhh!" and squash it, not pet it, but, "to each his own." If we all had the same tastes, needed the same stimuli, and shared identical values, no matter how sophisticated our world, we would be a society of complete bores, lacking the benefit of perspective, and more primitive than our ancient, cave-dwelling ancestors.

Tarantulas and Bird-Eating Spiders are huge, hairy creatures once thought to be very dangerous. They are only two of a large family of such spiders, many of them originating in the Americas. They are essentially harmless to man, though they will bite and their bite is painful, but not dangerous. Both these species must be handled with care, for they have very uncertain tempers. The bird-eating tarantula's bite is mildly toxic, much less so than that of the more popular Tarantula, whose bite can create a highly toxic condition in individuals who are sensitive to the poison it secretes.

Both species can conveniently be kept in a 10-gallon aquarium with a covered top. Both are carnivorous and both can be fed raw meat when in captivity. A piece the size of a marble will be consumed over a period of twenty-four hours and the tarantula will not need another feeding for a month. Bird-eating spiders eat mice, small birds, and large insects in in the wild.

HYRAXES OR CONEYS (ORDER *HYRACOIDEA*)

There are several species of *Hyraxes;* the tree, rock, and cape hyraxes are the best known. Though they appear to be rodents, these small creatures are not related to the rodent family at all. Uniquely they are more closely allied to the huge rhinoceros and to some long-extinct animals of monstrous bulk. Their nails are like small hooves and they are much like living fossils, retaining the characteristics of the archaic ungulates that roamed the earth thirty million years ago.

In appearance and size very much like a rodent, the Rock Hyrax (Heterohyrax brucei) *is actually more closely related to the rhinoceros. This little mammal is the coney mentioned in the Bible.*

The cape hyrax is a quiet creature that is easily tamed and has the appearance and actions of a rodent. Some of its teeth are also rodent-like. This hyrax is one of several small mammals lumped together under the general heading of *rock hyraxes* because they make their homes amid large rocks and boulders. They are about the size of rabbits and form a specific family and order. Most are nocturnal. Their habitat is tropical and they can be found in Africa, Arabia, and Syria. All make excellent pets if acquired when young. In South Africa I have seen native children playing with their pet Cape hyrax, and I have also seen little native children using sticks to keep the hyraxes away from grain being dried on the ground by the sun.

A pet hyrax should be kept in a cage large enough for exercise and with some piled rocks to make it feel at home. They are excellent climbers, so be sure your cage is covered. Feed grains of all kinds and rabbit-food pellets. The hyrax is a hardy little beastie but is tropical and needs a temperature of at least 75 degrees Fahrenheit. This little fellow, incidentally, is the coney mentioned in the Bible.

BATS (ORDER *CHIROPTERA*)

There is an aura of madness that seems to emanate from bats; and when they leave their foul caves at dusk, spewed forth from the dank darkness of their habitat, it is as though they have been vomited up from some noisome hell where unknown corruption lurks. If you conclude that I am not fond of bats, you are perfectly right. Yet I must admit that they are, for many reasons, fascinating creatures.

We know there are over two thousand forms of bats comprising the approximately five hundred species. They occur in all sections of the globe, tropical or temperate, and attain their greatest size in the warmest latitudes. Most of these flying mammals are rather small insectivores. In the Old World tropics there is a family of *Fruit Bats* that attain a wing spread of 5 feet, greater size than is attained by the *Fruit-eating Bats* of the American tropics, though there is a South American *Giant Bat* that boasts a 3-foot wing spread. (Its habitat extends also into Trinidad.) This huge creature is carnivorous and savagely attacks birds, reptiles, and small animals. The *Vampire Bat* is exclusively a New World creature—it is definitely not from Transylvania. There is also a species of long-nosed bat that feeds on the pollen of night-blooming flowers, a sort of Ferdinand of the bat family. All of the several dozen species of United States bats are harmless, insect-eating *Chiroptera*.

Bats are the only flying mammals. Since they have limited eyesight and are nocturnal, flying with great rapidity in the pitch-darkness, they have developed a unique kind of radar that keeps them from colliding

The Lump-nosed Bat (order Chiroptera), *". . . gargoyle faces of ancient hidden horrors . . ." The bat is the only flying mammal in the world.*

with one another or with other objects in the gloom of night. Most of them rest during the day, hanging upside down, attached to the roofs of caves, mines, and other dark noxious depths. The larger fruit bats roost in trees. The wings of the bat are actually hands with thin, elongated fingers connected by a membranous web that attaches to the hind legs.

Vampire Bats are the creatures that have given impetus to a series of horror movies that made a Hollywood star of Bela Lugosi in the role of Count Dracula, the human vampire. To add to this heinous reputation, vampires are the only mammals that feed exclusively upon the blood of other animals. Their sharp, specialized upper incisor teeth can inflict a painless wound that causes their victim's blood to flow. The vampire ghoulishly laps the gore with its thirsting tongue. No substitute food is acceptable to the vampire; it wants only blood.

I know of a woman who kept three vampires as pets and found it necessary to visit the local slaughterhouse once a day to obtain fresh blood with which to feed her three little noxious gnomes.

Many of the smaller harmless *fruit bats* and *insect-eating bats* have become pets. They are much like flying rodents. The larger *fruit bats* are also called *Flying Foxes* because of their facial resemblance to a fox.

Among the better-known species of bats are the *Leaf-nosed, Big Brown, Mastiff, Pipistrel, Red, Pallid, Silver-haired, Big-eared, Mexican Tree-tailed,* and *Hoary bat.* Many of these creatures have the gargoyle faces of ancient, hidden horrors dredged from the depths of a devil's tomb.

INSECTIVORES (ORDER *INSECTIVORA*)

These are small animals that feed largely on insects. The basic anatomy of some of these creatures, notably the *Solenodon* and the *Long-nosed Tenrec* reveals their close relationship to the earliest small mammals that appeared when the Age of the Reptiles was drawing to a close and the mammalian species were beginning to exert their dominance on earth. The close relationship between these two *Insectivora,* the solenodon and the tenrec—one a Haitian animal (a few are found in Cuba) and the other inhabiting Madagascar—also indicates the presence, sometime in the very remote past, of bridging areas of land between the continents as we know them today.

The *Old World Solenodon* is about the size of a cavy, with such a long pointed nose he can be best described as the Cyrano of the insectivores. Except for the nose they very much resemble a rat. These are rather rare animals, but on the island of Haiti I saw a young pet solenodon being carried around in the pocket of a young boy who, realizing my interest, promptly attempted to sell the creature to me. Like most beasts that have a definite linkage with primitive animal forms, the solenodon is not very bright. In captivity it prefers scraped or ground raw beef to any kind of prepared insect food.

The *Tenrecs* of Madagascar are similar to the solenodons, but some species display short spines like the hedgehog, to which they are also related, and they roll themselves into a protective ball when frightened.

Hedgehogs are also about the size of a cavy and are covered with sharp spines for protection. Like some of the tenrecs, they can roll themselves into a ball that becomes a veritable pincushion to anything or anyone that threatens them. There are over a dozen species of hedgehog inhabiting Africa, Asia, and Europe.

The *European Hedgehog* is found in Ireland, Great Britain, and the greater part of Europe. You can often see these little creatures filling the role of pets, particularly in old houses where their persistent hunting of roaches, beetles, and other insect pests makes them invaluable economical necessities to their owners.

ANTEATERS, ARMADILLOS, AND SLOTHS—EDENTATES (ORDER *XENARTHRA*)

Extremely divergent in form, the members of this family are either toothless or possess no front or incisor teeth. They are New World creatures, inhabiting tropical America, and are primitive placental mammals, the surviving remnants of ancient giant races that existed in prehistoric times.

The *Giant Anteater* and the *lamandua,* an arboreal anteater with a prehensile tail, are both edentates, but not generally considered in the pet category. Yet a young giant anteater, in the private zoo of my friend German Garcia y Garcia, has proven to be both amiable and docile, characteristics wanted in a pet. These strange creatures mature at over 75 pounds in weight.

This leaves the *armadillos* and *sloths* to consider. I have known of both species being made pets, though I must admit they were not what I would call wildly exciting, lively, or intellectually stimulating in that role.

Armadillos (order *Cingulata*) are armored edentates that inhabit tropical America. There are several different species all characterized by a jointed, bony, dermal skeleton of plates that are embedded in the skin and allow the animal to roll up into a tight, protective ball. There are three-banded, six-banded and nine-banded armadillos. They dig rather deep burrows and are nocturnal, prowling at night to feed on insects, carrion, and small rodents. In size armadillos range from nearly that of a rabbit to a giant species 5 feet long—too big for pet status consideration. These animals were introduced into Florida and the state is becoming overrun with them. The nine-banded species is found in southern Texas, Arizona, and southward to Brazil. The six- and three-banded armadillos are native to South America and the Guianas.

Prehistoric armadillos (Glyptodon) were so large that primeval man, if caught in the open in one of the cataclysmic storms that raged across a still-forming earth, could find adequate shelter under the dried-out shell of a deceased *glyptodon*. The present-day species has changed little from the ancient ancestral forms except in size. Armadillo meat is much sought after in certain areas. In Trinidad it is considered a gourmet delight and sells at an exceedingly high price per pound. It is rather good, tasting like delicate pork.

Your armadillo pet, if kept outdoors, should have a cement base to any enclosure in which it is kept or it will dig its way out. Feed dog food, meat, and occasionally a treat of mealworms and an insect mix that can be purchased commercially from a pet shop.

Sloths (family *Bradypodidae*) are extremely slow and deliberate in movement. In fact they seem to exist in an entirely different time sphere from any other animal on earth—as though they are visitors from some far-flung planet where the element of time differs drastically from our own. This is not their only peculiarity however. Among other things they share with bats the distinction of being the only two mammals that spend a large part of their lives hanging in an inverted position by their long, curved claws.

There are three genera of these sluggish arboreal edentates, the *Two-toed Sloth,* the *Three-toed Sloth* and the *Maned Sloth.* I leave it to your vivid imagination to arrive at a conclusion as to the differences between them. Actually only the two-toed sloth is pertinent to our interest as it is the only one of the three varieties that can thrive in captivity. From its appearance one would think this creature is related to the primates, but of course it is not. Another peculiarity of these very uncommon creatures is the microscopic algae that grow on their fur, lending them a greenish shade that is excellent protective coloration. Their almost complete inactivity undoubtedly aids in the algae formation.

Sloths are creatures of the warm climates, inhabiting tropical South

America. They cannot survive in cold climates unless given a completely tropical artificial habitat. All sloths feed on leaves in their arboreal environment. The three-toed sloth cannot live without being supplied with the large, thick leaves of the cecropia tree for food. But the two-toed sloth, much hardier than its more numerously-toed peer, can live well on a mixture of vegetables and fruits.

I have no idea how these creatures reproduce or continue their species. When one considers their many peculiarities, they have got to be the true oddballs of the animal kingdom. Though I have seen them kept as pets, I do not recommend them, for to my mind they have all the charm, animation, and intelligence of a worn fur coat.

You have been introduced in these pages to the many and varied creatures that have, through human curiosity and an inner need to reach out to other forms of life, been elevated to pet status. But I would be lax in my obligation to you if I did not repeat again (and for the last time, I promise) the pertinent warning I have expressed before. There is a difference between the domesticated animal that has been the dependent, companion, and pet of man for many satisfying generations and the wild animal that has behind it eons of independence from man and no acquired instinct of compatibility with humans, that has, through selection, become a part of its evolutionary format. Man has achieved dominance over all living things on this planet through ruthlessness and cold-blooded aggressiveness. Man was, and still is, the hunter supreme, thanks to his ability to reason and the weapons he has subsequently devised for his clever hands.

Wild animals are afraid of humans. Animals domesticated over many centuries are generally not afraid of man. To protect themselves from the danger that man represents the wild creatures use all their natural powers of defense when near man, lashing out with teeth and claws when frightened. This is a fact you must accept. Remember it when you make a pet of a wild creature. If acquired when very young, before its parents can instill in it the necessity for fear and savagery, a wild baby, if handled with care and affection, will usually respond in kind, seemingly accepting its role as a pet with the same enjoyment, poise, and lack of suspicion that the domesticated animal exhibits. But you must be constantly aware that the instinctive dread of man and the possibility of quick savage reaction to what it may consider danger is always present, buried beneath the surface but a constant part of its heritage. So be a bit careful with pets from the wild and try never to allow a situation to arise that will trigger that atavistic, hidden anxiety into defensive action.

CHAPTER
23

When the End Comes

There is always an end to everything. It is a universal law of nature that there must be a beginning and there must be an end, a completion: the trouble is that the end is always so final and from it we have no recourse.

When the pet you have loved dies, there is left an emptiness, a hurt, a wound that must be healed, and the quickest way to close the wound, to heal the hurt, and fill the emptiness is to procure another pet. In so doing you must not feel guilty; the new pet is not a substitute for the old one that has passed on. This is a completely new individual with its own character and its own ways to reach your heart.

We have a tendency to anthropomorphize, to ascribe to our pets human feelings and emotions because we love them and want them to be like us. But they are not like us. Animals live an instinctive life, while humans live a supposedly rational existence. There is a great, dark social gulf between us that we attempt, without complete success, to cross, but on which we sometimes, through our love and understanding, manage to shed some tiny light.

Death to your pet is a ceasing to be, a simple ending to existence, uncluttered by the orgiastic trappings of religious philosophy and false promises. The emotionalism, the wailing and mourning is supplied by you.

We are told that we should not—indeed cannot—feel the same about the passing of a pet as we can about the death of a human loved one, because the pet is an animal and we never had entered its inner world and, conversely, it had never really entered ours. In a way this is true. In another way, it is also utter nonsense. The closeness we share with our pets makes them individuals, endows them with more than simple animalistic values, so that often they become much more than just animals; sometimes they come to mean more to us than any human being.

So when they die, we truly mourn their journey into oblivion and we deeply miss them. Tears are tears whether they flood the eyes or just the heart. They are the high tide of our emotions, our farewell to a creature to whom we have given of ourselves and have received in return something precious. Remember, with a smile, the good things, the fine things you and your pet have shared. None of us want to remember with tears when a smile will do just as well.

From a philosophical viewpoint perhaps these creatures—our pets— and our association with them may come to mean more to our civilization than we can now imagine. Man's inhumanity to man and the beasts that share his world with him is a known fact. We—you and I and the rest of humanity—have not yet journeyed far enough from our primitive ancestors to realize the purity and beauty that is within our grasp and that shares with our inner being the bestiality of our human heritage. Our pets are simple animals, but man is a highly complicated, sophisticated one, who sees the paganism, the coldness, the hate, the savagery of races and religions mold cataclysmic wars that destroy millions of his peers. Understandably he becomes coldly cynical and distrustful. But perhaps the investment made by evolution in the long tedious task of fashioning *Homo sapiens* will not be wasted; perhaps there is hope for mankind. It lies in the philosophical and esthetic realms, in the mind- and soul-elevating appreciation of the arts, and in one other direction—the ability to care for, to give love and understanding to, another life-form, to a pet, and to come to learn something of the simple, devotional depth—without malice or lies—of the love returned by that pet. Through these resources perhaps mankind can overcome the cynical savagery within and elevate himself above the abyss of self-destruction.

Index

Index